Amines & Biomolecules

for JEE Main & Advanced

Study Package for
Chemistry

Includes Past
JEE & KVPY Questions

Useful for Class 12,
KVPY & Olympiads

Fully Solved

Dr. O. P. Agarwal

□ **Corporate Office : 45, 2nd Floor, Maharishi Dayanand Marg, Corner Market, Malviya Nagar, New Delhi-110017**

Tel. : 011-49842349 / 49842350

Typeset by Disha DTP Team

DISHA PUBLICATION
ALL RIGHTS RESERVED

For further information about the books from DISHA,
Log on to **www.dishapublication.com** or email to **info@dishapublication.com**

PREFACE

REVISED EDITION

It gives us immense pleasure and satisfaction to bring out the thoroughly revised and updated edition of the book **"Disha's Amines and Biomolecules"** The book has been designed to give a better look & feel and to make the text more lucid. The new pattern of JEE Main & Advanced has been kept in mind throughout.

The exercises at the end of each chapter have been designed in the flavour of the new pattern of JEE Main & Advanced. The question from the previous JEE papers have been incorporated in the different exercises. A separate section having past JEE questions is also provided at the end.

1. **Exercise 1 - MCQ with One correct option :** This exercise contains a collection of question, which has been very carefully selected and it is ensured that there is no repetition. The exercise contains a collection of questions, which has been very carefully selected and it is ensured that there is no repetition. The exercise has been designed so as to cover all the concepts involved in the chapter.

2. **Exercise 2 :** This exercise contains all the four new variety of questions which have been asked in the last 3-4 JEE examinations. These variety of questions are-

    (i) **MCQ's with one or more than one correct answers :** Around 20-30 well selected problems introduced in each chapter.

    (ii) **Comprehension based questions :** More than 50 passages which tests the student's comprehension and analytical ability have been added. All these are newly framed problems.

    (iii) **Matching type question :** Match the following type of question with multiple matching have been introduced in each chapter. These are unique and newly framed problems which will definitely pose a big challenge to the student. I feel that this type of problem is the best way to check a student's concepts.

    (iv) **Assertion & Reason type questions :** Assertion and Reason type of questions have been incorporated in each and every chapter.

3. **Exercise 3 - Subjective Problems :** This exercise contains a unique collection of subjective problems which will not only give practice to the students but will also help in revising the complete chapter.

In the end, We would like to request all readers to highlight the printing errors and come forward with suggestions for further improvement of the book.

DR. O.P. AGARWAL

CONTENTS

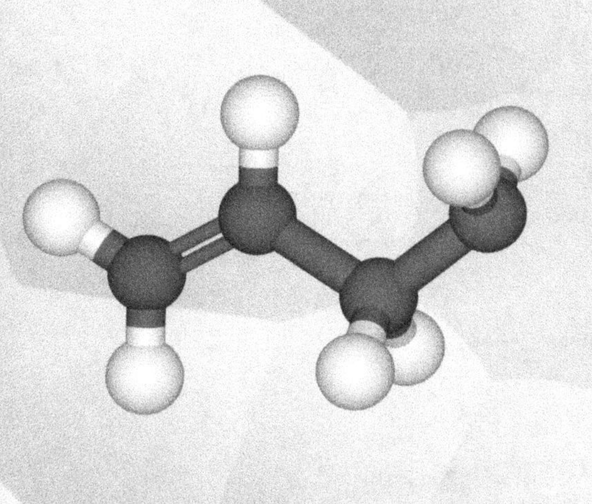

19

Aliphatic Amines

Nitrogen-containing compounds are essential to life and are ultimately derived from atmospheric nitrogen. Atmospheric nitrogen is reduced to ammonia, then converted into organic nitrogen compounds, the complete process is named as **nitrogen fixation**. The most important organic nitrogen compounds are **amines**.

19.1 Nomenclature

Amines are alkyl or aryl derivatives of ammonia in which one or more hydrogen atoms are replaced by alkyl or aryl groups. In **alkylamines**, nitrogen is attached to sp^3 hybridized carbon, while in **arylamines** nitrogen is attached to sp^2 hybridized carbon of a benzene or benzene-like ring.

$$R-\ddot{N}\!\!< \qquad\qquad Ar-N\!\!<$$

Alkylamine   Arylamine

Amines are **classified** as primary, secondary, or tertiary, according to the number of groups attached to the nitrogen atom.

$$\underset{\text{Ammonia}}{H-\underset{\underset{H}{|}}{\overset{\overset{H}{|}}{N}}-H} \qquad \underset{\text{Primary amine}}{R-\underset{\underset{H}{|}}{\overset{\overset{H}{|}}{N}}-H} \qquad \underset{\text{Secondary amine}}{R-\underset{\underset{H}{|}}{\overset{\overset{R'}{|}}{N}}-H} \qquad \underset{\text{Tertiary amine}}{R-\underset{\underset{R''}{|}}{\overset{\overset{R'}{|}}{N}}-R''}$$

Amines are named in two ways, either as *alkylamines* or as *alkanamines* (**chemical abstract names**). The latest vesion of the IUPAC rules accepts both.

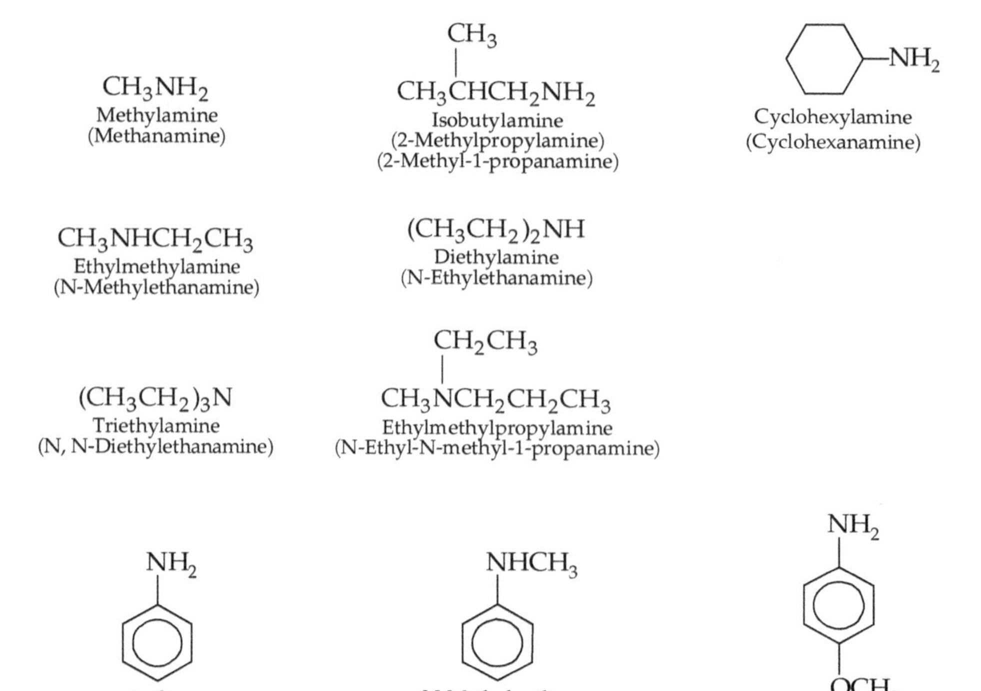

1° Amines	CH_3NH_2 Methylamine (Methanamine)	$CH_3CHCH_2NH_2$ (with CH_3 branch) Isobutylamine (2-Methylpropylamine) (2-Methyl-1-propanamine)	Cyclohexylamine (Cyclohexanamine)
2° Amines	$CH_3NHCH_2CH_3$ Ethylmethylamine (N-Methylethanamine)	$(CH_3CH_2)_2NH$ Diethylamine (N-Ethylethanamine)	
3° Amines	$(CH_3CH_2)_3N$ Triethylamine (N, N-Diethylethanamine)	$CH_3NCH_2CH_2CH_3$ (with CH_2CH_3 branch) Ethylmethylpropylamine (N-Ethyl-N-methyl-1-propanamine)	
Arylamines	Aniline (Benzenamine)	N-Methylaniline (N-Methylbenzenamine)	p-Ansidine (4-Methoxybenzenamine)

As replacement of 1, 2 or 3 hydrogen atoms of NH_3 gives amines, replacement of 1, 2, 3 or 4 hydrogen atoms of NH_4^+ give corresponding amine salts ; when all the four hydrogen atoms of NH_4^+ are replaced by alkyl groups it is known as **quaternary ammonium salt**. These are named by replacing —*amine* by —*ammonium* (or —*aniline* by —*anilinium*) and adding the name of the anion (chloride, nitrate, sulphate, etc.) For example,

$$CH_3NH_3^+Cl^- \qquad (C_2H_5NH_3^+)_2SO_4^{2-} \qquad C_6H_5NH_3^+Cl^-$$

Methylammonium chloride   Ethylammonium sulphate   Anilinium chloride

$$(CH_3)_3NH^+NO_3^- \qquad C_6H_5CH_2N^+(CH_3)_3I^-$$

Trimethylammonium nitrate   Benzyltrimethylammonium iodide (a quaternary ammonium salt)

TEST YOUR UNDERSTANDING - 19.1

1.   Give IUPAC names for the following compounds :

(a) $C_6H_5CH_2CH_2NH_2$ (b) $CH_2 = CHCH_2NH_2$ (c) $H_2NCH_2CHCH_3$ (with NH_2)   (d) cyclohexyl—$N(CH_3)_2$

(e) benzene ring with $CHMe_2$ and $CH_3NC_2H_5$ substituents   (f) benzene ring with NHC_2H_5, NO_2 and Cl substituents   (g) biphenyl with $NHCH_3$ groups   (h) benzene ring with $^+N(CH_3)_3CF_3COO^-$

2.   Write structure for the following compounds.

(a)   N-Methyl-1-butanamine

(b)   N, N-bis (1-chloroethyl)ethanamine

(c)   1, 5-Pentanediamine

(d)   1, 1, 1''-tri (chloroethyl)amine

(e)   N, N-Dicyclopropylcyclopropylamine

(f)   β-(3, 4-dihydroxyphenyl)ethylamine.

19.2 Preparation of Amines

19.2.1 Preparation of Amines from Alkyl Halides

(*i*) **By alkylation of ammonia** (*Ammonolysis of alkyl halides*). Alkyl halides react with ammonia by nucleophilic substitution to form the amine salt, from which free amine can be liberated by treatment with base, which may be NH_3 itself or OH^- added from outside.

$$H_3N: + R\text{—}X \xrightarrow{S_N2} H_3N^{\delta+} \text{---} R \text{---} X^{\delta-} \longrightarrow \underset{\text{1° Amine salt}}{H_3N^+\text{—}R \quad X^-}$$

$$\underset{\text{1° Amine}}{H_2O + R\text{—}NH_2} \xleftarrow{OH^-} R\text{—}N^+H_3 \xrightarrow{NH_3} \underset{\text{1° Amine}}{R\text{—}NH_2 + NH_4^+}$$

However, this method is of very limited synthetic application because multiple alkylations occur. The free primary amine can compete with ammonia and react with alkyl halide to form salt of a secondary amine.

$$\underset{\text{1° Amine}}{RNH_2} + RX \longrightarrow R_2NH_2^+X^- \xrightarrow{NH_3} \underset{\text{2° Amine}}{R_2NH} + NH_4^+X^-$$

Similarly, secondary amine may react with alkyl halide to give *tert*-amine. Even the *tert*-amine competes with ammonia to form a quaternary ammonium salt.

$$\underset{\text{2° Amine}}{R_2NH} + RX \longrightarrow R_3N^+HX^- \xrightarrow{NH_3} \underset{\text{3° Amine}}{R_3N} \xrightarrow{RX} \underset{\substack{\text{Quaternary} \\ \text{ammonium salt}}}{R_4N^+X^-}$$

Conversion of ammonia or 1° amine to quaternary ammonium salt is known as **exhaustive methylation**.

$$NH_3 \xrightarrow{RX} \underset{\text{1° Amine}}{RNH_2} \xrightarrow{RX} \underset{\text{2° Amine}}{R_2NH} \xrightarrow{RX} \underset{\text{3° Amine}}{R_3N} \xrightarrow{RX} \underset{\text{4° Ammonium salt}}{R_4N^+X^-}$$

Multiple alkylations, *i.e.* preparation of 2°, and 3° amines and quaternary ammonium salt, can be minimized by using a large excess of ammonia. In presence of large excess of ammonia, a molecule of RX is more likely to be attacked by one of the numerous ammonia molecules rather than one of the relatively few RNH_2 molecules. Further except the special case of methylamine, the primary amine can be separated from other products by distillation.

Because of their low reactivity, aryl halides do not normally react with ammonia under ordinary conditions. Aryl halides can be converted into amines, by ammonia, only (*a*) if the ring carries strongly electron-withdrawing group (*e.g.* —NO_2) at *o*- and *p*- positions to the halogen, or (*b*) if a high temperature or a strongly basic reagent is used.

(*ii*) **Alkylation of azide ion followed by reduction**. A much better method for preparing primary amine from an alkyl halide is *via* alkyl azide route. Azide is a very good nucleophile and reacts with primary and secondary alkyl halides to give alkyl azides which can be reduced to primary amine with sodium and alcohol or with $LiAlH_4$ or with H_2 in presence of Pt or Raney Ni.

$$R\text{—}X + \overset{..}{:}\!\!\underset{}{N} = N = \overset{..}{\underset{..}{N}}\!:^- \xrightarrow{S_N2} R\text{—}\overset{..}{N} = N^+ = \overset{..}{\underset{..}{N}}\!:^- \xrightarrow[\text{or } LiAlH_4]{\text{Na / alcohol}} R\text{—}\overset{..}{N}H_2$$
Azide ion   Alkyl azide

1, 2-Epoxycyclohexane $\xrightarrow{NaN_3}$ *trans–* $\xrightarrow{H_2/Pt}$ *trans*-2-Aminocyclohexanol

(*iii*) **The Gabriel synthesis.** Another method used for preparing primary amines from alkyl halides, an easily available starting material, without the formation of secondary and tertiary amines is the Gabriel synthesis. The key reagent of Gabriel synthesis, potassium phthalimide, is prepared by reacting phthalimide with KOH. Potassium phthalimide acts as a nucleophile and react with alkyl halides by S_N2 process to form an N-alkylphthalimide. Imides are diacyl derivatives of amines and can be hydrolysed by aqueous acid or base to liberate primary amine. However, more effective method for cleaving the imide to primary amine is reaction with hydrazine

Phthalimide   N-Potassium phthalimide (a nucleophile)

N-Alkylphthalimide   Phthalylhydrazide

(*i*)   Aryl halides can't be converted into arylamines because they do not undergo nucleophilic substitution with N-potassiophthalimide.

(*ii*)   Since phthalimide can undergo only a single alkylation, the formation of secondary and tertiary amines does not occur, and thus the Gabriel synthesis is a valuable method for the laboratory preparation of primary amines.

Further, like above two methods, Gabriel synthesis restricted the use of methyl, 1° and 2° alkyl halides because the 3° alkyl halides lead almost exclusively to elimination products.

TEST YOUR UNDERSTANDING - 19.2

1.   Which of the following amines can be prepared by the Gabriel synthesis ; give equations for it.

   (*a*)   Isobutylamine   (*b*)   Benzylamine   (*c*)   Aniline   (*d*) 2-Phenylethylamine

   (*e*)   *tert*-Butylamine   (*f*)   N-Methylbenzylamine.

19.2.2 Preparation of Amines by Reduction

Almost any nitrogen-containing organic compound can be reduced to amine. However, availability of a suitable precursor and the choice of an appropriate reducing agent determine whether a reaction can be used for preparing the amine or not.

Reduction of azides (described above), nitro, nitriles, oximes and amides. Reduction of an azide, a nitro, a nitrile or an oxime gives a primary amine ; while reduction of an amide can yield a primary, secondary, or tertiary amine.

(*a*)   Nitro group can be reduced to primary amines in two general ways : (*i*) by catalytic hydrogenation over Pt, Pd, or Ni, or (*ii*) by reduction with acid and relatively inexpensive metal like Fe, Sn, Zn or a metal salt like $SnCl_2$. This method is more important in preparing 1° aromatic amines, although it is equally suitable for the preparation of 1° aliphatic amines.

$$CH_3NO_2 \xrightarrow{\text{Sn, HCl}} CH_3NH_2 \; ; \; C_6H_5NO_2 \xrightarrow{\text{Sn—HCl}} C_6H_5NH_2$$

(*b*)
$$R—C \equiv N \xrightarrow{\text{LiAlH}_4 \text{ or H}_2, \text{ catalyst}} RCH_2NH_2$$
$$\text{Nitrile} \qquad\qquad\qquad\qquad \text{1° Amine}$$

Since nitriles can be prepared from alkyl halides by a nucleophilic substitution reaction with cyanide ion, the overall process $RX \rightarrow RC \equiv N \rightarrow RCH_2NH_2$, leads to primary amines that have one carbon atom more than the starting alkyl halide. Cyano groups in cyanohydrins are reduced under the same reaction conditions.

(c)

$$RCH = NOH \xrightarrow[\text{or Na in C}_2\text{H}_5\text{OH}]{\text{LiAlH}_4, \text{ or H}_2, \text{ catalyst}} RCH_2NH_2$$

Oxime　　　　　　　　　　　　　　1° Amine

Oximes, in turn, can be prepared from aldehydes and ketones.

(d)

$$\underset{\text{Amide}}{R-\overset{\overset{\displaystyle O}{\|}}{C}-NR_2{}'} \xrightarrow{\text{LiAlH}_4} \underset{\text{3° Amine}}{R-CH_2-NR_2{}'}$$

Here, if R′ = H, the product is a 1° amine, if one R′ = H and other R′ = an alkyl group the product is 2° amine. Amides, in turn, can be prepared from acid chlorides, acid anhydrides, and esters.

19.2.3 Preparation of Amines through Reductive Amination (*Reduction of imines*)

Imines are the products formed by the reaction of aldehydes and ketones with ammonia, 1° amine, or 2° amine. Imines can be reduced to amines by catalytic hydrogenation or LiAlH$_4$.

$$\underset{\text{Aldehyde or ketone}}{\overset{\overset{\displaystyle R'}{|}}{R-C=O}} + NH_3 \longrightarrow \underset{\text{Imine}}{\overset{\overset{\displaystyle R'}{|}}{R-C=NH}} \xrightarrow{\text{H}_2/\text{catalyst}} \underset{\text{Amine}}{\overset{\overset{\displaystyle R'}{|}}{R-CH-NH_2}}$$

The reaction can be carried out in a single operation by catalytic hydrogenation of a solution containing both ammonia and the carbonyl compound.

$$R-\overset{\overset{\displaystyle R'}{|}}{C}=O \quad
\begin{cases}
\xrightarrow[\text{[H]}]{\text{NH}_3} & \overset{\overset{\displaystyle R'}{|}}{R-CH-NH_2} \quad \text{1° Amine} \\[2em]
\xrightarrow[\text{[H]}]{\text{R"NH}_2} & \overset{\overset{\displaystyle R'}{|}}{R-CH-NHR"} \quad \text{2° Amine} \\[2em]
\xrightarrow[\text{[H]}]{\text{R"R"'NH}} & \overset{\overset{\displaystyle R'}{|}}{R-CH-NR"R"'} \quad \text{3° Amine}
\end{cases}$$

Reductive amination has been used successfully with a wide variety of aldehydes and ketones, both aliphatic and aromatic. For example,

(i) Cyclohexanone + NH$_3$ $\xrightarrow[\text{ethanol}]{\text{H}_2, \text{ Ni}}$ [imine, Not isolated] $\longrightarrow$ Cyclohexylamine (1° Amine)

(ii) $CH_3CH_2CHO + H_2N-$ (Aniline) $\xrightarrow[\text{ethanol}]{\text{H}_2, \text{ Ni}}$ [$CH_3CH_2CH=N-$] $\longrightarrow CH_3CH_2CH_2NH-$ N-Propylaniline (2° Amine)

Propanal

(iii) $CH_3CH_2CH_2CHO + HN\langle$ (Piperidine) $\xrightarrow[\text{ethanol}]{H_2,\ Ni}$ $\left[CH_3CH_2CH_2\overset{\overset{\displaystyle OH}{|}}{C}H{-}N\langle \rightleftharpoons CH_3CH_2CH_2CH = \overset{+}{N}\langle \right]$

Butanal   Piperidine   Carbinolamine   Iminium ion

$\longrightarrow CH_3CH_2CH_2CH_2{-}N\langle$

N-Butylpiperidine (3° amine)

Especially effective reducing agents for reductive aminations are sodium or lithium cyanoborohydride ($NaBH_3CN$ or $LiBH_3CN$). All that is required is to add sodium cyanoborohydride to an alcoholic solution of the carbonyl compound and an amine.

$$C_6H_5CHO \xrightarrow[\text{NaBH}_3\text{CN}]{CH_3CH_2NH_2} C_6H_5CH_2NHCH_2CH_3$$

Benzaldehyde   N-Benzylethylamine

Sodium cyanoborohydride (more toxic and less effective) has now-a-days been replaced by sodium triacetoxyborohydride, $Na(AcO)_3BH$ which is non-toxic and more effective. The $NaBH_3CN$ and $Na(AcO)_3BH$ are especially recommended while preparing 3° amines by reductive amination.

TEST YOUR UNDERSTANDING - 19.3

1.   Give reactions involved in the preparation of each of the following amine by reductive amination.

    (a)   Dibenzylamine   (b) N, N-Dimethylbenzylamine

    (c)   N-Benzylpiperidine   (d) α-Phenylethylamine   (e) β-Phenylethylamine.

2.   Reductive amination of a ketone is always a better method for the preparation of amines of the type R_2CHNH_2 than treatment of an alkyl halide with ammonia. Explain.

3.   Why sodium cyanoborohydride ($NaBH_3CN$) is considered to be a better reducing agent in reductive amination.

4.   (a)   Give steps involved in the conversion of acetyl chloride to ethyl amine.

    (b)   Give the product obtained in the following reactions :

    (i) [structure: 2-(3-aminopropyl)cyclohexanone] $\xrightarrow{H_2/Ni}$ [A]   (ii) [structure: 2-(2-aminoethyl)cyclohexanone] $\xrightarrow{H_2/Ni}$ [B]

    (iii) [aniline] NH_2 + [cyclohexanone] $\xrightarrow{H_2/Ni}$ [C] .

19.2.4 Hofmann Degradation of Amides

Amides, *with no substituent on the nitrogen,* react with solutions of bromine or chlorine in sodium hydroxide to yield amines. This reaction is called the *Hofmann rearrangement* or *Hofmann degradation.*

$$R{-}\overset{\overset{\displaystyle O}{||}}{C}{-}NH_2 + Br_2 + 4NaOH \longrightarrow RNH_2 + 2NaBr + Na_2CO_3 + 2H_2O$$

From the above reaction, it is evident that the carbonyl carbon atom of the amide is lost (as CO_3^{2-}) and the R group of the amide is attached to the nitrogen atom of the amide group, thus a primary amine having one carbon atom less than the amide is the final product.

Mechanism. The mechanism of the Hofmann rearrangement involves three stages :

(*i*)　　formation of N-bromoamide intermediate (steps 1 and 2),

(*ii*)　　rearrangement of the N-bromoamide to an isocyanate (steps 3 and 4), and

(*iii*)　　hydrolysis of the isocyanate (steps 5 and 6).

Steps 1 and 2. Amides of the type $RCONH_2$ are appreciably acidic in nature because their conjugate bases are stabilized by electron delocalization. Conjugate base of the amide reacts with bromine to form N-bromoamide.

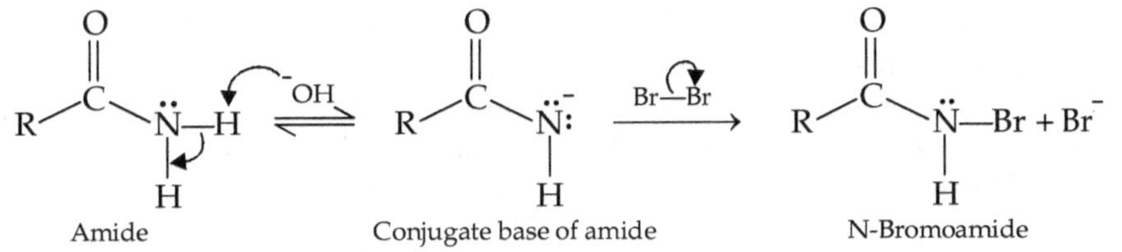

Amide   Conjugate base of amide   N-Bromoamide

Steps 3 and 4. Because of the presence of electron-withdrawing bromine, N-bromoamide is even more acidic than the starting amide, hence it easily undergoes deprotonation to form corresponding conjugate base. Due to the presence of electron-withdrawing Br as substituent, the nitrogen atom of the conjugate base of N-bromoamide becomes electron-deficient which causes the alkyl group to shift along with its bonding pair of electrons from acyl carbon to electron-deficient nitrogen. Actually, attachment of R to nitrogen helps in pushing out bromide ion. Migration of R— and elimination of bromide ion both take place simultaneously to form isocyanate.

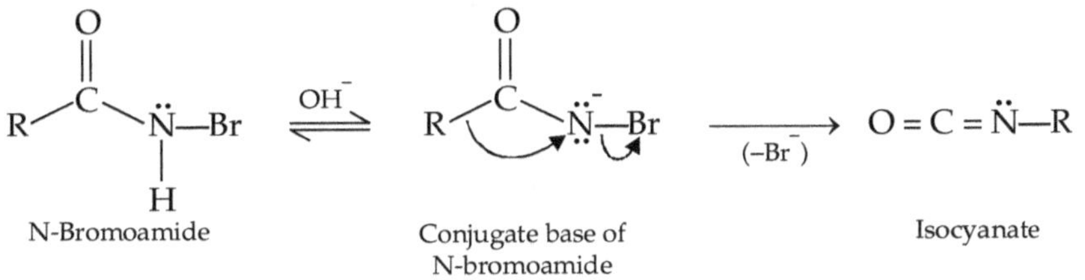

N-Bromoamide   Conjugate base of
N-bromoamide   Isocyanate

Note that the C—C bond cleavage and C—N bond formation take place simultaneously, and the migrating alkyl group does not become free. Hence if the R— group has chiral carbon, its configuration will be retained in the product (isocyanate and hence amine).

Steps 5 and 6. The isocyanate is quickly hydrolysed by base-catalyzed addition of water to form N-alkylcarbamic acid, which, being unstable, dissociates to an amine and carbon dioxide; CO_2 is then converted into CO_3^{2-} ion by base.

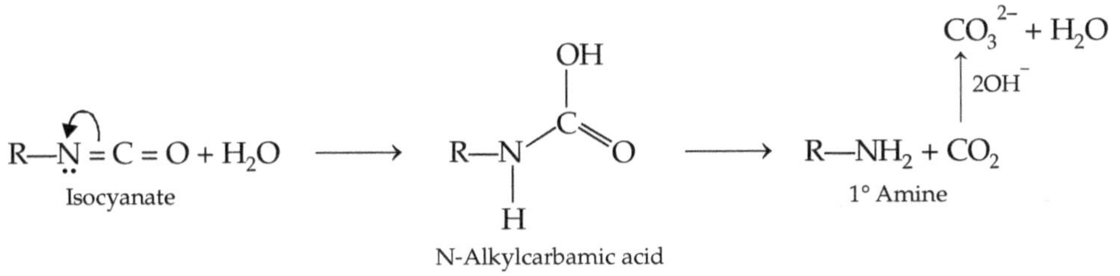

Isocyanate   N-Alkylcarbamic acid   1° Amine

Salient features of the Hofmann rearrangement.

(*i*)　　The method is equally suitable for the preparation of primary amines with 1°, 2°, or 3° alkyl groups, or aryl amines.

(*ii*)　　Only amides of the type $RCONH_2$ undergo Hofmann rearrangement. In other words, the amide nitrogen must have two protons attached to it ; of which one is replaced by bromine to give the N-bromo amide, while abstraction of the second by base is necessary to trigger the rearrangement. Thus amides of the type RCONH(R') although can form N-bromoamides, RCONBr(R'), under the reaction conditions, but these do not rearrange.

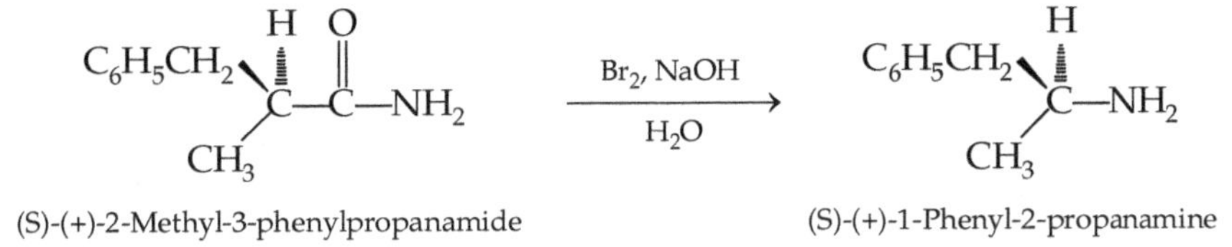

(S)-(+)-2-Methyl-3-phenylpropanamide   (S)-(+)-1-Phenyl-2-propanamine

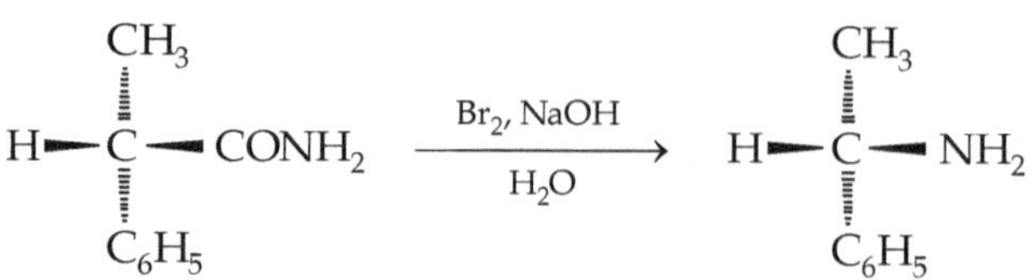

(+)-α-Phenylpropionamide   (−)-α-Phenylethylamine

Retention of configuration

(*iii*)   Rearrangement proceeds with *retention of configuration* at the migrating group.

(*iv*)   Isocyanates are formed as important intermediates. This can be proved if the reaction of an amide with bromine is carried out in methanol containing sodium methoxide instead of aqueous base. In such case, the product isolated is carbamate (ester of carbamic acid, $H_2N\ COOH$). Since **carbamates**, also known as **urethans**, are stable, these can be isolated.

$$CH_3(CH_2)_{14}CONH_2 \xrightarrow[CH_3OH]{Br_2,\ CH_3ONa} CH_3(CH_2)_{14}NHCOOCH_3$$

Hexadecanamide   Methyl N-pentadecylcarbamate

In such case, the isocyanate reacts with CH_3OH to form methyl carbamate.

$$RN = C = O + CH_3OH \longrightarrow RNHCOOCH_3$$

Isocyanate   Methyl N-alkylcarbamate

(*v*)   In the product $R{-}NH_2$, both hydrogen atoms are coming from OH^-, *i.e.* the two original H atoms of the $-CONH_2$ group are removed. Thus,

$$CH_3 - \overset{\overset{O}{\|}}{C} - NH_2 \xrightarrow{OD^- / Br_2} CH_3{-}ND_2$$

$$CH_3 - \overset{\overset{O}{\|}}{C} - ND_2 \xrightarrow{OH^- / Br_2} CH_3{-}NH_2$$

(*vi*)   Presence of electron-releasing substituent in the migrating alkyl group speeds up the migration of the alkyl group and hence the Hofmann rearrangement. Thus when the migrating group is aryl, the rate of degradation is increased by the presence of electron-releasing substituents in the ring, thus substituted amides show the following order of reactivity.

$$-OCH_3 > -CH_3 > -H > -Cl > -NO_2.$$

TEST YOUR UNDERSTANDING - 19.4

1.   Following amines are prepared by the reduction of an amide with $LiAlH_4$; provide the structure(s) of the parent amide(s) :

(*a*)      (*b*)   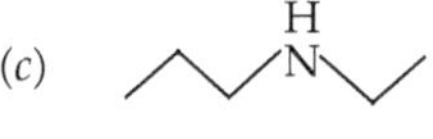   (*c*)   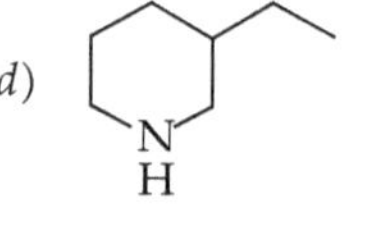   (*d*)   (*e*)   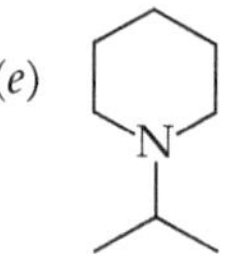

2.   (*a*)   Give the starting compound to prepare *n*-propylamine by reduction of following type of compound with $LiAlH_4$:

     (*i*)   A nitro compound   (*ii*)   An amide   (*iii*)   A nitrile   (*iv*)   An oxime   (*v*)   An azide.

   (*b*)   Which of these compounds are commonly reduced with

     (*i*)   Na and ethanol, and   (*ii*) H_2/Pt.

3.   Give reactions involved in the preparation of *n*-pentylamine from the alcohol having 5– or 6– carbon atoms by following methods.

   (*i*)   Ammonolysis of alcohols   (*ii*)   Gabriel synthesis   (*iii*)   Reduction of nitrile   (*iv*)   Reductive amination

   (*v*)   Hofmann degradation   (*vi*)   Amide reduction.

19.2.5 Preparation of Amines by Cutius and Schmidt Reactions

The Curtius rearrangement involves rearrangement of acyl azides to alkyl isocyanates. It resembles Hofmann rearrangement in the sense that the R— group migrates from the acyl carbon to the nitrogen atom as the leaving group departs, which is N_2 here (remember that N_2 is the best of all leaving groups since it is highly stable, nonbasic and escapes from the medium as it is a gas).

$$R-\underset{\underset{Cl}{}}{\overset{\overset{O}{\|}}{C}} \xrightarrow{NaN_3} R-\underset{\underset{N=N\equiv N}{}}{\overset{\overset{O}{\|}}{C}} \xrightarrow[(-N_2)]{} O=C=\ddot{N}-R \xrightarrow{H_2O} R-NH_2 + CO_2$$

$$\text{Isocyanate} \qquad\qquad \text{Amine}$$

Schmidt reaction involves the reaction of a carboxylic acid, hydrazoic acid and conc. H_2SO_4 to form amine *via* azide as intermedite

$$R-COOH + HN_3 \xrightarrow[\text{heat}]{\text{conc. } H_2SO_4} R-NH_2 + N_2 + CO_2$$

19.2.6 Preparation of Primary Amines by Lossen Rearrangement

Lossen rearrangement involves the conversion of a hydroxamic acid to primary amine by means of a base. Here also an isocyanate is formed as an intermediate

$$R-\underset{}{\overset{\overset{O}{\|}}{C}}-\underset{\underset{H}{|}}{N}-OH \xrightarrow[(-H^+)]{OH^-} \left[R-\overset{\overset{O}{\|}}{C}-\overset{..-}{N}-OH \right] \xrightarrow[(-OH^-)]{} \left[R-\overset{\overset{O}{\|}}{C}-\ddot{N}: \right] \longrightarrow O=C=N-R \xrightarrow[H_2O]{OH^-} R-NH_2 + CO_3^{2-}$$

$$\qquad\qquad\qquad\qquad\qquad \text{Nitrene} \qquad\qquad \text{Isocyanate}$$

19.2.7 Preparation of Primary Amine Containing a 3° Alkyl Group (Ritter Reaction)

Reaction of Me_3COH or $Me_2C=CH_2$ with HCN or RCN in conc. H_2SO_4 followed by hydrolysis gives primary amines.

$$(CH_3)_3COH \xrightarrow{H^+} (CH_3)_3C^+ \xleftarrow{H^+} (CH_3)_2C=CH_2$$

$$\textit{tert}\text{-Butanol} \qquad\qquad\qquad \text{Isobutene}$$

$$(CH_3)_3C^+ + :N\equiv CR \longrightarrow (CH_3)_3CN^+\equiv CR \xrightarrow[-H^+]{H_2O} (CH_3)_3CN-\underset{\underset{}{}}{\overset{\overset{H\ O}{|\ \|}}{C}}-R \xrightarrow{H_2O} (CH_3)_3CNH_2 + \qquad RCOO^-$$

$$\qquad\qquad\qquad\qquad\qquad\qquad\qquad\qquad\qquad \textit{tert}\text{-Butylamine} \quad (R = H \text{ or an alkyl group})$$

This method is especially useful for preparing 1° amines in which —NH_2 group is present on 3° carbon atom. Since such amines can't be prepared by reductive amination, nitrile reduction, oxime reduction, and Gabriel synthesis. However, Hofmann bromamide degradation can be used for preparing such amines.

19.2.8 By Leuckart Reaction

A ketone is heated with ammonium formate or dimethyl formamide (DMF) to form 1° and 3° amine respectively.

$$C_6H_5COCH_3 + HCOONH_4 \xrightarrow{\text{heat}} C_6H_5\underset{\underset{}{}}{\overset{\overset{NH_2}{|}}{C}}HCH_3 + H_2O + CO_2$$

$$(C_2H_5)_2CO + HCON(CH_3)_2 \xrightarrow{\text{heat}} C_2H_5-\overset{\displaystyle N(CH_3)_2}{\underset{\displaystyle}{CH}}-C_2H_5$$

DMF

Note that the reaction is similar to reductive amination.

19.2.9 By Grignard Reagents

$$RMgCl \ + \ ClNH_2 \ \longrightarrow \ RNH_2 \ + \ MgCl_2$$

      Chloramine   A 1° amine

$$RMgCl \ + \ ClNHR' \ \longrightarrow \ RNHR' \ + \ MgCl_2$$

  N-Alkylchloramine   A 2° amine

19.2.10 By the hydrolysis of Isocyanides and Isocyanates

$$RNC \ + \ 2H_2O \ \xrightarrow{\text{HCl}} \ RNH_2 \ + \ HCOOH$$

  Alkyl isonitrile

$$RNCO \ + \ 2KOH \ \xrightarrow{\text{heat}} \ RNH_2 + K_2CO_3$$

  Alkyl isocyanate

19.2.11 Special Methods for Preparing Secondary and Tertiary Amines

1. **By the reduction of isocyanides.** In this method one alkyl group is always methyl.

$$RNC + 4H \longrightarrow RNHCH_3 \quad \text{or} \quad RNC \xrightarrow{Na/C_2H_5OH} RNHCH_3$$

2. **Eschweiler-Clarke synthesis for tertiary amines.** This method is used for preparing a dimethyl 3° amine ($RNMe_2$). Primary or secondary amines are treated with formaldehyde and formic acid.

$$C_6H_5CH_2NH_2 + 2CH_2O + 2HCOOH \longrightarrow C_6H_5CH_2N(CH_3)_2 + 2H_2O + 2CO_2$$

$$(C_2H_5)_2NH + CH_2O + HCOOH \longrightarrow (C_2H_5)_2NCH_3 + H_2O + CO_2$$

Formic acid acts as a reducing agent by transferring its hydride ion to the electron-deficient carbon of formaldehyde and is oxidised to CO_2.

3. **Industrial methods.** Aniline, the most important of all amines, is prepared by following three methods :

(*a*) By the reduction of nitrobenzene by cheap reagents like Fe and dil. HCl or by catalytic hydrogenation.

(*b*) By treating chlorobenzene with ammonia at high temperature and high pressure in the presence of a catalyst

Methylamine, dimethylamine, and trimethylamine are synthesized from methanol and ammonia.

$$NH_3 \xrightarrow[\text{Al}_2\text{O}_3,\,450°C]{CH_3OH} CH_3NH_2 \xrightarrow[\text{Al}_2\text{O}_3,\,450°C]{CH_3OH} (CH_3)_2NH \xrightarrow[\text{Al}_2\text{O}_3,\,450°C]{CH_3OH} (CH_3)_3N$$

Methylamine   Dimethylamine   Trimethylamine

Function of Al₂O₃. Al_2O_3 is a Lewis acid and thus makes complexes with the O of ROH, making OH a better leaving group as H_2O.

TEST YOUR UNDERSTANDING - 19.5

1. How will you prepare $C_6H_5N(CH_3)_2$ from $C_6H_5NH_2$ in quantitative yield ?

19.3 Properties of Amines

1. Amines are moderately polar substances ; these are more polar than alkanes but less than alcohols. Thus amines have higher boiling points than alkanes and lower than alcohols of comparable molecular weight.

2. Molecules of primary and secondary amines can form strong hydrogen bonds to each other and to water or other hydroxylic solvents. However, tertiary amines although can form hydrogen bonds to water, their molecules do not form hydrogen bonds to each other. Hence

   (*a*) tertiary amines generally boil at lower temperatures than primary and secondary amines of comparable molecular weight. Among isomeric amines, primary amines have the highest boiling point, and tertiary amines the lowest.

   (*b*) lower amines (1°, 2° as well as 3°) are quite soluble in water.

3. Aniline, the simplest arylamine, is a liquid at room temperature. It is only slightly soluble in water and boils at 184°C. Other arylamines are less water-soluble and have higher boiling points than aniline.

TEST YOUR UNDERSTANDING - 19.6

1. Arrange the following isomeric amines in order of decreasing boiling points :
$$CH_3CH_2CH_2CH_2NH_2, \quad CH_3CH_2NHCH_2CH_3 \quad \text{and} \quad (CH_3)_2NC_2H_5.$$

2. Compare the dipole moments of the following compounds :
$$CH_3CH_2CH_2CH_2NH_2, \quad CH_3CH_2CH_2CH_2OH \quad \text{and} \quad CH_3(CH_2)_3CH_3.$$

3. Ethanolamine ($HOCH_2CH_2NH_2$) can form two different types of intramolecular H-bonding. Give their structures and discuss their relative importance.

4. *Optical isomerism in amines.* Like ammonia, nitrogen atom of most amines is sp^3 hybridised. The three substituents (alkyl groups or hydrogen atoms) occupy three corners of a tetrahedron, the fourth corner is occupied by an sp^3 orbital containing the unshared electron pair. Due to the presence of a free electron pair, the regular tetrahedral geometry (having bond angles of 109.5°) is somewhat distorted to trigonal pyramidal, having a bond angle less than 109.5°, *e.g.* 108° in trimethylamine.

If the three alkyl groups of a tertiary amine are different, the amine molecule will be chiral as hence should exist in two enantiomeric forms which should be resolvable. However, in practice, resolution is usually impossible because the two enantiomers interconvert rapidly.

Interconversion of amine enantiomers

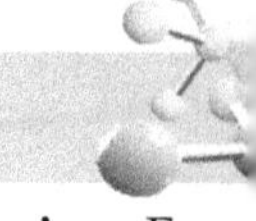

This interconversion, due to unshared pair of electrons, occurs through a **pyramidal** or **nitrogen inversion**. For most simple amines, the barrier to this interconversion is about 25 kJ mol^{-1} which is quite low to occur readily at room temperature. In other words, the two enantiomers of most of simple amines are interconverted readily at room temperature, and hence such amines can't be resolved, although they may have chiral nitrogen.

Ammonium salts do not have an unshared pair, hence they can't undergo inversion. Thus, quaternary ammonium salts having four different groups can be resolved into separate (relatively stable) enantiomers.

Enantiomers of quaternary ammonium salts (Resolvable)

TEST YOUR UNDERSTANDING - 19.7

1.   Which of the following compounds are (*i*) chiral, (*ii*) resolvable ?

(*a*) n-C$_3$H$_7$N(CH$_3$)C$_2$H$_5$

(*b*)   C$_6$H$_5$—N$^+$—O$^-$ with CH$_3$ above and C$_2$H$_5$ below

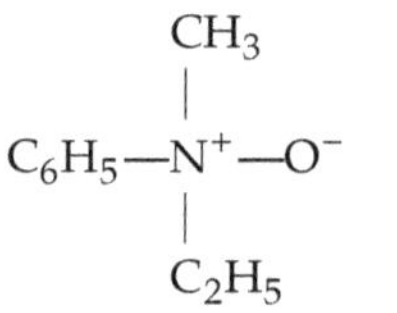

(*c*)   C$_3$H$_7$N$^+$(CH$_3$)$_2$C$_2$H$_5$ Br$^-$

(*d*)   CH$_3$CH$_2$CHN(CH$_3$)C$_2$H$_5$ with CH$_3$ above

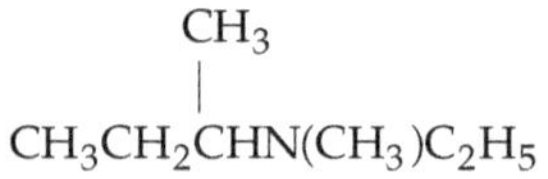

(*e*)   Me$_2$C———N̈CH$_3$ (cyclopropane ring with CH$_2$)

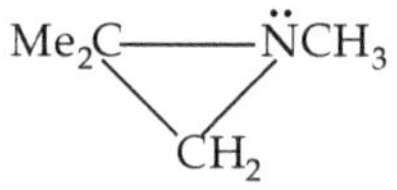

19.4   Reactions of Amines

Like ammonia, the three classes of amines contain nitrogen that bears an unshared pair of electrons. The tendency of nitrogen to share this pair of electrons is the sole reason for the entire chemical behaviour of amines, *i.e.* their basicity, their action as nucleophiles (in both aliphatic and acyl substitution) and the unusual high reactivity of aromatic rings bearing amino or substituted amino groups.

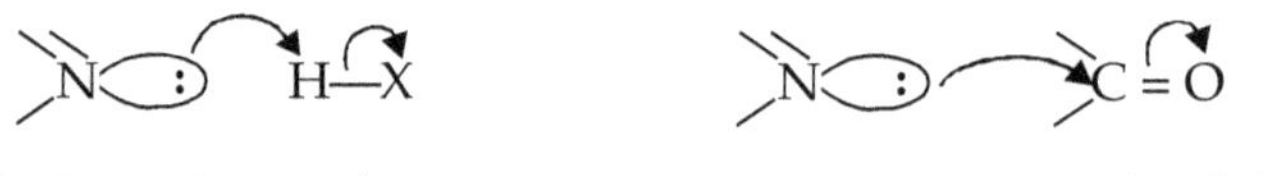

Amine acting as a base   Amine acting as a nucleophile

19.4.1   Basic and Nucleophilic Character of Amines

1.   **Basicity of amines.** Like ammonia, amines are converted into their salts by aqueous mineral acids and are liberated from their salts by aqueous hydroxides. Thus, like ammonia, amines are more basic than water and less basic than hydroxide ions.

$$RNH_2 \ + \ H_3O^+ \ \longrightarrow \ RNH_3^+ \ + \ H_2O$$

Stronger base   Weaker base

$$RNH_3^+ \ + \ OH^- \ \longrightarrow \ RNH_2 \ + \ H_2O$$

Stronger base   Weaker base

There are two conventions to measure the basicity of amines.

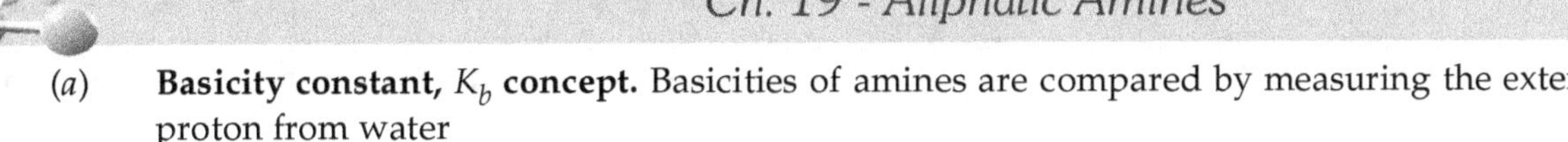

(a)   **Basicity constant, K_b concept.** Basicities of amines are compared by measuring the extent to which they accept proton from water

$$RNH_2 + H_2O \rightleftharpoons RNH_3^+ + OH^-$$

$$K_b = \frac{[RNH_3^+][OH^-]}{[RNH_2]} \; ; \; pK_b = -\log K_b$$

Here the basicity is expressed in terms of **basicity constant, K_b.** Each amine has its characteristic K_b, **the larger the K_b, the stronger is the base.**

(b)   **Acidity constant of the conjugate acid, K_a concept.** This is a convenient way for comparing the basic character of amines. The expression for this acidity constant is as follows.

$$RNH_3^+ + H_2O \rightleftharpoons RNH_2 + H_3O^+$$

$$K_a = \frac{[RNH_2][H_3O^+]}{[RNH_3^+]} \; ; \; pK_a = -\log K_a$$

If the amine is strongly basic, the aminium (or ammonium) ion will hold the proton tightly and consequently, will not be very acidic (indicated by its large pK_a value). On the other hand, if the amine in weakly basic, the aminium ion will not hold the proton tightly and will be much more acidic (indicated by its small pK_a value). In short, **the more basic the amine, the weaker is its conjugate acid and vice versa.**

TEST YOUR UNDERSTANDING - 19.8

1.   The K_b value for a base is 1×10^{-6} ; determine its pK_b value. Also calculate the K_a and pK_a values for its conjugate acid.

    Structure and basicity. Relation between structure and basicity of amines can well be understood by comparing the stabilities of amines with the stabilities of their ions ; **the more stable the ion relative to the parent amine, the more basic is the amine.**

1.   Since nitrogen is less electronegative than oxygen, and thus can better accommodate the positive charge of the ion, amines are more basic than alcohols, ethers, esters, etc.

2.   **Basicity of aliphatic amines.** An aliphatic amine is more basic than ammonia. This can be explained in two ways.

(a)   The alkyl group pushes electrons towards nitrogen (due to +I effect), and thus makes the lone pair of electrons more available for sharing with an acid.

$$R \longrightarrow \overset{..}{N}H_2 + H^+ \rightleftharpoons R \longrightarrow N^+H_3$$

R pushes electrons,   R pushes electrons,
makes unshared pair   stabilizes ion by
more available   neutralising charge

(b)   The alkyl group releases electrons and thus tends to disperse the positive charge of the alkylammonium ion and therefore stabilizes it. Since NH_4^+ (from NH_3) has no such alkyl group, it is not stabilised to such an extent as alkylammonium ion.

The above explanation is supported by the following relative basicities of the amines in the *gas phase.*

$$(CH_3)_3N \; > \; (CH_3)_2NH \; > \; CH_3NH_2 \; > \; NH_3 \quad \textbf{(Basicity in gas phase)}$$

However, in *aqueous solution*, the order of basicity of these amines (as shown below) is somewhat different.

$$(CH_3)_2NH \; > \; CH_3NH_2 \; > \; (CH_3)_3N \; > \; NH_3 \quad \textbf{(Basicity in aq. solution)}$$

The altered order of amine basicities in solution, as compared to those in the gas phase, is due to **solvation effects.**

Stability of the alkylammonium ions (conjugate acids of alkylamines) can be explained in the following two ways :

(*i*)   Dispersal of the positive charge by alkyl group(s). More the number of alkyl groups, more should be the stability of the alkylammonium ion and hence more is the basic character of the parent amine

$$CH_3 \to \overset{CH_3}{\underset{CH_3}{\overset{|}{N^+}H}} > CH_3 \to \overset{H}{\underset{CH_3}{\overset{|}{N^+}-H}} > CH_3 \to \overset{H}{\underset{H}{\overset{|}{N^+}-H}}$$

From $(CH_3)_3 \ddot{N}$ From $(CH_3)_2 \ddot{N}H$ From $(CH_3) \ddot{N}H_2$

(*ii*)   Formation of H-bond between H of the ammonium ion and O of H_2O, a solvent (*solvation effect*). Greater the number of H atoms on the N atom of the ammonium ion, more will be H-bonding and hence more will be the stability of the ammonium ion. Thus ammonium ion from *tert-*, *sec.-*, and primary amines have 1, 2 and 3 such H atoms, respectively ; hence the ammonium ion from *tert*-amines will be least stable. Actually poorer solvation of the ammonium ion formed from a tertiary amine more than compensates the electron-releasing effect of the three alkyl groups and makes the ammonium ion less stable and hence the parent *tert*-amine less basic than primary and secondary amines in aqueous solution.

$$CH_3 - \overset{CH_3}{\underset{H ------ OH_2}{\overset{|}{N^+}}} - H ------ OH_2 \qquad\qquad CH_3 - \overset{CH_3}{\underset{CH_3}{\overset{|}{N^+}}} ----- OH_2$$

Dimethylammonium ion   Trimethylammonium ion
(two protons on N available   (only one proton on nitrogen
for H-bonding).   available for H-bonding)
More stable from $(CH_3)_2NH$ **Less stable** from $(CH_3)_3N$

Secondary amines are more basic than either primary or tertiary amines because their conjugate acids possess the best combination of alkyl and hydrogen substituents to permit stabilization both by electron release from alkyl group and by solvation due to hydrogen bonding. Higher basic character of *tert*-amine than ammonia is due to electron-releasing effect of the three alkyl groups.

Basicity of arylamines. Arylamines, *e.g.* aniline and *p*-toluidine, are less basic than even ammonia what to speak of alkylamines. We can account for this effect, in part, on the basis of resonance. In arylamines, the lone pair of electrons on N is partly shared with the ring and is thus less available for sharing with a proton.

I   II   III   IV

Delocalization of the electron pair to the ring also stabilizes the parent compound, aniline.

When aniline accepts a proton, it becomes anilinium ion.

Aniline   Anilinium ion

Since N atom of anilinium ion does not have lone pair of electrons, structures corresponding to II, III and IV are not possible for the anilinium ion, and thus anilinium ion is considerably less stable than aniline. This greater stabilization of the reactant (aniline) as compared to product (anilinium ion) means that ΔH^0 for the reaction between aniline and water will be a larger positive quantity than that for the reaction between NH_3 and H_2O

$$\text{Aniline} + H_2O \longrightarrow \text{Anilinium ion} + OH^-$$

$$NH_3 + H_2O \longrightarrow NH_4^+ + OH^-$$

Hence, aniline will be the weaker base than ammonia. When the proton donor is a strong acid, arylamines (weak bases) can be completely protonated.

Another important effect in explaining the lower basicity of aromatic amines is the **electron-withdrawing effect of a phenyl group** because its carbon atoms are sp^2 hybridised which are more electronegative than the sp^3 hybridised carbon atoms of alkyl groups. Further, anilinium ion is less stable than the alkylammonium ion, again because of electron-withdrawing nature of the phenyl group which destabilizes the anilinium ion by intensifying the positive charge on N.

Positive charge on N intensified   Positive charge on N dispersed

Effect of substituents on basicity of aromatic amines. In general, electron-donating substituents on the aromatic ring increase the basicity of arylamines ; while electron-withdrawing groups decrease the basicity. Electron-releasing group tends to disperse the positive charge of the anilinium ion, and thus stabilizes the ion relative to the amine. On the other hand, electron-withdrawing group tends to intensity the positive charge of the anilinium ion, and thus destabilizes the ion relative to the amine.

Here $G = -NH_2, -OCH_3, -CH_3$

G releases electrons, stabilizes cation, increases basicity of the parent amine

Here $G = -NH_3^+, -NO_2, -SO_3^-, -COOH, -X$

G withdraws electrons, destabilizes cation, decreases basicity of the parent amine

Ortho effect. It is important to note that a group present in the *ortho* position to the $-NH_2$ group always weakens the basicity whether it is electron-releasing or electron-withdrawing. An electron-withdrawing substituent in the *ortho* position decreases the basicity to a much greater extent than the same group when present in *meta-* or *para*-position.

Since amines act as bases, they react with aqueous acids forming compounds called **aminium salts** ;in an aminium salt, the positively charged nitrogen atom is attached to at least one hydrogen atom.

$$CH_3CH_2NH_2 + HCl \xrightarrow{H_2O} CH_3CH_2NH_3^+Cl^-$$
Ethylaminium chloride

$$(CH_3CH_2)_3N + HI \xrightarrow{H_2O} (CH_3CH_2)_3NH^+I^-$$
Triethylaminium iodide

When the central nitrogen atom of a compound is positively charged but not attached to a hydrogen atom, the compound is called a **quaternary ammonium salt**. Since quaternary ammonium halides do not have an unshared electron pair on the nitrogen atom, these can not act as bases, *i.e.* they do not react with acids. However, quaternary ammonium

hydroxides are as strong bases as NaOH or KOH because they consist entirely of quaternary ammonium cations (R_4N^+) and hydroxide ions in the solid or in solution.

$$(CH_3)_4N^+ OH^- + HCl \longrightarrow (CH_3)_4N^+Cl^- + H_2O$$

Almost all alkylaminium and quaternary ammonium halides, nitrates, and sulphates are soluble in water (properties of salts). Thus although amines are water-insoluble, they dissolve in dilute aqueous HCl, HBr, HI or H_2SO_4 due to the formation of corresponding salts which are soluble in water. Parent amines can be regenerated from the soluble salt by making the salt solution alkaline. This difference in solubility behaviour between amines and their salts can be used both to detect amines and to separate them from non-basic compounds which do not react with aqueous acids.

$$\underbrace{RNH_2, \quad R_2NH, \quad \text{or} \quad R_3N}_{\substack{1° \text{ amine} \quad 2° \text{ amine} \quad 3° \text{ amine} \\ \text{Insoluble in water}}} \quad \underset{OH^-}{\overset{H^+}{\rightleftharpoons}} \quad \underbrace{RNH_3^+, \quad R_2NH_2^+, \quad \text{or} \quad R_3NH^+}_{\substack{\text{Corresponding aminium ion (salt)} \\ \text{Soluble in water}}}$$

TEST YOUR UNDERSTANDING - 19.9

1. 3-Aminopropanol, $H_2\ddot{N}CH_2CH_2CH_2\ddot{O}H$, can form conjugate acid, or conjugate base, or both ; write the possible structure for the same.

2. (a) What kind of reagents are used to form the conjugate base of an amine ?
   (b) Give the generic name for the conjugate base of an amine.

3. Write equations for the reaction of following hydrazines with an aqueous acid :
   (a) CH_3NHNH_2 (b) $C_6H_5NHNH_2$.

4. Name the factors that affect relative basicities.

5. Which one is more basic ?

(a) I (tetrahydroquinoline, N—H) or II (tetrahydroisoquinoline, NH)

(b) cyclohexylamine (NH_2) or 2-aminocyclohexanone (O, NH_2)

(c) $F_3CCH_2NH_2$ or $F_2CHCH_2NH_2$

(d) p-nitroaniline (NH_2, NO_2) or p-(trifluoromethyl)aniline (NH_2, CF_3)

(e) Aq. $(CH_3)_2NH$ or Aq. $(CH_3)_3N$

(f) $(CH_3)_2NH$ or $(CH_3)_3N$ in gas phase

(g) $Me_3CCH_2CH_2NH_2$ or $Me_3N^+CH_2CH_2NH_2$

(h) p-cyanoaniline (NH_2, $C \equiv N$) or p-nitroaniline (NH_2, NO_2)

(i) N,N-dimethylaniline (NMe_2) or 2,6-dimethyl-N,N-dimethylaniline (NMe_2, Me, Me)

6. Arrange the following in their decreasing basicity :
   (a) $CH_3NH^-Na^+$, $C_2H_5NH_2$, CH_3CONH_2 and $[(CH_3)_2CH]_3N$
   (b) $C_6H_5NH_2$, CH_3NH_2, $(C_6H_5)_2NH$, NH_3 and $(C_6H_5)_3N$
   (c) $CH_3CH_2NH_2$, $HOCH_2CH_2NH_2$, and $HOCH_2CH_2CH_2NH_2$
   (d) $CH_3CH = NH$, $CH_3CH_2NH_2$ and CH_3CN
   (e) $CH_3CH_2CH_2NH_2$, $CH_2 = CHCH_2NH_2$ and $CH \equiv CCH_2NH_2$
   (f) $C_6H_5CH_2NH_2$, $C_6H_{11}CH_2NH_2$ and p-$NO_2C_6H_4CH_2NH_2$
   (g) $CH_3CH_2NH_2$, CH_3CONH_2 and $C_6H_5CONH_2$.

7. Arrange the following in decreasing basic strength :

(*a*) $C_6H_5NH_2$, *p*-$NO_2C_6H_4NH_2$, *m*-$NO_2C_6H_4NH_2$, and *p*-$H_3COC_6H_4NH_2$

(*b*) $C_6H_5NH_2$, *o*-$NO_2C_6H_4NH_2$, *m*-$NO_2C_6H_4NH_2$, and *p*-$NO_2C_6H_4NH_2$

(*c*) $C_6H_5NH_2$, *o*-$CH_3OC_6H_4NH_2$, *m*-$CH_3OC_6H_4NH_2$, and *p*-$CH_3OC_6H_4NH_2$

(*d*) $C_6H_5NH_2$, *o*-$CH_3C_6H_4NH_2$, *m*-$CH_3C_6H_4NH_2$, and *p*-$CH_3C_6H_4NH_2$.

8. In terms of *s* character, amino N of guanidine should be more basic, but actually imino N is found to be more basic. Explain.

$$\underset{H_2N-\overset{\displaystyle \overset{NH}{\|}}{C}-NH_2}{}$$

9. Give the schematic representation involved in separating a mixture of the three water-insoluble liquids : aniline (b.p. 184°C), *n*-butylbenzene (b.p. 183°C), and *n*-valeric acid (b.p. 187°C).

Amines as resolving agents : Basic properties of amines has been applied in resolving (separating) the racemic forms of acidic compounds. Let us illustrate it by showing the resolution of a racemic form of an organic acid with the help of a single enantiomer of an amine, a resolving agent. The two enantiomeric components of the acid are converted into two salts. The two salts are not enantiomers, but diastereomers (the stereocenters of the acid portion of the two salts are enantiomerically related to each other, but the stereocenters of the amine portion are not). The diastereomers have different solubilities and thus can be separated by careful crystallization. The separated salts are then acidified with hydrochloric acid and the enantiomeric acids are obtained from the separate solutions. The amine remains in solution as its hydrochloride salt.

Resolution of the racemic form of an organic acid by the use of an optically active amine. Acidification of the separated diastereomeric salts causes the enantiomeric acids to precipitate (assuming they are insoluble in water) and leaves the resolving agent in solution as its conjugate acid.

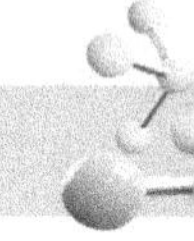

TEST YOUR UNDERSTANDING - 19.10

1. Give the schematic representation involved in the resolution of (±)-2-phenylpropanoic acid using (+)-*sec*-butylamine as the resolving agent.

2. **Reaction with alkyl halides (*Alkylation of amines*) :** Like ammonia, an amine (1°, 2° or 3°) can react with an alkyl halide to form next higher class of amine. Here, again it is the presence of electron pair on nitrogen which makes amines to behave as nucleophile and alkyl halides thus undergo nucleophilic substitutions.

$$R\overset{..}{N}H_2 + R'CH_2X \longrightarrow RN^+\!-\!CH_2R' \longrightarrow R\overset{..}{N}\!-\!CH_2R' + HX$$

1° Amine · 1° Alkyl halide · 2° Amine
(Nucleophile)

A second alkylation may follow, converting the secondary amine to a tertiary amine which may be alkylated to give a quaternary ammonium salt.

Because of its high reactivity towards nucleophilic substitution, methyl iodide is the most frequently used alkyl halide to proceed to the quaternary ammonium stage.

$$R\overset{..}{N}H_2 \xrightarrow{CH_3I} R\overset{..}{N}HCH_3 \xrightarrow{CH_3I} R\overset{..}{N}(CH_3)_2 \xrightarrow{CH_3I} RN^+(CH_3)_3I$$

1° Amine · 2° Amine · 3° Amine · Quaternary ammonium iodide

Quaternary ammonium salts are useful in synthetic organic chemistry as phase-transfer catalysts* and in the preparation of alkenes.

3. **Reaction with acid chlorides :** Like ammonia, amines (1° and 2°) react with acid chlorides of carboxylic acid or of sulphonic acids to form N-substituted amides.

$$RNH_2 + R'\!-\!\overset{\overset{\displaystyle O}{\|}}{C}\!-\!Cl \longrightarrow R'\!-\!\overset{\overset{\displaystyle O}{\|}}{C}\!-\!NHR$$

$$RNH_2 + Ar\!-\!\overset{\overset{\displaystyle O}{\|}}{\underset{\underset{\displaystyle O}{\|}}{S}}\!-\!Cl \longrightarrow Ar\!-\!\overset{\overset{\displaystyle O}{\|}}{\underset{\underset{\displaystyle O}{\|}}{S}}\!-\!NHR$$

$$(CH_3)_2NH + C_6H_5SO_2Cl \longrightarrow C_6H_5SO_2N(CH_3)_2$$

N, N-Dimethylbenzenesulphonamide

$$CH_3NH_2 + p\text{-}CH_3C_6H_4SO_2Cl \longrightarrow p\text{-}CH_3C_6H_4SO_2NHCH_3$$

p-Toluenesulphonyl chloride · N-Methyl-*p*-toluenesulphonamide
(Tosyl chloride)

In these reactions ammonia, 1° amine, or 2° amine serves as a nucleophile and attacks the carbonyl carbon or sulphur and displace chloride ion. Simultaneously, nitrogen loses a proton to a second molecule of ammonia or another base.

$$CH_3NH_2 + CH_3\!-\!\overset{\overset{\displaystyle O}{\|}}{C}\!-\!Cl \longrightarrow CH_3\!-\!\overset{\overset{\displaystyle O}{\|}}{C}\!-\!NHCH_3 + NH_4^+ + Cl^-$$

---

*   A small amount of a quaternary ammonium salt promotes the transfer of an anion from aqueous solution, where it is highly solvated, to an organic solvent, where it is much less solvated and much more reactive.

Tertiary amines, although basic and hence nucleophile, do not react with acid chlorides because they cannot lose a proton (to stabilize the product) after attaching themselves to carbon or sulphur. Hence for a reaction of amines with acid chlorides, there are two essential conditions : (*a*) amine should be nucleophilic to attack on the electron-deficient carbonyl C, (*b*) amine should possess a hydrogen atom on the nitrogen atom which is lost as proton to form the stable product (amide).

$$CH_3NH_2 + C_6H_5SO_2Cl \longrightarrow C_6H_5SO_2NHCH_3$$

$$(CH_3)_2NH + CH_3COCl \longrightarrow CH_3CON(CH_3)_2$$

$$(CH_3)_3N + CH_3COCl \quad or \quad C_6H_5SO_2Cl \longrightarrow No\ reaction$$

Acetylation is generally carried out using acetic anhydride rather than acetyl chloride. For example,

$$\bigcirc\!\!-NH_2 + (CH_3CO)_2O \xrightarrow{CH_3COONa} \bigcirc\!\!-NHCOCH_3 + CH_3COOH$$

Acetanilide

Schotten-Baumann reaction. Reaction of acid chloride or sulphonyl chloride of aromatic carboxylic acids or aromatic sulphonic acid with an amine (1° or 2° ; alphatic or aromatic) in presence of aqueous sodium hydroxide or pyridine to form substituted amides is known as Schotten-Baumann reaction.

$$C_6H_5NH_2 + C_6H_5COCl \xrightarrow{pyridine} C_6H_5CONHC_6H_5$$

Benzanilide

$$(n\text{-}C_3H_7)_2NH + C_6H_5SO_2Cl \xrightarrow{NaOH} C_6H_5SO_2N(C_3H_7\text{-}n)_2$$

N, N-Di-*n*-Propylbenzenesulphonamide

$$C_2H_5NHCH_3 \ + \ p\text{-}CH_3C_6H_4SO_2Cl \xrightarrow{aq.\ NaOH} p\text{-}CH_3.C_6H_4SO_2N(CH_3)C_2H_5$$

p-Toluene sulphonylchloride

Carboxamides as well as sulphonamides are easily hydrolysed to parent acid and amine. However, sulphonamides are hydrolysed more slowly than carboxamides (amides of carboxylic acids). Nucleophilic attack on a trigonal acyl carbon is relatively unhindered while that on a tetrahedral sulphonyl sulphur is relatively hindered. Moreover, the intermediate in the former is tetrahedral C, having octet of electrons, while that in the latter intermediate is a pentavalent sulphur, having dectet of electrons (a less stable system).

Tetrahedral C (stable octet)   Pentavalent S (unstable dectet)

4.   **Reaction with aldehydes and ketones :** Primary amines add (as nucleophiles) to the carbonyl group of an aldehyde or a ketone to form *carbinolamines,* which then dehydrate to form imines (also known as **Schiff's bases**) as the final product.

1° Amine   Aldehyde or Ketone   Carbinolamine   Imine

$$CH_3NH_2 + C_6H_5CHO \longrightarrow CH_3N = CHC_6H_5$$

N-Benzylidenemethylamine

$$(CH_3)_2CHCH_2NH_2 + \bigcirc\!\!=O \longrightarrow \bigcirc\!\!=NCH_2CH(CH_3)_2$$

N-Cyclohexylideneisobutylamine

Both the addition and elimination phase of the reaction are accelerated by acid catalysis.

Secondary amines add to aldehydes and ketones to form carbinolamines which can dehydrate to a stable product leading to a carbon-carbon double bond (difference from 1° amines which form product having carbon-nitrogen double bond).

$$R_2\ddot{N}H + \underset{2°\ Amine}{} \quad \underset{R''}{\overset{R'CH_2}{>}}C=O \longrightarrow R_2\ddot{N}-\underset{\underset{R''}{|}}{\overset{\overset{CH_2R'}{|}}{C}}-OH \xrightarrow{-H_2O} R_2N-C\underset{R''}{\overset{CHR'}{<}}$$

Carbinolamine — Enamine

Pyrrolidine + Cyclohexanone ⟶ N-(1-Cyclohexenyl)pyrrolidine

Pyrrolidine + Cyclopentanone ⟶ N-(1-Cyclopentenyl)pyrrolidine

This reaction is not given by *tert*-amines.

5. **Reaction with carbonyl chloride** to form *sym*-disubstituted urea.

$$2RNH_2 + Cl-\overset{\overset{O}{\|}}{C}-Cl \longrightarrow RNH-\overset{\overset{O}{\|}}{C}-NHR + 2HCl$$

This reaction is given only by 1°, and **not by 2° and 3° amines**.

6. **Reaction with isocyanates and isothiocyanates** to form disubstituted urea and thiourea respectively.

$$R\ddot{N}H_2 + \overset{\overset{O}{\|}}{C}=N-R' \longrightarrow R-\overset{+}{N}-C=N-R' \longrightarrow RNH-\overset{\overset{O}{\|}}{C}-NHR'$$

Unsymmetrical disubstituted urea

$$R\ddot{N}H_2 + \overset{\overset{S}{\|}}{C}=N-R' \longrightarrow RNH-\overset{\overset{S}{\|}}{C}-NHR'$$

Isothiocyanate

Unsymmetrical disubstituted thiourea

7. **Reaction with carbon disulphide.** Primary amines when warmed with carbon disulphide form a **dithiocarbamic acid** which is decomposed by mercuric chloride to give alkyl isothiocyanates, having mustard oil smell, along with black precipitate of mercuric sulphide. This reaction, known as **Hofmann mustard oil reaction**, is used as a test for 1° amines.

$$RNH_2 + S=C=S \longrightarrow S=C\underset{\backslash SH}{\overset{/NHR}{}} \xrightarrow{HgCl_2} R-N=C=S + HgS\downarrow + 2HCl$$

Dithiocarbamic acid — Isothiocyanate — Black

Secondary amines also react with CS_2 to form dithiocarbamic acids, but the latter do not react with mercuric chloride (difference from 1° amines).

$$R_2NH + S=C=S \longrightarrow S=C\underset{\backslash SH}{\overset{/NR_2}{}} \xrightarrow{HgCl_2} \text{No reaction}$$

Tertiary amines do not react with carbon disulphide.

8. **Carbylamine reaction of 1° amines.**

$$RNH_2 + CHCl_3 + 3KOH \longrightarrow R{-}N^+ \equiv C^-: + 3\,KCl + 3H_2O$$

An isocyanide
(foul smelling)

Recall that here the nucleophile RNH_2 attacks the electrophilic intermediate (dichlorocarbene, $:CCl_2$) formed by the action of a base on $CHCl_3$.

$$HCCl_3 \xrightarrow{OH^-} :CCl_3^- \xrightarrow{-Cl^-} :CCl_2$$

Dichlorocarbene

Since carbylamines have unpleasant smell which can be easily detected, the reaction is used to **identify primary amines.**

TEST YOUR UNDERSTANDING - 19.11

1. Give the structures for the products of the reaction of the following :

(*a*) $(CH_3)_2NH + C_6H_5COCl$
(*b*) $C_2H_5NH_2$ + Succinic anhydride
(*c*) $C_6H_5NHCH_3 + C_6H_5COOC_2H_5$
(*d*) $(CH_3)_2NH + C_6H_5SO_2Cl$
(*e*) $C_6H_5CH_2NH_2 + HCOOH \xrightarrow{heat}$
(*f*) $C_6H_5NH_2 + C_6H_5CHO$.

2. Complete the following :

(*a*) $CH_3COCH_2CH_3 + (CH_3)_2NH$

(*b*) 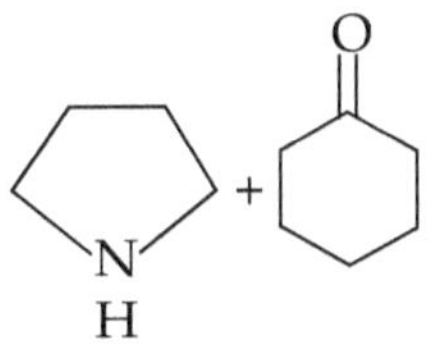 $\longrightarrow$ [A] $\xrightarrow{H_3O^+}$

9. **Reaction with nitrous acid.** Nitrous acid (HONO) is a weak, unstable acid. It is always prepared *in situ*, usually by treating sodium nitrite with an aqueous solution of a strong acid.

$$NaNO_2(aq) + HCl(aq) \longrightarrow NaCl(aq) + HONO(aq)$$

$$2NaNO_2(aq) + H_2SO_4(aq) \longrightarrow Na_2SO_4(aq) + 2HONO(aq)$$

Nitrous acid reacts with all classes of amines, although different product is obtained from different class of amines. Reaction of nitrous acid with all amines (1°, 2°, or 3°, aliphatic, or aromatic) involves electrophilic attack by nitrosyl cation, NO^+ followed by displacement of H^+. This attack occurs at position of highest electron density which is N atom in 1° and 2° amines, and *para-* or *ortho*-carbon atom of the highly reactive ring in case of aromatic 3° amines.

Formation of nitrosyl cation by the reaction of $NaNO_2$ with HCl

$$^-O{-}N=O \xrightarrow{H^+} HO{-}N=O \xrightarrow{H^+} H\overset{+}{O}(H){-}N=O \longrightarrow {}^+N=O + H_2O$$

Nitrite ion (from $NaNO_2$) — Nitrous acid — Protonated nitrous acid

$\downarrow Cl^-$

$$H_2O + Cl{-}N=O \longrightarrow {}^+N=O + Cl^-$$

(better leaving group) — Nitrosyl chloride

Primary aromatic amines react with nitrous acid to form diazonium salts. This is one of the most important reactions in organic chemistry because the arenediazonium salts, although unstable, are far more stable than aliphatic diazonium salts. They do not decompose at an appreciable rate in solution at temperature below 5°C.

$$Ar{-}NH_2 + NaNO_2 + 2HX \longrightarrow Ar{-}N^+ \equiv N : X^- + NaX + 2H_2O$$

1° Aromatic amine — Arenediazonium salt (stable below 5°C)

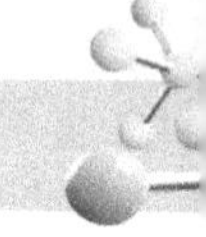

Details of preparation and synthetic importance of aromatic diazonium salts will be discussed in the next chapter.

Primary aliphatic amines also react with nitrous acid to yield aliphatic diazonium salts. However, aliphatic diazonium salts are quite unstable and decompose spontaneously, even at low temperatures, by losing nitrogen to form carbocations (hence the reaction is commonly known as **deamination**). The carbocations, in turn, produce a mixture of alkenes, alcohols, and alkyl halides.

$$CH_3CH_2CH_2NH_2 \xrightarrow[HCl]{HONO} [CH_3CH_2CH_2N_2{}^+Cl^-] \longrightarrow CH_3CH_2CH_2{}^+ + N_2 + Cl^-$$

$$CH_3CH = CH_2 \xleftarrow{-H^+} CH_3CH_2CH_2{}^+ \longrightarrow CH_3{}^+CHCH_3 \xrightarrow{-H^+} CH_3CH = CH_2$$

Propene $\downarrow H_2O, \text{ or } Cl^-$ $\downarrow H_2O, \text{ or } Cl^-$

$CH_3CH_2CH_2OH$ or $CH_3CH_2CH_2Cl$ $CH_3CHOHCH_3$ or $CH_3CHClCH_3$
1-Propanol   1-Chloropropane   2-Propanol   2-Chloropropane

Since the reaction yields a complex mixture of products, it is of little synthetic importance. However, since the evolution of nitrogen is quantitative, diazotisation of 1° aliphatic amines is used in detecting the presence of $-NH_2$ group, especially in amino acids and proteins.

Secondary amines, both aliphatic and aromatic, react with nitrous acid to yield N-nitrosoamines which useually separate from the reaction mixture as oily yellow liquids.

$$(CH_3)_2NH + HONO \longrightarrow (CH_3)_2N-N = O$$

Dimethylamine   N-Nitrosodimethylamine

$$C_6H_5NHCH_3 + HONO \longrightarrow C_6H_5N(CH_3)N = O$$

N-Methylaniline   N-Nitroso-N-methylaniline

Nitrosamines are easily hydrolysed by dil. HCl back to form 2° amines. An important property of nitrosamines is their reaction with phenol and conc. H_2SO_4 to form green coloured solution which changes to deep blue on adding aq. NaOH (**Libermann's nitroso reaction**, used as a test for 2° amines).

N-Nitrosoamines are cancer-causing agents (**carcenogens**). We encounter several nitrosamines in the environment, *e.g.*

$$(CH_3)_2NN = O$$

N-Nitrosodimethylamine   N-Nitrosopyrrolidine   N-Nitrosonornicotine
(formed during tanning of leather;   (formed when bacon, cured   (present in tobacco smoke)
also found in beer and herbicides)   with $NaNO_2$, is fried)

Nirosamines are probably also synthesized within our body. Enzyme-catalyzed reduction of $NO_3{}^-$ gives $NO_2{}^-$ which combines with amines present in the body to form N-nitrosamines. In the human body, HONO is also formed by the action of gastric HCl on nitrites ingested in foods ; HONO then can react with 2° amino group to form N- nitrosamine.

Aliphatic tertiary amines form $R_3N^+-N = O$ type of compounds which do not have any amino H, hence stable at low temperature. These compounds are of little importance.

Tertiary aromatic amines undergo ring substitution almost exclusively at the para position (electrophilic aromatic substitution).

$$\text{C}_6\text{H}_5-N(CH_3)_2 \xrightarrow{HONO} ON-\text{C}_6\text{H}_4-N(CH_3)_2$$

p-Nitroso-N, N-dimethylaniline

Since nitrosonium ion, NO^+ (produced *via* H_2O^+-NO or $NOCl$) is very weak electrophile, nitrosation ordinarily occurs only in very strongly activated aromatic rings, *viz.* rings bearing dialkylamino ($-NR_2$) or hydroxy ($-OH$) group.

TEST YOUR UNDERSTANDING - 19.12

1. Give the various possible products obtained by the reaction of nitrous acid on :

   (*a*)　2, 2-dimethylpropylamine,　　(*b*)　1, 1-dimethylpropylamine, and　(*c*)　benzylamine.

2. Write down the structures of the alcohols produced by the reaction of nitrous acid on *sec*-butylamine.

3. N-Nitrosamines are stabilized by electron delocalization. Write the two most stable resonance forms of N-nitrosodimethylamine, $(CH_3)_2NO$

4. N-Methylaniline and N, N-dimethylaniline give different products with nitrous acid. Comment.

5. Give the structure of the products obtained by the reaction of nitrous acid on the following.

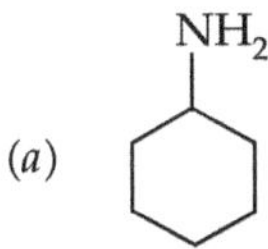

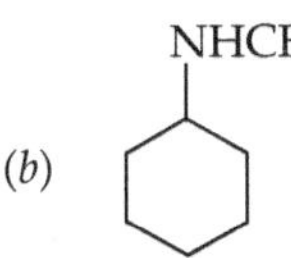

---

10. **Oxidation of amines.** Amines are usually oxidized at N, rather than at C in RCH_2OH. Primary and secondary aliphatic amines are although oxidisable, in most cases useful products are not obtained. Complicated side reactions often occur, causing the formation of complex mixtures.

(*a*)
$$CH_3CH_2NH_2 \xrightarrow{KMnO_4} \underset{\text{Aldimine}}{CH_3CH = NH} \xrightarrow{H^+} CH_3CHO$$

$$(CH_3)_2CHNH_2 \xrightarrow[\text{Caro's acid}]{H_2SO_5} \underset{\text{Ketoxime}}{(CH_3)_2C = NOH}$$

$$(CH_3)_3CNH_2 \xrightarrow{H_2SO_5} (CH_3)_3CN = O$$

(*b*)
$$\underset{\text{Dimethylamine}}{(CH_3)_2NH} \xrightarrow{H_2SO_5} \underset{\text{Dimethylhydroxylamine}}{(CH_3)_2NOH}$$

$$2(CH_3)_2NH \xrightarrow{KMnO_4} \underset{\text{Tetramethylhydrazine}}{(CH_3)_2N—N(CH_3)_2}$$

Tertiary amines can be oxidized quantitatively by H_2O_2 or a peroxy acid to tetiary amine oxides, R_3N^+—O^-, a dipolar ion or Zwitterion.

$$R_3N: \xrightarrow{H_2O_2 \text{ or } RCOOOH} R_3\overset{+}{N}—\overset{..}{\underset{..}{O}}{}^{-}$$

Tertiary amine oxides containing a β-hydrogen atom, on heating, undergo a useful elimination reaction to form alkenes (**Cope reaction**).

Cope elimination. Tertiary amine oxides, prepared by treating tertiary amines with hydrogen peroxide, containing β-hydrogen atom, when heated undergo the elimination of a dialkylhydroxylamine and form alkene.

$$RCH_2CH_2N(CH_3)_2 \xrightarrow{H_2O_2} RCH_2CH_2\overset{\overset{\displaystyle :\overset{..}{O}{}^{-}}{|}}{\underset{\underset{\displaystyle CH_3}{|}}{N}}{}^{+}\!\!—CH_3 \xrightarrow{150°C} RCH = CH_2 + \underset{\text{N, N-Dimethylhydroxylamine}}{\overset{\overset{\displaystyle OH}{|}}{N(CH_3)_2}}$$

The cope elimination is a *syn* elimination and proceeds through a cyclic transition state.

$$R—\overset{\overset{\displaystyle H}{|}}{\underset{\underset{\displaystyle H}{|}}{C}}—CH_2—\overset{\overset{\displaystyle O^-}{|}}{\underset{\underset{\displaystyle CH_3}{|}}{N}}{}^{+}\!\!—CH_3 \xrightarrow{heat} R—\overset{\overset{\displaystyle H------O^-}{}}{\underset{\underset{\displaystyle H}{|}}{C}}CH_2\overset{}{\underset{\underset{\displaystyle CH_3}{|}}{N}}{}^{+}\!\!—CH_3 \longrightarrow R—CH = CH_2 + HON(CH_3)_2$$

TEST YOUR UNDERSTANDING - 19.13

1.   Identify the compounds [A] to [G] in the following reactions :

(a) [cyclohexane with CH$_2$NMe$_2$ group] $\xrightarrow{H_2O_2}$ [A] $\xrightarrow{heat}$ Alkene [B]   (b) [cyclohexene with NMe$_2$ group] $\xrightarrow{H_2O_2}$ [C] $\xrightarrow{heat}$ Alkene [D]

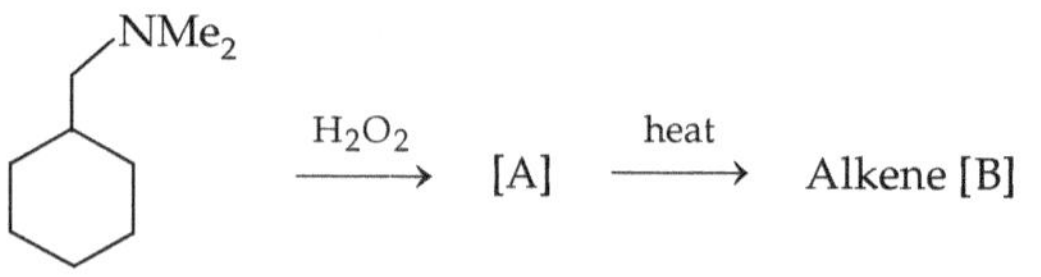

(c) $C_2H_5\overset{O^-}{\underset{CH_3}{N^+}}CH_2CH_2CH_3$ $\xrightarrow{heat}$ Alkene [E] + Alkene [F]   (d) $C_6H_{11}\ CH_2\overset{O^-}{N^+}(CH_3)_2$ $\xrightarrow{heat}$ [G]

Arylamines are very easily oxidized by a variety of reagents, including the oxygen in air. Further, here oxidation is not confined to the amino group but also occurs in the ring (the electron-releasing ability of the —NH$_2$ group makes the ring electron rich, and hence especially susceptible to oxidation). The oxidation of other oxidizable functional group on an aromatic ring cannot be usually accomplished when an amino group is present on the ring, because ring is oxidized first.

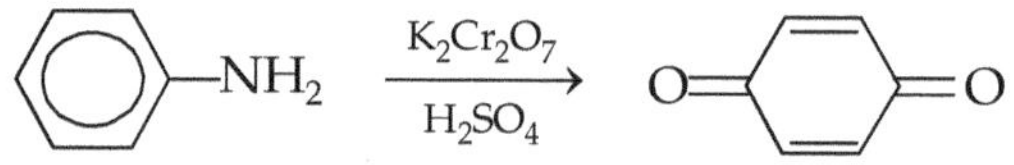

[benzene ring with —NH$_2$] $\xrightarrow[H_2SO_4]{K_2Cr_2O_7}$ [O=cyclohexadiene=O]

Aniline   *p*-Benzoquinone

19.4.2 Ring Substitution in Aromatic Compounds

In the preceding reactions No. 1 to 10, the amine acts as a nucleophile by donating its electron pair to an electrophilic reagent. However, in ring substitution, electron pair on nitrogen makes *ortho* and *para* carbon atoms of the ring nucleophilic.

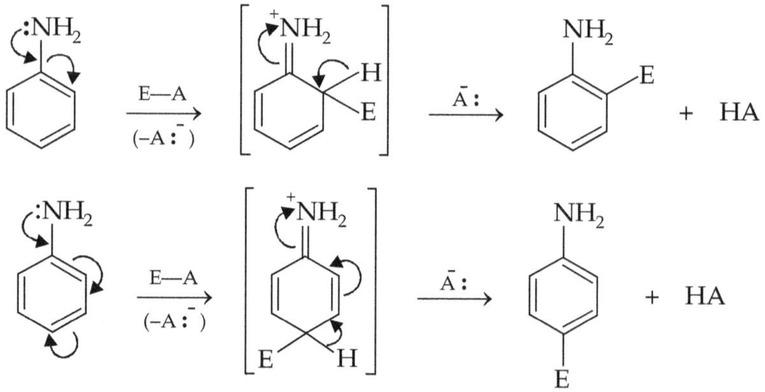

[reaction mechanism scheme showing ortho and para substitution of aniline with E—A]

Due to presence of electron pair on nitrogen, the —NH$_2$, —NHR or —NR$_2$ group acts as an activating group and an *o*- and *p*-director in electrophilic aromatic ring substitution. The important examples of electrophilic substitution in aromatic ring will be discussed in aniline.

19.4.3 Reactions of Quaternary Ammonium Salts

(i) *Formation of quaternary (4°) ammonium hydroxides.* When an aqueous solution of a 4° ammonium halide is treated with silver oxide, silver halide precipitates out, and a solution of quaternary ammonium hydroxide is formed.

$$2R_4N^+X^- + Ag_2O + H_2O \longrightarrow 2R_4N^+OH^- + 2AgX\downarrow$$

4° Ammonium halide

4° Ammonium hydroxide
(a very strong base, like NaOH)

(ii) *Hofmann elimination.* When a quaternary hydroxide is heated strongly (to 125°C or higher), it decomposes to form an alkene and a tertiary amine.

$$CH_3CHCH_2CH_3 \xrightarrow{\text{heat}} CH_2 = CHCH_2CH_3 + (CH_3)_3N + H_2O$$
$$\mid$$
$$N^+(CH_3)_3OH^-$$

1-Butene(95%)

This reaction, known as **Hofmann elimination,** is an E2 reaction in which hydroxide ion functions as a base. A novel aspect of the Hofmann elimination is its *regioselectivity.* Elimination in alkyltrimethylammonium hydroxides proceeds in the direction that gives the less substituted alkene (opposite to Saytzeff rule) ; this is known as **Hofmann rule** *or* **Hofmann orientation**.

$$\overset{\beta}{CH_2}-\overset{\alpha}{CH}-\overset{\beta}{CH_2}CH_3 \xrightarrow[-\text{(CH}_3)_3\text{N}]{\text{heat} \atop -\text{H}_2\text{O},} CH_2 = CH-CH_2CH_3 + CH_3CH = CHCH_3$$

Butene-1 (95%)   Butene-2 (5%)

The base (OH⁻) attacks the most acidic hydrogen ; a primary hydrogen atom is more acidic because its carbon atom bears only one electron-releasing group. Alternatively, it is the less sterically hindered β hydrogen that is attacked by the base (OH⁻ or any other base). Methyl groups are deprotonated in preference to methylene groups which in turn are deprotonated in preference to methines. In case the 4° ammonium hydroxide does not have any β-hydrogen, alkene formation is impossible, rather alcohol is formed by S_N2 reaction.

$$HO^- + CH_3 - N^+(CH_3)_3 \xrightarrow{\text{heat}} CH_3OH + (CH_3)_3N\text{:}$$

Thus remember that although most eliminations involving neutral substances tend to follow *Saytzeff rule,* eliminations with charged substances tend to follow *Hofmann rule* and yield mainly the least substituted alkenes.

Conversion of an amine (1°, 2°, or 3°) to the fully methylated product, *i.e.* quaternary ammonium salt is known as **Hofmann exhaustive methylation.** Exhaustive Hofmann methylation followed by reaction with silver oxide and then heating to give an alkene has been used for determining the structure of an amine and compounds having nitrogen in the ring.

4-Methylpyridine

3-Methyl-1, 4-pentadiene   3-Methyl-1, 3-pentadiene
(**More stable,** conjugated diene)

TEST YOUR UNDERSTANDING - 19.14

1. Write down the structure of the various alkenes obtained :

(a) during dehydrohalogenation of $n\text{-}C_3H_7CHBrCH_3$, and

(b) Hofmann elimination of $n\text{-}C_3H_7CH(CH_3)N^+Me_3OH^-$.

2. Give the structure of the major alkene formed during heating following salts :

(a) $(CH_3)_3CCH_2C(CH_3)_2$
$\quad\quad | $
$\quad\quad N^+(CH_3)_3OH^-$

(b) $CH_3CH_2\overset{+}{N}(CH_3)_2CH_2CH_2CH_3$
$\quad\quad\quad\quad OH^-$

(c) cyclopentane$-C(CH_3)_2-N^+(CH_3)_3\ OH^-$

(d) $CH_3CH_2CHCH_3\ OC_2H_5^-$
$\quad\quad\quad | $
$\quad\quad\quad \overset{+}{S}(CH_3)_2$

(e) 3-methyl-1,1-dimethylpiperidinium OH^-

(f) $C_6H_{11}N^+Me_2(CH_2CH_2CH_3)OH^-$.

3. Write down the structures of the alkenes formed on E2 elimination from

(a) 1-ethyl-2-methylpropyltrimethylammonium ion.

(b) diethyldi-n-propylammonium ion

(c) dimethylethyl-2-chloroethylammonium ion

(d) dimethylethyl-n-propylammonium ion.

Mention the major product, if any, in each case.

4. Predict the structures of the main products (A) and (B) in the following reactions :

$$\text{(a)}\quad CH_3CH_2-\underset{\underset{CH_3}{|}}{\overset{\overset{CH_3}{|}}{C}}-S^+(CH_3)_2\ OC_2H_5^-\ \xrightarrow[\text{ethanol}]{\text{heat in}}\ A$$

Dimethyl-*tert*-pentylsulphonium ethoxide

$$\text{(b)}\quad CH_3CH_2-\underset{\underset{CH_3}{|}}{\overset{\overset{CH_3}{|}}{C}}-S^+(CH_3)_2I^-\ \xrightarrow[\text{ethanol}]{\text{heat in}}\ B$$

5. Predict and account for the product of Hofmann elimination of

(a) $PhCH_2CH_2N^+(CH_3)_2OH^-$
$\quad\quad\quad\quad\quad | $
$\quad\quad\quad\quad\quad CH_2CH_3$

(b) $CH_3CH_2N^+-C(CH_3)_3OH^-$.
$\quad\quad\quad\quad |\quad\quad\quad\quad | $
$\quad\quad\quad\quad CH_3 \quad\quad\ CH_3$

(with CH_3 above the N)

19.5 Analysis of Amines

Amines are characterized by their basicity. A water-insoluble compound that dissolves in cold dil. HCl, or a water-soluble compound (not a salt) whose aqueous solution turns red litmus blue must be an amine. The nature of amine (primary, secondary, or tertiary) can best be distinguished from each other by the **Hinsberg test** which is based upon the formation of sulphonamide.

1.   **The Hinsberg test.** The amine is shaken with benzenesulphonyl chloride (also known as **Hinsberg reagent**) in the presence of aqueous potassium hydroxide. Each type of amine gives a different set of visible results.

(i) A clear solution is obtained in case of primary amines.

(ii) A precipitate is obtained in case of secondary amines.

(iii) No apparent change is observed in case of water-insoluble tertiary amine.

When the above mixture (amine + $C_6H_5SO_2Cl$ + aq. KOH) is acidified with HCl, again different set of results is observed in the three types of amines.

(a) A precipitate is obtained in case of primary amine.

(b) No change is observed in case of secondary amine.

(c)   A clear solution is obtained in case of tertiary amine.

In short,

$$1° \text{ Amine} + C_6H_5SO_2Cl \xrightarrow{\text{aq. KOH}} \text{Clear solution} \xrightarrow{\text{HCl}} \text{Precipitate}$$

$$2° \text{ Amine} + C_6H_5SO_2Cl \xrightarrow{\text{aq. KOH}} \text{Precipitate} \xrightarrow{\text{HCl}} \text{No change}$$

$$\underset{\text{(water insoluble)}}{3° \text{ Amine} + C_6H_5SO_2Cl} \xrightarrow{\text{aq. KOH}} \underset{\text{(water insoluble)}}{3° \text{ Amine}} \xrightarrow{\text{HCl}} \text{Water soluble clear salt sol.}$$

Chemistry of the Hinsberg test.

$$\underset{\textbf{1° Amine}}{RNH_2} + C_6H_5SO_2Cl \xrightarrow{OH^-} \underset{\substack{\text{N-Substituted sulphonamide} \\ \text{(acidic H on N)}}}{[C_6H_5SO_2NHR]} \xrightarrow{KOH} \underset{\text{Clear solution}}{C_6H_5SO_2N^-RK^+} \xrightarrow{H^+} \underset{\text{Precipitate}}{C_6H_5SO_2NHR}$$

$$\underset{\textbf{2° Amine}}{R_2NH} + C_6H_5SO_2Cl \longrightarrow \underset{\substack{\text{N, N-Disubstituted} \\ \text{sulphonamide} \\ \text{(no acidic H)}}}{C_6H_5SO_2NR_2 \downarrow} \xrightarrow{KOH} \text{No reaction} \xrightarrow[\text{room temp.}]{H^+} \text{No reaction}$$

Remember that N, N-disubstituted sulphonamides are hydrolysed to give parent amine when heated with an acid.

$$C_6H_5SO_2NR_2 \xrightarrow[\text{(ii) } OH^-]{\text{(i) } H_3O^+, \text{ heat}} C_6H_5SO_2O^- + R_2NH$$

$$\underset{\textbf{3° Amine}}{R_3N} + \underset{\text{Insoluble}}{C_6H_5SO_2Cl} \xrightarrow{OH^-} R_3N \xrightarrow{HCl} \underset{\text{Clear solution}}{R_3N^+Cl^-}$$

2.   Primary amines can also be detected by the following tests.

(a)   **Carbylamine test.** Unpleasant smelling carbylamine is formed when a 1° amine (aliphatic or aromatic) is treated with alkaline chloroform solution.

(b)   **Mustard oil reaction.** Primary amines (aliphatic or aromatic) form isothiocyanates having mustard oil like smell.

(c)   **Reaction with nitrous acid :**

(i)   *Aliphatic primary amines* evolve quantitative amount of N_2 and form alcohols, when treated with nitrous acid.

(ii)   *Primary aromatic amines*, when treated with nitrous acid at low temperatures (0–5°C), are converted into **diazonium salts** which yield highly coloured azo compounds upon treatment with β-naphthol (a phenol) in presence of sodium hydroxide.

19.6   Separation of Mixture of Amines

As described earlier, Hofmann ammonolysis of alkyl halide and alcohol, gives a mixture of 1°, 2° and 3° amines along with quaternary ammonium salt. The four can be separated easily. First of all, the mixture is distilled over KOH when all the three types of amines distil over leaving behind quaternary ammonium salt as residue.

$$RNH_2 + R_2NH + R_3N + R_4N^+I^- \xrightarrow[\text{distil}]{KOH} \begin{cases} \rightarrow RNH_2 + R_2NH + R_3N \text{ (Distillate)} \\ \rightarrow R_3N^+OH^- \text{ (Residue)} \end{cases}$$

The mixture of the three types of amines collected as distillate can be separated into the individual type by the following methods.

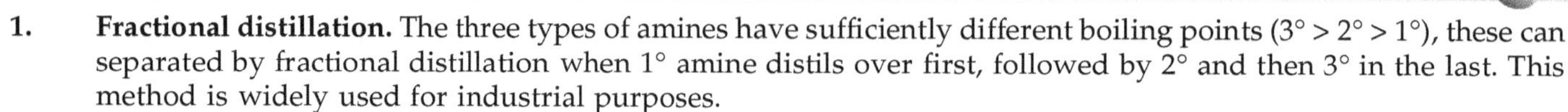

1. **Fractional distillation.** The three types of amines have sufficiently different boiling points ($3° > 2° > 1°$), these can separated by fractional distillation when $1°$ amine distils over first, followed by $2°$ and then $3°$ in the last. This method is widely used for industrial purposes.

2. **Hofmann method.** The mixture is treated with diethyl oxalate, also known as **Hofmann reagent**, when $1°$ amine forms oxamide (solid), $2°$ amine forms oxamic ester (liquid), while the $3°$ amine does not react.

$$
\begin{array}{l}
\text{COOC}_2\text{H}_5 \\
| \\
\text{COOC}_2\text{H}_5
\end{array}
+
\begin{array}{l}
\text{HNHR} \\
\\
\text{HNHR}
\end{array}
\longrightarrow
\begin{array}{l}
\text{CONHR} \\
| \\
\text{CONHR}
\end{array}
+ \; 2\text{C}_2\text{H}_5\text{OH}
$$

Diethyl oxalate $1°$ Amine (2 moles)   N, N'-Dialkyloxamide (**solid**)

$$
\begin{array}{l}
\text{COOC}_2\text{H}_5 \\
| \\
\text{COOC}_2\text{H}_5
\end{array}
+ \; \text{HNR}_2
\longrightarrow
\begin{array}{l}
\text{CONR}_2 \\
| \\
\text{COOC}_2\text{H}_5
\end{array}
+ \; \text{C}_2\text{H}_5\text{OH}
$$

Diethyl oxalate $2°$ Amine (1 mole)   Dialkyloxamic ester (**liquid**)

The mixture containing dialkyloxamide (solid), dialkyloxamic ester, and unreacted $3°$ amine is filtered.

Recovery of $1°$ amine. The solid oxamide is distilled over potassium hydroxide, when primary amine distils over leaving potassium oxalate (a a salt) as residue.

$$
\begin{array}{l}
\text{CONHR} \\
| \\
\text{CONHR}
\end{array}
+ \; 2\text{KOH} \xrightarrow{\text{distil}}
\begin{array}{l}
\text{COOK} \\
| \\
\text{COOK}
\end{array}
; \quad \textbf{RNH}_2
$$

(Residue)   (Distillate)

Recovery of $2°$ and $3°$ amine. The filtrate containing oxamic ester and $3°$ amine is fractionally distilled when **tertiary amine** having low boiling point distils first. Secondary amine is then recovered from the oxamic ester by distilling over potassium hydroxide.

$$
\begin{array}{l}
\text{CONR}_2 \\
| \\
\text{COOC}_2\text{H}_5
\end{array}
+ \; 2\text{KOH} \xrightarrow{\text{distil}}
\begin{array}{l}
\text{COOK} \\
| \\
\text{COOK}
\end{array}
; \quad \textbf{R}_2\textbf{NH} + \text{C}_2\text{H}_5\text{OH}
$$

Residue   Distillate

3. **Hinsberg method.** This method is based upon the difference in solubility of benzensulphonamides, formed by the reaction of $1°$ and $2°$ amines with benzenesulphonyl chloride, also known as **Hinsberg reagent**, in aqueous KOH and ether (recall that $3°$ amines do not react with the reagent).

Details of chemistry of the $1°$ and $2°$ amines with the reagent has already been discussed in Hinsberg's test. Hence, here only an outline involved in the separation of the three amines is given.

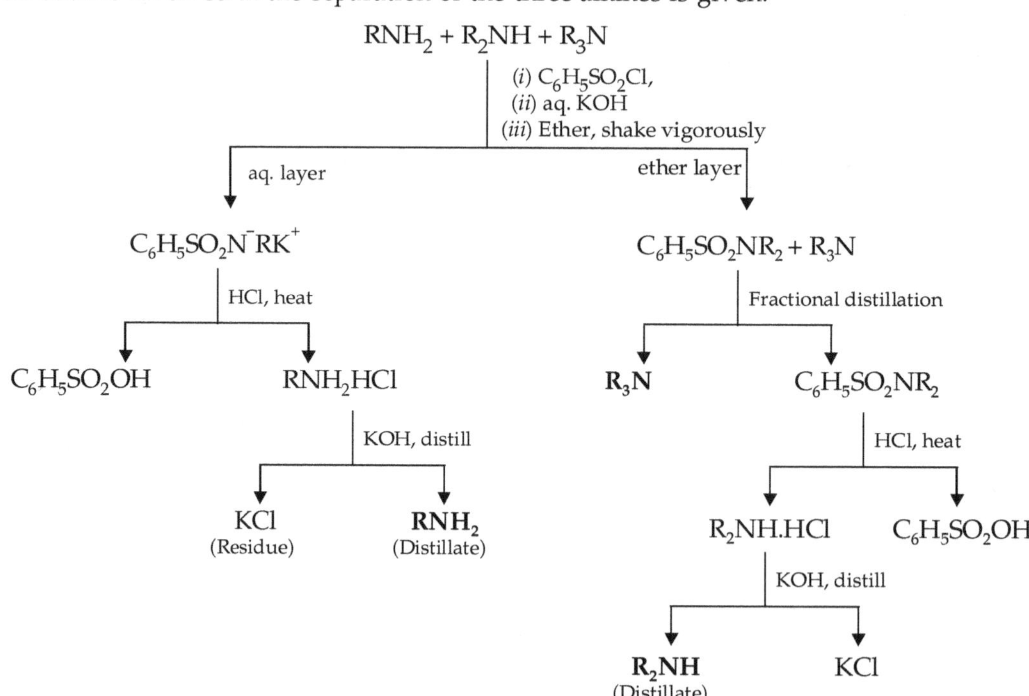

TEST YOUR UNDERSTANDING - 19.15

1.   What are limitations of Hinsberg test ?
2.   Distinguish among RNH_2, R_2NH and R_3N using succinic anhydride as the reagent.

19.7   Illustrative Examples

Example 1 :

Identify the bracketed compounds in the following reactions :

(i) $n\text{-}C_3H_7COOH \xrightarrow{LiAlH_4} [A] \xrightarrow{PBr_3} [B] \xrightarrow[\text{(ii) CuI}]{\text{(i) Li}} [C] \xrightarrow{n\text{-}C_3H_7COCl} [D] \xrightarrow[H_2/Ni]{NH_3} [E]$

(ii) $C_6H_5SO_2Cl \xrightarrow{CH_3NH_2} [A] \xrightarrow{NaOH} [B] \xrightarrow{CH_3Br} [C] \xrightarrow{H_3O^+} [D] + [E]$

(iii)   cyclohexyl$-CH_2NH_2 \xrightarrow[CH_3I]{\text{excess of}} [A] \xrightarrow[H_2O]{Ag_2O} [B]$

(iv)   cyclohexyl$-NH_2 \xrightarrow[CH_3I]{\text{excess of}} [A] \xrightarrow[H_2O]{Ag_2O} [B] \xrightarrow{\text{heat}} [C] + (CH_3)_3N \xrightarrow{\text{heat}} [C] + [D]$

(v) $C_6H_5NH_2 \xrightarrow{2CH_3I} [A] \xrightarrow{HNO_2} [B] \xrightarrow{NaOH} [C] + [D]$

(vi)   phthalimide-NK $\xrightarrow{Br(CH_2)_2COO^-} [A] \xrightarrow[\text{(ii) H}^+]{\text{(i) OH}^-} [B]$ (vii)   cyclohexyl$-NH_2 \xrightarrow[HCl]{NaNO_2} [A] + [B] + [C]$

(viii) $\xrightarrow{[A]} [B] \xrightarrow{CH_3NH_2} [C] \xrightarrow{NaBH_3CN} \text{—NHCH}_3$

(ix)   cyclohexyl$-OH \xrightarrow{PBr_3} [A] \xrightarrow{NH_3} [B] \xrightarrow{\text{oxid.}} [C] \xrightarrow{NH_3} [D] \xrightarrow{H_2/Ni} [E]$

(x)   phenyl$-OH \xrightarrow{\text{oxidation}} [A] \xrightarrow{NH_3} [B] \xrightarrow{H_2/Ni} [C]$

(xi) $HOCH_2CH_2CH_2OH \xrightarrow{1\,eq.\,SOCl_2} [A] \xrightarrow{KCN} [B] \xrightarrow{SOCl_2} [C] \xrightarrow{H_2/Ni} [D] \xrightarrow{NaOH} [E]$

(xii) $2\,CH_2\!-\!CH_2 \text{(epoxide)} \xrightarrow{NH_3} [A] \xrightarrow{P_2O_5} [B]$

(xiii)   (epoxide)$+ (CH_3)_3N \xrightarrow{H_2O} [A] \xrightarrow{\substack{\text{(a strong base)}}} [B] \xrightarrow{CH_3COCl} [C]$

(xiv) $(CH_3)_2CHCHO \xrightarrow[\text{base}]{CH_2O} [A] \xrightarrow[H^+]{CN^-} [B] \xrightarrow[H^+]{H_2O} [C] \longrightarrow [D] \xrightarrow{H_2NCH_2CH_2COOH} [E]$

(xv) $H_2C\!-\!CH_2 \text{(epoxide)} \xrightarrow{(C_2H_5)_2NH} [A] \xrightarrow{p\text{-}O_2NC_6H_4COCl} [B] \xrightarrow{H_2,\,Ni} [C]$

Solution :

(i) $n\text{-}C_3H_7CH_2OH,$ $n\text{-}C_3H_7CH_2Br,$ $(n\text{-}C_3H_7CH_2)_2CuLi,$ $n\text{-}C_3H_7CH_2COC_3H_7\text{-}n,$ $n\text{-}C_3H_7CH_2\overset{\overset{\displaystyle NH_2}{|}}{C}HC_3H_7\text{-}n$
      [A]   [B]   [C]   [D]   [E]

(ii) $C_6H_5SO_2NHCH_3,$ $C_6H_5SO_2\overset{-}{N}CH_3,$ $C_6H_5SO_2N(CH_3)_2,$ $C_6H_5SO_2OH + (CH_3)_2NH_2^{+}$
      [A]   [B]   [C]   [D]   [E]

(iii)

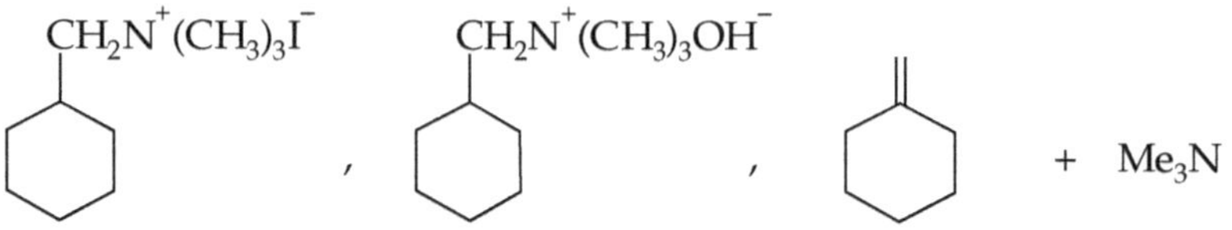

      [A]   [B]   [C] $+ \;\; Me_3N$ [D]

(iv)

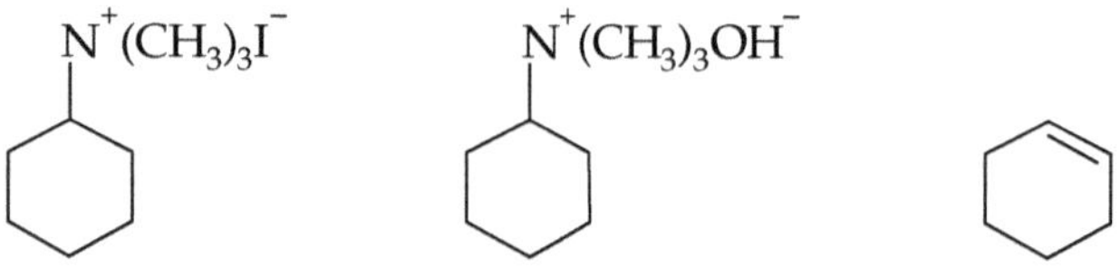

      [A]   [B]   [C]

(v)

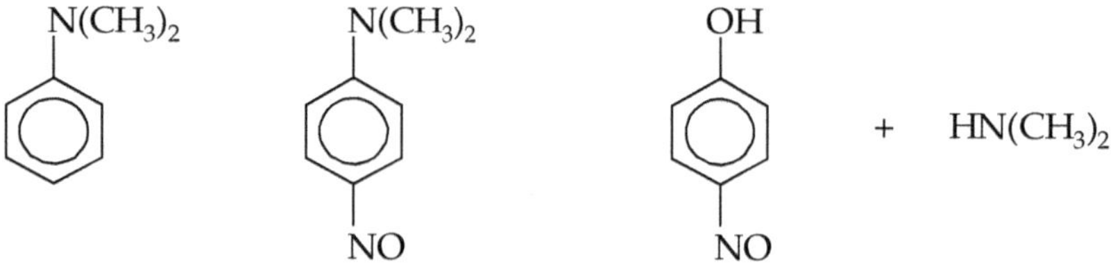

      [A]   [B]   [C] $+ \;\; HN(CH_3)_2$ [D]

(vi) $\text{Phthalimido-}N(CH_2)_2COO^{-}$ $H_3N^{+}(CH_2)_2COOH$

      [A]   [B]

(vii) $\xrightarrow[(-N_2)]{}$ (Unstable) $\longrightarrow$ [A] $+$ [B] $+$ [C]

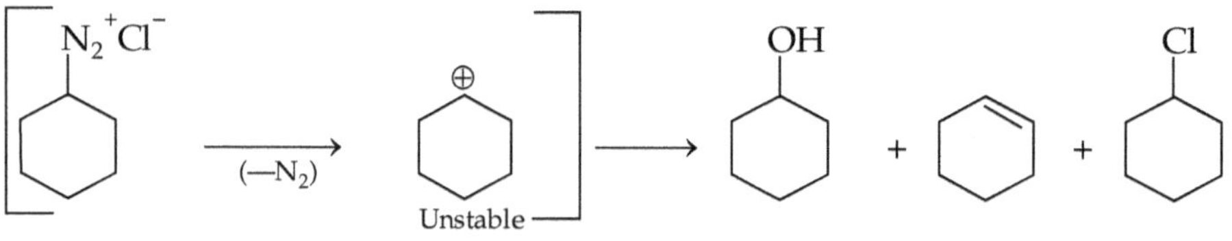

(viii)   PCC (Pyridinium chlorochromate) $\sim\!\!\!\sim\!CHO$ $\sim\!\!\!\sim\!CH=NCH_3$

      [A]   [B]   [C]

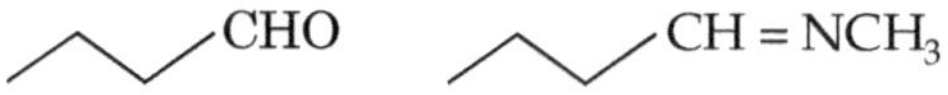

(ix) $\xrightarrow[(-HBr)]{NH_3}$ 2° amine   A   B

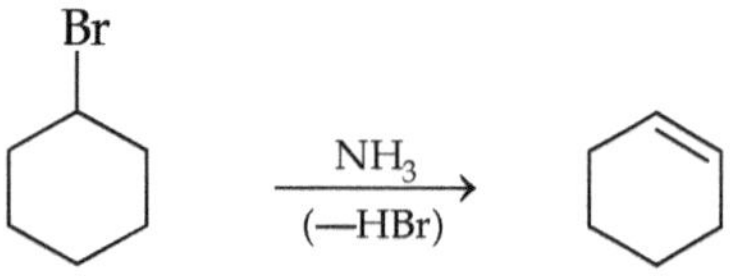

(x)   A   ,   B   ,   C

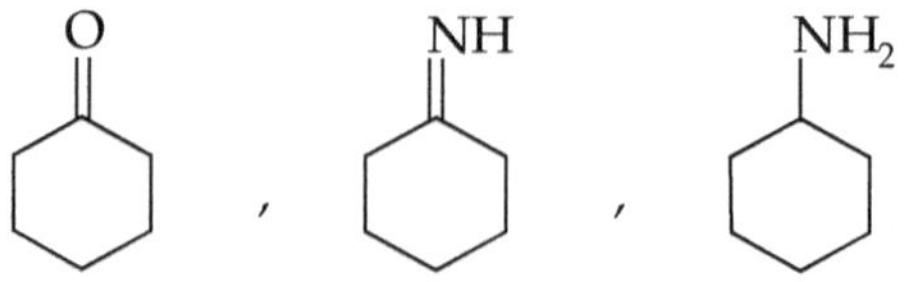

(xi)

$$\underset{\text{OH}}{\diagdown}\text{Cl}\;,\quad \underset{\text{OH}}{\diagdown}\text{CN}\;,\quad \underset{\text{Cl}}{\diagdown}\text{CN}\;,\quad \underset{\text{Cl}\quad \text{NH}_2}{\diagdown}\;,\quad \underset{\underset{H}{N}}{\diagup}$$

　　　[A]　　　　　　[B]　　　　　　[C]　　　　　　[D]　　　　　　[E]

(xii)　$HOCH_2CH_2NHCH_2CH_2OH$　or

　　　　　　　　　　　　　[A]　　　　　　　　　　　　　[B] Morpholine

(xiii)

$$\triangle\!\!\!\diagdown O \;+\; N(CH_3)_3 \longrightarrow {}^-OCH_2CH_2N^+(CH_3)_3 \xrightarrow{H_2O} HOCH_2CH_2N^+(CH_3)_3OH^-$$

　　　　　　　　　　　　　　　　　　　[A]　　　　　　　　　　　　　　　[B]

$$\longrightarrow CH_3\overset{\overset{\displaystyle O}{\|}}{C}OCH_2CH_2N^+(CH_3)_3OH^-$$

[C]

(xiv)　$(CH_3)_2\overset{\overset{\displaystyle CH_2OH}{|}}{C}CHO$　　$(CH_3)_2\overset{\overset{\displaystyle CH_2OH}{|}}{\underset{\underset{\displaystyle OH}{|}}{C}}CHCN$　　$(CH_3)_2\overset{\overset{\displaystyle CH_2OH}{|}}{\underset{\underset{\displaystyle OH}{|}}{C}}-CH-\overset{\overset{\displaystyle OH}{|}}{C}=O$

　　　　[A]　　　　　　　　　[B]　　　　　　　　γ-Hydroxy acid [C]

$(CH_3)_2\overset{\overset{\displaystyle CH_2CO}{|}}{\underset{\underset{\displaystyle OH}{|}}{C}}-CH(CH_3)_2$

γ-Lactone [D]

$$\overset{\overset{\displaystyle CH_2OH}{|}}{\underset{\underset{\displaystyle OH}{|}}{C}}-CH-\overset{\overset{\displaystyle O}{\|}}{C}-NHCH_2CH_2COOH$$

[E]

(xv)　$HOCH_2CH_2N(C_2H_5)_2$

[A]

Benzene ring with $COOCH_2CH_2N(C_2H_5)_2$ and NO_2 — [B]

Benzene ring with $COOCH_2CH_2N(C_2H_5)_2$ and NH_2 — [C]

Example 2 :

Write down the structure of the amine in the following two cases :

(a)　$CH_3COOH \xrightarrow[\text{(ii) KOD, Br}_2]{\text{(i) NH}_3\text{, heat}} A$　　　　　(b)　$CH_3COOH \xrightarrow[\text{(ii) KOH/Br}_2]{\text{(i) ND}_3\text{, heat}} B$

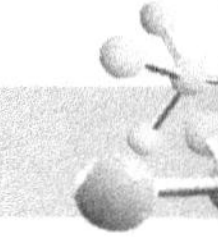

Solution :

The two reactions will give methyl amine, but having different isotopes of hydrogen in the amino group. It can be easily understood by the mechanism of Hofmann degradation.

$$CH_3-\overset{\overset{O}{\|}}{C}-OH \quad\xrightarrow{NH_3,\,heat}\quad CH_3-\overset{\overset{O}{\|}}{C}-NH_2 \quad\xrightarrow{Br_2}\quad CH_3-\overset{\overset{O}{\|}}{C}-\underset{Br}{NH} \quad\xrightarrow{OH^-}\quad CH_3-\overset{\overset{O}{\|}}{C}-\overset{\ominus}{N}\,Br \quad\xrightarrow{rearrangement}\quad \underset{Isocyanate}{CH_3-N=C=O} \quad\xrightarrow{2\,OD^-}\quad CH_3-ND_2$$

$$CH_3-\overset{\overset{O}{\|}}{C}-OH \quad\xrightarrow{NH_3,\,heat}\quad CH_3-\overset{\overset{O}{\|}}{C}-ND_2 \quad\xrightarrow{Br_2}\quad CH_3-\overset{\overset{O}{\|}}{C}-\underset{Br}{ND} \quad\xrightarrow{OH^-}\quad CH_3-\overset{\overset{O}{\|}}{C}-\overset{\ominus}{N}\,Br \quad\xrightarrow{rearrangement}\quad \underset{Isocyanate}{CH_3-N=C=O} \quad\xrightarrow{2\,OD^-}\quad CH_3-NH_2$$

Example 3 :

Give steps involved in the following conversions.

(i)   **Propene into allylamine.**

(ii) Succinic anhydride to β-alanine (β-aminopropionic acid)

(iii)   1, 3-Butadiene to hexamethylenediamine, one of the raw materials for the manufacture of nylon-6, 6.

(iv)   Ethylamine to (a) methylethylamine, and (b) dimethylethylamine

(v)   *n*-Butanol to *n*-hexylamine

(vi) Ethyl cyanide to ethylamine

(vii) $H_3C-\!\!\bigcirc\!\!-NO_2 \longrightarrow H_2N-\!\!\bigcirc\!\!-NO_2$

(viii) $H_3CO-\!\!\bigcirc \longrightarrow H_3CO-\!\!\bigcirc\!\!-\overset{\overset{CH_3}{|}}{C}HNH_2$

(ix) $\bigcirc\!\!-CH_3 \longrightarrow \bigcirc\!\!-CH_2CH_2NH_2$

(x) $\bigcirc\!\!-CH_3 \longrightarrow \bigcirc\!\!-CH_2\overset{+}{N}Me_3Cl^-$

(xi) cyclohexanol (–OH) $\longrightarrow$ cyclohexylamine (–NH$_2$)

(xii) cyclohexanol (–OH) $\longrightarrow$ cyclopentylamine (–NH$_2$)

Solution :

(i) $CH_2 = CHCH_3 \xrightarrow{Cl_2, 400°C} CH_2 = CHCH_2Cl \xrightarrow{NH_3} CH_2 = CHCH_2NH_2$

(ii) Succinic anhydride $\xrightarrow{NH_3} H_2N\overset{O}{\underset{||}{C}}CH_2CH_2\overset{O}{\underset{||}{C}}OH \xrightarrow[\text{(ii) } H^+]{\text{(i) NaOBr}} H_2NCH_2CH_2\overset{O}{\underset{||}{C}}OH$ (β–Alanine)

(iii) $CH_2 = CHCH = CH_2$ (1, 3–Butadiene) $\xrightarrow[\text{(1, 4–addition)}]{Cl_2} ClCH_2CH = CHCH_2Cl \xrightarrow{H_2, Ni} Cl(CH_2)_4Cl$

$\xrightarrow{2\,KCN} NC(CH_2)_4CN \xrightarrow{H_2, Ni} H_2NCH_2(CH_2)_4CH_2NH_2$ (Hexamethylenediamine)

(iv) (a) $CH_3CH_2NH_2$ (Ethylamine) $\xrightarrow[\text{KOH}]{CHCl_3} CH_3CH_2NC \xrightarrow{H_2/Pt} CH_3CH_2NHCH_3$ (Methylethylamine)

(b) $CH_3CH_2NH_2$ (Ethylamine) $\xrightarrow[\text{HCOOH}]{H_2C=O} CH_3CH_2N(CH_3)_2$ (Dimethylethylamine)

(v) $n\text{-}C_3H_7CH_2OH$ (n-Butanol) $\xrightarrow[\text{(ii) Mg, ether}]{\text{(i) PBr}_3} n\text{-}C_3H_7CH_2MgBr \xrightarrow[\text{oxide}]{\text{ethylene}} n\text{-}C_3H_7CH_2CH_2CH_2OH \xrightarrow{NH_3} n\text{-}C_3H_7CH_2CH_2CH_2NH_2$ (n-Hexylamine)

(vi) CH_3CH_2CN (Ethyl cyanide) $\xrightarrow{H_3O^+} CH_3CH_2COOH \xrightarrow{NH_3,\,heat} CH_3CH_2CONH_2 \xrightarrow{NaBrO} CH_3CH_2NH_2$ (Ethylamine)

(vii) $p\text{-nitrotoluene} \xrightarrow[\text{(ii) } H^+]{\text{(i) KMnO}_4,\,OH^-} p\text{-nitrobenzoic acid} \xrightarrow[\text{(ii) NH}_3]{\text{(i) SOCl}_2} p\text{-nitrobenzamide} \xrightarrow{NaOBr} p\text{-nitroaniline}$

(viii) anisole $\xrightarrow[\text{AlCl}_3]{CH_3COCl} \text{4-methoxyacetophenone} \xrightarrow{NH_3} \text{imine (HN=CCH}_3\text{)} \xrightarrow{H_2, Ni} \text{H}_2\text{NCHCH}_3 \text{ derivative}$

(ix) toluene $\xrightarrow{NBS} \text{benzyl bromide (CH}_2\text{Br)} \xrightarrow{KCN} \text{CH}_2\text{CN} \xrightarrow{LiAlH_4} \text{CH}_2\text{CH}_2\text{NH}_2$

(x) toluene $\xrightarrow{Cl_2,\,light} \text{benzyl chloride (CH}_2\text{Cl)} \xrightarrow{Me_3N} \text{CH}_2\overset{+}{N}Me_3Cl^-$

(xi)

Cyclohexanol $\xrightarrow[\text{H}_2\text{SO}_4]{\text{K}_2\text{Cr}_2\text{O}_7}$ (cyclohexanone) $\xrightarrow[\text{(ii) H}_2/\text{Pt}]{\text{(i) NH}_3}$ Cyclohexylamine

(xii)

Cyclohexanol $\xrightarrow{\text{H}_2\text{SO}_4}$ (cyclohexene) $\xrightarrow[\text{heat}]{\text{KMnO}_4,\ \text{H}^+}$ (COOH–COOH) $\xrightarrow[\text{heat}]{\text{BaO}}$ (=O) $\xrightarrow[\text{(ii) H}_2,\ \text{Pt}]{\text{(i) NH}_3}$ Cyclopentylamine

---

Example 4 :

Give all steps involved in the reaction of nitrous acid with ethylamine.

Solution :

Nitrous acid gives nitrosonium ion (an electrophile).

$$\text{HO—N}=\text{O} \xrightarrow{\text{H}^+} \text{H}_2\text{O}^+\text{—N}=\text{O} \longrightarrow \text{H}_2\text{O} + \text{N}^+ = \text{O}$$

Nucleophilic attack of the electron pair of the amine on the nitrosonium ion produces N-nitrosomine which undergoes a series of proton transfer to form a diazocation as the final product.

$$\text{C}_2\text{H}_5\text{—N:} + \overset{+}{\text{N}} = \ddot{\text{O}} \longrightarrow \text{C}_2\text{H}_5\text{—}\overset{+}{\text{N}}\text{—N} = \ddot{\text{O}} \xrightarrow[(-\text{H}^+)]{\text{H}_2\text{O}} \text{C}_2\text{H}_5\text{—N—}\ddot{\text{N}} = \ddot{\text{O}} \xrightarrow{\text{H}_3\text{O}^+}$$

N-Nitrosamine

$$\text{C}_2\text{H}_5\text{—N—}\overset{+}{\text{N}} = \text{OH} \xrightarrow[(-\text{H}^+)]{\text{H}_2\text{O}} \text{C}_2\text{H}_5\text{—N} = \text{N—OH} \xrightarrow{\text{H}_3\text{O}^+} \text{C}_2\text{H}_5\text{—N} = \text{N—}\overset{+}{\text{O}}\text{H}_2 \longrightarrow \text{C}_2\text{H}_5\text{—}\overset{+}{\text{N}} \equiv \text{N:}$$

Ethyl diazoic acid   Ethyl diazonium cation

Example 5 :

Write down the final product in the following reaction, giving steps involved.

(1-hydroxymethyl cyclopentanol, –OH, –CH₂NH₂) $+$ HONO $\longrightarrow$

Solution :

(–OH, –CH₂NH₂) $\xrightarrow{\text{HONO}}$ (–OH, –CH₂N₂⁺) $\xrightarrow{(-\text{N}_2)}$ (–OH, –CH₂⁺)

1° Carbocation

$\xrightarrow{\text{rearrangement}}$ (–OH, CH₂ ring) $=$ (cyclohexyl –OH cation) $\xrightarrow{-\text{H}^+}$ (cyclohexenol –OH) $\longrightarrow$ (cyclohexanone =O)

3° Carbocation

Example 6 :

How will you distinguish between each of the following pairs by simple chemical tests.

(a) **Aniline and cyclohexylamine**

(b) $(CH_3)_4N^+Cl^-$ **and** $(CH_3)_3NH^+Cl^-$

(c) $(CH_3)_4N^+OH^-$ **and** $(CH_3)_2NCH_2OH$

(d) $(C_6H_5NH_3)_2\,SO_4$ **and** p-$N^+H_3C_6H_4SO_3^-$.

Solution :

(a) At low temperature, aniline $(C_6H_5NH_2)$, on treatment with HONO, undergoes diazotisation to form diazonium salt which form highly coloured azo dyes on addition of β-naphthol. Cyclohexylamine $(C_6H_{11}NH_2)$ also forms diazonium salt with nitrous acid but the salt, cyclohexyl-N_2^+ is unstable, even at low temperatures and evolves N_2 detected by its bubbles.

(b) Add conc. NaOH and heat the mixture, when only $(CH_3)_3NH^+Cl^-$ is changed into the volatile free base, $(CH_3)_3\,N$, detected by its typical ammonia-like odour.

$$(CH_3)_3N^+HCl^- \xrightarrow{\text{Conc. NaOH, heat}} (CH_3)_3N + NaCl + H_2O$$

$$(CH_3)_4N^+Cl^- \xrightarrow{\text{Conc. NaOH, heat}} \text{No reaction}$$

However, remember that $Me_4N^+OH^-$ gives Me_3N, on thermal decomposition.

(c) $(CH_3)_4N^+OH^-$ is a strong base and its solution turns red litmus blue. It also gives a white precipitate of $Ba(OH)_2$ when $BaCl_2$ is added. The other compound, Me_2NCH_2OH is a covalent alcohol.

(d) Only $(C_6H_5NH_3)_2^{2+}\,SO_4^{2-}$ gives white precipitate of $BaSO_4$, on adding $BaCl_2$. The other compound is a sulphonate which does not give precipitate with Ba^{2+}.

Example 7 :

Suggest a structural formula for an optically active amine, $C_8H_{11}N$, which evolves nitrogen on treatment with nitrous acid.

Solution :

Molecular formula, $C_8H_{11}N$, of the compound indicates that it has four degree of unstauration (a saturated compound with 8 carbons would have the formula $C_8H_{19}N$) which points out the presence of a benzene ring. Further, since the amine evolves N_2 with HONO, it should be 1°. Further, since the amine is optically active, it will have chiral carbon, hence its two other substituents should be H and CH_3.

$$
\begin{array}{c}
NH_2 \\
| \\
C_6H_5\text{—}C\text{—}H \quad (C_8H_{11}N) \\
| \\
CH_3
\end{array}
$$

Example 8 :

Deduce the structures of the following amines from the products obtained from exhaustive methylation and Hofmann elimination.

(a) **Amine of the molecular formula $C_5H_{13}N$ reacts with 1 mole of methyl iodide and finally gives propene.**

(b) **Amine of the formula $C_5H_{13}N$ reacts with 2 moles of methyl iodide and gives ethene and a 3° amine which in turn reacts with 1 mole of CH_3I and give propene.**

Solution :

(a) The amine is a 3° amine because it reacts with only 1 mole of CH_3I. Formation of propene indicates that one of the alkyl groups is C_3H_7- (n- or iso-). Hence amine $(C_5H_{13}N)$ should be $C_3H_7N(CH_3)_2$.

(b) Given reactions indicate that amine is a 2° amine. Separate formation of ethene and propene shows that the two alkyl groups are C_2H_5 and C_3H_7. Hence amine is $C_3H_7NHC_2H_5$.

Example 9 :

A resolvable amine (A) when subjected to exhaustive methylation, it takes up 3 equivalents of methyl iodide and the product when heated gives an alkene (B). Alkene (B) on ozonolysis yields an equimolar mixture of methanal and butanal. Suggest the structure of the amine (A).

Solution :

$$A \xrightarrow[\text{(ii) heat}]{\text{(i) } 3CH_3I} B \xrightarrow{O_3} H_2C=O + O=CHCH_2CH_2CH_3$$

    (amine)   (alkene)   Methanal   Butanal

(i)   Nature of alkene (B) can be evaluated from its ozonolysis products.

$$H_2C=O + O=CHCH_2CH_2CH_3 \xleftarrow{O_3} H_2C=CHCH_2CH_2CH_3$$

   Methanal   Butanal   Alkene, B

(ii)   Since the amine takes up 3° equivalents of CH_3I, to form 4° ammonium ion, it must be 1° amine which can be either I or II.

$$H_2NCH_2CH_2CH_2CH_2CH_3 \qquad\qquad H_3C\overset{\overset{\displaystyle NH_2}{|}}{C}HCH_2\,CH_2CH_3$$

      I (Achiral)   II (Chiral)

    However, resolvable nature of the amine indicates that it is II, and not I which is optically inactive.

Example 10 :

A carboxylic acid A ($C_5H_{10}O_2$) when heated with hydrazoic acid in presence of conc. H_2SO_4 gives a compound B which on treatment with alkaline chloroform forms another compound C. Compound C gives following reactions.

(i)   On hydrolysis in presence of acid, it gives compound B and methanoic acid.

(ii)   On reduction it gives tert-butylmethylamine.

Identify compound A and give all reactions.

Solution :

Let us summarise the give reactions.

$$\underset{\substack{(-COOH\ group)}}{A,\ C_5H_{10}O_2} \xrightarrow[\text{conc. } H_2SO_4]{N_3H} B \xrightarrow[\text{KOH}]{CHCl_3} C \xrightarrow{\text{reduction}} (CH_3)_3CNHCH_3$$

$$\downarrow H_3O^+$$

$$HCOOH + B$$

Reactions of the compound C indicate that it should be an isonitrile, Me_3CNC. Hence B should be corresponding amine and A corresponding carboxylic acid.

$$(CH_3)_3CNHCH_3 \xleftarrow{\text{reduction}} (CH_3)_3CNC \xleftarrow[\text{KOH}]{CHCl_3} (CH_3)_2CNH_2 \xleftarrow{} (CH_3)_3CCOOH$$

   tert-Butylmethyl amine   C (Isonitrile)   B (1°amine)   A

EXERCISE 19.1 (MCQ - ONE option correct)

1. Pick up the incorrect name, if any
 (a) N-methylaniline (b) N-methylbenzenamine
 (c) methylaniline (d) All are correct.

2. Which of the following is more correct ?
 (a) $RX + NH_3 \text{ (excess)} \rightleftharpoons RNH_3^+ + X^-$
 (b) $RX + NH_3 \text{ (excess)} \rightleftharpoons RNH_2 + NH_4^+$
 (c) Both are equal important
 (d) $RX + NH_3 \text{ (excess)} \rightleftharpoons R_4N^+ + X^-.$

3. Cyclohexanol can be converted into cyclohexylamine by following two routes. Which of the following methods is expected to give good yield of cyclohexylamine ?

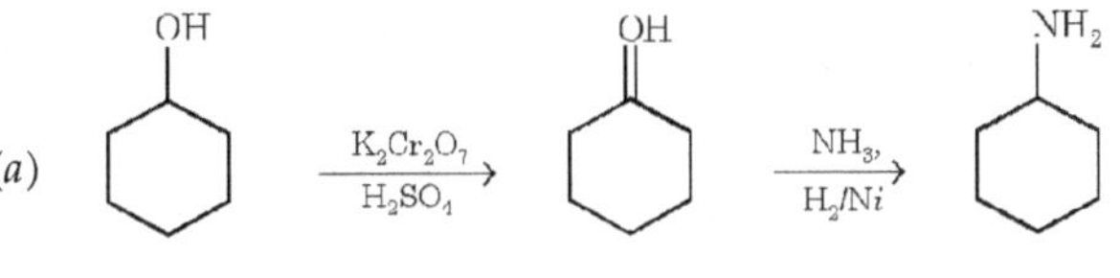

(a)

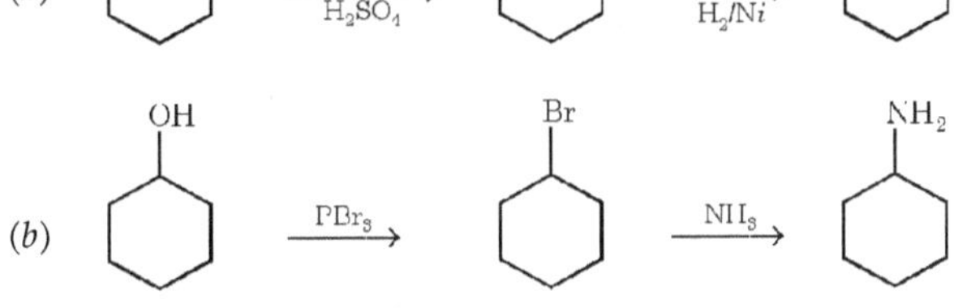

(b)

 (c) Both are equally suitable
 (d) Neither of the two.

4. Best method for preparing 1° amines from alkyl halides is by
 (a) Hofmann bromamide reaction
 (b) Gabriel phthalimide reaction
 (c) Both are equally good
 (d) Reaction with NH_3.

5. Which is the best method for preparing N, N-dimethylaniline from aniline ?
 (a) $C_6H_5NH_2 + CH_3I \longrightarrow$
 (b) $C_6H_5NH_2 + CH_3OH \xrightarrow{H^+}$
 (c) $C_6H_5NH_2 + CH_2O \xrightarrow{HCOOH}$
 (d) Both (a) and (b) are equally good.

6. Ethyl cyanide can be converted to ethylamine by
 (a) reduction with Sn and HCl
 (b) Reduction with $LiAlH_4$
 (c) Acidic hydrolysis followed by heating with ammonia and then alkaline bromine
 (d) None.

7. Predict the nature of the product P

$$C_6H_5CONH_2 \xrightarrow{Br_2/OD^-} P$$

 (a) $C_6H_5NH_2$ (b) C_6H_5NHD
 (c) $C_6H_5ND_2$ (d) All the three.

8. The tertiary amine, $CH_3\overset{\underset{\displaystyle |}{C_2H_5}}{C}HN(CH_3)(C_2H_5)$, is
 (a) resolvable due to the presence of chiral N atom
 (b) resolvable due to the presence of chiral C atom
 (c) both (a) and (b)
 (d) non-resolvable.

9. Which of the following species is basic in nature ?
 (a) $(CH_3CH_2)_4N^+Br^-$ (b) $(CH_3CH_2)_4N^+OH^-$
 (c) Both (d) None.

10. Which of the following is most basic ?

(a) 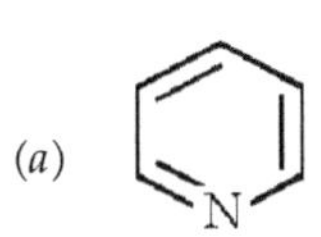 (b) 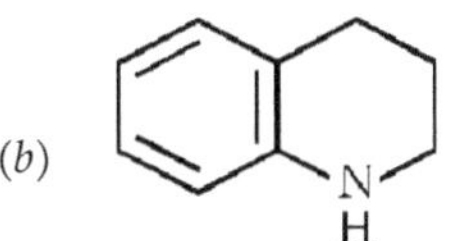

(c) 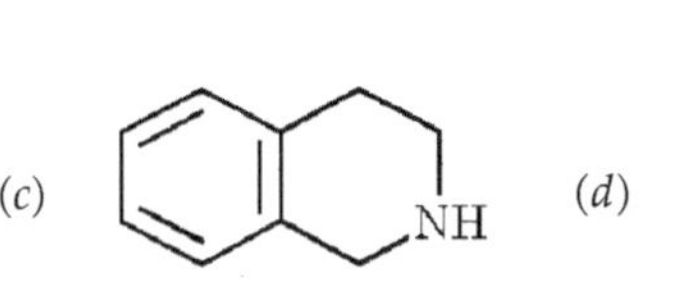 (d)

11. Which of the following is most basic in gas phase ?
 (a) NH_3 (b) $CH_3CH_2NH_2$
 (c) $(CH_3CH_2)_2NH$ (d) $(CH_3CH_2)_3N.$

12. The correct order of decreasing basic character of the four amines (I to IV) is

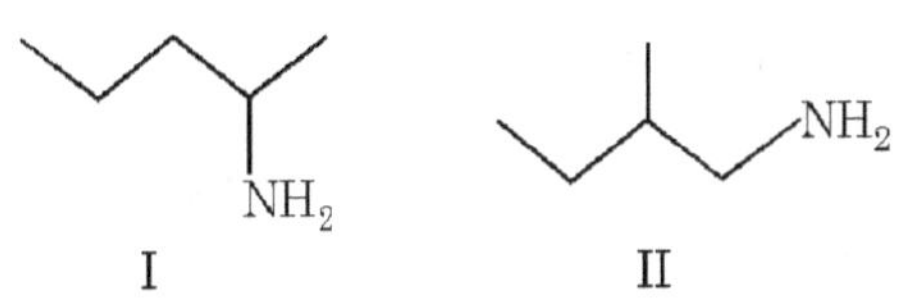

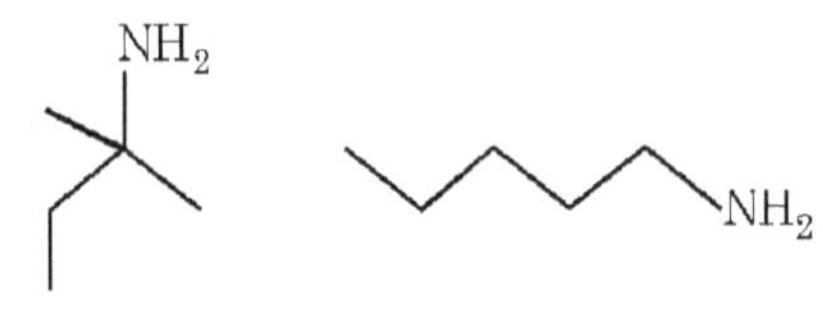

 (a) I > II > III > IV
 (b) IV > II > III > I
 (c) III > II > I > IV
 (d) All are equal since all are 1° amines.

13. Which of the following is most volatile ?
 (a) $n\text{-}C_3H_7NH_2$ (b) $CH_3NHC_2H_5$
 (c) $(CH_3)_3N$ (d) $CH_3OH.$

14. The correct arrangement of decreasing dipole moment of the following three compounds is
 CH_3CH_2OH (I) ; $CH_3CH_2NH_2$ (II), $CH_3CH_2CH_3$ (III)

 (a) I > II > III (b) III > II > I
 (c) II > III > I (d) II > I > III.

15. Which of the following in least basic ?
 (a) $FCH_2CH_2NH_2$ (b) $CH_3CH_2NH_2$
 (c) $ClCH_2CH_2NH_2$ (d) All are equally basic.

16. Which of the following can form salt with aqueous acids ?
 (a) $CH_3\overset{..}{N}H_2$ (b) $CH_3CO\overset{..}{N}H_2$
 (c) Both (d) None

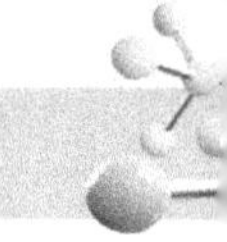

17. Phenylhydrazine hydrochloride, $C_6H_5NHNH_3^+Cl^-$, an important carbonyl reagent is formed by treating phenylhydrazine, $C_6H_5NHNH_2$ with aq. hydrochloric acid. What product you expect when methylhydrazine, CH_3NHNH_2 is treated with aq. hydrochloric acid ?
    (a) $CH_3NHNH_3^+Cl^-$
    (b) $CH_3N^+H_2NH_2Cl^-$
    (c) Both
    (d) No reaction.

18. Predict about the relative boiling point of the following two amines.

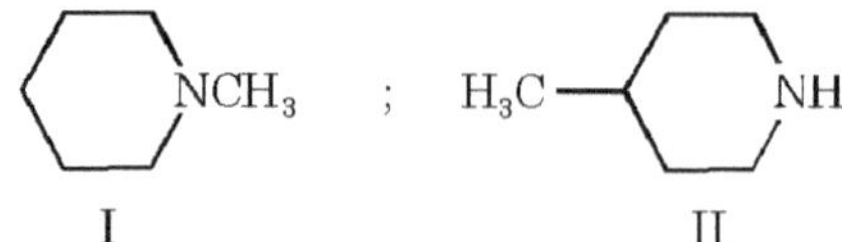

      I   II

    (a) Boiling point of I > II
    (b) Boiling point of II > I
    (c) Both should have equal boiling points
    (d) It can't be predicted.

19. A nitro group in the *para* or *ortho* to the amino group decreases the basicity of the —NH_2 group by
    (a) destabilizing the corresponding anilinium ion
    (b) stabilizing the parent amine
    (c) both of the above factors
    (d) None of the above statement is correct.

20. Which one of the following is better nitrosating agent ?
    (a) HONO
    (b) NOCl
    (c) Both are equal
    (d) None.

21. N, N-Dimethylaniline is converted to *p*-nitroso-N, N-dimethylaniline easily by
    (a) H_2O^+—NO
    (b) HO—NO
    (c) Both are equal
    (d) None.

22. Which of the following amine is more reactive ?
    (a) $CH_3CH_2NH_2$
    (b) $HOCH_2CH_2NH_2$
    (c) Both are equal reactive
    (d) It can't be predicted.

23. Which of the following amine will react with BF_3 ?
    (a) $(CH_3)_3N$
    (b) $(C_6H_5)_3N$
    (c) Both
    (d) None.

24. Glycine (aminoacetic acid) can best be prepared by the reaction of potassium phthalimide with
    (a) chloroacetic acid
    (b) ethyl chloroacetate
    (c) either of the two
    (d) acetic acid.

25. How many alkenes can be formed when *n*-butylamine is treated with nitrous acid ?
    (a) 1
    (b) 2
    (c) 3
    (d) 0.

26. Predict the nature of P in the following reaction
$$Me_3CCH_2NH_2 \xrightarrow{HONO} P \text{ (main product)}$$
    (a) Me_3CCH_2OH
    (b) $Me_2CCH=CH_2$
    (c) $Me_2C(OH)C_2H_5$
    (d) $Me_3CCH_2NH(NO)$.

27. 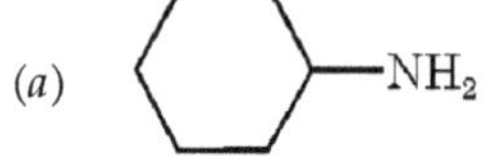 Cl + NH_3 ⟶ A. Here A is

    (a) 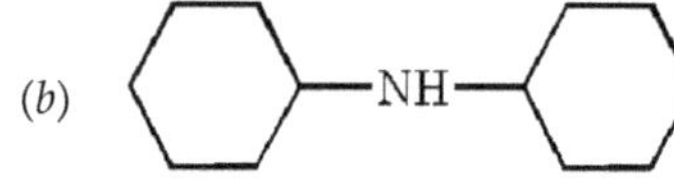NH_2
    (b) NH
    (c) Both (a) and (b)
    (d)

28. X. Here X is

    (a)
    (b)
    (c)
    (d)

29. In the compound given below the correct order of the acidity of the positions X, Y and Z is
    (a) Z > X > Y
    (b) X > Y > Z
    (c) X > Z > Y
    (d) Y > X > Z

30. In the following reaction,
$$CH_3NH_2 + CHCl_3 + KOH$$
⟶ Nitrogen containing compound + $KCl + H_2O$.
The nitrogen containing compound is
    (a) $CH_3-NH-CH_3$
    (b) $CH_3-C\equiv N$
    (c) $CH_3 \overset{+}{N} \equiv \overset{-}{C}$
    (d) $CH_3 - \overset{-}{N} \equiv \overset{+}{C}$

31. The correct order of basicities of the following compounds is
    1. $CH_3 - C \begin{smallmatrix} NH \\ \\ NH_2 \end{smallmatrix}$
    2. $CH_3 - CH_2 - NH_2$
    3. $(CH_3)_2NH$
    4. $CH_3 - \overset{O}{\overset{\|}{C}} - NH_2$
    (a) 2 > 1 > 3 > 4
    (b) 1 > 3 > 2 > 4
    (c) 3 > 1 > 2 > 4
    (d) 1 > 2 > 3 > 4

32. Which one of the following is the strongest base in aqueous solution ?
    (a) Methylamine
    (b) Trimethylamine
    (c) Aniline
    (d) Dimethylamine.

33. The correct order of increasing basic nature for the bases NH_3, CH_3NH_2 and $(CH_3)_2NH$ is
    (a) $(CH_3)_2NH < NH_3 < CH_3NH_2$
    (b) $NH_3 < CH_3NH_2 < (CH_3)_2NH$
    (c) $CH_3NH_2 < (CH_3)_2NH < NH_3$
    (d) $CH_3NH_2 < NH_3 < (CH_3)_2NH$

34. Ethyl isocyanide on hydrolysis in acidic medium generates
    (a) propanoic acid and ammonium salt
    (b) ethanoic acid and ammonium salt
    (c) methylamine salt and ethanoic acid
    (d) ethylamine salt and methanoic acid

35. Which one of the following methods is neither meant for the synthesis nor for separation of amines?
(a) Curtius reaction (b) Wurtz reaction
(c) Hofmann method (d) Hinsberg method

36. Introduction of a methyl group in ammonia markedly increases the basic strength of ammonia in aq. solution, introduction of the second methyl group increases only marginally the basic strength of methyl amine in water. This is due to
(a) different type of hybridisation in the two amines
(b) protonated dimethyl amine is more solvated than methyl amine
(c) protonated dimethyl amine is more solvated than the protonated methyl amine
(d) protonated dimethyl amine is less stable than the protonated methyl amine

37.  $\xrightarrow{\text{heat}}$ Z; Z is

(a) 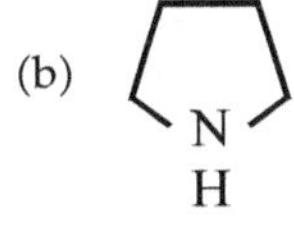

(b) 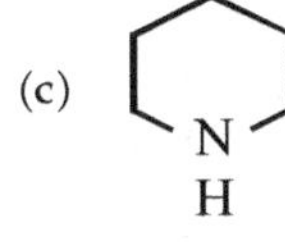

(c) 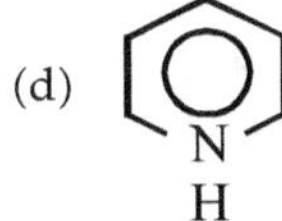

(d)

38. The relative order of basic character of the following compounds is

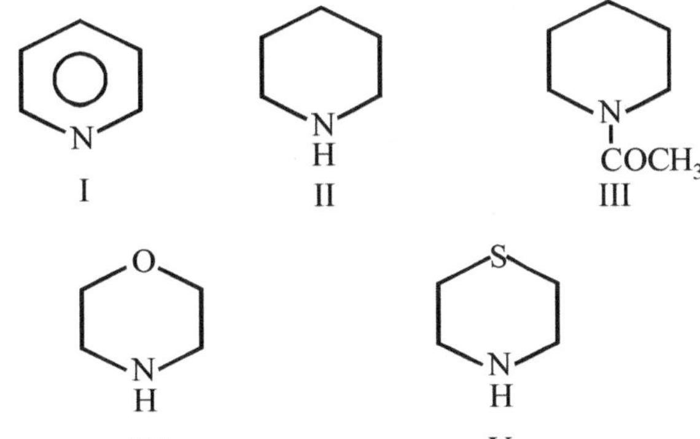

(a) II > I > III > IV > V (b) II > III > IV > V > I
(c) II > V > IV > I > III (d) II > IV > V > III > I

39. In the following reaction, the reagent X should be

$$RCOOH + [X] \xrightarrow{\text{conc. } H_2SO_4} RNH_2$$

(a) NH_3 (b) HN_3
(c) either of the two (d) None of the two

40. Benzamide and benzyl amine can be distinguished by
(a) cold dil. NaOH
(b) cold dil. HCl
(c) both a & b
(d) $NaNO_2$, HCl, 0°C, then β-naphthol

41. Which of the following is true regarding basic character of pyridine and pyrrole?
(a) Pyrrole is more basic because its nonbonding electrons occupy sp^3 orbital

(b) Pyridine is more basic because its nonbonding electrons is not a part of aromatic sextet.
(c) Both are equally basic
(d) Pyridine is less basic because it is 3° amine

42. The correct order of decreasing basic character of the three aliphatic primary amines is

(a) I > II > III (b) III > II > I
(c) I > II ≈ III (d) I = II ≡ III

43. Which of the statement is true regarding the basicity of the following two primary amines ?

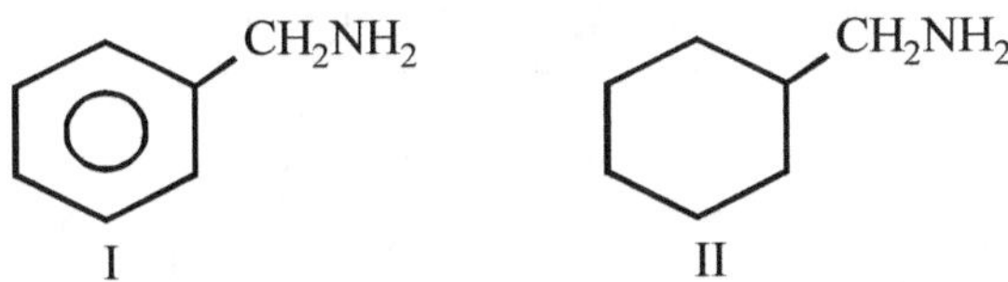

(a) Both are equally basic because both are 1° amines
(b) I > II because it is an aromatic amine
(c) II > I because it is an aliphatic amine
(d) I < II because of difference in the nature of β-carbon

44. Pyrrole and pyridine both are basic and form salts with acids?

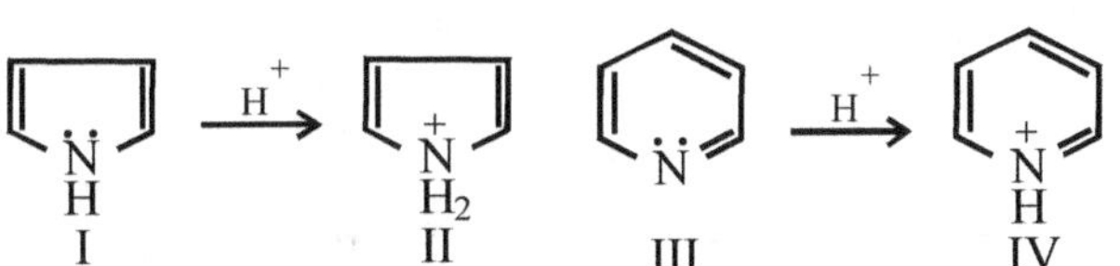

Which of the following statement is true regarding the aromatic character of the four species?
(a) All the four are aromatic
(b) I, III and IV are aromatic
(c) I, II and III are aromatic
(d) I and III are aromatic

45. Which of the following leads to carbon-carbon double bond?
(a) 1° Amine + RCHO → (b) 2° Amine + R_2CO →
(c) 2° Amine + RCHO → (d) both b & c

46. Which of the following will react most readily with NaOH to form ethanol ?

(a) $(CH_3)_4 N^+ I^-$ (b) $(CH_3)_4 S^+ I^-$

(c) $(CH_3)_3 CCl$ (d) CH_3OCH_3

47. In Hofmann bromamide degradation, one of the important steps is the migration of
(a) an alkyl group without its electron pair to electron deficient N atom
(b) an alkyl group with its electron pair to electron deficient O atom
(c) an alkyl group with its electron pair to electron rich N atom
(d) an alkyl group with its electron pair to electron deficient N atom

48. $(CH_3)_3C - \overset{\overset{\displaystyle O}{\|}}{C} - NH_2 \xrightarrow[\text{(ii)}D_2O]{\text{(i) } OD^-/Br_2}$ Product P is

(a) $(CH_3)_3 CNH_2$ (b) $(CH_3)_3 CNHD$
(c) $(CH_3)_3 CND_2$ (d) no reaction

49.

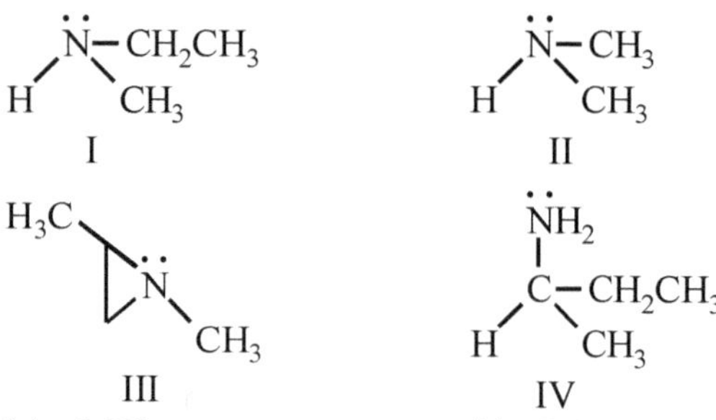

(a)   [structure: CH₃ with N(CH₃)₂ and vinyl group]

(b)   [structure with N(CH₃)₂ and terminal alkene]

(c)   [structure with N(CH₃)₂ and CH₃]   (d)   None

50. Which of the following is one of the intermediates in Hofmann, Curtius, Schmidt and Lossen reaction ?

(a) $R\overset{+}{C}O$ (b)   RNCO

(c)   RCNO   (d) $R\overset{-}{CONH}$

51. Which of the following is not formed as an intermediate in the Hofmann rearrangement?

$$R-CONH_2 \xrightarrow{Br_2 / NaOH} RNH_2$$

(a) $R-\overset{O}{\overset{||}{C}}-\overset{H}{\overset{|}{N}}Br$ (b) $R-\overset{O}{\overset{||}{C}}-\overset{..}{N}{}^{-}-Br$

(c) $R-\overset{O}{\overset{||}{C}}-\overset{..}{N}{:}$ (d)   All the three are formed

52. How many structural isomers of a Grignard reagent are possible for preparing *n*-butane by reaction with ethyl amine ?

(a)   1   (b)   2

(c)   3   (d)   4

53. [phthalimide structure] NR $\xrightarrow[\text{(ii) HCl}]{\text{(i) NH}_2\text{NH}_2.\text{H}_2\text{O}}$ Product is

(a)   [benzene ring with CONH₂·HCl and CONH₂·HCl]

(b)   [benzene ring with CONHNH₂ and CONH₂]

(c)   [phthalimide-type ring structure]

(d)   [benzene ring with COOH and COOH]

54. The basic character of ethyl amine, diethyl amine and triethyl amine in chlorobenzene is

(a) $C_2H_5NH_2 < (C_2H_5)_2NH < (C_2H_5)_3N$

(b) $C_2H_5NH_2 < (C_2H_5)_3N < (C_2H_5)_2NH$

(c) $(C_2H_5)_3N < (C_2H_5)_2NH < C_2H_5NH_2$

(d) $(C_2H_5)_3N < C_2H_5NH_2 < (C_2H_5)_2NH$

55. The correct order of decreasing basic character of the three aliphatic primary amines is

[structures: I — propyl NH₂; II — butenyl NH₂; III — propargyl NH₂]

(a)   I > II > III   (b)   III > II > I

(c)   I > II ≈ III   (d)   I = II ≡ III

56. The correct order of increasing basicity is

$$CH_3CH_2NH_2 \quad CH_3\overset{NH}{\overset{||}{C}}NH_2 \quad CH_3\overset{O}{\overset{||}{C}}NH_2$$
$$\text{I} \quad\quad\quad\quad \text{II} \quad\quad\quad\quad \text{III}$$

(a)   II < III < I   (b)   I ≈ III < II

(c)   I < II < III   (d)   III < I < II

57. $CH_3CH_2CH_2NH_2 \xrightarrow[0°C]{NaNO_2, HCl} P$. P is

(a) $CH_3CH_2CH_2OH$ (b) $(CH_3)_2CHCl$

(c)   Both (a) and (b)   (d)   Reaction not possible

58. Which of the following amines can be resolved into two enantiomers?

[structures: I, II, III, IV]

(a)   I, IV   (b)   I, II

(c)   I, III, IV   (d)   III, IV

59. Which of the following statement is false?

(a)   Dimethyl amine as well as trimethyl amine are soluble in water

(b)   Trimethyl amine forms hydrogen bond neither with itself nor with water.

(c)   Trimethyl amine can act as hydrogen bond acceptor only, while dimethyl amine can serve as both a hydrogen bond donor and acceptor

(d)   All the three statements are false

60. Which of the following leads to carbon-carbon double bond?

(a)   1° Amine + RCHO →   (b)   2° Amine + R₂CO →

(c)   2° Amine + RCHO →   (d)   both b & c

61. Predict the possible number of alkenes and the main alkene in the following reaction.

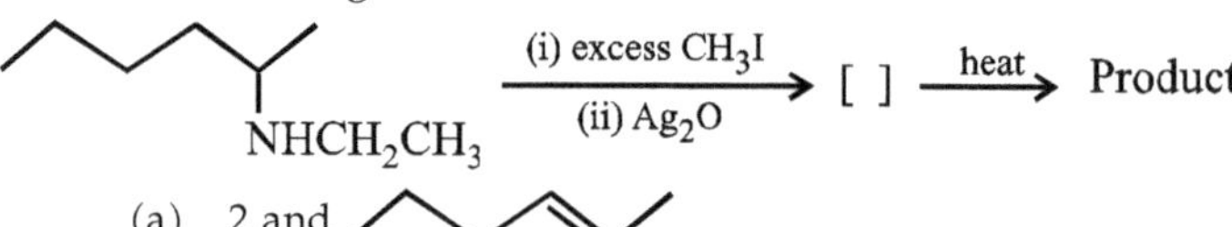

(a)   2 and [alkene structure]

(b)   2 and [alkene structure]

(c)   3 and $H_2C = CH_2$

(d)   2 and $H_2C = CH_2$

62. In Hofmann bromamide degradation, one of the important steps is the migration of

(a)   an alkyl group without its electron pair to electron deficient N atom

(b)   an alkyl group with its electron pair to electron deficient O atom

(c)   an alkyl group with its electron pair to electron rich N atom

(d)   an alkyl group with its electron pair to electron deficient N atom

63. Identify (C) and (D) in the following series of reactions

$$CH_3NH_2 \xrightarrow[CH_3I]{\text{excess of}} [A] \xrightarrow{AgOH} [B] \xrightarrow{heat} [C]+[D]$$

(a) $(CH_3)_3COH, CH_3NH_2$ (b) $(CH_3)_2C = CH_2, CH_3NH_2$

(c) $(CH_3)_3N, CH_3OH$ (d) $(CH_3)_2C=CH_2, CH_3OH$

64. Which of the following is hydrolysed to give secondary amine -

(a)   Alkyl cyanide   (b) $H-\overset{O}{\overset{||}{C}}-N(CH_3)_2$

(c)   Nitro paraffins   (d)   Acid amide

65. Which of the following does not yield an amine -

(a) $R - X + NH_3 \rightarrow$

(b) $R - CH = N - OH + [H] \xrightarrow[C_2H_5OH]{Na}$

(c) $R - CN + H_2O \rightarrow$ (d) $RCONH_2 + 4[H] \rightarrow$

66. Which of the following amine does not react with Hinsberg reagent ?

(a) Neopentylamine (b) Isopropylamine

(c) Triethylamine (d) Ethylmethylamine

67. The major product of the following reaction is

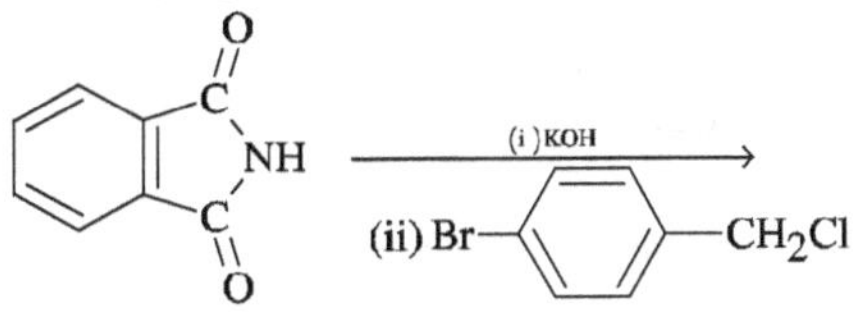

(reaction scheme with phthalimide)

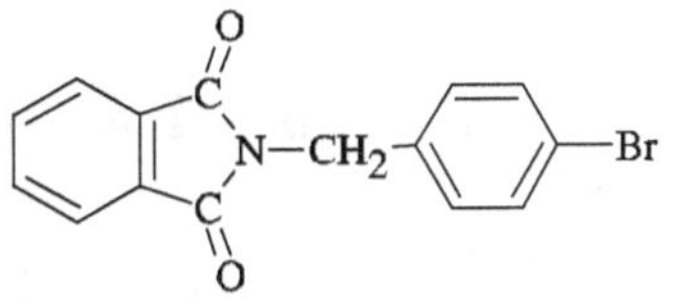

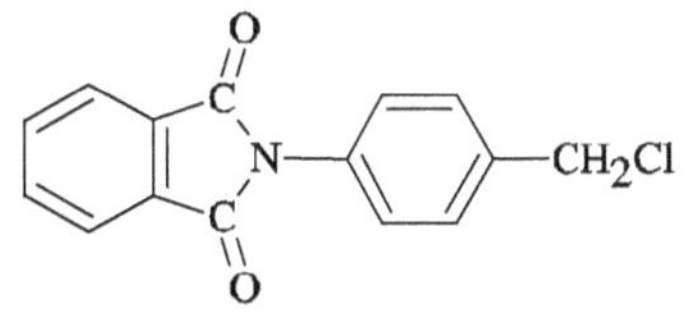

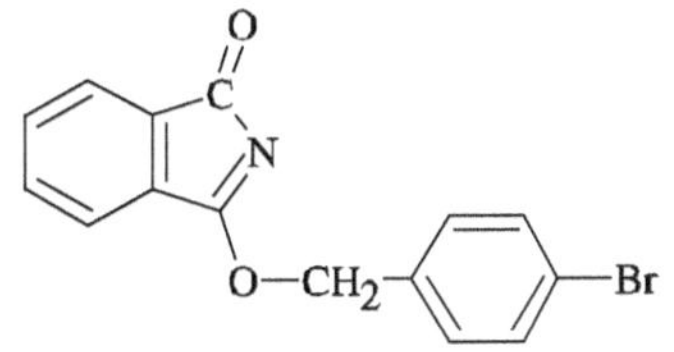

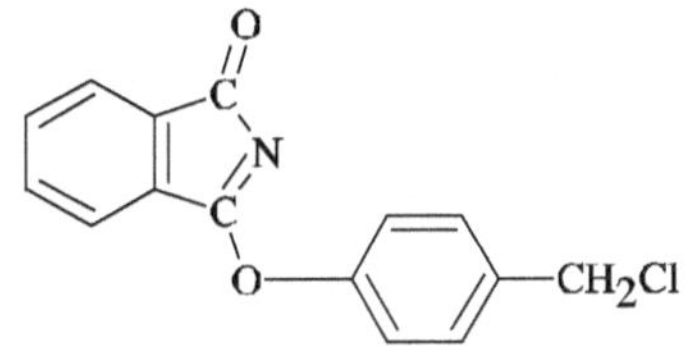

EXERCISE 19.2   (MCQ 1 or >1 option correct, Passage based, Matching, A/R)

DIRECTIONS for Q. 1 to Q. 22 : Multiple choice questions with one or more than one correct option(s).

1. Which of the following amine can be prepared by Gabriel method?

(a) $CH_3CH_2NH_2$ (b) $(CH_3)_2CHNH_2$

(c) $(CH_3)_3CNH_2$ (d) $C_6H_5NH_2$

2. Which of the following can't be used as an alkylating agent for an amine ?

(a) CH_3CH_2Cl (b) $CH_2 = CHCl$

(c) C_6H_5Cl (d) $(CH_3)_3CCl$

3. $(CH_3)_3CNH_2$ can't be prepared by

(a) reductive amination (b) oxime reduction

(c) Hofmann degradation (d) Gabriel synthesis.

4. Guanidine, $(NH_2)_2 C = NH$, is said to be the strongest nitrogen containing organic base because

(a) it has two $-NH_2$ groups

(b) it has three nitrogen atoms that can be protonated

(c) it is less stable as compared to the protonated species

(d) its conjugate acid is very much stable due to three equivalent structures.

5. Quaternary ammonium salts are used

(a) as phase transfer catalysts

(b) in preparing alkenes

(c) for preparing 3° amines

(d) preparing 2° amines

6. Which of the following is not true

Hinsberg test is applicable to

(a) all amines

(b) liquid amines soluble in water

(c) liquid amines insoluble in water

(d) solid amines insoluble in water.

7. Primary, secondary and tertiary amines may be separated by using

(a) benzene sulphonyl chloride

(b) diethyl oxalate

(c) sulphonyl chloride

(d) acetyl chloride

8. $CH_3CH_2CH_2NH_2 \xrightarrow{HNO_2} A(mixture)$

Mixture can contain

(a) $CH_2CH_2CH_2OH$ (b) $CH_3\underset{\underset{OH}{|}}{C}H.CH_3$

(c) 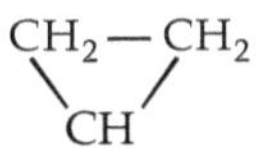 (cyclopropane structure) (d) $CH_3CH = CH_2$

9. $\underset{(x)}{C_4H_{11}N} + HNO_2 \longrightarrow C_4H_{10}O(3° \text{ alcohol})$; hence X will give :

(a) carbyl amine reaction

(b) Hofmann mustard oil reaction

(c) diazonium salt (as the intermediate) with HNO_2

(d) none is correct

10. Mixture of 1°, 2° and 3° amines can be separated by :

(a) Hinsberg's method

(b) Hofmann's method

(c) distillation

(d) chromatography

11. Which is /are correct reaction(s) :

(a) 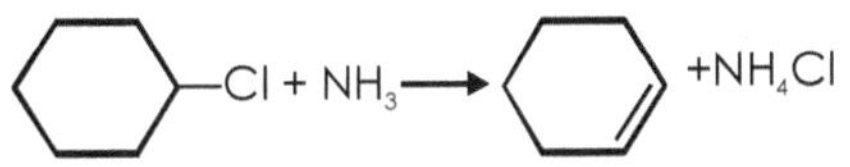 (cyclohexyl chloride) $-Cl + NH_3 \longrightarrow$ (cyclohexene) $+NH_4Cl$

(b) 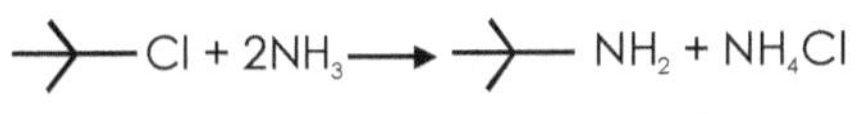 $\rightarrow\!\!-Cl + 2NH_3 \longrightarrow \rightarrow\!\!- NH_2 + NH_4Cl$

(c)  $\rightarrow\!\!-Cl + NH_3 \longrightarrow \prec NH_4Cl$

(d)  $\diagup\!\!\diagdown NH_2 + HNO_2 \xrightarrow{0°C} \uparrow OH$

12.

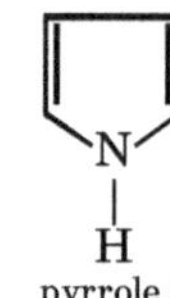 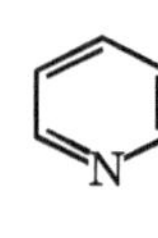 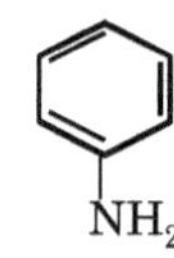

pyrrole I   pyridine II   aniline III

which is/are correct statements?

(a)   I is more basic than II
(b)   II is more basic than I and III
(c)   III is more basic than II
(d)   all are aromatic bases

13.   In the reaction $2X + B_2H_6 \rightarrow [BH_2(X)_2]^+ [BH_4]^-$ the amine(s) X is (are)

(a) NH_3 (b) CH_3NH_2
(c) $(CH_3)_2NH$ (d) $(CH_3)_3N$

14.   Reaction of $R-\overset{\overset{\displaystyle O}{||}}{C}-NH_2$ with a mixture of Br_2 and KOH gives R-NH_2 as the main product. The intermediates involved in this reaction are :

(a) $R-\overset{\overset{\displaystyle O}{||}}{C}-NHBr$ (b) $R-NHBr$

(c) $R-N=C=O$ (d)   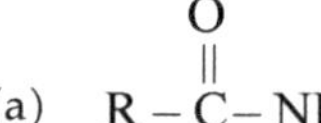

15.   Which of the following compound can be methylated by diazomethane ?

(a) C_2H_5COOH
(b) $C_2H_5NH_2$
(c) C_6H_5OH
(d) $CH_3COCH_2COOC_2H_5$

16.   Which of the following amine can be prepared by Gabriel method ?

(a) $CH_3CH_2NH_2$ (b) $(CH_3)_2CHNH_2$
(c) $(CH_3)_3CNH_2$ (d) $C_6H_5NH_2$

17.   Which of the following can't be used as an alkylating agent for an amine ?

(a) CH_3CH_2Cl (b) $CH_2=CHCl$
(c) C_6H_5Cl (d) $(CH_3)_3CCl$

18.   Which of the following can exist as inner salt ?

(a)   *p*-Aminobenzenesulphonic acid
(b)   *p*-Aminobenzoic acid
(c)   Aminoacetic acid
(d)   Alanine

19.   Which of the following reacts with nitrous acid ?

(a)   Acetamide
(b)   2-Nitrobutane
(c)   2-Methyl-2-nitropropane
(d)   Diethylamine

20.   Which of the following intermediates are likely to be formed when 2-methylpropyl amine is treated with nitrous acid ?

(a) $(CH_3)_2CH\overset{+}{C}H_2$ (b) $(CH_3)_3C\overset{+}{O}H_2$

(c) $(CH_3)_2CHCH_2\overset{+}{O}H_2$ (d) $(CH_3)_2\overset{+}{C}CH_3$

21.   Carbenes are the reactive intermediates in

(a)   Reimer Tiemann reaction
(b)   Wittig reaction
(c)   Hofmann bromamide reaction
(d)   Carbylamine reaction

22. $\underset{(X)}{C_4H_{11}N} + HONO \longrightarrow \underset{(3°\ alcohol)}{C_4H_{10}O}$

X should

(a)   give carbylamine reaction
(b)   undergo diazotisation
(c)   react with water
(d)   give Hofmann bromamide reaction

INSTRUCTION for Q. 23 to Q. 38 : Read the passages given below and answer the questions that follow.

PASSAGE 1

An optically active naturally occurring toxic liquid $C_8H_{17}N$ (X), in hemlock that was said to cause Socrates death dissolves in aq. HCl and gives no gas with nitrous acid. It gives a precipitate with benzenesulphonyl chloride in presence of NaOH. when treated with excess of methyl iodide, then with moist oxide and finally heated, it gives a compound (Y). Compound (Y) is treated similarly as (X) and which finally gives two nitrogen free compounds.

23.   What conclusion you will draw when we say that the original compound does not give any precipitate with $C_6H_5SO_2Cl$ in presence of NaOH?

(a)   It may be 1° amine   (b)   It may be 3° amine
(c)   Either of the two   (d)   Neither of the two

24.   The above set of reactions indicate that N is present in the

(a)   side chain   (b)   ring
(c)   either of the two   (d)   none of the two

PASSAGE 2

Primary aliphatic amines also react with nitrous acid to yield aliphatic diazonium salts. However, aliphatic diazonium salts are quite unstable and decompose spontaneously, even at low temperatures, by losing nitrogen to form carbocations (hence the reaction is commonly known as **deamination**). The carbocations, in turn, produce a mixture of alkenes, alcohols, and alkyl halides.

$$CH_3CH_2CH_2NH_2 \xrightarrow[HCl]{HONO} [CH_3CH_2CH_2N_2{}^+Cl]$$

$$\longrightarrow CH_3CH_2CH_2{}^+ + N_2 + Cl^-$$

$$CH_3CH=CH_2 \xleftarrow{-H^+} CH_3CH_2CH_2{}^+ \longrightarrow CH_3{}^+CHCH_3$$

$$\xrightarrow{-H^+} \underset{Propene}{CH_3CH=CH_2}$$

25.   The reaction of $CH_3CH_2CH_2NH_2$ with nitrous acid is used in detecting the presence of $-NH_2$ group in amino acids and proteins because this test is based on the fact

(a)   a green colour is obtained
(b)   a red colour is obtained in the final stage
(c)   a characteristic change in colour is observed
(d)   nitrogen is evolved quantitatively

26. Which of the following product is also formed in the above reaction?

(a) $CH_3CH_2CH_2Cl$ (b) $CH_3CHOHCH_3$

(c) $CH_3CHClCH_3$ (d) All the three

27. Which type of product is likely to be formed when $CH_3CH_2CH_2NH_2$ in the above case is replaced by $C_6H_5CH_2NH_2$?

(a) An alkene   (b) An alcohol

(c) Both (a) and (b)   (d) None of the two

PASSAGE 3

The conversion of an amide to an amine with one carbon atom less by the action of alkaline hypohalite is known as Hofmann degradation.

$$RCONH_2 + Br_2 + 4KOH \longrightarrow RNH_2$$

The most important feature of the reaction is the rearrangement of N-bromamide anion to isocyanate :

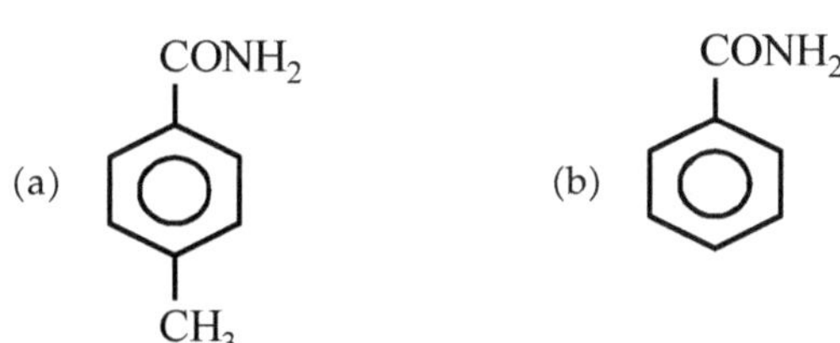

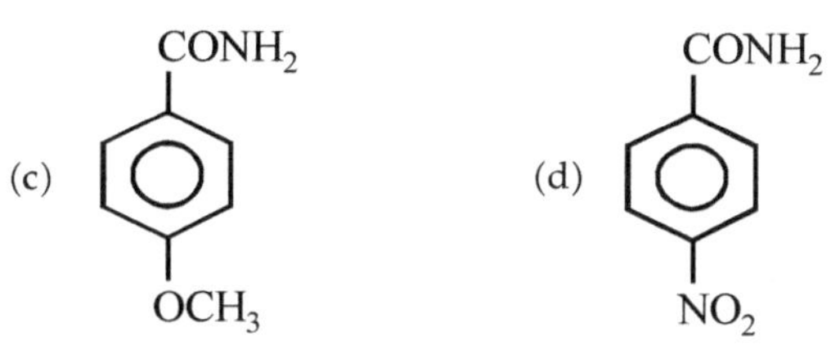

Hofmann reaction is accelerated if the migrating group is more electron-releasing.

28. Which step is the driving force in the above reaction to proceed in right direction?

(a) conversion of I to II

(b) conversion of II to III

(c) conversion of III to RNH_2

(d) All

29. Which of the following can undergo Hofmann reaction most easily?

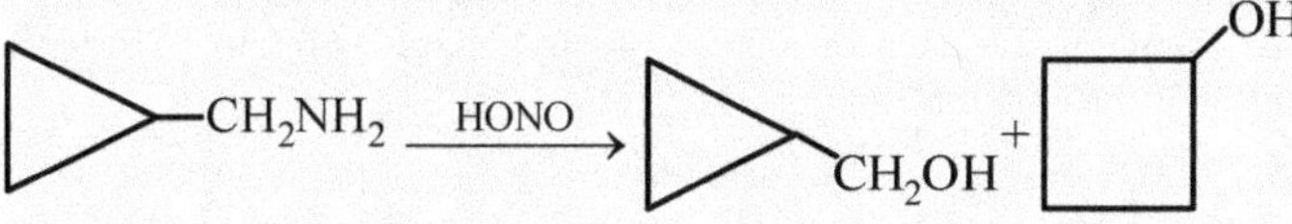

30.

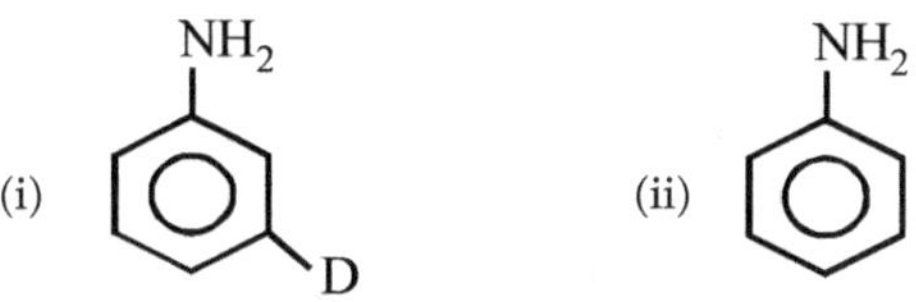

$(+) - \alpha$-Phenylpropionamide

(a) $(+) -$ (b) $(-) -$

(c) $50 : 50$ racemic   (d) non-$50 : 50$ racemic

31. Predict the product in the following reaction :

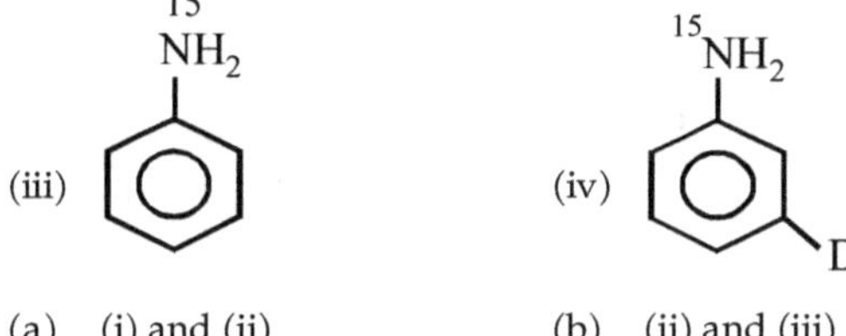

(a) (i) and (ii)   (b) (ii) and (iii)

(c) (i) and (iii)   (d) All the four

PASSAGE 4

Nitrous acid reacts with amines forming different products depending upon the type of amine. Aliphatic primary amines react with HONO forming alcohol as the major product, other products being alkene and alkyl halide. Certain cyclic primary amines can undergo ring expansion or ring contraction on treatment with HONO again forming alcohol as the major product.

Aromatic primary amines when treated with HONO undergo diazotization to form diazonium salt as the stable product.

32. Which of the following statement is not true ?

(a) All primary amines first form diazonium salt when treated with nitrous acid.

(b) All aliphatic primary amines when treated with nitrous acid form primary alcohols as the major product

(c) The three classes of amines give different products on treatment with nitrous acid.

(d) None of the three

33. 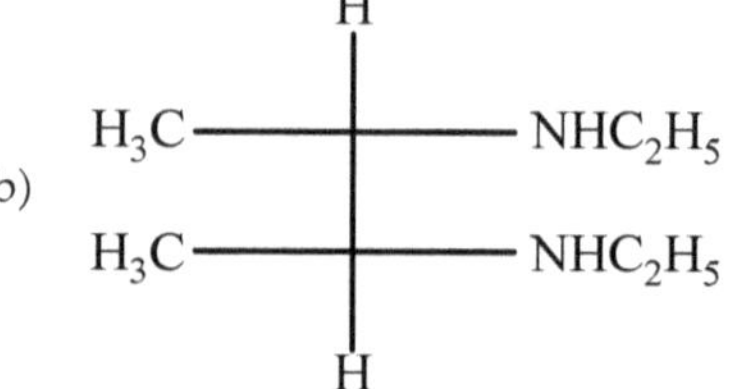 (cyclobutylamine) $\xrightarrow{\text{HONO}}$ P.   Product P may be

(a) (cyclobutanol, with OH)

(b) (cyclopropyl)–CH_2OH

(c) (cyclopentyl)–OH

(d) (cyclopropyl)–OH

34. (cyclopentane with OH and CH_2NH_2) $\xrightarrow[\text{HCl}]{\text{NaNO}_2}$ Stable product Z may be

(a) (cyclobutane with two CH_2OH)

(b) (cyclohexane with OH)

(c) (cyclohexane with two OH)

(d) (cyclohexanone)

35. $(+)-CH_3\overset{\overset{\displaystyle NH_2}{|}}{C}HCH_2CH_3 \xrightarrow{\text{HONO}}$ Product is

(a) enantiomer of the original compound
(b) diastereomer of the original compound
(c) racemic mixture of the original compound
(d) $(+)-$ isomer

PASSAGE 5

Like ammonia, an amine (1°, 2° or 3°) can react with an alkyl halide to form next higher class of amine. Here, again it is the presence of electron pair on nitrogen which makes amines to behave as nucleophile and alkyl halides thus undergo nucleophilic substitutions.

$$\underset{\substack{\text{1° Amine}\\(\text{Nucleophile})}}{R\ddot{N}H_2} + \underset{\text{1° Alkyl halide}}{R'CH_2X} \longrightarrow RN^+\!\!\underset{|}{\overset{|}{-}}CH_2R' \quad \overset{H}{\underset{H}{|}} \quad X^-$$

$$\longrightarrow \underset{\text{2° Amine}}{R\underset{H}{\ddot{N}}\!-\!CH_2R'} + HX$$

A second alkylation may follow, converting the secondary amine to a tertiary amine which may be alkylated to give a quaternary ammonium salt.

36. Identify the product(s) obtained when $Br(CH_2)_4Br$ is heated with 1 equivalent of ethyl amine

(a) Br—(chain)—$NHCH_2CH_3$

(b) C_2H_5NH—(chain)—NHC_2H_5

(c) Br—(chain)—$N(CH_2CH_3)(CH_2)_4Br$

(d) (N-ethylpyrrolidine)

37. Identify the product(s) obtained when $Br(CH_2)_4Br$ is heated with excess of methyl amine

(a) $Br(CH_2)_3CH_2\overset{\overset{\displaystyle |}{\displaystyle (CH_2)_4Br}}{N}CH_3$

(b) $Br(CH_2)_3CH_2\overset{\overset{\displaystyle Br^-(CH_2)_4Br}{\displaystyle |}}{\underset{\overset{\displaystyle |}{\displaystyle (CH_2)_4Br}}{N^+}}CH_3$

(c) (N-methylpyrrolidine, with CH_3)

(d) $\underset{H}{H_3C\overset{\displaystyle N}{}}$—(chain)—$NHCH_3$

38. (aziridine with CH_3 groups) $+ C_2H_5NH_2 \longrightarrow Z$, here Z is

(a) $\begin{array}{c}H\\H_3C-\!\!\overset{|}{\underset{|}{\,}}\!\!-NHC_2H_5\\H_5C_2HN-\!\!\overset{|}{\underset{|}{\,}}\!\!-CH_3\\H\end{array}$

(b) $\begin{array}{c}H\\H_3C-\!\!\overset{|}{\underset{|}{\,}}\!\!-NHC_2H_5\\H_3C-\!\!\overset{|}{\underset{|}{\,}}\!\!-NHC_2H_5\\H\end{array}$

(c) Both of these
(d) None of the two

Instructions for Q. 39 to Q. 45 : Following questions are Multiple Matching type Questions :

39.

Column - I (Reagent/Reaction)	Column - II (Product)
(A) Reductive amination	(a) 1° amines
(B) Isonitriles	(b) 2° amines
(C) Hofmann rearrangement	(c) 3° amines
(D) Alkyl azides	(d) Isocyanate is formed as intermediate

40.

Column - I	Column - II
(A) Tertiamine oxide	(a) Regioselective
(B) Hofmann elimination	(b) Stereospecific
(C) Cope elimination	(c) Zwitterion
(D) Mustard oil reaction	(d) Isothiocyanates

41. Match the following in which reactions match with the name given on RHS in any way, i.e reactant, product, intermediate or reagent.

Column I	Column II
(A) Beckmann rearrangement	(a) Isocyanate
(B) Hofmann bromamide rearrangement	(b) Amide
(C) Curtius reaction	(c) Amine
(D) Fries reaction	(d) AlCl$_3$

42. Match each of the compounds in **Column I** with its characteristic reaction(s) in **Column II**.

Column I	Column II
(A) $CH_3CH_2\ CH_2CN$	(a) Reduction with Pd–C/H$_2$
(B) $CH_3\ CH_2\ OCOCH_3$	(b) Reduction with SnCl$_2$/HCl
(C) CH_3–CH= CH–CH$_2$OH	(c) Development of foul smell on treatment with chloroform and alcoholic KOH
(D) $CH_3CH_2CH_2CH_2NH_2$	(d) Reduction with diisobutylaluminium hydride(DIBAL-H)
	(e) Alkaline hydrolysis

43.

Column I	Column II
(A) Allylic rearrangement	(a) Carbanions
(B) Hofmann rearrangement	(b) Electron deficient species
(C) Wittig reaction	(c) Carbocations
(D) Carbylamine reaction	(d) Carbenes

44.

Column - I	Column - II
(A) Hofmann degradation	(a) Amides
(B) Beckmann rearrangement	(b) Isocyanates
(C) Curtius rearrangement	(c) NaOH/Br$_2$
(D) Lossen rearrangement	(d) RCON$_3$

45. Match the column correctly –

Column I	Column II
(A) Conversion of amide	(a) Quaternary salt to amine
(B) Conversion of primary amine to isocyanide	(b) Schmidt reaction
(C) Tetraethylammonium iodide	(c) Carbylamine reaction
(D) $RCOOH + N_3H + H_2SO_4$	(d) Hofmann's bromamide reaction.

Instructions for Q. 46 to 54 : Following questions are Assertion and Reasoning Type Questions :

Note : Each question contains STATEMENT-1 (Assertion) and STATEMENT-2 (Reason). Each question has 5 choices (a), (b), (c), (d) and (e) out of which ONLY ONE is correct.

(a) Statement-1 is True, Statement-2 is True; Statement-2 is a correct explanation for Statement-1.

(b) Statement-1 is True, Statement-2 is True; Statement-2 is NOT a correct explanation for Statement-1.

(c) Statement -1 is True, Statement-2 is False.

(d) Statement -1 is False, Statement-2 is True.

(e) Statement -1 is False, Statement-2 is False.

46. **Statement 1 :** Amines are basic in nature

Statement 2 : The lone pair of electron is present on nitrogen atom.

47. **Statement 1 :** In order to convert R – Cl to pure R–NH$_2$. Gabriel pthalimide synthesis can be used.

Statement 2: With proper choice of alkyl halides, pthalimide synthesis can be used to prepare 1°, 2° or 3° amines.

48. **Statement 1:** In Hofmann bromide reaction, the amine formed has one carbon atom less than the parent 1° amide.

Statement 2: N-methyl acetamide undergoes hofmann bromamide reaction.

49. **Statement 1:** Ammonia is less basic than water.

Statement 2 : Nitrogen is less electronegative than oxygen.

50. **Statement-1 :** 1° Amides react with Br$_2$ + NaOH to give 1° amines with one carbon atom less than the parent amide.

Statement-2 : The reaction occurs through intermediate formation of acylnitrene.

51. **Statement-1 :** In order to convert R–Cl to pure R–NH$_2$, Gabriel-phthalimide synthesis can be used.

Statement-2 : With proper choice of alkyl halides, phthalimide synthesis can be used to prepare 1°, 2° or 3° amines.

52. **Statement-1 :** Acetamide reacts with Br$_2$ in presence of methanolic CH$_3$ONa to form methyl N-methylcarbamate.

Statement-2 : Methyl isocyanate is formed as an intermediate which reacts with methanol to form methyl N-methylcarbamate.

53. **Statement-1:** 1°, 2° and 3° amines are hydrogen-bonding donors, while 1° and 2° amines are hydrogen-bonding acceptors.

Statement-2 : Low molecular weight amines are soluble in water.

54. **Statement-1 :** Hofmann elimination gives alkene

Statement-2 : Alkenes are less acidic than NH$_3$

EXERCISE 19.3 (Subjective Problems)

1. Write down the structures, names and type (1°, 2°, 3°) of

(a) the isomeric amines of the formula $C_4H_{11}N$

(b) the isomeric amines having benzene nucleus of the formula C_7H_9N.

(c) the five isomeric cyclic compounds having the molecular formula C_4H_9N.

2. Give the structural formulas of the following compounds.

(a) *sec*- Butylamine

(b) β-Phenylethylamine

(c) Diphenylamine

(d) N, N-Dimethylaminocyclohexane

(e) Tetra-isobutylammonium iodide

(f) *sec*-Butylammonium benzoate

(g) Ethyl 3-(N-methylamino)-2-butenoate.

3. Mention the sequence of reagents used in the preparation of *n*-propylamine from each of the following compounds.

(a) *n*-Propyl bromide   (b) *n*-Propyl alcohol

(c) Ethanol   (d) *n*-Butanol

(e) *n*-Butyramide

Mention which of the above corresponding compound can be used for preparing aniline and benzylamine ?

4. Prepare *n*-propylamine by

(a) alkyl halide amination

(b) reductive amination

(c) amide reduction

(d) nitrile reduction

(e) Hofmann rearrangement, and

(f) Curtius reaction.

5. Gabriel synthesis is not recommended for preparing following amines, explain.

(a) *tert*-Butylamine

(b) Neopentylamine

(c) Diethylamine

(d) *p*-Toluidine.

6. Identify compounds A to D.

(a)
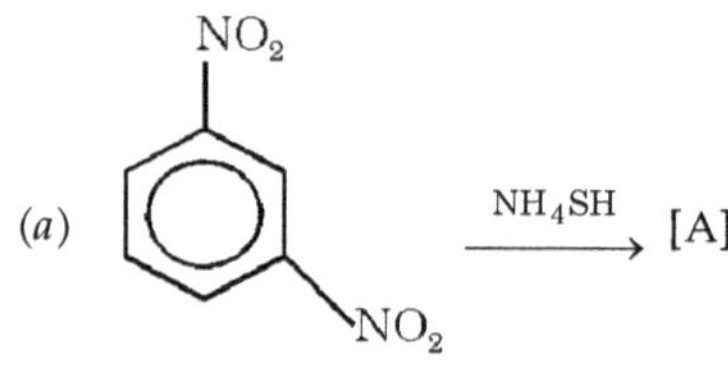

(b) $CH_2 = CHCH_2Li \xrightarrow{NaN_3} [B] \xrightarrow{H_2/pt} [C] \xrightarrow{LiAlH_4} [D]$

7. Give the structures for the products of the reductive amination with H_2/Ni of

(a) CH_3CHO with (i) NH_3, (ii) $C_2H_5NH_2$, and (iii) $C_2H_5NHCH_3$

(b) $(CH_3)_2CO$ with (i) NH_3, (ii) $C_2H_5NH_2$, and (iii) $C_2H_5NHCH_3$.

8. (a) What are the advantages of reductive amination over the reaction of alkyl halides with amines.

(b) How can you ensure a good yield of RR′NH (a 2° amine) from RNH_2 and R′ X ?

9. Two α, ω-diamines have been isolated from the rotting flesh ; one has the molecular formula $C_4H_{12}N_2$ and the other $C_5H_{14}N_2$. Give two methods for preparing each of them from α, ω-dihalides.

10. Write chemical equations for the reactions of CH_3NH_2 with (i) H_2O, (ii) $HCl(g)$, (iii) B $(CH_3)_3$.

11. Compare the basicities of

(a) $C_6H_5NH_2$, $(C_6H_5)_2NH$, NH_3, and cyclohexyl—NH_2.

(b) aniline, *p*-methyoxyaniline, *p*-nitroaniline

(c) benzylamine, *m*-chlorobenzylanine, *m*-ethylbenzylamine,

(d) *p*-chloro-N-methylaniline, 2, 4-dichloro-N-methylaniline, 2, 4, 6-trichloro-N-methylaniline.

12. Which is more basic : an aqueous solution of trimethylamine or an aqueous solution of tetramethylammonium hydroxide ?

13. What do you expect about the solubility of N-nitrosoamines in aq. HCl ?

14. Give the structure of the compound formed, if any, when ethylamine is treated with

(a) acetic acid   (b) isobutyryl chloride

(c) dil. NaOH   (d) benzyl bromide

(e) chlorobenzene   (f) 2,4,6-trinitrochlorobenzene

(g) phthalic anhydride   (h) acetone, H_2/Ni

(i) sodium chloroacetate.

15. Compare the behaviour of ethylamine, diethylamine and triethylamine with each of the following reagents.

(a) dil. HCl   (b) methyl iodide

(c) acetic anhydride   (d) benzenesulphonyl chloride

(e) $NaNO_2$ + aq. HCl.

16. Compare and account for the products obtained from thermal decomposition of following compounds.

(a) $[(CH_3)_3 N^+C_2H_5]$ OH^-

(b) $(CH_3)_4N^+OH^-$

(c) $C_6H_5N^+Me_3OH$

(d)
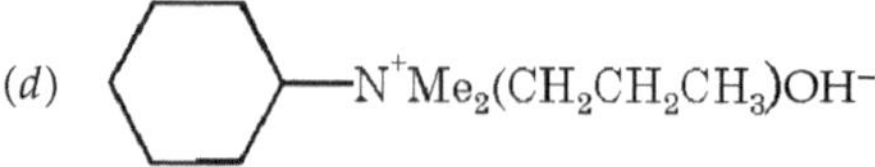

17. Give structures and names of the principal products obtained from the action, if any, of sodium nitrite and hydrochloric acid on each of the following.

(a) *n*-Propylamine   (b) 2-Amino-3-methylbutane

(c) 4, 4′-Diaminodiphenyl   (d) N, N-Dimethylaniline

(e) Sulphanilic acid   (f) Benzylamine.

18. Give the structures of all possible products obtained by the action of sodium nitrite and hydrochloric acid on

    (*a*) isobutylamine, and   (*b*) neopentylamine.

19. Write the equation involved in the formation of nylon-6, 6 when hexamethylenediamine is heated with adipic acid, Addition of a drop of HCl on the fabric nylon-6, 6 makes a hole, explain the chemistry involved.

20. Name the reagent or test used to distinguish between the following pairs.

    (*a*) $n\text{-}C_3H_7NH_2$ and $(n\text{-}C_3H_7)_2NH$

    (*b*) $(n\text{-}C_3H_7)_2\,NH$ and $(n\text{-}C_3H_7)_3N$

    (*c*) Me_3NHCl and Me_4NCl

    (*d*) $Me_2NCH_2CH_2OH$ and Me_4NOH

    (*e*) $C_6H_5NH_2$ and $C_6H_5NHCOCH_3$

    (*f*) $C_6H_5NH_3Cl$ and $p\text{-}ClC_6H_4NH_2$

    (*g*) $C_6H_5NH_2$ and 2, 4, 6-trinitroaniline

    (*h*) $C_2H_5NH_3Cl$ and $NH_2CH_2CH_2Cl$

    (*i*) $C_2H_5NH_3HSO_4$ and $C_2H_5NHSO_2C_6H_5$.

21. Describe the simple chemical tests that can be used to distinguish among members of each of the following set :

    (*a*) Aniline, benzylamine and N, N-dimethylbenzylamine

    (*b*) Formamide, benzonitrile and N, N-dimethylaniline

    (*c*) Nitrobenzene, *m*-tolunitrile and N, N-dimethyl-*m*-toluidine.

22. An organic solid compound A ($C_{13}H_{11}ON$) is insoluble in aqueous NaOH and aqueous HCl. However, its prolonged heating with aqueous NaOH gives a liquid (B) and a solution of compound (C). Compound B can be separated from C by steam distillation, its solution in hydrochloric acid gives a red solid on treatment with sodium nitrite followed by β-naphthol. Acidification of C gives white precipitate of the compound D ($C_7H_6O_2$) which on distillation with soda lime gives benzene. Identify compound A and give reactions to explain all reactions.

SOLUTIONS

EXERCISE 19.1

1	(c)	11	(d)	21	(a)	31	(b)	41	(a)	51	(d)	61	(c)
2	(b)	12	(b)	22	(a)	32	(d)	42	(a)	52	(b)	62	(d)
3	(a)	13	(c)	23	(a)	33	(b)	43	(d)	53	(c)	63	(c)
4	(b)	14	(a)	24	(b)	34	(d)	44	(b)	54	(a)	64	(b)
5	(b)	15	(a)	25	(b)	35	(b)	45	(d)	55	(a)	65	(c)
6	(c)	16	(a)	26	(c)	36	(d)	46	(a)	56	(d)	66	(c)
7	(c)	17	(b)	27	(d)	37	(c)	47	(d)	57	(c)	67	(a)
8	(b)	18	(b)	28	(c)	38	(c)	48	(c)	58	(d)		
9	(b)	19	(c)	29	(b)	39	(b)	49	(b)	59	(b)		
10	(c)	20	(b)	30	(c)	40	(b)	50	(b)	60	(d)		

1. Methylaniline can be $C_6H_5NHCH_3$, o-, m- and p-$CH_3C_6H_4NH_2$.

2. $RX + NH_3$ (excess) $\longrightarrow RNH_2 + HX$; $NH_3 + HX \longrightarrow NH_4^+ + X^-$.

3. Reaction of 2° halide with ammonia (a base) is always accompanied by some elimination product.

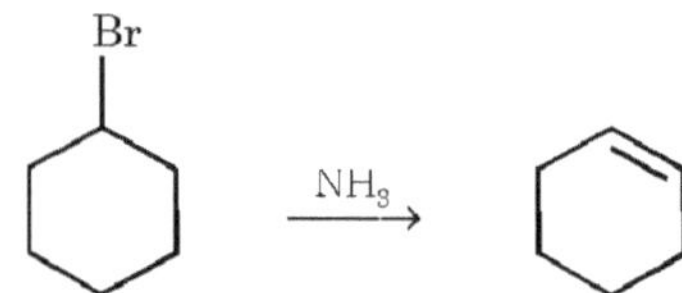

4. In Hofmann's method, the starting material is amide (not amine). Reaction of alkyl halide with ammonia may lead to the formation of a mixture of amines (1°, 2° and 3°).

5. In option (a), $C_6H_5NH_2 + CH_3I$ may form 4° salt as a by product. In option (c), CH_2O is converted to CH_2O^+H which may cause electrophilic aromatic substitution.

6. $CH_3CH_2CN \xrightarrow{H^+} CH_3CH_2COOH \xrightarrow{NH_3} CH_3CH_2COONH_4 \xrightarrow{heat} CH_3CH_2CONH_2 \xrightarrow{Br_2, OH^-} CH_3CH_2NH_2$.

7. Consult mechanism of Hofmann's Bromamide reaction.

8. Although N is also chiral but its three substituents interconvert due to lone pair of electrons on nitrogen, hence it should be non-resolvable due to chiral N.

9. $R_4N^+OH^-$ behaves like NaOH or KOH.

10. In options (a), (b) and (d), lone pair of electrons is involved in delocalization because of presence of π electrons in the conjugate position.

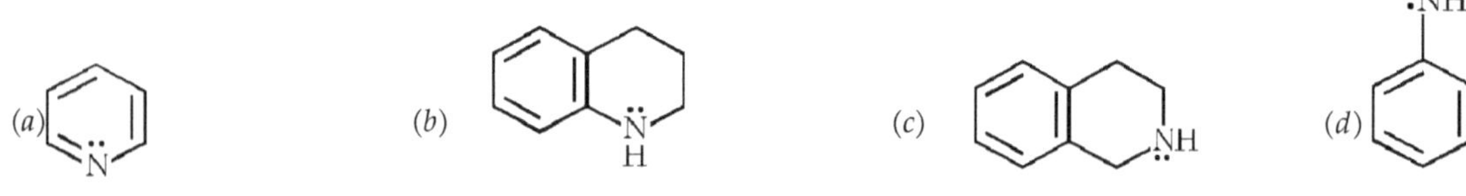

11. In gas phase, solvation effect is absent, hence basicity is due to alkyl group.

12. Steric factor. More is crowding near the —NH_2 group lesser is its capacity to accept H^+.

13. *tert*-Amine molecules can not associate because of absence of H-bonding.

14. Electronegativity of O, N and C follows the order : O > N > C.

15. (i) Fluorine decreases electron density on N. (ii) F stabilizes the conjugate acid, $FCH_2CH_2NH_3^+$, by dispersing +ve charge on N.

16. In $CH_3-\overset{\overset{O}{\|}}{C}-\overset{..}{N}H_2$, electron pair is delocalized.

17. $C_6H_5NHNH_2 + HCl \longrightarrow C_6H_5NHNH_3^+Cl^-$ $CH_3NHNH_2 + HCl \longrightarrow CH_3N^+H_2NH_2Cl^-$.

Electron releasing character of the —CH_3 group increases electron density on the first N.

18. In II, intermolecular H-bonding between similar molecules is possible, while this is not so in I.

19. (a)

—M, —I effect of the —NO_2 group increases +ve charge on N, hence destabilize the intermediate

(b)

Delocalization of electron on N of the —NH_2 group stabilizes the amine

20. In NOCl, Cl^- is a weak base hence good leaving group.

21. H_2O is less basic, hence good leaving group than OH^-.

22. Intramolecular H-bonding decreases nucleophilicity and hence reactivity of the —NH_2 group.

23. $(C_6H_5)_3$ N: does not react with BF_3 because of delocalization of electrons on N to three benzene rings.

24. Chloroacetic acid protonates phthalimide.

25. $CH_3CH_2CH_2CH_2NH_2 \xrightarrow{\text{HONO}} CH_3CH_2CH_2\overset{+}{C}H_2 \longrightarrow CH_3CH_2\overset{+}{C}H CH_3$

                               1° carbocation   2° carbocation

$\longrightarrow CH_3CH = CHCH_3 \quad + \quad CH_3CH_2CH = CH_2$

cis- and *trans*- Butene-2   Butene-1

26. $Me_3CCH_2NH_2 \xrightarrow{\text{HONO}} Me_3C\overset{+}{C}H_2 \longrightarrow Me_2\overset{+}{C}CH_2CH_3 \longrightarrow Me_2C(OH)CH_2CH_3.$

                            1° carbocation   3°carbocation

27. 2° Halides mainly undergo elimination with base like NH_3.

28.

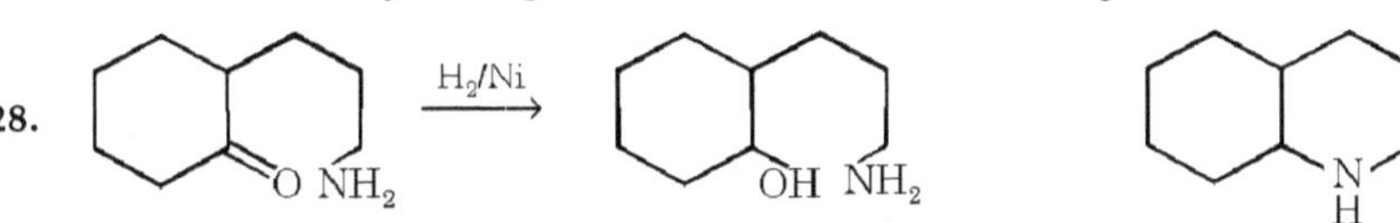

29. **(b)** (i) Position (X) is most acidic due to – COOH group.

          (ii) –NH_3^+ group at position Y is more acidic than at Z because of presence of electron withdrawing – COOH group in close proximity. Hence – NH_3^+ group at position Z is least acidic.

30. **(c)** This is an example of carbylamine reaction

$CHCl_3 + RNH_2 + KOH$

$\longrightarrow R - \overset{+}{N} \equiv C^- + 3KCl + 3H_2O$

31. **(b)**

The protonated form of II would be III which is more stable because here the contributing structures (III) and (IV) are equivalent.

In $CH_3 - \overset{..}{N}H - CH_3$, the availability of electron pair increases due to the +I effect of two CH_3 groups while in $CH_3CH_2NH_2$, +I effect of only one ethyl group is operative.

In $CH_3 - \underset{O}{\overset{||}{C}} - NH_2$, the electron availability on nitrogen decreases due to resonance as shown below

$CH_3 - \underset{O}{\overset{||}{C}} - \overset{..}{N}H_2 \longleftrightarrow CH_3 - \underset{O^-}{\overset{|}{C}} = \overset{\oplus}{N}H_2$

Therefore, the order of basic strength would be $1 > 3 > 2 > 4$.

32. **(d)** Aromatic amines are less basic than aliphatic amines. Among aliphatic amines the order of basicity is 2° > 1° > 3°. The electron density is decreased in 3° amine due to crowding of alkyl group over N atom which makes the approach and bonding by a proton relatively difficult. Therefore the basicity decreases. Further Phenyl group show – I effect, thus decreases the electron density on nitrogen atom and hence the basicity.

∴ dimethylamine (2° aliphatic amine) is strongest base among given choices.

∴ The correct order of basic strength is

Dimethylamine > Methyl amine > Trimethyl amine > Aniline.

33. **(b)** The alkyl groups are electron releasing group ($+ I$), thus increases the electron density around the nitrogen thereby increasing the availability of the lone pair of electrons to proton or lewis acid and making the amine more basic. Hence more the no. of alkyl group more basic is the amine. Therefore the correct order is

$$NH_3 < CH_3NH_2 < (CH_3)_2N$$

34. **(d)** Ethyl isocyanide on hydrolysis form primary amines.

$$CH_3CH_2N \overset{+}{\equiv} C + H_2O \xrightarrow{H^+}$$

$$CH_3CH_2NH_2 + HCOOH$$

Therefore it gives only one mono chloroalkane.

35. **(b)** Wurtz reaction is for the preparation of hydrocarbons from alkyl halide

$$RX + 2Na + XR \longrightarrow R - R + 2NaX$$

36. **(d)** The basic character of an amine in water is determined by (i) electron availability on the N atom and (ii) the extent of stabilization of the cation (protonated amine) due to solvation by hydrogen bonding

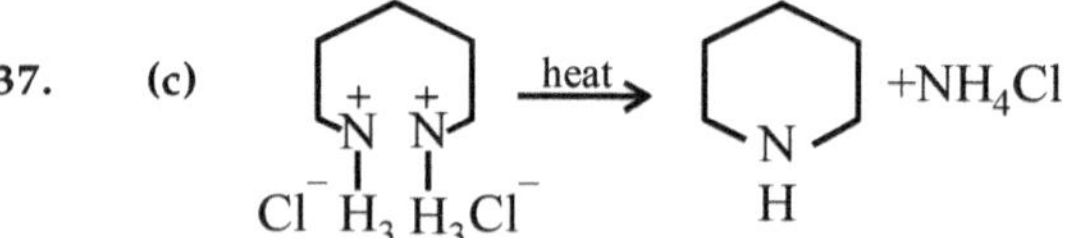

Methyl amine   Protonated methyl amine, $CH_3\overset{+}{N}H_3$
(Highly stabilized)

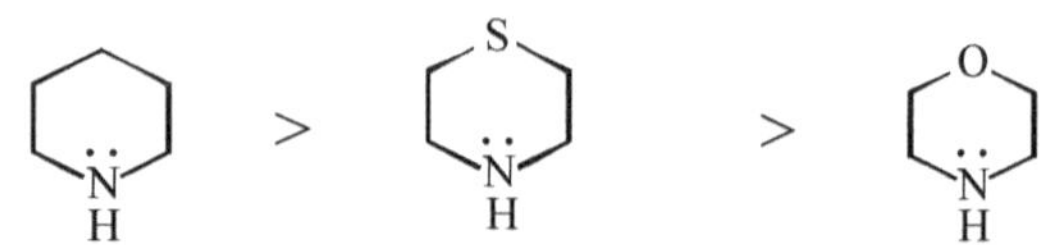

Dimethyl amine   Protonated dimethyl amine
(Lesser stabilized than $CH_3\overset{+}{N}H_3$)

37. **(c)** 

38. **(c)**

No delocalisation of *e* pair > Presence of S (electronegative element decreases *e* density on N) > O is more electronegative than S, hence further decreases availability of *e* pair on N

N is sp^3 hybridised

> N is sp^2 hybridised > (N, with $H_3C-\overset{C}{\underset{\parallel}{}}\!=\!O$, *e* pair on N delocalised to O)

39. **(b)** Reaction is an example of **Schmidt reaction** in which carboxylic acids are heated with hydrazoic acid in presence of a mineral acid to form primary amines.

$$RCOOH + HN_3 \xrightarrow{\text{conc. } H_2SO_4} RNH_2 + CO_2$$

40. **(b)** Cold dil. NaOH does not attack to either of the compound, while cold dil. HCl reacts only with benzyl amine $C_6H_5CH_2NH_2$.

41. **(a)** The four compounds differ in two respects : Compounds II has sp^3 hybridised N, compounds I and III have sp^2 while compound IV has sp hybridised N. Now we know that greater the s character of an orbital, more tightly its electrons are held and hence lesser will be their availability for protonation causing weak basic character. Thus the basic character of the three N's is $sp^3N > sp^2\,N > sp\,N$. However, in pyrrole electrons on N are part of aromatic sextet, i.e., these are delocalised and hence lesser available for protonation and thus pyrrole is a weaker base than pyridine because in pyridine nonbonding electrons present in sp^2 orbital do not form a part of aromatic sextet. Thus the basic character should be in the following order.

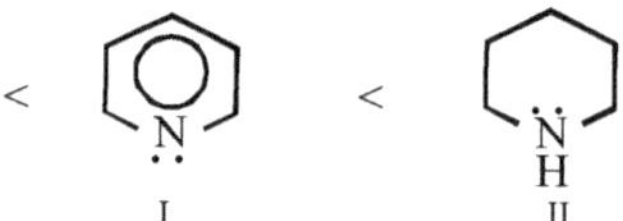

42. **(a)** Note the point of difference in the given compounds which here lies at β-carbon. In I, II, III, the β-carbon atoms are sp^3, sp^2 and sp hybridised respectively which in turn cause the difference in their s character. We know that more is the s character of an atom, greater will be its electron-withdrawing nature. Thus sp (50% s character) hybridised carbon is most electron-withdrawing, while sp^3 (25% s character) is least electron-withdrawing. Further, we know that presence of an electron-withdrawing group decreases basicity of an amine. Thus

I ($\beta - C\ sp^3$ hybridised) > II ($\beta - C\ sp^2$) > III ($\beta - C\ sp$)

43. **(d)** Here again the two amines differ in the nature of β-carbon atom

II > I

44. **(b)**

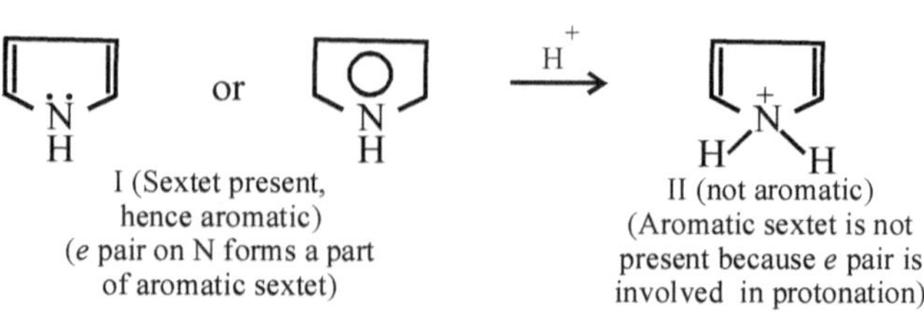

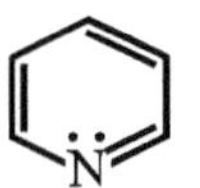

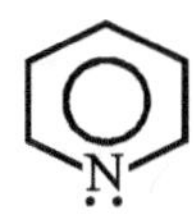

III (sextet present, hence aromatic)
(*e* pair on N, not a part of sextet)

IV (sextet present, hence aromatic)

45. **(d)**

$$RNH_2 + \!\!\!>\!\!C=O \longrightarrow \!\!\!>\!\!C\!\!<^{OH}_{NHR} \xrightarrow{-H_2O} \!\!\!>\!\!C=NR$$

1° Amine | Aldehyde/ketone | Carbinolamine | Imine (Schiff's base)

$$R_2NH + \!\!\!^{CH_3}_{R}\!\!>\!\!C=O \longrightarrow \!\!\!^{CH_3}_{R}\!\!>\!\!C\!\!<^{NR_2}_{OH} \longrightarrow \!\!\!^{CH_2}_{R}\!\!>\!\!C=NR_2$$

2° Amine | Aldehyde / ketone (R = H) (R=Alkyl) | Carbinolamine | Enamine

46. **(a)** Due to greater electronegativity of N over S, positive charge on N will make the methyl groups more electron-deficient than that on positively charged S. Therefore,

$(CH_3)_4N^+I^-$ will undergo nucleophilic substitution more readily than the sulphur analogue.

$$HO^- + \;CH_3\!\!\rightarrow\!\!N^+(CH_3)_3 \longrightarrow CH_3OH + (CH_3)_3N$$

47. **(d)** For this one should remember that Hofmann's degradation involves migration to electron deficient nitrogen atom, hence the alkyl group will migrate with its bonding pair of electrons.

$$R-\overset{O}{\overset{||}{C}}-\overset{..}{N}H_2 \xrightarrow{^-OBr} R-\overset{O}{\overset{||}{C}}-\overset{..}{N}HBr \xrightarrow{OH^-} R-\overset{O}{\overset{||}{C}}-\overset{..}{\underset{..}{N}}-Br$$

Amide

$$\longrightarrow \overset{O}{\underset{}{\overset{||}{R\!\!\div\!\!C}}}-\overset{..}{N} \longrightarrow O=C=\overset{..}{N}R \xrightarrow{H_2O} RNH_2 + CO_3^{2-}$$

Alkyl isocyanate | Amine

(note that N is electron-deficient)

48. **(c)** Remember that in Hofmann rearrangement, the two original H atoms of the –CONH₂ group are removed by base (OH⁻) and new H's are derived from H₂O.

$$(CH_3)_3C-\overset{O}{\overset{||}{C}}-NH_2 \xrightarrow[(ii)D_2O]{(i)OD^-/Br_2} (CH_3)_3C-ND_2$$

49. **(b)**

50. **(b)** $R-N=C=O$ (Alkyl isocyanate) is the common intermediate in the four reactions.

51. **(d)** All the three are formed.

53. **(c)** The reaction is an example of hydrazinolysis.

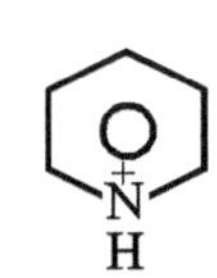

54. **(a)** In presence of chlorobenzene, hydrogen bonding is not possible between the protonated amine and the solvent and thus the stabilization factor (solvation effect) is absent. Hence basicity is explained on the basis of the number of electron releasing groups in an amine.

55. **(a)** Note the point of difference in the given compounds which here lies at β-carbon. In I, II, III, the β-carbon atoms are sp^3, sp^2 and sp hybridised respectively which in turn cause the difference in their s character. We know that more is the s character of an atom, greater will be its electron-withdrawing nature. Thus sp (50% s character) hybridised carbon is most electron-withdrawing, while sp^3 (25% s character) is least electron-withdrawing. Further, we know that presence of an electron-withdrawing group decreases basicity of an amine. Thus

I ($\beta - C\ sp^3$ hybridised) | II ($\beta - C\ sp^2$) | III ($\beta - C\ sp$)

56. **(d)** II is most basic because delocalisation of electron pair leads to negative charge on N making it electron-rich and hence liable to be attacked by proton very easily. Moreover, the corresponding protonated species is very much stable because of equivalent contributing structures.

Species III is least basic because of delocalisation of electron pair on N, making it less available for protonation. Species I lies in mid-way, thus

$$CH_3-\overset{O}{\overset{||}{C}}-\overset{..}{N}H_2 < CH_3CH_2\!\!\rightarrow\!\!\overset{..}{N}H_2 < CH_3-\overset{\overset{..}{N}H}{\overset{||}{C}}-\overset{..}{N}H_2$$

III | I | II

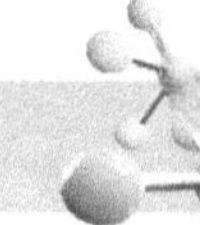

57. **(c)** Although aliphatic 1° amines form diazonium salts, these are unstable and decompose to alkyl carbocation which can form variety of normal as well as rearranged products

$$CH_3CH_2CH_2NH_2 \xrightarrow[0°C]{HONO} \left[CH_3CH_2CH_2N_2^+Cl^- \right]_{Unstable}$$

$$\rightarrow CH_3CH_2\overset{+}{C}H_2 + N_2 + Cl^-$$

$$CH_3CH_2CH_2OH \xleftarrow{H_2O} CH_3CH_2\overset{+}{C}H_2 \longrightarrow$$
$$1° \text{ Carbocation}$$

$$\cdot CH_3\overset{+}{C}HCH_3 \xrightarrow{Cl^-} CH_3\overset{\overset{\displaystyle Cl}{|}}{C}HCH_3$$
$$2° \text{ Carbocation}$$

58. **(d)** Most of the simple amines those having smaller alkyl (groups) can't be resolved , although they may contain three different alkyl groups.

59. **(b)** Hydrogen bonding is a strong intermolecular attraction between an electrophilic O–H or N–H hydrogen atom and a pair of non-bonding electrons. Thus a hydrogen bond requires both a **hydrogen bond donor** (a molecule having O–H or N–H group) and a **hydrogen bond acceptor** (a molecule having lone pair of electrons). Thus dimethyl amine can serve as hydrogen bond donor due to N–H group as well as hydrogen bond acceptor due to lone pair of electrons on N. Such molecules can form hydrogen bond with themselves and also with water (or other hydrogen bond donor). On the other hand, trimethyl amine can serve only as hydrogen bond acceptor since it has lone pair of electrons but not hydrogen on N. Hence it can form hydrogen bond with water but not with themselves.

Acting as H–bond donor

Acting as H–bond acceptor

Trimethyl amine only as H– bond acceptor

60. **(d)**

$$RNH_2 + \underset{\text{Aldehyde/ketone}}{\overset{\displaystyle}{>}C=O} \longrightarrow \underset{\text{Carbinolamine}}{>C\overset{\displaystyle OH}{\underset{\displaystyle NHR}{}}} \xrightarrow{-H_2O} \underset{\substack{\text{Imine} \\ \text{(Schiff's base)}}}{>C=NR}$$

1° Amine

$$R_2NH + \underset{\substack{\text{Aldehyde / ketone} \\ (R = H) \ (R=Alkyl)}}{\overset{\displaystyle CH_3}{\underset{\displaystyle R}{>}}C=O} \longrightarrow \underset{\text{Carbinolamine}}{\overset{\displaystyle CH_3}{\underset{\displaystyle R}{>}}C\overset{\displaystyle NR_2}{\underset{\displaystyle OH}{}}} \longrightarrow \underset{\text{Enamine}}{\overset{\displaystyle CH_2}{\underset{\displaystyle R}{>}}C=NR_2}$$

2° Amine

61. **(c)** The given amine has three β-hydrogens, hence it can form three alkenes of which least substituted ($H_2C=CH_2$) will be the major product (Hofmann product or Hofmann elimination).

(from β₁)   (from β₂)   + $H_2C = CH_2$ (from β₃)

In Hofmann elimination H atom (in the form of proton) is eliminated from that β carbon atom which has maximum number of H atom(s). This is due to the fact that Hofmann elimination (an example of E2 reaction) requires anti-coplanar arrangement of the β H atom and the leaving group. Further, higher the chances for this arrangement to remain in staggered conformation more will be the ease of elimination. Thus greater the number of H atom at β position, higher will be the chances for Me_3N^+– and H atom to remain in this particular conformation (anti-coplanar arragnement of Me_3N^+ – and H atom in staggered conformation).

62. **(d)** For this one should remember that Hofmann's degradation involves migration to electron deficient nitrogen atom, hence the alkyl group will migrate with its bonding pair of electrons.

$$R-\overset{\overset{\displaystyle O}{||}}{C}-\overset{\displaystyle ..}{N}H_2 \xrightarrow{^-OBr} R-\overset{\overset{\displaystyle O}{||}}{C}-\overset{\displaystyle ..}{N}HBr \xrightarrow{OH^-} R-\overset{\overset{\displaystyle O}{||}}{C}-\overset{\displaystyle ..}{N}^-Br$$
Amide

$$\longrightarrow \overset{\overset{\displaystyle O}{||}}{R}-C-N \longrightarrow O=C=NR \xrightarrow{H_2O} RNH_2 + CO_3^{2-}$$

(note that N is electron-deficient)   Alkyl isocyanate   Amine

63. **(c)** $$CH_3NH_2 \xrightarrow[\text{excess}]{CH_3I} \underset{(A)}{(CH_3)_4N^+I^-} \xrightarrow{AgOH}$$

$$\underset{(B)}{\cdot(CH_3)_4N^+OH^-} \xrightarrow{heat} \underset{(C) \text{ and } (D)}{(CH_3)N + CH_3OH}$$

64. **(b)** Alkyl cyanides, nitroparaffins and acid amides on hydrolysis give carboxylic acids.

$$\overset{\overset{\displaystyle O}{||}}{H}-C-N(CH_3)_2 \longrightarrow \overset{\overset{\displaystyle O}{||}}{H}-C-OH + HN(CH_3)_2$$

65. **(c)** RCN on hydrolysis yields RCOOH (acid)

66. **(c)** **Hinsberg's reagent** is benzene sulphonyl chloride. A **tertiary amine** does not react with **Hinsberg's** reagent and remains insoluble in aqueous KOH when it is treated with Hinberg's reagent in presence of excess of KOH.

67. **(a)**

EXERCISE 19.2

>1 CORRECT OPTION	1	(a,b)	2	(b,c,d)	3	(a,b,d)	4	(c,d)	5	(a,b,c)
	6	(a,b,d)	7	(a, b)	8	(a, b, c, d)	9	(a, b, c)	10	(a, b, c, d)
	11	(a, c, d)	12	(b, d)	13	(a, b, c)	14	(a, c)	15	(a, c, d)
	16	(a, b)	17	(b, c, d)	18	(a, c, d)	19	(a, b, d)	20	(b, d)
	21	(a, b, d)	22	(a, b, c)						
PASSAGE 1	23	(c)	24	(b)						
PASSAGE 2	25	(d)	26	(d)	27	(c)				
PASSAGE 3	28	(b)	29	(c)	30	(a)	31	(c)		
PASSAGE 4	32	(b)	33	(a, b)	34	(d)	35	(c)		
PASSAGE 5	36	(a, d)	37	(c, d)	38	(a)				
MATCH THE FOLLOWING	39	(A) - (a, b, c), (B) - (a, b), (C) - (a, d), (D) - (a)								
	40	(A) - (c), (B) - (a), (C) - (b, c), (D) - (d)								
	41	(A) - (b) ; (B) - (a, b, c) ; (C) (a, c) ; (D) - (d)								
	42	(A) - (a, b, d, e) ; (B) - (a, d, e) ; (C) a ; (D) - ©								
	43	(A) - (b, c) ; (B) - (b) ; (C)- (a) ; (D) - (b)								
	44	(A) - (a, b, b) ; (B) - (a) ; (C) -(b, d) ; (D) - (b)								
	45	(A) - (d) ; (B) - (c) ; (C)-(a) ; (D) - (b)								
A/R	46	(a)	47	(c)	48	(c)	49	(d)	50	(a)
	51	(c)	52	(a)	53	(b)	54	(b)		

1. For the preparation of Me_3CNH_2, the required alkyl halide is Me_3CX which will react with potassium phthalimide, a strong base, to form alkene rather than substituted product. For preparing $C_6H_5NH_2$, C_6H_5Cl will be the starting halide in which Cl is non-reactive.

2. Vinyl and aryl halides do not undergo S_N2 reactions, unless activated by electron withdrawing group (in the *o*- and *p*-position in case of aryl halides). 3° Halides form alkenes on elimination.

3. In **reductive amination method**, products can have only CH_3, a 1°C, or 2°C bonded to N as in CH_3NH_2, RCH_2NH_2 or R_2CHNH_2 respectively. In the **reduction of oxime**, amine formed can have only 1° or 2°C bonded to N. In **Gabriel phthalimide method**, the required Me_3CCl would undergo elimination (E2) rather than substitution (S_N2).

4. On the basis of hybridisation, N (sp^3) of NH_2 with less *s* character should be more basic than N (sp^2) of the imino (= NH) group. However, N of imino group is more basic and it is this nitrogen which is protanated because its conjugate acid is resonance hybrid of three equivalent structures which accounts its unusual stability.

Guidanine

Conjugate acid of guanidine

Unusual stability of the conjugate acid of guanidine explains why guanidine is the strongest organic known base

5. Consult text.

6. Hinsberg test is applicable to liquid amines which are insoluble in water because water solubility of the amine decreases nucleophilicity of nitrogen.

13. **(a,b,c)** Lower amines like NH_3, CH_3NH_2 and $(CH_3)_2NH$ break diborane molecule unsymmetrically, while larger amines like $(CH_3)_3N$, C_5H_5N break diborane in symmetrical manner.

$$B_2H_6 + 2NH_3 \longrightarrow [H_2B(NH_3)_2]^+ [BH_4]^-$$

$$B_2H_6 + 2NH_3 \longrightarrow 2H_3B \longleftarrow N(CH_3)_3$$

14.   **(a, c)**   This is an example of Hoffmann degradation of amides.

$$R-\overset{\overset{O}{\|}}{C}-NH_2 + Br_2 \rightarrow R-\overset{\overset{O}{\|}}{C}-NHBr + HBr$$

$$R-\overset{\overset{O}{\|}}{C}.NHBr + KOH \rightarrow R-\overset{\overset{O}{\|}}{C}.N^-Br + H_2O + KBr$$

$$R-\overset{\overset{O}{\|}}{C}.N^- Br \xrightarrow{\;-Br^-\;} R-\overset{\overset{O}{\|}}{C}.N \xrightarrow{\text{rearrangement}} R-N=C=O \xrightarrow{\;H_2O\;} R-NH_2$$

15.   **(a,c,d)**   Diazomethane is used for methylating acidic groups ; compound IV has enolic —OH group, hence it can also be methylated by CH_2N_2.

16.   **(a,b)**   For the preparation of Me_3CNH_2, the required alkyl halide is Me_3CX which will react with potassium phthalimide, a strong base, to form alkene rather than substituted product. For preparing $C_6H_5NH_2$, C_6H_5Cl will be the starting halide in which Cl is non-reactive.

17.   **(b,c,d)**   Vinyl and aryl halides do not undergo S_{N^2} reactions, unless activated by electron withdrawing group (in the *o-* and *p*-position in case of aryl halides). 3° Halides form alkenes on elimination.

18.   **(a,c,d)**   In p-$NH_2C_6H_4COOH$, —COOH group is very weak so it can't transfer H^+ to the weakly basic amino group. All other three form zwitterions.

19.   **(a,b,d)**   *tert*-Nitro compounds (Me_3CNO_2) do not react with HONO because they do not have any α-H. The three others react with HONO as usual.

$$\underset{\text{2-Nitrobutane}}{CH_3-\overset{\overset{NO_2}{|}}{C}HCH_2CH_3} \xrightarrow{\;HONO\;} \underset{\underset{NO}{|}}{CH_3-\overset{\overset{NO_2}{|}}{C}-CH_2CH_3}$$

Pseudonitrol (blue)

28.   **(b)**   Species II (acylnitrene) is electron-deficient (N has only 6 electrons), hence it has a tendency to get its octet completed by the migration of alkyl group.

29.   **(c)** $-OCH_3$ is more electron-releasing hence when the migrating aryl group has $-OCH_3$ in the para postion, its migration is accelerated.

30.   **(a)**   The migrating group (the group attached to C of the $-CONH_2$ part) never becomes free, so optical activity of the reactant is maintained.

31.   **(c)**   Since phenyl group (migrating group) does not become free, no cross product [i.e., (ii) and (iv)] is formed.

43.   **A-b, c; B-b; C-a; D-b, d**

   (A)   Allylic rearrangements involve the migration of the double bond (and the functional group, if present) from one position to other. These reactions proceed through SN^1, SN^2, SE^1 and SE^2 mechanism; SN^1 involves carbocations (electron-deficient species), while SE^1 involves carbanion.

   (B)   Hofmann rearrangement involves nitrene $(R-\overset{\overset{O}{\|}}{C}-\overset{..}{N}:)$ intermediate in which nitrogen is electron deficient.

   (C)   Aldol condensation involves the attack of base on aldehyde or ketone, the reaction will involve the formation of carbanion.

   (D)   Carbylamine reaction involves the formation of dichlorocarbene $(:CCl_2)$ as intermediate which is electron deficient.

50.   **(a)**   **R** is the correct explanation of **A**.

51.   **(c)**   **Correct R :** Only primary aliphatic amines can be prepared by Gabriel phthalimide reaction.

52.   **(a)**   **R** is the correct explanation of **A**.

EXERCISE 19.3

1. (*a*) 1° Amines **CH$_3$(CH$_2$)$_2$CH$_2$NH$_2$**　　CH$_3$CHCH$_2$CH$_3$ (with NH$_2$)　　CH$_3$CHCH$_2$NH$_2$ (with CH$_3$)　　**(CH$_3$)$_3$CNH$_2$**

　　　　　n-Butylamine　　　　*sec*-Butylamine　　　Isobutylamine　　　*tert*-Butylamine

2° Amines　　CH$_3$NHCH$_2$CH$_2$CH$_3$　　CH$_3$NHCHCH$_3$ (with CH$_3$)　　CH$_3$CH$_2$NHCH$_2$CH$_3$

　　　　Methylpropylamine　　　Methyl isopropylamine　　　Diethylamine

3° Amines　　CH$_3$CH$_2$NCH$_3$ (with CH$_3$)

　　　　Ethyldimethylamine

(*b*) **1° Amines**　　C$_6$H$_5$CH$_2$NH$_2$　　　*o*-, *m*-, and *p*-CH$_3$C$_6$H$_4$NH$_2$

　　　　　　　Benzylamine　　　　　　Toluidines

　　2° Amines　　C$_6$H$_5$NHCH$_3$

　　　　　　N-Methylaniline

(*c*)

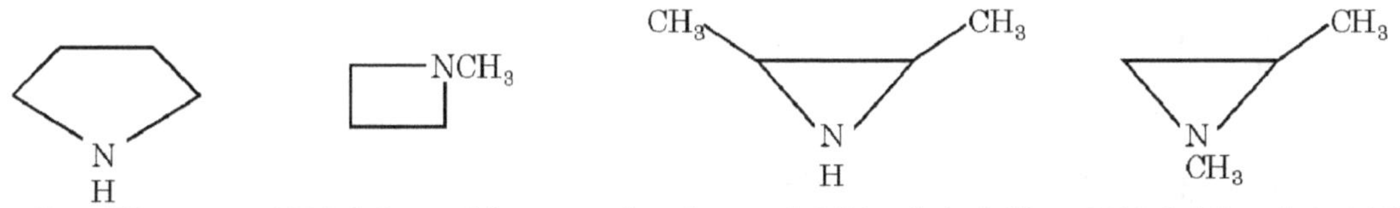

Pyrrolidine or Azacyclopentane (2° amine)　　N-Methylazacyclobutane 3°(amine)　　*cis*-and *trans*- 2, 3-Dimethylaziridine (2° amine)　　N-Methyl-2-methylaziridine (3° amine)

2. (*a*)

(*b*) C$_6$H$_5$CH$_2$CH$_2$NH$_2$

(*c*) C$_6$H$_5$—NH—C$_6$H$_5$

(*d*)

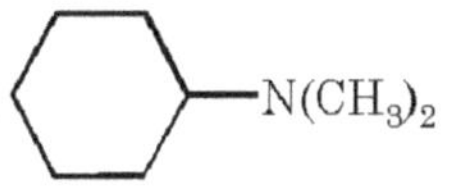

(*e*) [(CH$_3$)$_2$CHCH$_2$]$_4$ N$^+$I$^-$

(*f*)

(*g*) CH$_3$C = CHCOOC$_2$H$_5$ (with NHCH$_3$)

3. (*a*) excess of NH$_3$　　　　　　　　(*b*) C$_6$H$_5$NHCrO$_3$Cl (for oxidising —CH$_2$OH to —CHO), NH$_3$, H$_2$/Ni

(*c*) HBr, NaCN, H$_2$/Ni　　　　　　(*d*) K$_2$Cr$_2$O$_7$, SOCl$_2$, NH$_3$, Br$_2$/NaOH

(*e*) Br$_2$/NaOH.

Aniline can be prepared only from C$_6$H$_5$Cl and that too under very vigorous conditions. Benzylamine can be prepared from all of the corresponding compounds except (*c*).

4. (*a*) CH$_3$CH$_2$CH$_2$Br + NH$_3$ (excess) $\longrightarrow$ CH$_3$CH$_2$CH$_2$NH$_2$

(*b*) CH$_3$CH$_2$CHO + NH$_3$ $\xrightarrow{\text{H}_2/\text{Ni}}$ CH$_3$CH$_2$CH$_2$NH$_2$

(*c*) CH$_3$CH$_2$CONH$_2$ $\xrightarrow{\text{LiAlH}_4}$ CH$_3$CH$_2$CH$_2$NH$_2$

(*d*) CH$_3$CH$_2$CN $\xrightarrow[\text{(ii) H}_2\text{O}]{\text{(i) LiAlH}_4}$ CH$_3$CH$_2$CH$_2$NH$_2$

(*e*) CH$_3$CH$_2$CH$_2$CONH$_2$ $\xrightarrow{\text{Br}_2/\text{KOH}}$ CH$_3$CH$_2$CH$_2$NH$_2$

(*f*) CH$_3$CH$_2$CH$_2$COCl $\xrightarrow{\text{NaN}_3}$ CH$_3$CH$_2$CH$_2$CON$_3$ $\xrightarrow[\text{H}_2\text{O}]{\text{heat}}$ CH$_3$CH$_2$CH$_2$NH$_2$

5. Recall that Gabriel phthalimide involves S_N2 reaction in one of the steps, so halides unreactive in S_N2 reaction (*e.g.* $CH_2 = CHX$, ArX) cannot be used.

(*a*) For preparing *tert*-butylamine, the corresponding *tert*-butyl chloride, being 3°, undergoes elimination reaction.

(*b*) For preparing neopentylamine, the corresponding alkyl halide (neopentyl chloride, Me_3CCH_2Cl) is sterically himdered at the carbon bearing Cl, so it can't undergo S_N2 reaction.

(*c*) In potassium phthalimide, only one alkyl group can be introduced, hence Gabriel synthesis is used only for preparing 1° and not for 2° and 3° amines.

(*d*) For preparing *p*-toluidine, the corresponding halide would be p-$BrC_6H_4CH_3$ in which Br is not activated for nucleophilic substitution ; had there been an electron-withdrawing group as in p-$BrC_6H_4NO_2$, Br must have been replaced to form p-$NH_2C_6H_4NO_2$.

6. (*a*) 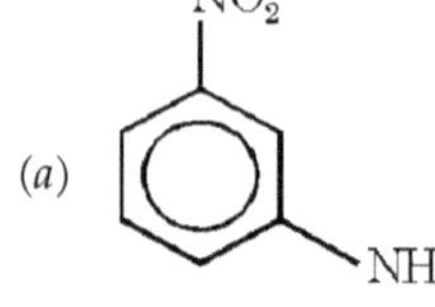   (*b*) $CH_2 = CHCH_2N_3$, $CH_3CH_2CH_2NH_2$ $CH_2 = CHCH_2NH_2$

         [A]   [B]   [C]   [D]

7. (*a*) (*i*) $CH_3CH_2NH_2$,   (*ii*) $CH_3CH_2NHC_2H_5$,   (*iii*) $CH_3CH_2N(CH_3)C_2H_5$

     (*b*) (*i*) $(CH_3)_2CHNH_2$,   (*ii*) $(CH_3)_2CHNHC_2H_5$,   (*iii*) $(CH_3)_2CHN(CH_3)C_2H_5$

8. (*a*) Although both processes give the same kind of products, in reductive amination successive amination is more easily controlled. Moreover, reductive amination can be successfully used for preparing amines having *sec*-alkyl group by taking corresponding ketone as one of the starting materials. Ammonolysis method can't be used for preparing such amines because the starting halide would be R_2CHX which may undergo E2 elimination under the given conditions.

(*b*) By using excess of RNH_2. However, this technique is useful only when the amine is relatively inexpensive.

9. Structural formula for the two α, ω-diamines (two —NH_2 groups present on the terminal carbon atoms) can be written as below.

$C_4H_{12}N_2$: H_2NCH_2—$[C_2H_4]$—CH_2NH_2 or $H_2NCH_2CH_2CH_2CH_2NH_2$

                                          Putrescine

$C_5H_{14}N_2$: H_2NCH_2—$[C_3H_6]$—CH_2NH_2 or $H_2NCH_2CH_2CH_2CH_2CH_2NH_2$

                                          Cadaverine

Synthesis of $C_4H_{12}N_2$.

(*i*) $Br(CH_2)_4Br \xrightarrow{\ NH_3\ } H_2N(CH_2)_4NH_2$

(*ii*) $BrCH_2CH_2Br \xrightarrow{\ KCN\ } NCCH_2CH_2CN \xrightarrow{\ Na/C_2H_5OH\ } H_2N(CH_2)_4NH_2$

Synthesis of $C_5H_{14}N_2$. (*i*) From $Br(CH_2)_5Br$; (*ii*) From $Br(CH_2)_3Br$.

10.   (*i*) $CH_3NH_2 + H_2O \rightleftharpoons CH_3NH_3^+ + OH^-$

         (*ii*) $CH_3NH_2 + HCl(g) \longrightarrow CH_3NH_3^+Cl^-(s)$

         (*iii*) $CH_3\overset{..}{N}H_2 + B(CH_3)_3 \longrightarrow CH_3\underset{H_2}{N^+}{-}B^-(CH_3)_3$

11. Aliphatic amines are more basic than aromatic amines. Electron-releasing groups raise basicity, while electron-withdrawing groups lower basicity.

(*a*) $cyclo$-$C_6H_{11}NH_2$ > NH_3 > $C_6H_5NH_2$ > $(C_6H_5)_2NH$

12. In aqueous solution of $(CH_3)_4N^+OH^-$, the base is OH^-, which is much stronger than $(CH_3)_3N$.

13. N-Nitrosoamines are insoluble in aq. HCl because nitroso group (N = O) behaves like C = O in delocalizing electron density and weakening the basicity.

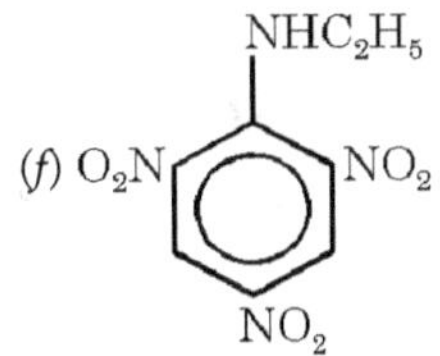

14. (a) $C_2H_5NH_3^+{}^-OCOCH_3$ (b) $(CH_3)_2CHCONHC_2H_5$ (c) No reaction

(d) $C_2H_5NHCH_2C_6H_5$, $C_2H_5N(CH_2C_6H_5)_2$, $C_2H_5N^+(CH_2C_6H_5)_3\ Br^-$

(e) No reaction

(f) 2,4,6-trinitro-N-ethylaniline (O_2N, NO_2, NO_2 substituted, NHC_2H_5)

(g) 2-($CONHC_2H_5$)benzoic acid ($COOH$ / $CONHC_2H_5$)

(h) $C_2H_5NHCHMe_2$ (i) $C_2H_5NHCH_2COO^-Na^+$

15. (a) All the three form soluble ammonium salts

$C_2H_5NH_2HCl$ or $C_2H_5NH_3^+Cl^-$, $(C_2H_5)_2NH_2^+Cl^-$, $(C_2H_5)_3N^+HCl^-$

(b) All the three form quaternary ammonium salts

(c) $C_2H_5NHCOCH_3$ $C_2H_5N(CH_3)COCH_3$ No reaction, $(C_2H_5)_3N$

    Neutral amide   Neutral amide   Basic

        Insoluble in dil. acid or base   Soluble in H^+, insoluble in base

(d) $C_2H_5NHSO_2C_6H_5$ $(C_2H_5)_2NSO_2C_6H_5$ $(C_2H_5)_3N$ (No reaction)

    Acidic   Neutral   Basic

    Soluble in aq.base   Insoluble in acid or base   Insoluble in base, soluble in acid

(e) $C_2H_5OH + N_2$ $(C_2H_5)_2N—N = O$ No reaction.

16. (a) $[(CH_3)_3N^+C_2H_5]OH^- \xrightarrow{\text{heat}} (CH_3)_3N + CH_2 = CH_2 + H_2O$

(b) $HO^- + CH_3—N(CH_3)_3 \longrightarrow HOCH_3 + N(CH_3)_3$

(c) $C_6H_5—N^+Me_3OH^- \xrightarrow{\text{heat}} C_6H_5—NMe_2 + MeOH$

There is no β hydrogen, hence alkene is not formed.

(d) cyclohexyl-$\overset{+}{N}(Me)(Me)CH_2CH_2CH_3\ OH^- \xrightarrow{\text{heat}}$ cyclohexene $+ Me_2NCH_2CH_2CH_3$ (Minor) and cyclohexyl-$NMe_2 + CH_2 = CHCH_3$ (Major)

17. (a) n-C_3H_7OH, $(CH_3)_2CHOH$, $CH_3CH = CH_2$, n-C_3H_7Cl, $(CH_3)_2CHCl$

(b) $CH_3\overset{NH_2}{\underset{|}{CH}}\overset{CH_3}{\underset{|}{CH}}CH_3 \xrightarrow{\text{HONO}} CH_3\overset{+}{CH}\overset{CH_3}{\underset{|}{CH}}CH_3 \longrightarrow CH_3CH_2\overset{CH_3}{\underset{|}{\overset{+}{C}}}CH_3 \longrightarrow CH_3CH = \overset{CH_3}{\underset{|}{C}}CH_3 + CH_3CH_2\overset{CH_3}{\underset{|}{\underset{|}{C}}}CH_3$ with OH

            2° Carbocation   2-Methyl-2-butene   *tert*-Pentyl alcohol

                                       (2-Methyl-2-butanol)

(c) $Cl^-{}^+N_2$—C_6H_4—C_6H_4—$N_2^+Cl^-$ (d) $O = N$—C_6H_4—NEt_2

(e) ^-O_3S—C_6H_4—N_2^+ (f) $C_6H_5CH_2OH + N_2$

18. (a) $(CH_3)_2CHCH_2NH_2 \xrightarrow[(-N_2)]{HONO}$ CH$_3$—C(H)(CH$_3$)—$\overset{+}{C}H_2 \longrightarrow$ CH$_3$—$\overset{\oplus}{C}$(CH$_3$)—CH$_3$

tert-Butyl cation

$(CH_3)_2CHCH_2OH + (CH_3)_2CHCH_2Cl$
$+ (CH_3)_2C = CH_2$

$(CH_3)_2C = CH_2 + (CH_3)_3—COH$
$+ (CH_3)_3Cl$

(b) CH$_3$—C(CH$_3$)(CH$_3$)—CH$_2$NH$_2$ $\xrightarrow[(-N_2)]{HONO}$ CH$_3$—C(CH$_3$)—CH$_2{}^+ \longrightarrow$ CH$_3$—$\overset{+}{C}$(CH$_3$)—CH$_2$CH$_3$

$\xrightarrow[\text{or} —H^+]{(i)\ OH^-}$ CH$_3$—C(OH)(CH$_3$)—CH$_2$CH$_3$ + CH$_3$—C(CH$_3$) = CHCH$_3$ + CH$_2$ = C(CH$_3$)—CH$_2$CH$_3$

19. HOOC (CH$_2$)$_4$COOH + H$_2$N (CH$_2$)$_6$NH$_2 \longrightarrow$ Salt $\xrightarrow[-H_2O]{heat}$ —C(=O)—(CH$_2$)$_4$C(=O)—NH (CH$_2$)$_6$ NH—C(=O)(CH$_2$)$_4$C(=O) NH (CH$_2$)$_6$NH—

Adipic acid   Hexamethylenediamine   A polyamide (Nylon 6, 6)

Addition of HCl causes hydrolysis of the amide linkage and thus the polymer chain is cleaved which appears in the form of a hole.

20. (a) Hinsberg test   (b) Hinsberg test

(c) Me$_3$N$^+$HCl$^- \xrightarrow{OH^-}$ Me$_3$N   ;   Me$_4$N$^+$Cl$^- \xrightarrow{OH^-}$ Me$_4$N$^+$OH$^-$

(odour or basic nature)

(d) CrO$_3$/H$_2$SO$_4$ positive only for Me$_2$NCH$_2$CH$_2$OH which is an alcohol

(e) C$_6$H$_5$NH$_2$ (being basic) dissolves in aq. HCl ; C$_6$H$_5$NHCOCH$_3$ is neutral and hence insoluble in aq. HCl

(f) AgNO$_3$ gives AgCl only with C$_6$H$_5$NH$_3{}^+$Cl$^-$

(g) aq. HCl which dissolves only C$_6$H$_5$NH$_2$; 2, 4, 6-trinitroaniline being very very weak base does not dissolve in aq. HCl

(h) AgNO$_3$ which gives AgCl only with C$_2$H$_5$NH$_3{}^+$Cl$^-$

(i) (i) BaCl$_2$ which gives BaSO$_4$ precipitate only with C$_6$H$_5$NH$_3{}^+$HSO$_4{}^-$

(ii) Water which dissolves only salt, *i.e* C$_6$H$_5$NH$_3{}^+$HSO$_4{}^-$.

21. (a)(i) Aniline gives red compound with HONO (cold) + β-naphthol.

(ii) Benzylamine (C$_6$H$_5$CH$_2$NH$_2$) and N, N-dimethylbenzylamine (C$_6$H$_5$CH$_2$NMe$_2$) can be differentiated by HONO or Hinsberg test

(b) Formamide (HCONH$_2$) is soluble in water, N, N-dimethylaniline is soluble in aq. HCl, but the neutral nitrile (C$_6$H$_5$CN) is insoluble

(c) Only N, N-dimethyl-*m*-toluidine is soluble in aq. HCl, hot aq. NaOH gives NH$_3$ with the nitrile (*m*-tolunitrile), while C$_6$H$_5$NO$_2$ is unreactive.

22. C$_6$H$_5$NHCOC$_6$H$_5$ $\xrightarrow[heat]{aq.\ NaOH}$ C$_6$H$_5$NH$_2$ + $^+$Na$^-$OOCC$_6$H$_5$

Benzanilide (A)   (B)   (C)

$^+$Na $^-$OOCC$_6$H$_5$ $\xrightarrow{H^+}$ HOOCC$_6$H$_5$ $\xrightarrow[lime]{Soda}$ C$_6$H$_6$

(C)   (D)   Benzene

20

Aromatic Amines and Diazonium Salts

When 1°, 2°, or 3° amino group is directly attached to benzene nucleus, compunds are known as **aromatic amines** *or* **aryl amines**

NH_2 Aniline, 1° (Aminobenzene)

NHR N-Alkylaniline (2° amine)

NRR' N, N-Dialkylaniline (3° amine)

(R and R' may be any alkyl or aryl (group)

One should note that when amino group is indirectly attached to benzene ring, the compound is called as aryl substituted aliphatic amine. In such compounds, —NH_2 group behaves as that of aliphatic amines.

NH_2, CH_3 — *o*-Toluidine (*o*-Methylaniline)

NH_2, NH_2 — *o*-Phenylenediamine

Aromatic amines

CH_2NH_2 — Benzylamine (1°)

CH_2NHCH_3 — N-Methylbenzylamine (2°)

Aryl substituted aliphatic amine

20.1   Preparation of Aryl Amines

Most of the methods used for preparing aromatic amines are very similar to that used for aliphatic amines.

1. **Reduction of nitro compounds.** The most widely used method for preparing aromatic amines is the reduction of the nitro group to the amino group. This reduction can be achieved by catalytic hydrogenation, or most frequently with an acid and a metal (Fe, Zn, Sn) or a metal salt like $SnCl_2$.

$$C_6H_5NO_2 \xrightarrow[\text{or (i) Fe, HCl, (ii) OH}^-]{\text{H}_2\text{, Catalyst}} C_6H_5NH_2$$

Nitrobenzene   Aniline

p-Nitrotoluene   *p*-Toluidine

m-Nitroacetophenone   *m*-Aminoacetophenone

Remember that $LiAlH_4$ does not reduce $PhNO_2$ to $PhNH_2$.

Since nitro compounds are readily prepared by direct nitration, the primary aromatic amines obtained by the reduction of these nitro compounds are readily converted into diazonium salts ; the diazonium group, in turn, can be replaced by a large number of other groups. This route gives a common and most useful method for introducing different groups in benzene nucleus.

$$Ar{-}H \longrightarrow Ar{-}NO_2 \longrightarrow Ar{-}NH_2 \longrightarrow Ar{-}N_2^{+} \longrightarrow \text{Other compounds.}$$

TEST YOUR UNDERSTANDING - 20.1

1.   Give steps involved in the following conversions.

     (a)   Toluene to *p*-toluidine   (b)   *o*-Isopropylaniline from benzene

     (c)   *m*-Aminoacetophenone from benzene   (d)   4-Isopropyl-1, 3-benzenediamine from benzene.

     (e)   Toluene to *p*-aminobenzoic acid.

Selective reduction of one nitro group of a dinitro compound can often be achieved by NH_4HS or through the use of carefully measured amount of hydrogen sulphide in aqueous (or alcoholic) ammonia

m-Dinitrobenzene   *m*-Nitroaniline

Remember that

(*i*)　use of an excess amount of H_2S may result in the reduction of more than one nitro group.

(*ii*)　it is always not possible to predict which —NO_2 group will be reduced, *e.g.*

2.　**Hofmann degradation.**

$$C_6H_5CONH_2 \xrightarrow{Br_2/NaOH} C_6H_5NH_2$$
Benzamide　　　　　　Aniline

3.　**Curtius reaction**

$$C_6H_5COOH \xrightarrow[\text{heat}]{N_3H,\ conc.\ H_2SO_4} C_6H_5NH_2 + CO_2 + N_2$$

4.　By acidic hydrolysis of isocyanides. $C_6H_5NC \xrightarrow{H_3O^+} C_6H_5NH_2 + HCOOH$

5.　By reduction of azobenzene.

Azobenzene　　　　　　　　Hydrazobenzene　　　　　　　　Aniline

$$ArN = NAr \xrightarrow[\text{(mild reduction)}]{Sn,\ NaOH} ArNH—NHAr \xrightarrow[\text{(vigorous reduction)}]{(i)\ SnCl_2,\ H_3O^+,\ (ii)\ OH^-} 2ArNH_2$$

6.　**Hofmann Martius rearrangement.** When a 3° or 2° aromatic amine hydrochloride is heated, it is converted into primary amine hydrochloride.

N, N-Dimethylaniline
hydrochloride

7.　**Commercially,** aniline is prepared by passing ammonia over chlorobenzene in presence of Cu_2O as catalyst and under pressure and at 200°C.

$$C_6H_5Cl + NH_3 \xrightarrow[\text{pressure, 200°C}]{Cu_2O} C_6H_5NH_2$$

Like aliphatic secondary amines, aromatic secondary amines can be prepared by reducing the corresponding isocyanide. $C_6H_5NC \longrightarrow C_6H_5NHCH_3$.

20.2 Properties of Aryl Amines

Aryl amines give most of properties of aliphatic amines in exactly similar fashion, *viz.* solubility, basicity, alkylation, acetylation, benzoylation, carbylamine reaction, condensation with aldehydes to form Schiff base, oxidation etc. Two properties deserve special attention, *viz.* reaction with nitrous acid and electrophilic substitution.

1. **Reaction with nitrous acid.** As is aliphatic amines, each class of aromatic amine yields a different kind of product when treated with nitrous acid, HONO. Primary aromatic amines react with nitrous acid to yield arene diazonium salts.

$$ArNH_2 + NaNO_2 + 2HX \xrightarrow{cold} Ar{-}N \equiv N^+X^- + NaX + 2H_2O$$

$$\text{1° Aromatic amine} \qquad\qquad \text{Arenediazonium salt}$$

Although arenediazonium salts are far more stable than aliphatic diazonium salts, especially at low temperatures (0–5°C), they slowly decompose even at low temperature, hence always used immediately after preparation.

Why arenediazonium ions are more stable than alkyldiazonium ions ? This is due to two factors.

(a) Electron-release from the *ortho* and *para* positions of the ring stabilizes the arenediazonium ions.

(b) The arene cation, Ar^+, is very difficult to be formed as compared to R^+ from $RN^+ \equiv N$.

Secondary amines, both aliphatic and aromatic, react with nitrous to form N-nitrosamines which shown Libermann's nitroso reaction

$$C_6H_5NHCH_3 + NaNO_2 + HCl \longrightarrow C_6H_5N(NO)CH_3$$

$$\text{N-Methylaniline} \qquad\qquad \text{N-Nitroso-N-methylaniline}$$

Tertiary aromatic amines undergo ring substitution discussed in electrophilic substitution.

2. **Electrophilic Substitution.** Arylamines contain two functional groups, the amino group and the aromatic ring. The reactivity of the amino group is affected by its aryl substituent, and the reactivity of the ring is affected by its amino group. The same electron delocalization that reduces the basicity and the nucleophilicity of an arylamine nitrogen increases the electron density in the aromatic ring and thus makes arylamines extremely reactive towards electrophilic aromatic substitution.

We know that the $-NH_2$, $-NHR$, and $-NR_2$ groups are ortho, para-directing and exceedingly powerful activating groups in electrophilic aromatic substitution. These effects are due to the formation of the especially stable intermediate carbocations I and II, in which every atom (except hydrogen) has a complete octet of electrons.

Thus the chief problem encountered in electrophilic substitution with aromatic amines is that *they are hightly reactive.* For example,

(a) In halogenation substitution tends to occur at every available *ortho* and *para* position and thus monohalogenated product can't be prepared

(b)   Nitric acid not only nitrates, but also oxidizes the highly reactive ring as well, with loss of much material as dark-coloured tar. Furthermore, in the strongly acidic nitration medium, the amine is converted into anilinium ion ($—NH_3^+$) ; substitution is thus controlled not by the $—NH_2$ group but by the $—NH_3^+$ group which, because of its positive charge, directs the entering group to the *meta-* position instead of *ortho*, and *para-*.

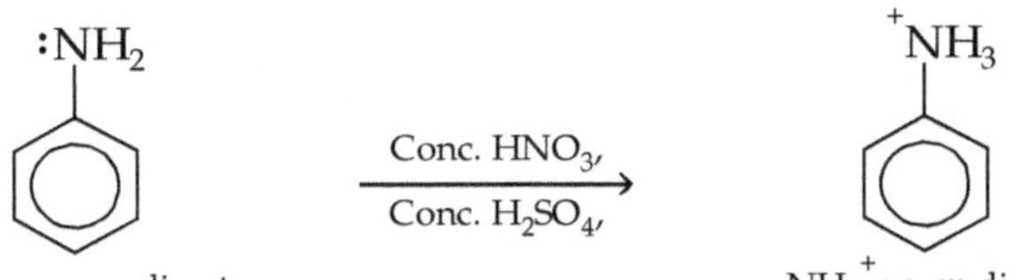

$$:NH_2 \xrightarrow[\text{Conc. } H_2SO_4,]{\text{Conc. } HNO_3,} \overset{+}{N}H_3$$

$—NH_2$ gp. *o, p*-director $—NH_3^+$ gp. *m*-director

However, all these difficulties are overcome by protecting the amino group by acetylation, with either acetyl chloride or acetic anhydride. Acetylation ($—NH_2 \longrightarrow NHCOCH_3$) converts $—NH_2$ group to acetamido ($—NHCOCH_3$) group which is *o, p*-directing but lesser activating toward electrophilic aromatic substitution than the parent $—NH_2$ group.

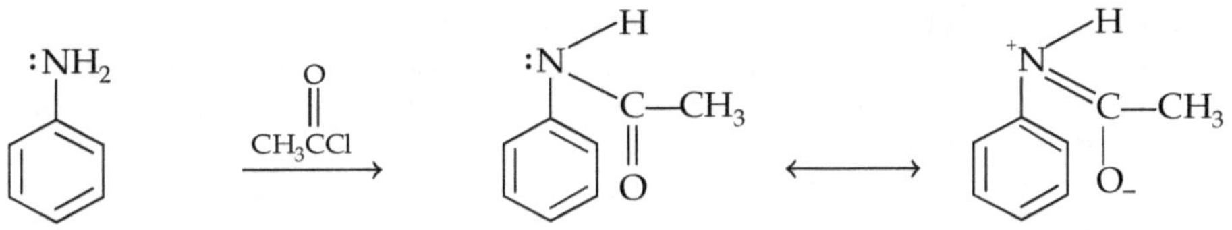

Aniline
(electron pair can delocalize only to benzene ring making *o, p*-positions highly reactive)

Acetanilide Resonance in acetanilid due to amide group (note that electron pair on N can also delocalize to amide group, hence $—NHCOCH_3$ gp. becomes weak activator than the $—NH_2$ group)

Thus protection of the amino group of an arylamine moderates the reactivity of the $—NH_2$ group and permits nitration (or halogenation) of the ring to be achieved in the required *o, p*-positions. Another important feature of the N-acetyl protecting group is that after it has served its purpose, it may be removed by hydrolysis (acidic or basic) liberating the parent amino group (*deprotection*).

Bromination

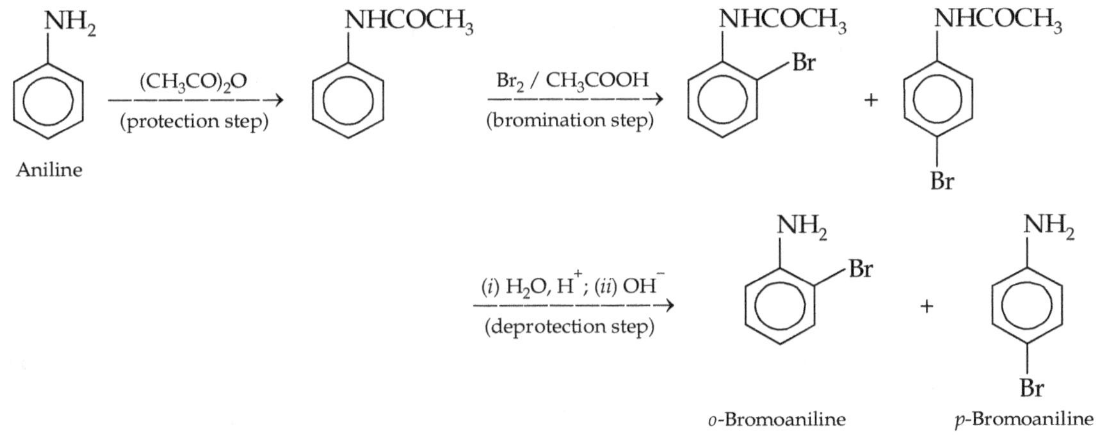

Aniline $\xrightarrow[\text{(protection step)}]{(CH_3CO)_2O}$ (acetanilide) $\xrightarrow[\text{(bromination step)}]{Br_2 / CH_3COOH}$ (o-NHCOCH₃-Br) + (p-NHCOCH₃-Br)

$\xrightarrow[\text{(deprotection step)}]{(i) H_2O, H^+; (ii) OH^-}$ *o*-Bromoaniline + *p*-Bromoaniline

Nitration

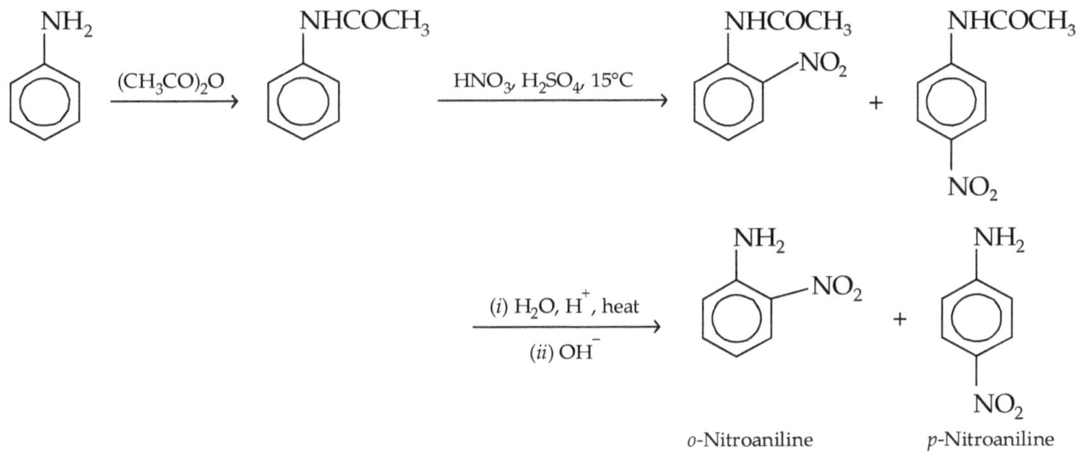

$NH_2 \xrightarrow{(CH_3CO)_2O} NHCOCH_3 \xrightarrow{HNO_3, H_2SO_4, 15°C}$ (o-NHCOCH₃-NO₂) + (p-NHCOCH₃-NO₂)

$\xrightarrow[\text{(ii) OH}^-]{(i) H_2O, H^+, \text{heat}}$ *o*-Nitroaniline + *p*-Nitroaniline

Sulphonation

Aniline is usually sulphonated by **"baking"** the salt, anilinium hydrogen sulphate at 180–200°C ; the main product is the *para* isomer-

NH_2 $\xrightarrow{H_2SO_4}$ $NH_3^+ HSO_4^-$ $\xrightarrow[(-H_2O)]{180-200°C}$ $NHSO_3H$ $\xrightarrow[\text{3 hours}]{180-200°C}$ $NH_3^+ \cdots SO_3^-$

Aniline   Anilinium hydrogen sulphate   Sulphamic acid   Sulphanilic acid

It is believed that sulphonation of amines proceeds by a mechanism that is entirely different from ordinary aromatic substitution.

Sulphanilic acid (*p*-Aminobenzenesulphonic acid) is a salt of special type, called a *dipolar ion** (*sometimes called a* Zwitterion). It is formed by the reaction of on acidic group ($-SO_2OH$) and a basic group ($-NH_2$) that are part of the same molecule, hence it is also called *inner salt*. It is interesting to note that its properties are different from that of a typical amine and a sulphonic acid. Such properties are (*a*) high melting point, (*b*) insolubility in water and organic solvents, (*c*) solubility in aqueous NaOH, and (*d*) insolubility in aqueous HCl. These properties can be explained on the basis of its structure.

(*a*)   High melting point is due to its ionic nature.

(*b*)   Insolubility in organic solvents is also due to its ionic nature. Its insolubility in water is typical of dipolar salts. Not all salts dissolve in water.

(*c*)   Its solubility in aq. NaOH is because of transference of H^+ from the weakly acidic $-NH_3^+$ group to strongly basic OH^- ion to form *p*-aminobenzene sulphonate ion (II), which, like most sodium salts, is soluble in water.

No reaction $\xleftarrow{HCl}$ $NH_3^+ \cdots SO_3^-$ $\xrightarrow{OH^-}$ $NH_2 \cdots SO_3^-$

I (Insoluble in water)   II (Soluble in water)

(*d*)   Its insolubility in aq. HCl is due to the fact that the $-SO_3^-$ ion is too weak base to accept H^+ from strong acids (recall that sulphonic acids are strong acids, hence their anions are very weak bases).

TEST YOUR UNDERSTANDING - 20.2

1.   Account for the fact that *p*-aminobenzoic acid, *p*-$NH_2C_6H_4COOH$, does not exist as a dipolar ion, although 2-aminoethanoic acid (glycine) exists as a dipolar ion.

Friedel-Crafts reactions are normally not successful to unprotected anilines.

$NHCOCH_3$, CH_2CH_3 $\xrightarrow[AlCl_3]{CH_3COCl}$ $NHCOCH_3$, CH_2CH_3 , $COCH_3$

2-Ethylacetanilide   4-Acetamido-3-ethylacetophenone

---

*   A dipolar ion is formed only when a molecule contains both an amino as well as an acidic group, and the amine is more basic than the anion of the acid.

Coupling reaction. Aniline having a strongly activating ($-NH_2$) group undergoes coupling reaction with benzenediazonium salt (a weak electrophile).

$$ArN_2^+ \quad + \quad \text{(C}_6\text{H}_5)-NH_2 \xrightarrow{H^+} Ar-N=N-\text{(C}_6\text{H}_4)-NH_2$$

A weak electrophile   A strongly activated ring   *p*-Aminoazobenzene

Nitrosation. In an electrophilic aromatic nitrosation, the attacking reagent is *nitrosonium ion.* The nitrosonium ion is a very weak electrophile and hence nitrosation can take place only in rings bearing powerfully activating dialkylamino ($-NR_2$) or hydroxy ($-OH$) group, *i.e.,* in *tert*-amines and phenols.

$$\text{N(CH}_3)_2\text{-C}_6\text{H}_5 \xrightarrow{^+NO} \text{N(CH}_3)_2\text{-C}_6\text{H}_4\text{-NO}$$

N, N-Dimethylaniline   *p*-Nitroso–*N, N*– dimethylaniline

TEST YOUR UNDERSTANDING - 20.3

1. Complete the following reaction by supplying structure to the bracketed compounds.

(a) [o-diaminobenzene] + Glyoxal $\longrightarrow$ [E]

(b) [o-diaminobenzene] $\xrightarrow[\text{HONO, 5°C}]{\text{1 mol of}}$ [F]

(c) Aniline $\xrightarrow{C_6H_5CHO}$ [G] $\xrightarrow{HNO_3}$ [H] + [I] $\xrightarrow{H_3O^+}$ [J] + [K] + [L]

2. Arrange the following amines in their decreasing basic character.

(a) [aniline], [cyclohexylamine] and [benzylamine]

(b) [aniline], [pyridine] and [pyrrole]

20.3 Preparation and Reactions of Diazonium Salts

When a primary aromatic amine dissolved or suspended in cold aqueous mineral acid, is treated with sodium nitrite, arenediazonium salts are formed.

$$Ar-NH_2 \quad + \quad NaNO_2 + 2HX \xrightarrow{0-5°C} Ar-N \equiv N^+X^- + NaX + 2H_2O$$

1° Aromatic amine   A diazonium salt

As described earlier, aryl diazonium ions are substantially more stable than alkyl diazonium ions, and are of enormous synthetic value. The important synthetic reactions of diazonium salts may be divided into two classes. (*a*) *replacement reactions*, in which nitrogen is lost as N_2 and its place is taken by some other atom or group, and (*b*) *coupling reactions*, in which the nitrogen is retained in the product.

1. **Reactions involving replacement of $-N^+ \equiv N$.** Diazonium group can be replaced easily be any one of a number of groups or atoms like $-F, -Cl, -Br, -I, -CN, -OH, -H,$ and $-NO_2$. Most of these replacement reactions do not require any special and drastic condition ; simply the requisite reagent is added to the solution of diazonium salt which is then gently warmed. The required substituted compound is formed along with the evolution of nitrogen.

$$Ar-N^+ \equiv N +: Z \longrightarrow Ar-Z + N_2$$

(a)   *Replacement of the —N_2^+ group by —Cl, —Br, or —CN (the Sandmeyer reaction).* Arenediazonium salts react with cuprous chloride, cuprous bromide, and cuprous cyanide to give products in which diazonium group has been replaced by —Cl, —Br, and —CN respectively. These reactions are known as **Sandmeyer reactions.**

$$Ar—N_2^+X^- \xrightarrow{CuX} Ar—X + N_2 \ (X = —Cl, —Br, —or—CN)$$

Sometimes the synthesis is carried out by a modification known as the **Gattermann reaction,** in which copper powder and hydrogen halide (HCl or HBr) are used in place of cuprous halide.

(b)   *Replacement by —NO_2 group*

$$Ar—N^+_2Cl^- + NaNO_2 \xrightarrow[Cu^{2+} \text{ or } Cu_2O]{NaHCO_3} Ar—NO_2 + N_2$$

(c)   *Replacement by —I.* This can simply be achieved by mixing the diazonium salt with potassium iodide at room temperature.

$$Ar—N_2^+X^- + I^- \longrightarrow Ar—I + N_2 + X^-$$

(d)   *Replacement by —F.* The diazonium group can be replaced by fluorine by treating the diazonium salt with fluoroboric acid (HBF_4). The precipitated diazonium fluoroborate is isolated, dried and heated until decomposition occurs to yield the aryl fluoride. This reaction is known as **Balz-Schiemann reaction.**

$$Ar—N_2^+X^- \xrightarrow{HBF_4} Ar—N_2^+BF_4^-\downarrow \xrightarrow{heat} Ar—F + BF_3 + N_2$$

(e)   *Replacement by —OH.* Diazonium salts react with water, of course slowly at low temperature, even ice cold, and vigorously at room or high temperature to yield phenols and this is the reason why these salts are used immediately after preparation.

$$Ar—N_2^+X^- + H_2O \xrightarrow{heat} Ar—OH + N_2 + H^+$$

This is the most general method for the preparation of phenols. Sulphuric acid is normally used instead of hydrochloric acid in the diazotization steps so as to minimise the competition with water for capture of the cationic intermediate ; HSO_4^- is less nucleophilic than Cl^-.

As we shall see later, the phenol so formed may undergo coupling reaction with the unreacted diazonium salt. Since this coupling takes place easily in alkaline medium, we can minimize this further by making the solution more acidic ; for which diazonium solution is added slowly to a large volume of boiling dil. H_2SO_4.

Diazonium group can be replaced by —OH group also by adding cuprous oxide to a dilute solution of the diazonium salt containing a large excess of cupric nitrate.

$$Ar—N_2^+ HSO_4^- \xrightarrow[Cu^{2+}, H_2O]{Cu_2O} Ar—OH$$

This variation of Sandmeyer reaction is a much simpler and safer procedure than the above older method for preparing phenol.

(f)   *Replacement by hydrogen (deamination via diazotization).* This can be brought about by a number of reducing agents, *e.g.*, H_3PO_2, C_2H_5OH, $NaBH_4$, or Na_2SO_3; most useful of these is *hypophosphorous acid, H_3PO_2.*

$$Ar—N_2^+X^- + H_3PO_2 + H_2O \longrightarrow Ar—H + H_3PO_3 + HX$$

Aniline can directly be converted to benzene by carrying out its diazotization in presence of hypophosphorous acid for which amine is dissolved in hypophosphorous acid and sodium nitrite is added (diazonium salt is reduced as fast as it is formed).

$$Ar—NH_2 \xrightarrow{H_3PO_2, NaNO_2} Ar—H + N_2 + H_2O$$

Replacement of —NH_2 group *via* the diazonium group by hydrogen is very useful reaction because introduction of —NH_2 group (precursor of —N_2X) can be used to introduce the new group in a *p*-position which is sometimes not possible by direct reaction as illustrated in the following preparation.

(g)   *Replacement by phenyl group (Gattermann reaction)* :

Preparation of *m*-bromotoluene : Here the two *o, p*-directing groups are situated *meta* for each other, hence neither bromination of toluene nor methylation of bromobenzne would yield the required *m*-bromotoluene.

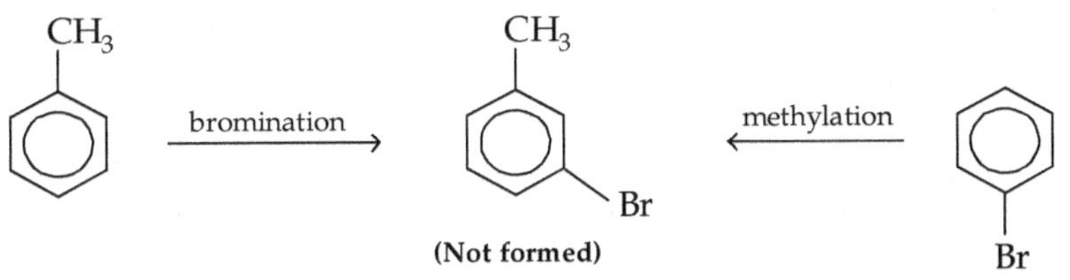

(Not formed)

However, this can be prepared from toluene in the following way.

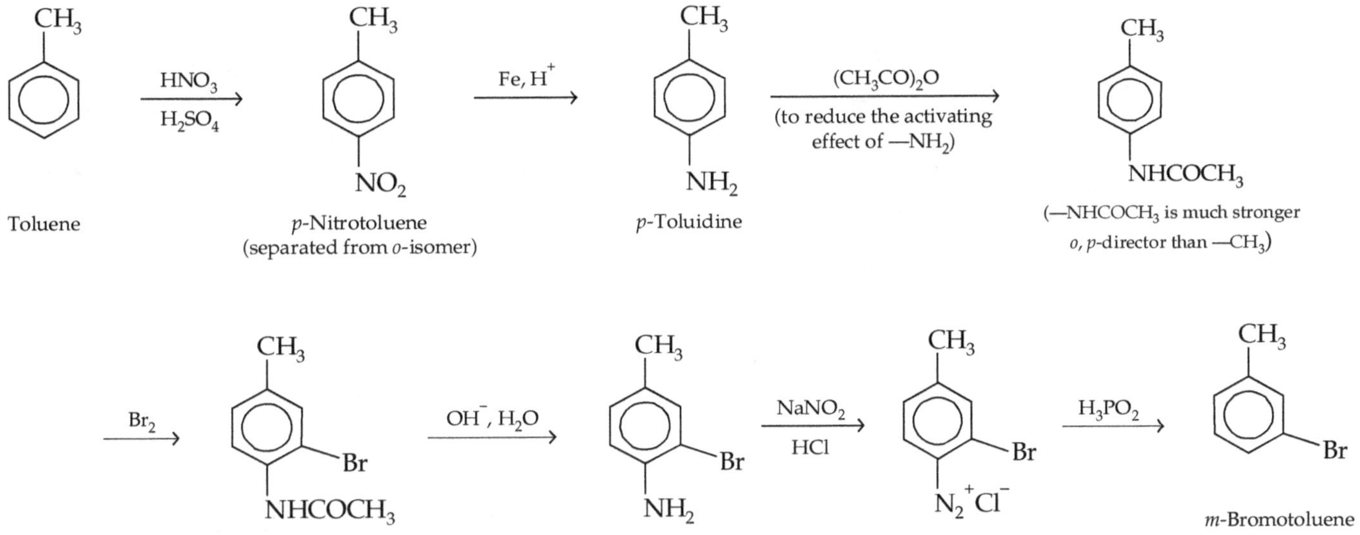

Toluene → *p*-Nitrotoluene (separated from *o*-isomer) → *p*-Toluidine → (—NHCOCH$_3$ is much stronger *o, p*-director than —CH$_3$)

m-Bromotoluene

TEST YOUR UNDERSTANDING - 20.4

1. In diazotisation of arylamines, excess of mineral acid is used. Explain.

2. Complete the following by supplying structures to the bracketed compounds.

(*a*)

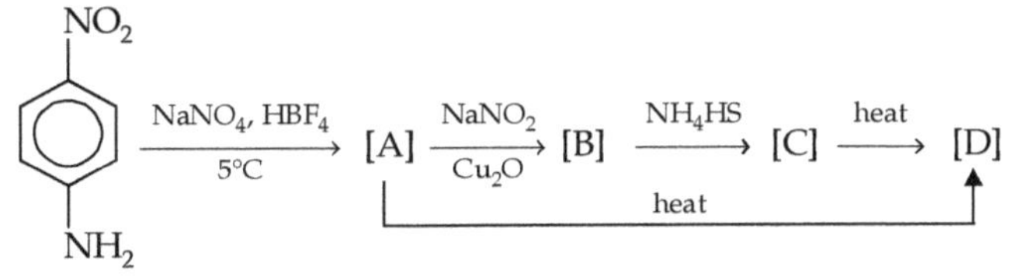

(*b*)

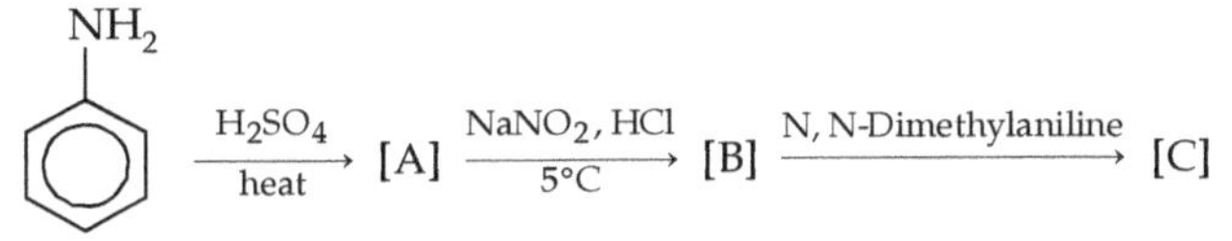

3. Give intermediate steps to carry out the following transformations.

  (*a*) Toluene to *p*-toluic acid   (*b*) Nitrobenzene to *m*-bromophenol

  (*c*) *p*-Nitroaniline to 1, 2, 3-tribromobenzene   (*d*) Benzene to 1, 3, 5-tribromobenzene

  (*e*) Benzene to *m*-bromochlorobenzene   (*f*) Aniline to *p*-dinitrobenzene

  (*g*) C$_6$H$_5$NH$_2$ to C$_6$H$_5$D.

4. Direct bromination of toluene gives a mixture of *o*- and *p*-bromotoluenes which are very difficult to separate, so devise a scheme that can be used for converting toluene to *o*- and *p*-bromotoluenes.

2. **Coupling reactions of diazonium salts.** Like nitrosonium ion ($^+$NO), arenediazonium ions (ArN_2^+) are weak electrophiles, and are thus capable of attacking only very reactive rings. Hence the aromatic ring undergoing attack by the diazonium ion must contain a powerfully electron-releasing group, generally —OH, —NR_2, —NHR, —or NH_2. Substitution mainly occurs *para* to the activating group.

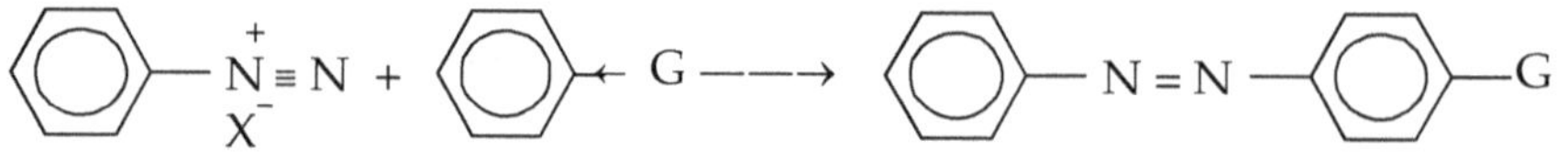

$$\left(\text{G} = \begin{array}{l} \text{—NH}_2\text{, —NHR} \\ \text{—NR}_2\text{, or —OH} \end{array}\right)$$

An azo compound

(*a*) Couplings between arenediazonium cation, and phenols take place most rapidly in *slighlty* alkaline solution. In alkaline medium, an appreciable amount of phenol is present as a phenoxide ion which is more reactive toward electrophilic substitution than the parent phenol.

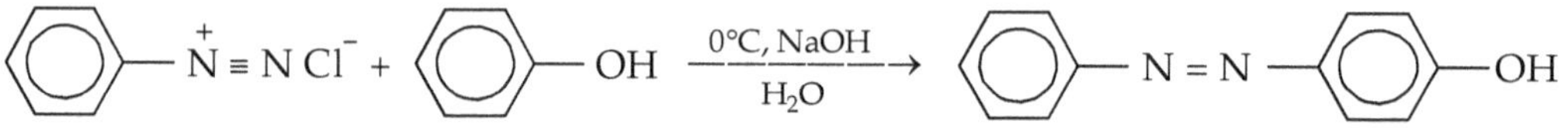

p-Hydroxyazobenzene

However, the solution should not be too alkaline because in strongly alkaline medium the arenediazonium ion exists in equilibrium with an un-ionized diazohydroxide and diazotate ; neither of these couple.

$$Ar—N \equiv N^+ OH^- \underset{H^+}{\overset{NaOH}{\rightleftharpoons}} Ar—N = N—OH \underset{H^+}{\overset{NaOH}{\rightleftharpoons}} Ar—N = N—O^- Na^+$$

Arenediazonium ion	Diazohydroxide	Diazotate ion
(**couples**)	(does not couple)	(does not couple)

(*b*) Couplings between arenediazonium cation and amines take place mostly in *slightly* acidic solutions (pH 5–7).

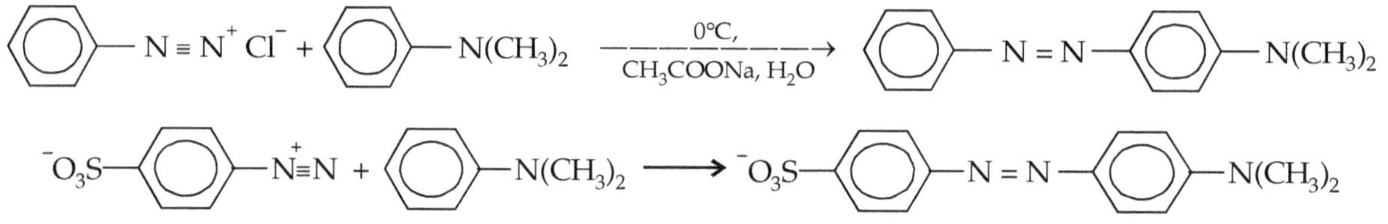

Methyl orange

The higher acidity increases the amount of protonated amine which is unreactive toward electrophilic substitution

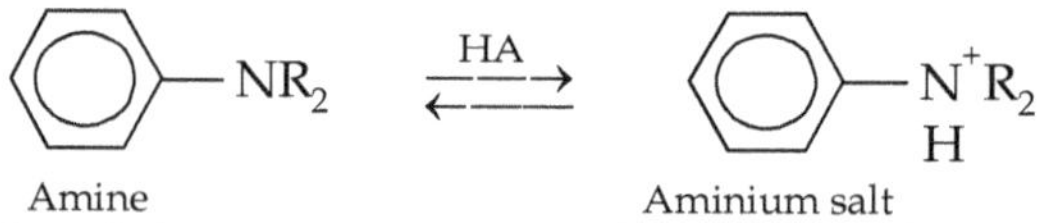

Amine	Aminium salt
(**couples**)	(does not couple)

Azo compounds are usually intensely coloured because the azo linkage (—N = N—) brings the two aromatic rings into conjugation. This gives an extended system of delocalized π electrons and allows absorption of light in the visible region. Because of their intense colours, many azo compounds are extensively used as dyes. Azo compounds undergo reduction in the following manner.

(*i*) $Ar—N = N—Ar' \xrightarrow[\text{(mild reduction)}]{Sn, NaOH} \overset{\text{H \quad H}}{Ar—N—N—Ar'}$
A hydrazo compound

(*ii*) $Ar—N = N—Ar' \xrightarrow[\text{(vigorous reduction)}]{\text{(i) SnCl}_2, H^+ ; \text{(ii) OH}^-} ArNH_2 + H_2NAr'$

Azo compounds can exist in *cis* and *trans* forms ; the former being less stable due to steric strain.

cis-Azobenzene   *trans*-Azobenzene

3. **Reduction.** Arenediazonium salts are reduced to phenylhydrazine hydrochloride by means of $SnCl_2$ and HCl or with sodium sulphite.

$$C_6H_5\!-\!N \equiv N^+ \, Cl^- \xrightarrow[\text{or } Na_2SO_3]{SnCl_2, HCl} C_6H_5NHNH_2 . HCl$$

Benzenediazonium chloride   Phenylhydrazine hydrochloride

 **20.4** **Illustrative Examples**

Example 1 :

Supply the structure of bracketed compounds in each of the following conversions.

(a)   [A] Acid $\xrightarrow{\text{[B]}/\text{Conc. } H_2SO_4}$ [C] $\xrightarrow[5°C]{NaNO_2, HCl}$ [D] $\xrightarrow{CuCl}$ *p*-Nitrochlorobenzene

(b) $C_6H_6 \xrightarrow[AlCl_3]{C_2H_5Br}$ [A] $\xrightarrow[H_2SO_4]{HNO_3}$ [B] $\xrightarrow{NBS}$ [C] $\xrightarrow[NH_3]{\text{excess}}$ [D]

(c) $C_6H_5NH_2 \xrightarrow{(CH_3CO)_2O}$ [A] $\xrightarrow{ClSO_2OH}$ [B] $\xrightarrow{NH_3}$ [C] $\xrightarrow[(ii) OH^-]{(i) H_3{}^+O}$ [D]

(d)   [B] $\xleftarrow[H^+]{C_6H_5N_2{}^+Cl^-}$ HO—⟨benzene⟩—NH_2 $\xrightarrow[OH^-]{C_6H_5N_2{}^+Cl^-}$ [A]

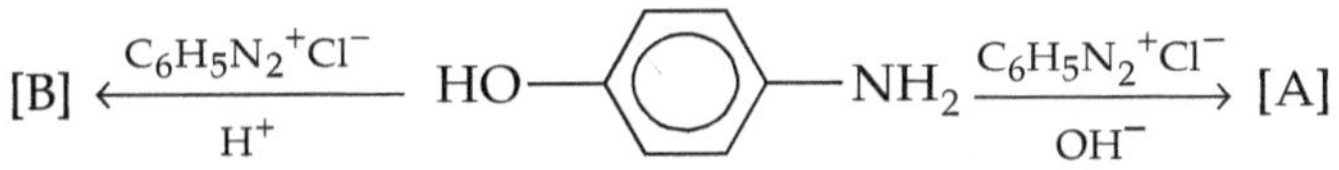

(e)   (structure: o-ethyl-N-acetylaniline with C_2H_5 and $NHCOCH_3$ substituents) $\xrightarrow[H_2SO_4]{HNO_3}$ [A] $\xrightarrow{OH^-}$ [B] $\xrightarrow{Cl_2}$ [C]

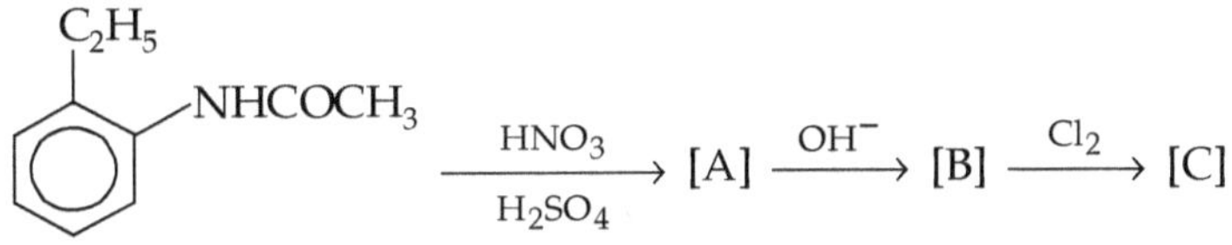

Solution :

(a)   Proceed backward with the structure of the knwon compound, *p*-nitrochlorobenzene and the knwon reagent.

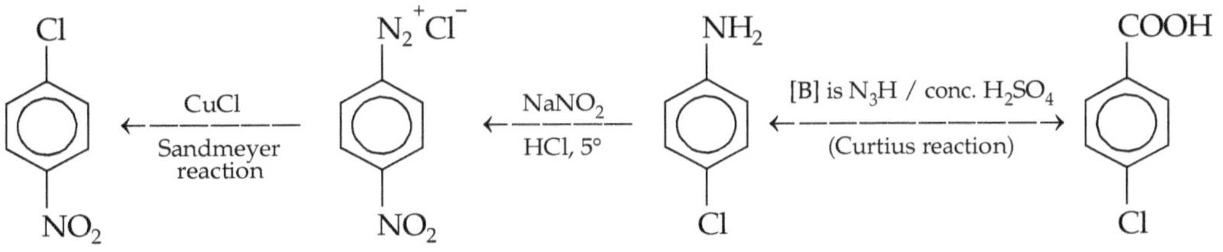

Cl⟨ring⟩NO₂ $\xleftarrow[\substack{\text{Sandmeyer}\\\text{reaction}}]{CuCl}$ N₂⁺Cl⁻⟨ring⟩NO₂ $\xleftarrow[HCl, 5°]{NaNO_2}$ NH₂⟨ring⟩Cl $\xleftarrow[\text{(Curtius reaction)}]{\text{[B] is } N_3H / \text{conc. } H_2SO_4}$ COOH⟨ring⟩Cl

                 [D]   [C]   [A]

(b) CH_2CH_3⟨ring⟩ [A]   ; CH_2CH_3⟨ring⟩NO_2 [B]   ; $CH(Br)CH_3$⟨ring⟩NO_2 [C]   ; $CH(NH_2)CH_3$⟨ring⟩NO_2 [D]

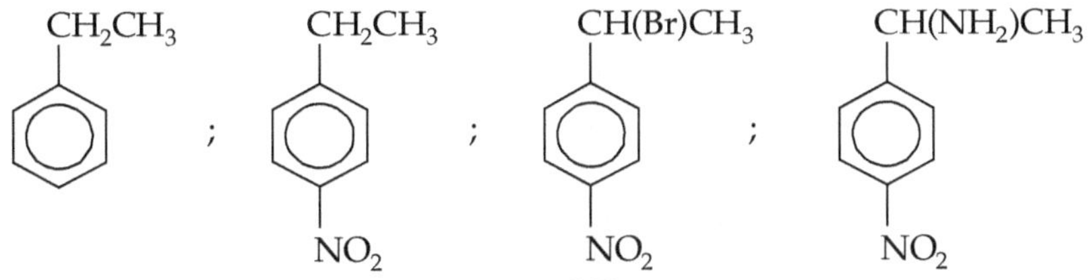

(c) NHCOCH_3 (benzene ring) ; NHCOCH_3 (benzene ring with SO_2Cl) ; NHCOCH_3 (benzene ring with SO_2NH_2) ; NH_2 (benzene ring with SO_2NH_2)

(d) $\text{HO}-$(ring)$-\text{NH}_2$, $\text{N}=\text{NC}_6\text{H}_5$ **[A]**   ; $\text{HO}-$(ring)$-\text{NH}_2$, $\text{N}=\text{NC}_6\text{H}_5$ **[B]**

(e) C_2H_5, NHCOCH_3, O_2N ring **[A]** ; C_2H_5, NH_2, O_2N ring **[B]** ; C_2H_5, NH_2, O_2N, Cl ring **[C]**

Example 2 :
Give steps involved in the following conversions.
(a) $\text{C}_6\text{H}_5\text{NH}_2$ to $\text{C}_6\text{H}_5\text{D}$

(b) C_6H_6 to optically active *sec*-butylbenzene

(c)   Aniline to benzoic acid.

(d)   (benzene) $\longrightarrow$ (benzene ring with NH_2 and CH_2NH_2)

(e)   (C_2H_5, NH_2, O_2N, Cl ring) $\longrightarrow$ (C_2H_5, Cl, Cl ring)

(f)   Benzene to ethyl *m*-fluorophenyl ketone

(g)   (isopropylbenzene) $----\rightarrow$ (isopropylbenzene with NO_2)

Solution :

(a) $\text{C}_6\text{H}_5\text{NH}_2 \xrightarrow[\text{HCl, 5°C}]{\text{NaNO}_2} \text{C}_6\text{H}_5\text{N}_2{}^+\text{Cl}^- \xrightarrow{\text{DPH}_2\text{PO}_2} \text{C}_6\text{H}_5\text{D}$

(b)   (benzene) $+ \text{ClCH}$ $\genfrac{}{}{0pt}{}{\text{CH}_3}{\text{CH}_2\text{CH}_3}$ *sec*-Butyl chloride $\xrightarrow{\text{AlCl}_3}$ (benzene with $\text{CH}\genfrac{}{}{0pt}{}{\text{CH}_3}{\text{C}_2\text{H}_5}$) racemate $\xrightarrow[\substack{(ii)\ \text{Sn, HCl}\\(iii)\ \text{OH}^-}]{(i)\ \text{HNO}_3,\ \text{H}_2\text{SO}_4}$ (ring with $\text{CH}\genfrac{}{}{0pt}{}{\text{CH}_3}{\text{C}_2\text{H}_5}$ and NH_2) reacemate

$\xrightarrow[\substack{(+)\text{- or }(-)\text{-}\\\text{tartaric acid}}]{\text{resolve with}}$ (ring with $\text{CH}\genfrac{}{}{0pt}{}{\text{CH}_3}{\text{C}_2\text{H}_5}$ and NH_2) separated enantiomers $\xrightarrow[\substack{(ii)\ \text{H}_3\text{PO}_2}]{(i)\ \text{HONO, 5°C}}$ (ring with $\text{CH}\genfrac{}{}{0pt}{}{\text{CH}_3}{\text{C}_2\text{H}_5}$) separated *sec*-Butylbenzenes

(c) Aniline $\xrightarrow[\text{5°C}]{\text{HONO}}$ [benzenediazonium, N_2^+] $\xrightarrow{\text{CuCN}}$ [CN] $\xrightarrow{\text{hydrolysis}}$ Benzoic acid (COOH)

(d) Benzene $\xrightarrow[\text{H}_2\text{SO}_4]{\text{HNO}_3}$ [NO_2] $\xrightarrow[\text{(ii) (CH}_3\text{CO)}_2\text{O}]{\text{(i) Sn, HCl}}$ [$NHCOCH_3$] $\xrightarrow[\text{H}_2\text{SO}_4]{\text{HNO}_3}$ [$NHCOCH_3$ / NO_2]

$\xrightarrow{\text{OH}^-}$ [NH_2 / NO_2] $\xrightarrow[\text{(ii) OH}^-]{\text{(i) Sn, HCl}}$ [NH_2 / NH_2] $\xrightarrow[\text{(ii) CuCN}]{\text{(i) HONO, 5°C}}$ [CN / CN] $\xrightarrow{\text{LiAlH}_4}$ [CH_2NH_2 / CH_2NH_2]

(e) [C_2H_5, NH_2, Cl, O_2N] $\xrightarrow[\text{(ii) CuCl}]{\text{(i) HONO, 5°C}}$ [C_2H_5, Cl, Cl, O_2N] $\xrightarrow[\text{(ii) HNO}_2\text{, 5°C}]{\text{(i) Sn, HCl ; OH}^-}$ [C_2H_5, Cl, Cl, $^-ClN_2^+$] $\xrightarrow{\text{H}_3\text{PO}_2}$ [C_2H_5, Cl, Cl]

(f) Benzene $\xrightarrow[\text{AlCl}_3]{\text{CH}_3\text{CH}_2\text{COCl}}$ [$COCH_2CH_3$] $\xrightarrow[\text{(ii) Fe, HCl ; OH}^-]{\text{(i) HNO}_3\text{, H}_2\text{SO}_4}$ [$COCH_2CH_3$ / NH_2]

$\xrightarrow{\text{HONO, 5°C}}$ [$COCH_2CH_3$ / $N_2^+Cl^-$] $\xrightarrow[\text{(ii) heat}]{\text{(i) HBF}_4}$ [$COCH_2CH_3$ / F] Ethyl *m*-fluorophenyl ketone

(g) Isopropylbenzene (Cumene) $\xrightarrow[\text{(ii) Fe, HCl ; OH}^-]{\text{(i) HNO}_3\text{, H}_2\text{SO}_4}$ [isopropyl / NH_2] $\xrightarrow{\text{CH}_3\text{COCl}}$ [isopropyl / $NHCOCH_3$]

$\xrightarrow[\text{(ii) OH}^-]{\text{(i) HNO}_3\text{, H}_2\text{SO}_4}$ [isopropyl / NO_2 / NH_2] $\xrightarrow{\text{HONO, 5°C}}$ [isopropyl / NO_2 / N_2^+] $\xrightarrow{\text{H}_3\text{PO}_2}$ [isopropyl / NO_2] *m*-Isopropylnitrobenzene

Example 3 :

An unknown compound X containing nitrogen and chlorine is readily soluble in water to give a solution that turns blue litmus red. Titration of X with standard sodium hydroxide gives a neutralization equivalent of 129.

When compound X is treated with aq.NaOH, a liquid containing nitrogen but no chlorine separates out. Liquid Y gives a red precipitate on treatment with nitrous acid and β-naphthol under suitable conditions. Assign structure to X and Y.

Solution :

Solubility of the compound X in water, and its reaction with NaOH to form Y with the loss of chlorine indicates that X is the hydrochloric acid salt. Further compound Y (not having chlorine) seems to be 1° primary aromatic amine due to its reaction with HCl (diazotisation) and β-naphthol (coupling) to form red precipitate. The 1° aromatic amine hydrochloride should be $C_6H_5NH_3{}^+Cl^-$, indicated by its N.E. 129.

$$C_6H_5NH_3{}^+Cl^- + H_2O \longrightarrow C_6H_5NH_2 + H_2O + HCl$$

$$\text{(X) NE = 129} \qquad\qquad \text{(Y)}$$

$$C_6H_5NH_3{}^+Cl^- + NaOH \longrightarrow C_6H_5NH_2 + H_2O + NaCl$$

$$\text{(X)} \qquad\qquad\qquad \text{(Y)}$$

Example 4 :

Deduce structure of the compound (A) of the formula $C_7H_7NO_2$ which is insoluble in dil. acid and base. On vigorous oxidation, it gives compound (B), $C_7H_5NO_4$ which is soluble in dil. aqueous $NaHCO_3$ and gives two isomeric monochloro substitution products.

Solution :

Since the compound (A), $C_7H_7NO_2$ is insoluble in dil. acid and base, and its nitrogen is not removed on oxidation, so it should contian —NO_2 group as one of the substitutents which is present as such in B. Hence the other substituent in B ($C_7H_5NO_4$) should be —COOH as indicated by its solubility in aq. $NaHCO_3$. So, the compound B, $C_7H_5NO_4$ is $C_6H_4(NO_2)COOH$. The two substituents must be present in *para* to each other so as to explain the formation of two isomeric monochloro substitution products. Thus (A) should be *p*-nitrotoluene

COOH — Two possible sites — vigorous oxidation — NO_2 — (B) — R — NO_2 — or — CH_3 — NO_2 — (A)

Example 5 :

Deduce a possible structure for the compund (A) of the formula C_8H_9NO which is insoluble in dil. acid and base. On treatment with $KMnO_4$ in H_2SO_4 , it gives compound B, which is free of nitrogen, soluble in aqueous $NaHCO_3$ and gives only one mononitro substitution product.

Solution :

$$[A] \xrightarrow[\;H_2SO_4\;]{\;KMnO_4\;} [B] \xrightarrow{\;nitration\;} \text{One mononitro derivative}$$

$$C_8H_9NO \qquad\qquad \text{(soluble in aq. } NaHCO_3\text{)}$$

Students are advised to start the problem from any knwon reaction fact or strucutre given in the problem. For example, in the present question it is given that compound [B] is soluble in aq. $NaHCO_3$, so it must contain —COOH group. Further it is given that (B) forms only one mononitro derivative which indicates that it should contian two —COOH groups and that too in *para* to each other.

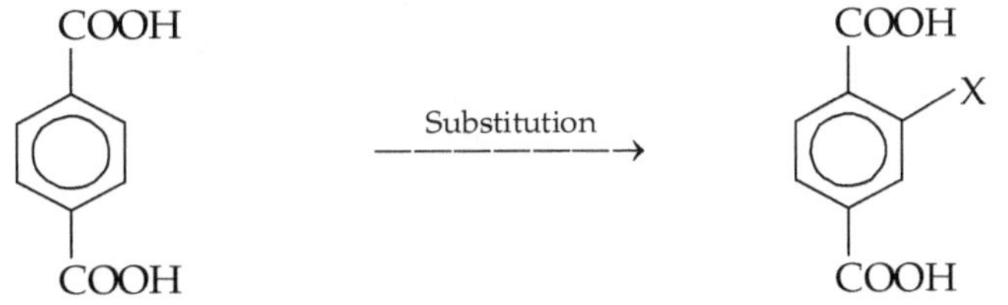

COOH

Substitution →

COOH
X
COOH

(B) All four positions
are equivalent

Now since compound B is obtained by acidic –$KMnO_4$ oxidation of A, A should have two substituents and one substituent must contain nitrogen in such form which is insoluble in acids and bases and is liable to be converted to —COOH group by $KMnO_4 + H_2SO_4$.

The nitrogen containing group which coincides with all the given* characteristics is —$CONH_2$. Hence the other substituent in A (C_8H_9NO) should be —CH_3 and that too in *para* position to explain the formation of B.

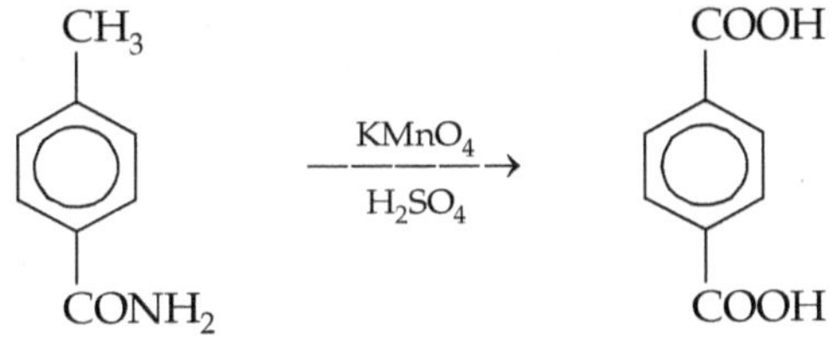

CH_3

$KMnO_4$ → H_2SO_4

COOH

$CONH_2$

(A) C_8H_9NO

COOH

(B)

Example 6 :

An azo compound (X) is cleaved by stannous chloride to form two amines, namely 2-methyl-4-aminophenol (A) and 3-bromo-4-aminotoluene (B). Deduce the structure of the azo compound. Can both of the amines (A and B) be used for preparing the parent azo compound by coupling reaction, if so give the synthesis of the azo compound.

Solution :

In such questions, first draw structures of both of amines in such a way that their amino groups face each other. Now replace the two amino groups by azo linkage, —N = N—.

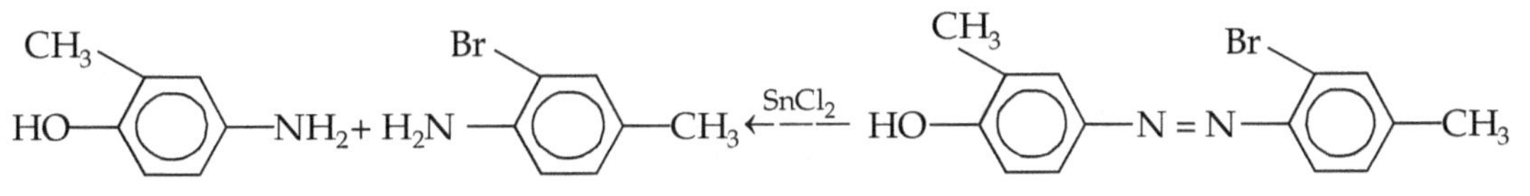

CH_3
HO—⟨ ⟩—NH_2 + H_2N—⟨ ⟩—CH_3
Br

$\xleftarrow{SnCl_2}$

CH_3
HO—⟨ ⟩—N = N—⟨ ⟩—CH_3
Br

(A)　　　　(B)　　　　(X)

The two possible pairs that can be used for preparing the azo compound X by coupling are

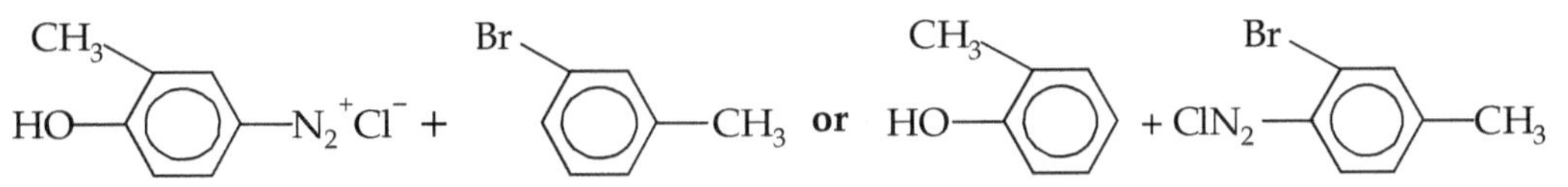

CH_3
HO—⟨ ⟩—$N_2^+Cl^-$ + ⟨ ⟩—CH_3
Br

or

CH_3
HO—⟨ ⟩ + ClN_2—⟨ ⟩—CH_3
Br

(From amine A)　　　　(From amine B)

However, the first combination is not feasible because the benzene ring does not bear reactive —OH or —NH_2 group, *i.e.*, it is not sufficiently reactive to be attacked by the electrophilic diazonium cation.

---

*　Other important N containing groups are —NO_2 (not removed by $KMnO_4 + H_2SO_4$), —NH_2, —$NHCOCH_3$, etc. (liable to destroy the benzene ring).

Example 7 :

A nitrobenzene derivative (A) of the formula $C_8H_9NO_2$ when treated with metallic tin and NaOH, it forms compound (B). Compound B rearranges to an aromatic diamine (C) on treatment with strong mineral acid. Compound (C) is treated first with nitrous acid at low temperature and then heated with ethanol to give 3, 3'-diethyldiphenyl. Deduce the structure of the compound (A) and write the reactions involved.

Solution :

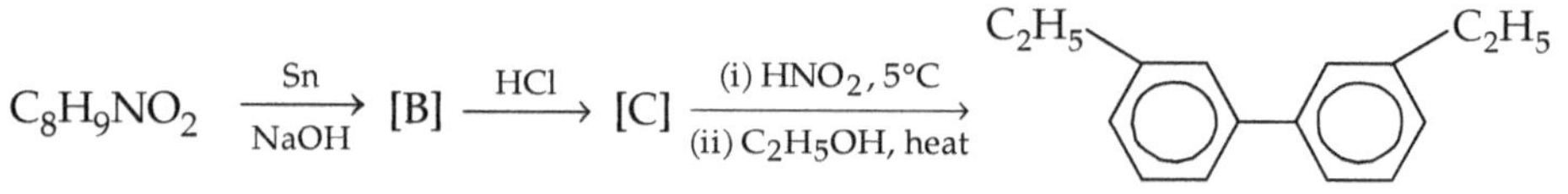

$$C_8H_9NO_2 \xrightarrow[\text{NaOH}]{\text{Sn}} [B] \xrightarrow{\text{HCl}} [C] \xrightarrow[\text{(ii) C}_2\text{H}_5\text{OH, heat}]{\text{(i) HNO}_2, 5°C}$$

[A] $C_6H_5NO_2.C_2H_4$

The above series of reactions lead to following points.

(*i*)   Compound (C) is a diamine and is formed by treating [B] with strong HCl, involving rearrangement, [C] must have two —NH_2 groups in para positions.

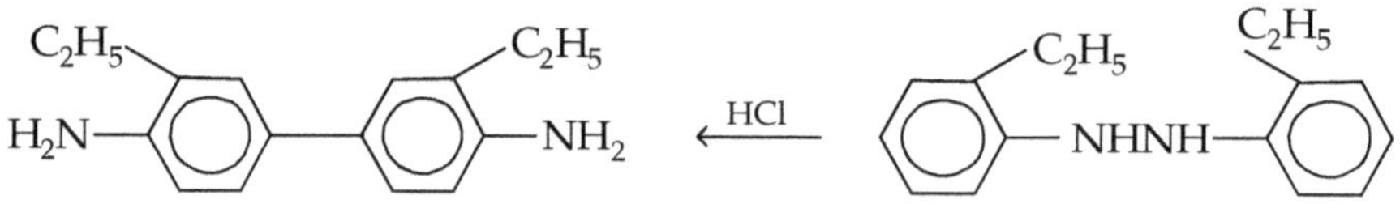

Thus the compound [B] must be a substituted hydrazobenzene with undergoes rearrangement (benzidine rearrangement) on treatment with strong mineral acid.

(*ii*)   Formation of hydrazobenzene by the reduction of compound A with Sn and OH⁻ indicates that A must be 2-ethylnitrobenzene.

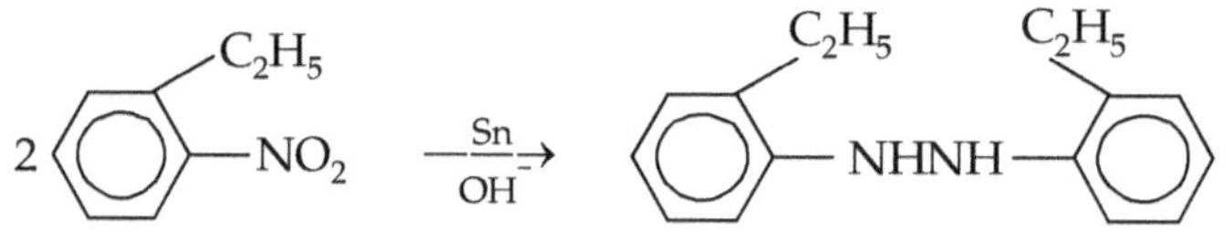

Example 8 :

Pyridine undergoes electrophilic substitution at position 3 rather than at 2 or 4. Explain.

Solution :

Due to the presence of N in ring, pyridine behaves like a strongly deactivated benzene (e.g. nitrobenzene), thus positions 2 and 4 are deactivated towards electrophiles. This is evident by the fact that Friedel–Crafts reactions fail while other electrophilic substitutions require unusually strong conditions. Thus formation of 3-substituted product (the relatively less deactivated position) can be explained by higher stability of the corresponding intermediate.

Attack at 3-position :

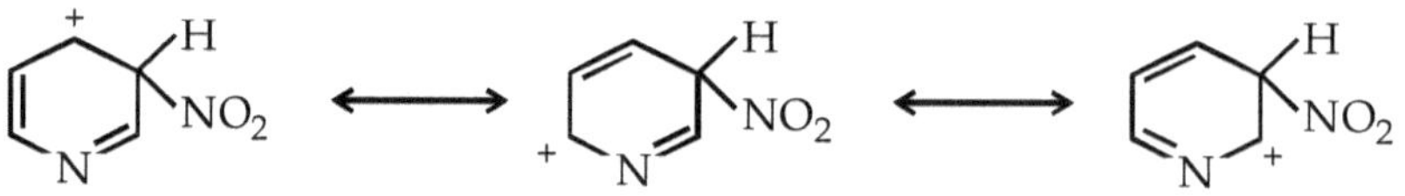

Attack at 2-position :

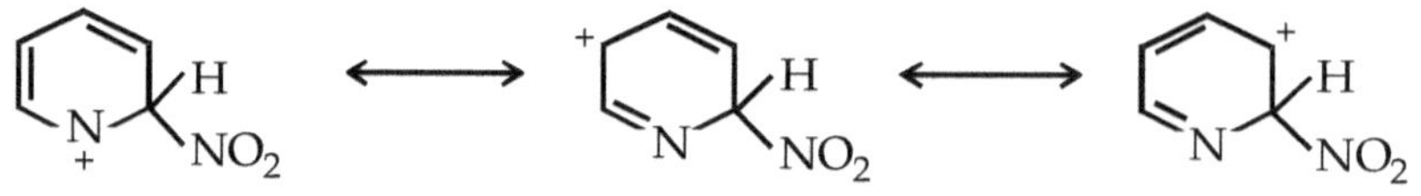

No octet on N **(Unfavourable)**

Thus the intermediate corresponding to 2- (as well as 4-) substituted product is less stable than the 3-substituted intermediate.

Example 9 :

2-Chloropyridine when treated with sodium methoxide gives 2-methoxypyridine, while no such reaction occurs with 3-chloropyridine. Explain.

Solution :

This is an example of nucleophilic substitution, recall that pyridine is deactivated toward attack by electrophiles, it is activated toward attack by nucleophiles. Thus if a good leaving group is present either at 2 or 4 position, a nucleophile can attack and displace the leaving group. The intermediate due to attack at 2 or 4 position is stabilized by delocalization of the negative charge, since this stabilization is not possible if attack occurs at the 3-position, 3-chloropyridine is not converted to 3-methoxypyridine.

Nucleophilic attack at C-2

Similar situation arises in case of 4-chloropyridine.

Nucleophilic attack at C-3 (not observed)

None of the structure has –ve charge on N (hence unfavouable situation)

Example 10 :

Propose mechanism for the following reaction.

You may use an acid or a base, wherever you require.

Solution :

Example 11 :

Draw all the resonating structures of the 2-substituted intermediate obtained by treating pyrrole in acetic anhydride (CH_3CO^+ is the electrophile). Is there any difference in the relative stability of these structures?

Solution :

Every atom has a full octet
(especially stable)

Example 12 :

An optically active naturally occurring toxic liquid $C_8H_{17}N$ (X), in hemlock that was said to cause Socrates death dissolves in aq. HCl and gives no gas will nitrous acid. It gives a precipitate with benzenesulphonyl chloride in presence of NaOH. when treated with excess of methyl iodide, then with moist oxide and finally heated, it gives a compound (Y) $C_{10}H_{21}N$. Compound (Y) is treated similarly as (X) and finally gives 1, 4-octadiene and 1, 5-octadiene. Suggest structure to (X) and)(Y) and explain all the reactions. Is there any possible structural isomer of (X); if so give the complete set of reaction with this?

Solution :

(*i*)   The given reactions (solubility in aq. HCl, no gas with HONO and a precipitate with $C_6H_5CO_2Cl$ / NaOH) indicate that the given compound is a secondary amine.

(*ii*)   Since the given compound eliminates nitrogen by two sequence of Hofmann degradation, N must be present in the ring.

(*iii*)   Formation of two unbranched alkenes as the final products indicates that the alkyl group or groups consisting of 3-C must be present on the α-carbons and it must be unbranched. Two possibilities arise : (a) one CH_3 and one C_2H_5 groups are present on the two α-carbons, (b) one n-C_3H_7 group is present on one of the α-carbons. However,

EXERCISE 20.1 (MCQ - ONE option correct)

1. Which of the following is not a property of sulphanilic acid ?
(a) It is soluble in *aq*.NaOH
(b) It is soluble in *aq*. HCl
(c) It is insoluble in organic solvents
(d) It does not melt but decomposes.

2. H_3C—⬡—N = N—⬡—NMe_2 can be produced

by coupling reaction of which of the following pair?

(a) H_3C—⬡—NH_2 + ⬡—NMe_2

(b) H_3C—⬡ + H_2N—⬡—NMe_2

(c) Both (a) and (b)
(d) Neither of the two.

3. Arrange the following compounds in decreasing order of coupling with benzenediazonium chloride.

OH	O$^-$	NH_3^+	NH_2
⬡	⬡	⬡	⬡
(I)	(II)	(III)	(IV)

(a) IV > I > II > III
(b) II > I > IV > III
(c) II > IV > I > III
(d) II > III > IV > I.

4. Arrange the following diazonium cation in decreasing order of coupling with phenol.

N_2^+	N_2^+	N_2^+	N_2^+
⬡	⬡	⬡	⬡—NO_2
	CH_3	NO_2	NO_2
(I)	(II)	(III)	(IV)

(a) I > II > III > IV
(b) IV > III > II > I
(c) IV > III > I > II
(d) II > I > III > IV.

5. Predict the nature of P in the following reaction.

NH_2-⬡-CH_3 + NO_2-⬡ ——→ P

(a) O=⬡=O
(b) O_2N—HN—⬡—CH_3
(c) H_2N—⬡—CHO
(d) H_2N—⬡—COOH

6. Predict the product [B] in the following series of reactions.

$C_6H_5NH_2 \xrightarrow[KOH]{CHCl_3} [A] \xrightarrow{H_3O^+} [B]$

(a) $C_6H_5CH_2NH_2$
(b) C_6H_5COOH
(c) $C_6H_5NHCH_3$
(d) $C_6H_5NH_2$.

7. How many diazo group will be introduced when resorcinol is treated with excess of benzenediazonium chloride in alkaline medium ?
(a) 1
(b) 2
(c) 3
(d) Nil.

8. ⬡(NH_2) $\xrightarrow[\text{Conc. } H_2SO_4]{\text{Conc. } HNO_3}$ X. Here X is mainly

(a) *o*-Nitroaniline
(b) *p*-Nitroaniline
(c) a mixture of (a) and (b)
(d) *m*-Nitroaniline.

9. What should be the final product in the following reaction ?

O_2N—⬡—NH_2 + 2ICl ——→ Main product

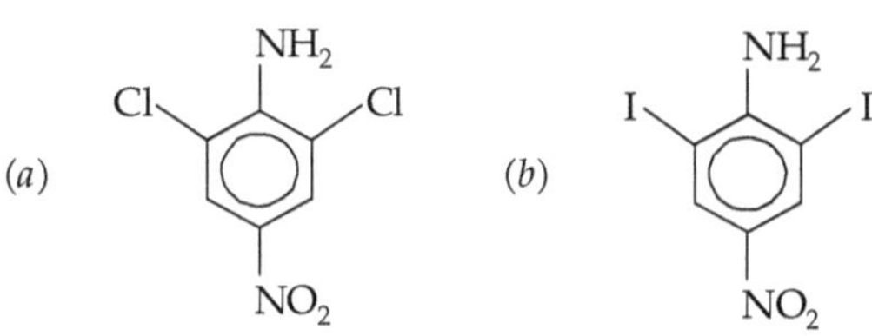

(a) [structure with NH_2, Cl, Cl, NO_2]
(b) [structure with NH_2, I, I, NO_2]
(c) [structure with NH_2, I, Cl, NO_2]
(d) No reaction.

10. Which of the following has lowest pK_b value ?
(a) Benzylamine
(b) Aniline
(c) Acetanilide
(d) *p*-Nitroaniline

11. Which of the following is stronger than aniline ?

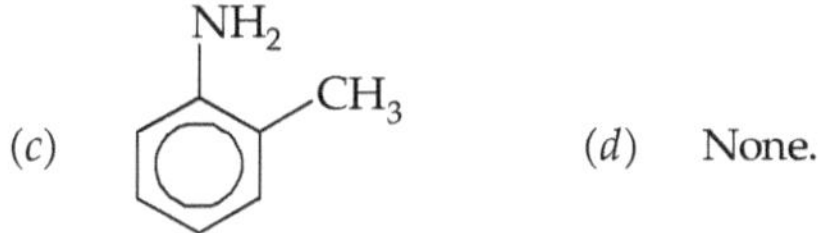

(a) [NHCOCH$_3$ structure]
(b) [NH_2 / COCH$_3$ structure]
(c) [NH_2 / CH$_3$ structure]
(d) None.

12. The increasing order of pK_b values for the three anilines (I, II and III) is

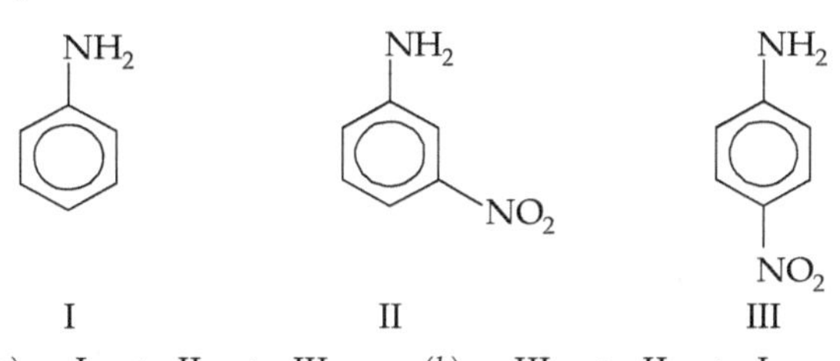

I — [NH_2 structure]
II — [NH_2 / NO_2 structure]
III — [NH_2 / NO_2 structure]

(a) I < II < III
(b) III < II < I
(c) I < III < II
(d) II < I < III.

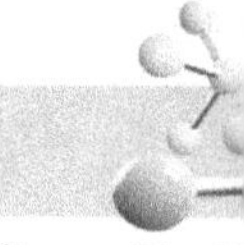

13. Arrange the following amines according to their decreasing K_b values.

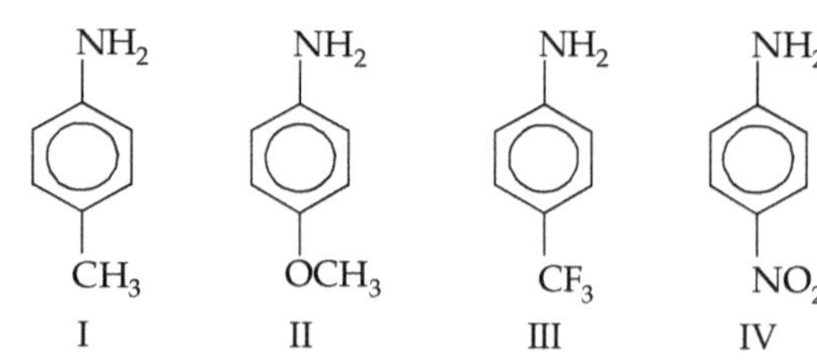

    I   II   III   IV

(a) I > II > III > IV
(b) IV > III > II > I
(c) II > I > III > IV
(d) II > I > IV > III.

14. Of the four orders given below for the basic character of the four compounds, which one is correct order ?

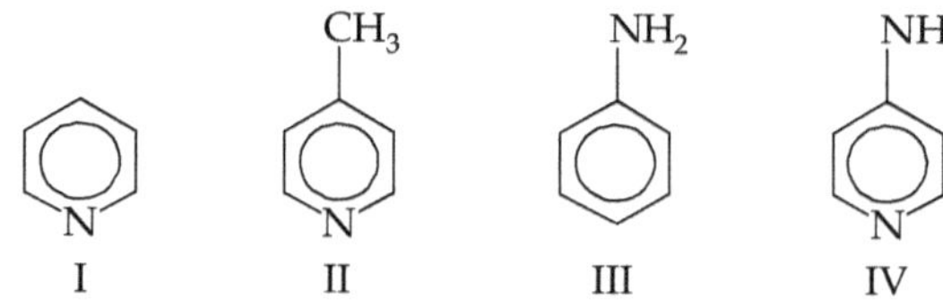

    I   II   III   IV

(a) IV > III > II > I
(b) IV > I > II > III
(c) IV > II > I > III
(d) I > II > IV > III.

15. The correct order for decreasing basic character of the four amines I to IV is

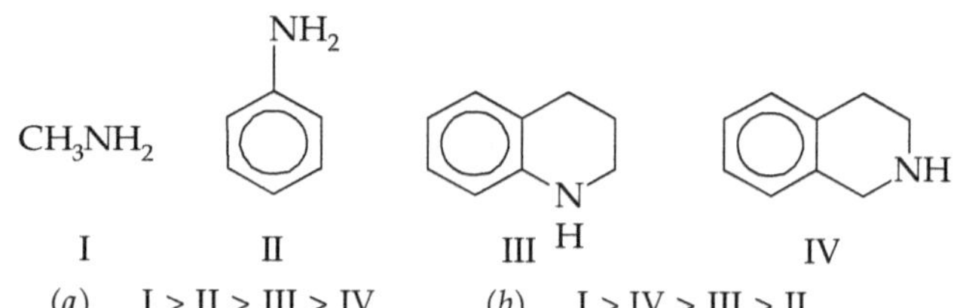

    I   II   III   IV

(a) I > II > III > IV   (b) I > IV > III > II
(c) I > II > IV > III   (d) IV > I > III > II.

16. Which of the following is most basic, and which one is least ?

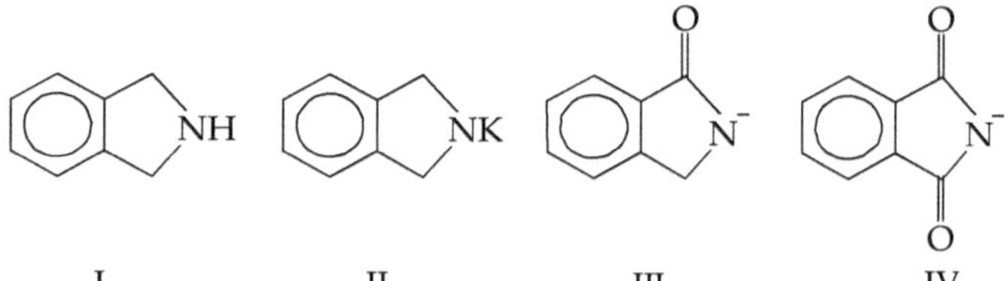

    I   II   III   IV
(a) II and IV respectively (b) II and I respectively
(c) I and II respectively (d) IV and I respectively.

17. When a 2°aromatic amine hydrochloride is heated, it leads to the formation of 1° amine hydrochloride, the reaction is known as
(a) Hofmann degradation
(b) Fries migration
(c) Hofmann Martius rearrangement
(d) None of the three.

18. Fluorobenzene can be prepared from aniline *via* diazotisation, the reaction is known as
(a) Sandmeyer reaction   (b) Gattermann reaction
(c) Schiemann reaction   (d) Modified Sandmeyer reaction

19. Benzenediazonium chloride on reaction with phenol in weakly basic medium gives
(a) diphenyl ether   (b) *p*-hydroxyazobenzene
(c) chlorobenzene   (d) benzene.

20. A positive carbylamine test is given by
(a) N, N-dimethylaniline
(b) 2,4-dimethylaniline
(c) N-methyl-*o*-methylaniline
(d) *p*-methylbenzyl amine

21. Which of the following statement is not correct regarding aniline?
(a) It is less basic than ethylamine
(b) It can be steam distilled
(c) It reacts with sodium to give hydrogen
(d) It is soluble in water

22. Benzenediazonium chloride on reaction with phenol in weakly basic medium gives
(a) diphenyl ether   (b) *p*-hydroxyazobenzene
(c) chlorobenzene   (d) benzene

23. The correct stability order of the following resonance structures is

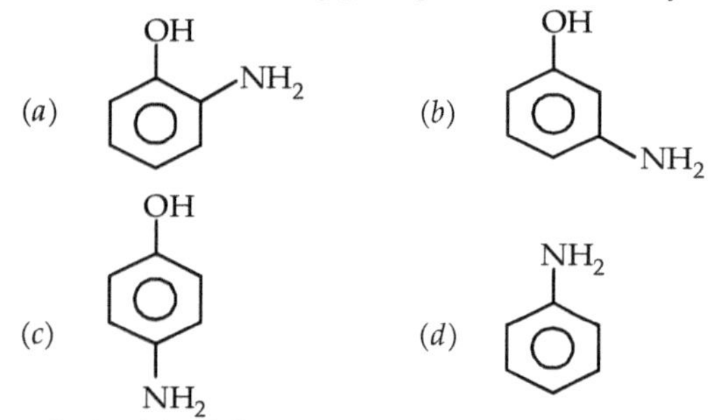

(a) I > II > IV > III   (b) I > III > II > IV
(c) II > I > III > IV   (d) III > I > IV > II

24. Which of the following gives paracetamol on acylation?

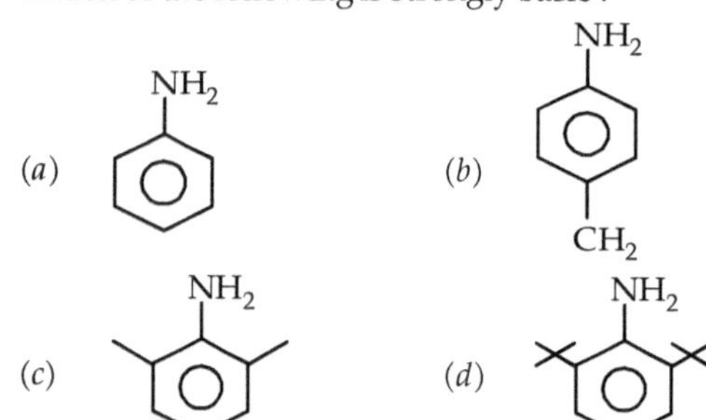

25. Which of the following is strongly basic :

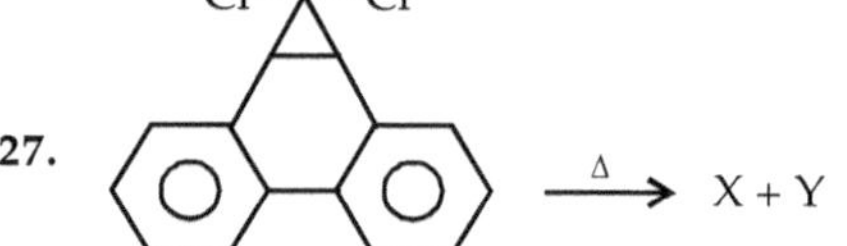

26. Which of the following statements is not correct?
(a) Aliphatic amines are stronger bases than ammonia
(b) Aromatic amines are stronger bases than ammonia
(c) The alkyl group in alkyl ammonium ion stabilizes the ion more relative to the amine
(d) The aryl group in aryl ammonium ion stabilizes the ion less relative to the amine

27.

Regarding X and Y which of the following statement is/are correct?
I. Both X and Y are aromatic
II. One of them is anti-aromatic
III. All the carbon in X and Y are sp^2 hybridized
IV. One of the above species can give addition reaction with

pyrrole and can produce   as a major product.

(a) I, III   (b) I, III, IV
(c) III, IV   (d) II, IV

28. Benzenediazonium chloride forms coloured compound when treated with :
(a) Phenol   (b) Cresol
(c) Resorcinol   (d) All of the above

29. Which of the following statements is correct?
(a) Reaction of stereoisomeric alcohol with $SOCl_2$ in presence of pyridine gives the product with retention of configuration
(b) Solvolysis of secondary substrate is found to depend upon only the nucleophilic power of solvent not upon the ionization power of solvent.
(c) p-Aminobenzoic acid exists as Zwitterion in aqueous solvent
(d) Coupling of diazonium salt with phenol is carried out in mildly alkaline solution and with amines in mildly acidic solution

30. Which of the following substances represent a colourless substance?

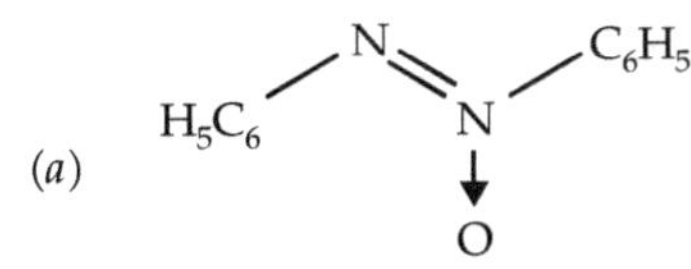

(a)

(b)

(c)

(d) None of the above

31. Pyrrole and pyridine both are basic and form salts with acids?

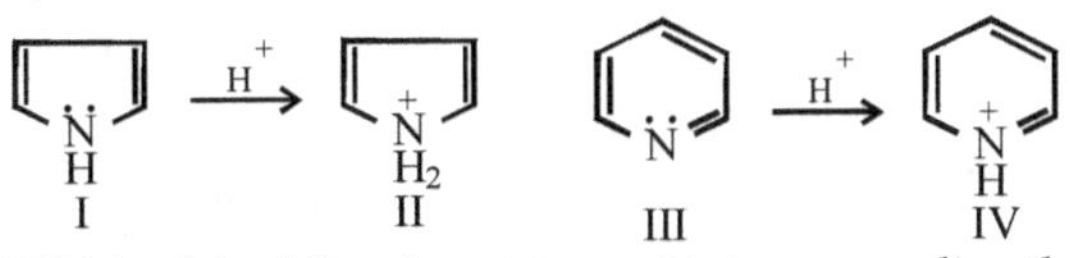

Which of the following statement is true regarding the aromatic character of the four species?
(a) All the four are aromatic
(b) I, III and IV are aromatic
(c) I, II and III are aromatic
(d) I and III are aromatic

32. Electrophilic aromatic substitution of pyridine resembles with
(a) benzene　　(b) aniline
(c) nitrobenzene　　(d) none of these

33. For the diazonium ions, the order of reactivity towards diazo-coupling with phenol in the presence of dil.NaOH is

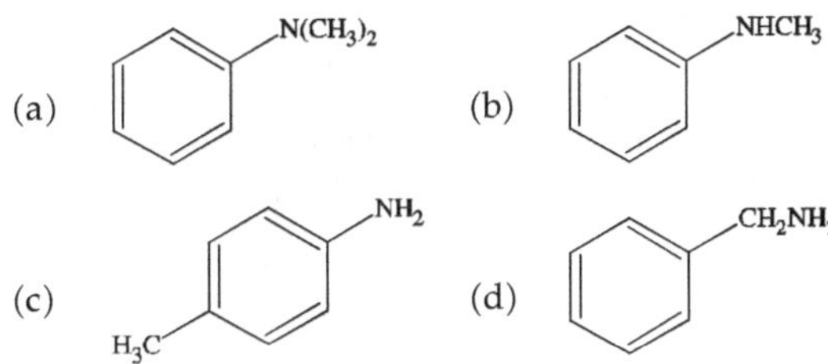

(a) I < IV < II < III　　(b) IV < II < I < III
(c) I < II < IV < III　　(d) III < IV < II < I

34. When aniline is treated with acetyl chloride in presence of anhydrous aluminium chloride, the main product is
(a) o - aminoacetophenone　(b) p-aminoacetophenone
(c) both (a) and (b)　　(d) m-aminoacetophenone

35. Benzenediazonium chloride when treated with phenols gives azo dyes, to get best result the pH of the medium should be
(a) around 4　　(b) around 8
(c) around 10　　(d) 12

36. Amongst the compounds given, the one that would form a brilliant colored dye on treatment with $NaNO_2$ in dil. HCl followed by addition to an alkaline solution of β-naphthol is

(a) $N(CH_3)_2$ 　　(b) $NHCH_3$

(c) NH_2 　　(d) CH_2NH_2

EXERCISE 20.2 (MCQ 1 or >1 option correct, Passage based, Matching, A/R)

DIRECTIONS for Q. 1 to Q. 15 : Multiple choice questions with one or more than one correct option(s).

1. Which of the following reaction can be used for preparing aniline?
(a) $C_6H_5COOH \xrightarrow{N_3H,\ conc.\ H_2SO_4}$
(b) $C_6H_5NC \xrightarrow{H_3O^+}$
(c) $C_6H_5NC \xrightarrow{LiAlH_4}$
(d) $C_6H_5CONH_2 \xrightarrow{Br_2/NaOH}$

2. Examine the following two structures for the anilinium ion, predict which of the following statement is FALSE regarding the two canonical structures for anilinium ion?

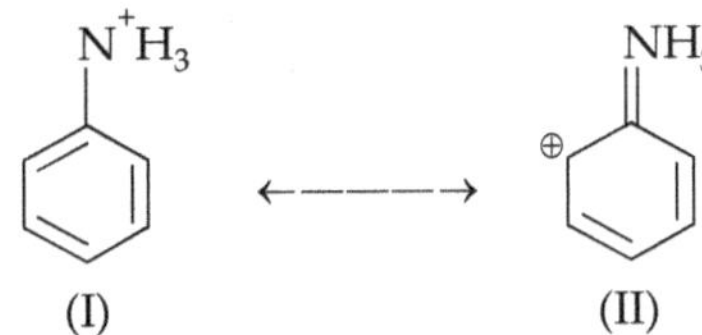

(a) II is not an acceptable canonical structure because carbocations are less stable than ammonium ions.
(b) II is not acceptable canonical structure because nitrogen has 10 valence electrons.
(c) II is not acceptable canonical structure because it is non-aromatic.
(d) II is acceptable structure.

3. Which of the following can exist as inner salt ?
(a) p-Aminobenzenesulphonic acid
(b) p-Aminobenzoic acid
(c) Aminoacetic acid
(d) Alanine

4. Which of the following pairs show coupling reaction ?

(a)

(b)

(c)

(d) Diazotised sulphanilic acid + Dimethylaniline

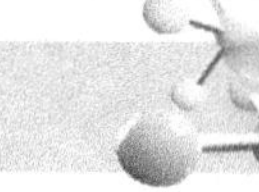

5. Which of the following statement is false regarding following reaction ?

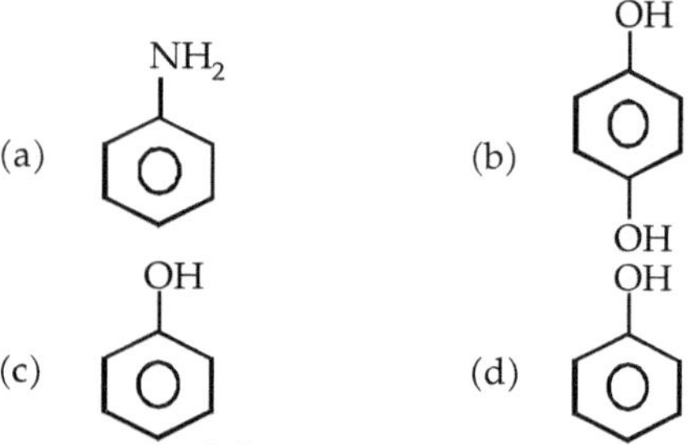

$+ NH_3 \quad \xrightarrow[\text{pressure}]{\text{heat}}$

(a) No reaction is possible because —Cl is present on benzene ring.

(b) A nucleophilic substitution will take place in which both —Cl will be replaced by two —NH_2 groups.

(c) A nucleophilic substitution will take place in which only —Cl attached on C_1 will be replaced by —NH_2.

(d) A nucleophilic substitution will take place in which only —Cl attached on C_4 will be replaced by —NH_2.

6. Libermann's nitroso reaction is used for testing
(a) 1° amine   (b) 2° amine
(c) phenol   (d) 3° amine.

7. Which of the following statement is true regarding reaction of *p*-aminophenol with arenediazonium chloride?

$$HO-\underset{5\quad 6}{\overset{3\quad 2}{\bigcirc}}-NH_2 + ArN_2^+\,Cl^- \longrightarrow$$

(a) Reaction takes place at position 2 in presence of HCl.
(b) Reaction takes place at position 3 in presence of NaOH.
(c) No reaction occurs.
(d) Four azo groups can be introduced in the molecule.

8. *p*-Chloraniline and aniline hydrochloride can't be distinguished by
(a) Sandmeyer reaction   (b) $NaHCO_3$
(c) $AgNO_3$ (d) Carbylamine test.

9. Oxidation of A gives p-benzoquinone. A can be :

(a) [structure: aniline, NH_2]
(b) [structure: hydroquinone, OH and OH]
(c) [structure: phenol, OH]
(d) [structure: catechol, OH and OH]

10. Among the following statements on the nitration of aromatic compounds, the correct ones are
(a) the rate of nitration of benzene is almost the same as that of hexadeutrobenzene.
(b) the rate of nitration of toluene is greater than that of benzene.
(c) the rate of nitration of benzene is greater than that of hexadeutrobenzene
(d) nitration is an electrophilic substitution reaction.

11. When nitrobenzene is treated with Br_2 in presence of $FeBr_3$, the major product formed is *m*-bromonitrobenzene. Statements which are related to obtain the *m*-isomer are
(a) The electron density on meta carbon is more than that on ortho and para positions
(b) The intermediate carbonium ion formed after initial attack of Br^+ at the meta position is least destabilised
(c) Loss of aromaticity when Br^+ attacks at the ortho and para positions and not at meta position
(d) Easier loss of H^+ to regain aromaticity from the meta position than from ortho and para positions.

12. $\bigcirc-\overset{x}{\ddot{N}}=\overset{y}{\ddot{N}}-\bigcirc-\overset{z}{\ddot{N}}H_2$ .....(P)

The correct statements about the compound (P) is/are :
(a) Nitrogen (x) is most basic in nautre
(b) The lone pair of electrons of nitrogen (z) is delocalized in the aromatic ring
(c) All the nitrogen atoms x, y and z are sp^2 hybridized
(d) The compound 'P' has stereoisomers

13. The correct orders are :

(a) [structures: o-toluic acid > benzoic acid] ......acid strength

(b) [structures: o-toluic acid > benzoic acid] ..... rate of decarboxylation by soda lime

(c) [structures: o-ethylaniline > aniline] ..... basic strength

(d) [structures: N,N-dimethyl-o-xylidine > 2-amino-1,3-dimethylbenzene] > .... basic strength

14. The feasible reactions are :

(a) [structure reaction with $NaBH_4$ giving CH_2NH_2]

(b) [phenol with O_2N, NO_2, NO_2 + $NaHCO_3$ → O_2N, NO_2, NO_2 with ONa $+CO_2\uparrow+H_2O$]

(c) [7-azaindole + HCl → protonated product $Cl^\ominus$]

(d) $\underset{\overset{|}{CH_3}}{\overset{\overset{\displaystyle CH_3}{|}}{CH_3-C-Br}} \xrightarrow{\text{Na/ether}} \underset{}{\overset{\overset{\displaystyle CH_3}{|}}{CH_3-C}}=CH_2+ \underset{\overset{|}{CH_3}}{\overset{\overset{\displaystyle CH_3}{|}}{CH_3-C-H}}$

15. In which reaction, major product formed is correct

(a) [structure with NH_2 and $Br_2/NaOH$ → NH_2 product $+CHBr_3+CO_2$, with $COO^\ominus$]

(b) [phenol with $CHBr_3+NaOH$ → salicylaldehyde with OH, CHO]

(c) [cyclopentane with CH_3, CH_2-NH_2, OH + HNO_2 → cyclohexanone with CH_3]

(d) $R-\underset{\overset{\|}{O}}{C}-NH_2 \xrightarrow{HNO_2} R-\underset{\overset{\|}{O}}{C}-OH$

PASSAGE 1

2-Chloropyridine when treated with sodium methoxide gives 2-methoxypyridine. The intermediate is stabilized by delocalization of the negative charge; since this type of stabilization is not possible if attack occurs at the 3-position, hence 3-chloropyridine is not converted into 3-methoxypyridine.

16. Which of the three resonating structures is especially stable?
   (a)   I   (b)   II
   (c)   III   (d)   none

17. The unstability of the corresponding intermediate from 3-chloropyridine is because of the fact that
   (a)   the intermediate has lesser number of canonical structures
   (b)   none of the canonical structure has negative charge on N
   (c)   both of the above reasons
   (d)   none of the two

18. What would happen if 2-chloropyridine is replaced by 4-chloropyridine?
   (a)   2-Methylpyridine will be formed
   (b)   3-Methoxypyridine will be formed
   (c)   4-Methoxypyridine will be formed
   (d)   No reaction

PASSAGE 2

Primary aromatic amines react with nitrous acid to yield arenediazonium salts.

$$\underset{\substack{1^\circ \text{ aromatic} \\ \text{aniline}}}{ArNH_2} + NaNO_2 + 2HX \xrightarrow{\text{cold}} \underset{\substack{\text{Arenediazonium} \\ \text{salt}}}{Ar-N \equiv N^+X^-} + NaX + 2H_2O$$

Although arenediazonium salts are far more stable than aliphatic diazonium salts, especially at low temperature (0 - 5°), they slowly decompose even at low temperature, hence always used immediately after preparation.

Secondary amines, both aliphatic and aromatic, react with nitrous to form N-nitrosoamines which show Libermann's nitroso reaction

$$\underset{\text{N-Methylaniline}}{C_6H_5NHCH_3} + NaNO_2 + HCl \longrightarrow C_6H_5N(NO)CH_3$$

Aryldiazonium ions are substantially more stable than alkyldiazonium ions, and are of enormous synthetic value. The important synthetic reactions of diazonium salts may be divided into two classes. (a) replacement reaction, in which nitrogen is lost as N_2 and its place is taken by some other atom or group, and (b) coupling reactions, in which the nitrogen is retained in the product.

19. Arenediazonium ions are more stable than alkyldiazonium ions because
   (a)   resonance stabilization of the corresponding cation
   (b)   the arene cation, Ar^+ is very difficult to be formecd
   (c)   both the above factors
   (d)   none of the two

20. $$C_6H_5NH_2 \longrightarrow C_6H_5N_2X^- \xrightarrow{H_2O} C_6H_5OH + N_2 + H^+$$
In the preparation of the above diazonium salt, use of H_2SO_4 is preferred to HCl because
   (a)   sulphuric acid is a stronger acid
   (b) HSO_4^- is less nucleophilic than Cl^-
   (c)   sulphuric acid absorbs water
   (d)   None of the three

21. Coupling reaction is not in feasible in
   (d)   All are feasible

22. Which of the following statement is false?
   (a)   Coupling between arenediazonium cation and amines take place in strongly acidic conditions
   (b)   Coupling between arenediazonium cation and phenols takes place in slightly alkaline medium
   (c)   Both are correct
   (d)   Neither is correct

23. In strongly alkaline medium, the arenediazonium cation exists in the following equilibrium

$$\underset{I}{Ar-N=N^+\ OH^-} \underset{H^+}{\overset{NaOH}{\rightleftharpoons}} \underset{II}{Ar-N=N-OH} \underset{H^+}{\overset{NaOH}{\rightleftharpoons}} \underset{III}{Ar-N=N-O^-Na^+}$$

Which of the above can undergo coupling reaction?
   (a)   I   (b)   II
   (c)   III   (d)   II and III

PASSAGE 3

p-Amino-N, N-dimethylaniline is added to a strongly acidic solution of **X**. The resulting solution is treated with a few drops of aqueous solution of **Y** to yield blue coloration due to the formation of methylene blue. Treatment of the aqueous solution of **Y** with the reagent potassium hexacyanoferrate(II) leads to the formation of an intense blue precipitate. The precipitate dissolves on excess addition of the reagent. Similarly, treatment of the solution of **Y** with the solution of potassium hexacyanoferrate (III) leads to a brown coloration due to the formation of **Z**.

24. The compound **X** is
   (a) $NaNO_3$ (b)   NaCl
   (c) Na_2SO_4 (d) Na_2S

25. The compound **Y** is
   (a) $MgCl_2$ (b) $FeCl_2$
   (c) $FeCl_3$ (d) $ZnCl_2$

26. The compound **Z** is
   (a) $Mg_2[Fe(CN)_6]$ (b) $Fe[Fe(CN)_6]$
   (c) $Fe_4[Fe(CN)_6]_3$ (d) $K_2Zn_3[Fe(CN)_6]_2$

Instructions for Q. 27 to 29 : Following questions are Multiple Matching type Questions :

27. *Column - I*
    Basic compound

    Column - II
    pK$_a$ of ammonium ions

(A) $\langle$Ph$\rangle$—NH$_2$ (a)   0.4

(B) NH$_3$ (b)   4.63

(C) (pyrrolidine) NH   (c)   5.25

(D) (pyrrole) NH   (d)   9.26

(E) (pyridine) N   (e)   11.27

28. *Column - I*
(A) Aldehyde + Zn(Hg) + conc. HCl

Column - II
(a) distinguish between primary and other amines

(B) Carbylamine reaction   (b) White precipitate

(C) Schiff bases   (c) Hydrocarbon

(D) 2, 4, 6-tri bromo-aniline   (d) Antioxidation

29. *Column - I*   *Column - II*

(A) p-Cl-C$_6$H$_4$-COOH + HN$_3$ $\xrightarrow{\text{Conc. H}_2\text{SO}_4}$ p-Cl-C$_6$H$_4$-NH$_2$ (a) pH 5 - 7

(B) C$_6$H$_5$—NH$_2$ + C$_6$H$_5$N$_2^+$ $\longrightarrow$ Azo dye.   (b) Curtius reaction

(C) C$_6$H$_5$—OH + C$_6$H$_5$N$_2^+$ $\longrightarrow$ Azo dye.   (c) Sulphanilic acid

(D) Methyl orange   (d) pH 9 - 10

Instructions for Q. 30 to 42 : Following questions are Assertion and Reasoning Type Questions :

Note : Each question contains STATEMENT-1 (Assertion) and STATEMENT-2 (Reason). Each question has 5 choices (a), (b), (c), (d) and (e) out of which ONLY ONE is correct.

(a) Statement-1 is True, Statement-2 is True; Statement-2 is a correct explanation for Statement-1.

(b) Statement-1 is True, Statement-2 is True; Statement-2 is NOT a correct explanation for Statement-1.

(c) Statement -1 is True, Statement-2 is False.

(d) Statement -1 is False, Statement-2 is True.

(e) Statement -1 is False, Statement-2 is False.

30. **Statement-1 :** Benzene diazonium chloride does not give tests for nitrogen.
Statement-2 : Loss of N$_2$ gas takes place during heating.

31. **Statement-1 :** Anilinium chloride is more acidic than ammonium chloride.
Statement-2 : Anilinium ion is resonance-stabilized.

32. **Statement-1 :** p-O$_2$N—C$_2$H$_5$COCH$_3$ is prepared by Friedel Craft's acylation of nitrobenzene.
Statement-2 : Nitrobenzene easily undergoes electrophilic substitution reaction.

33. **STATEMENT - 1 :** Aniline on reaction with NaNO$_2$ / HCl at 0°C followed by coupling with β-naphthol gives a dark blue precipitate.
STATEMENT - 2 : The colour of the compound formed in the reaction of aniline with NaNO$_2$/HCl at 0°C followed by coupling with β-naphthol is due to the extended conjugation.

34. **Statement 1 :** pK$_b$ for aniline is more than that of methylamine.
Statement 2 : Higher pK$_b$ means less basic.

35. **Statement 1 :** Amino group is o- and p-directing in aromatic electrophilic substitution reactions, aniline on nitration gives a substantial amount of m-nitroaniline.
Statement 2 : Direct nitration of aniline gives a substantial amount of p-nitroaniline

36. **Statement 1 :** Diazonium salts of aromatic amines are more stable than those of aliphatic amines.
Statement 2 : Diazonium ion shows resonance.

37. **Statement 1 :** Ethylamine is soluble in water, whereas aniline is not.
Statement 2 : Ethylamine forms hydrogen bonds with water molecules.

38. **Statement 1 :** Aniline undergo Friedel-Crafts reaction.
Statement 2 : Aniline forms salt with aluminium chloride (a lewis acid) which is used as a catalyst.

39. **Statement 1 :** Gabriel phthalimide synthesis is preferred for synthesising aliphatic primary amines.
Statement 2 : Aryl halides undergo nucleophilic substitution with the anion formed by phthalimide.

40. **Statement 1 :** Toluene undergoes diazo coupling with Ph $\overset{\oplus}{\text{N}_2}$
and O$_2$N—C$_6$H$_3$(NO$_2$)—$\overset{\oplus}{\text{N}}$≡N.

Statement 2 : Ar$\overset{\oplus}{\text{N}_2}$ is a weak electrophile and undergoes diazo coupling only with highly activated ring.

41. **Statement 1 :** In strongly acidic medium aniline becomes less reactive towards electrophilic reagent.
Statement 2 : NH$_2$ group is ortho and para directing.

42. **Statement - 1 :** In strongly acidic solutions, aniline becomes more reactive towards electrophilic reagents.
Statement-2 : The amino group being completely protonated in strongly acidic solution, the lone pair of electrons on the nitrogen is no longer available for resonance.

Instructions for Q. 43 to 45 : Following questions are Integer Type Questions :

43. 1,4-dinitrobenzene $\xrightarrow{\text{NH}_4\text{SH}}$ $\xrightarrow[\text{excess}]{\text{Br}_2/\text{H}_2\text{O}}$ $\xrightarrow[\text{HCl}]{\text{NaNO}_2}$ $\xrightarrow{\text{CuBr–HBr}}$ $\xrightarrow{\text{Sn/HCl}}$ $\xrightarrow{\text{Br}_2/\text{H}_2\text{O}}$ major end product.

Find the total number of halogen atoms present in the major end product.

44. Ph – NH$_2$ $\xrightarrow[\text{0–5°C}]{\text{NaNO}_2/\text{HCl}}$ Ph–NH$_2$ $\xrightarrow{\text{dil. HCl}}$ (X)

Find the sum of number of nitrogen atoms present in (X) and the total number of stereoisomers of (X) formed.

45. Ph(H)C=N–OH $\xrightarrow{\text{H}^{(+)}/\text{H}_2\text{O}/\Delta}$ A $\xrightarrow{\text{dil. H}_2\text{SO}_4}$ B+C

$\downarrow$ H$_2$O

E $\xleftarrow[\text{2. Cu / HBr}]{\text{1. NaNO}_2/\text{H}^+}$ D $\xleftarrow{\text{Br}_2}$ B is insoluble layer

E has how many halogens ?

EXERCISE 20.3 (Subjective Problems)

1. Write down structures of the following compounds.
(a) *p*-Toluidine
(b) Anilinium chloride
(c) N, N-Diethylaniline
(d) 2, 4-Dimethylaniline
(e) Benzylamine
(f) Diphenylamine
(g) *p, p'*-Diaminodiphenyl
(h) N-*n*-Propylaniline.

2. Compare the behaviour of aniline, N-methylaniline and N, N-dimethylaniline toward each of the following reagents.
(a) Dil. HCl
(b) excess of CH_3I
(c) C_6H_5COCl + pyridine
(d) $C_6H_5SO_2Cl$ + *aq.* KOH
(e) Bromine water.

3. Give structures and names of the principal organic products expected from the action of sodium nitrite and hydrochloric acid on each of the following compound.
(a) *o*-Toluidine
(b) N-Methylaniline
(c) N, N-Dimethylaniline
(d) 4, 4'-Diaminodiphenyl
(e) Benzylamine
(f) Sulphanilic acid.

4. Write balanced equations for the following reactions.
(a) Benzanilide + *aq.* NaOH (boiling)
(b) Methyl formate + aniline

(c) *m*-Nitro–N–methylaniline + HONO
(d) *m*-Toluidine + aq. Br_2 (excess)
(e) *p*-Toluidine + aq. Br_2 (excess)
(f) $p\text{-}CH_3C_6H_4NHCOCH_3$ + HNO_3 + H_2SO_4
(g) Benzanilide + Br_2 + Fe.

5. Complete the following.

(a) $C_6H_5COOH \xrightarrow{PCl_5} [A] \xrightarrow{NH_3} [B] \xrightarrow{P_2O_5} [C] \xrightarrow{H^+,\ heat} [D]$

(b) $C_6H_5NH_2 + [E] + [F] \longrightarrow C_6H_5NHCONHC_6H_5$

(c) 2, 4-Dinitroaniline $\xrightarrow[5°C]{NaNO_2,\ HCl} [G] \xrightarrow{anisole} [H]$

(d) Aniline $\xrightarrow{Br_2\ water} [I] \xrightarrow[(ii)\ C_2H_5OH]{(i)\ NaNO_2,\ HCl,\ 5°C} [J]$

(e) $CH_3CONHC_6H_5 \xrightarrow{Br_2,\ Fe} [K] + [L]$.

SOLUTIONS

EXERCISE 20.1

1	(b)	6	(d)	11	(c)	16	(a)	21	(d)	26	(b)	31	(b)	36	(b)
2	(a)	7	(c)	12	(a)	17	(c)	22	(b)	27	(c)	32	(c)		
3	(c)	8	(d)	13	(c)	18	(c)	23	(b)	28	(d)	33	(b)		
4	(c)	9	(b)	14	(c)	19	(b)	24	(c)	29	(d)	34	(d)		
5	(c)	10	(a)	15	(d)	20	(b)	25	(c)	30	(c)	35	(b)		

1. In the Zwitterion of sulphanilic acid, the $-SO_3^-$ is too weakly basic (its conjugate acid $-SO_3H$ is a strong acid) to accept H^+ from strong acids, hence it does not dissolve in HCl.

2. Arenediazonium cation is a weak electrophile, hence it can couple only with those compounds which bear powerful electron-releasing group like $-OH$, $-NH_2$, $-NHR$, or $-NR_2$. Hence toluene, having weak electron-releasing $-CH_3$ group can't couple with diazonium cation.

3. Coupling reaction between arenediazonium cation and an aromatic compound is an electrophilic substitution reaction in which, $C_6H_5N_2^+$, a weak electrophile reacts with the benzene compound having highly activating group. More is the activating (electron-releasing) character of the group, easier will be coupling. Hence
$$-O^- > -NH_2 > -OH > -NH_3^+.$$

4. Electorn-withdrawing groups (like $-NO_2$) make arenediazonium cation more electron-deficient, *i.e.*, strong electrophile, while electron-releasing group makes diazonium cation a weak electrophile.

5. $C_6H_5NO_2$ oxidizes CH_3 of $p\text{-}NH_2C_6H_4CH_3$ to CHO and itself reduced to $C_6H_5NH_2$.

6. $C_6H_5NH_2 \xrightarrow{CHCl_3,\ KOH} C_6H_5NC \xrightarrow{H_3O^+} C_6H_5NH_2 + HCOOH$

7.

Resorcinol has one *para* and two *ortho* positions free.

8. Aniline in presence of acids undergoes protonation to form $C_6H_5NH_3^+$ in which $-NH_3^+$ group is *m*-directing.

9. Iodine chloride is an electrophilic reagent and because of high electronegativity of Cl it gives rise to I^+ and Cl^-. Hence

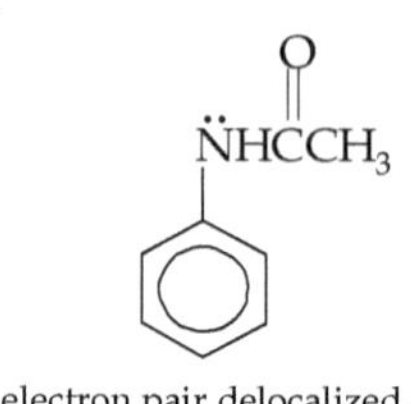

10. Lower the pK_b value of an amine, more is its basic character.

(a) $CH_2\ddot{N}H_2$ (benzyl)
Electron pair localized, hence most basic

(b) $\ddot{N}H_2$ (aniline)
Electron pair delocalized

(c) $\ddot{N}HCCH_3$ (acetanilide)
electron pair delocalized on ring as well as on —CO—gp.

(d) $\ddot{N}H_2$ ... NO_2
electron pair highly delocalized due to —NO_2 gp.

11. Presence of electron-withdrawing gp. (—$COCH_3$) in *o*, *p*-position decreases basicity while that of electron-releasing gp. (—CH_3) increases basic character of the aromatic amine. Acetanilide is weaker than aniline because here electron pair on N is also delocalized to the —CO— part in addition to benzene ring. The same is also true to p-$CH_3CO.C_6H_4.NH_2$.

12. The basic character and hence K_b values of the three anilines follows the order

I   >   II (NO_2)   >   III (NO_2)

I
e pair is delocalized only to ring

II
e pair is delocalized only to ring, but —I effect of —NO_2 also decreases basicity

III
e pair is delocalized to ring as well as to —NO_2 gp. ; —I effect of —NO_2 further decreases basicity

Since higher the K_b value of an amine, lower is pK_b value ; thus the pK_b values of the three anilines will be of the order : I < II < III.

13. II (OCH_3) > I (CH_3) > III (CF_3) > IV (NO_2)

II
—OCH_3 increases basic character due to + M effect of the —OCH_3 gp.

I
—CH_3 increases basic character due to + I effect of the —CH_3 gp.

III
—CF_3 decreases basic character due to —I effect of the —CF_3 gp.

IV
–NO_2 decreases basic character due to —M and —I effects of the —NO_2 gp.

14. IV > II > I > III

IV
e pair on N of the ring not involved in sextet ; also e pair on —NH_2 delocalized to N of the ring

II
e pair of N of the ring not involved in sextet; +I effect of —CH_3 further increases e density

I
e pair on N is not involved in sextet

III
e pair on N is delocalized to ring

15. IV > I > III > II

IV
2° Amine, e pair localized

I
1° Amine, e pair localized

III
2° Amine, e pair delocalized

II
1° Amine, e pair delocalized

16. II has maximum electrons density on N and it is localized ; in IV electrons are delocalized due to two —C = O groups.

17. $N(CH_3)_2HCl$ $\xrightarrow{\text{heat}}$ $NHCH_3HCl$ (CH_3) $\xrightarrow{\text{heat}}$ $NH_3.HCl$ (CH_3, CH_3)

The above reaction is an example of Hofmann Martius rearrangement.

18. Theoretical question.

19.

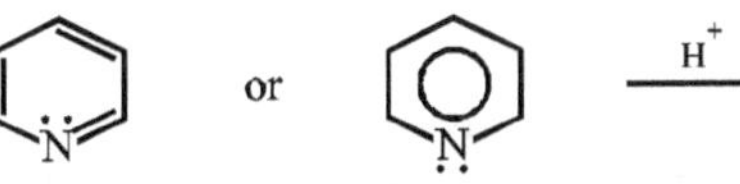

25. The conjugate acid of (d) exhibits steric inhibition of resonance.

26. Aromatic amines are less basic than ammonia.

27.

$\ddot{C}Cl_2$ (Singlet carbon)

28. All have electron donating group attached to the ring which makes dye formation favourable.

31.

I (Sextet present, hence aromatic)
(*e* pair on N forms a part of aromatic sextet)

II (not aromatic)
(Aromatic sextet is not present because *e* pair is involved in protonation)

III (sextet present, hence aromatic)
(*e* pair on N, not a part of sextet)

IV (sextet present, hence aromatic)

32. Pyridine resembles a strongly deactivated benzene, here the deactivation is due to electron-withdrawing effect of the electrongative N atom from 2-and 4 - positions making 3-positions to be more vulnerable for the attack of an electrophile. Remember that the nonbonding electrons on N are perpendicular to the π-system (they are present in sp^2 orbital), these are not involved in delocalisation, i.e., they can't stabilize the positively charged intermediate.

33. Presence of electron withdrawing group in arene diazonium ions enhances the electrophilic character of the ion and thus increases coupling.

34. In presence of $AlCl_3$ (a Lewis acid), aniline is converted into anilinium cation, which being *m*-directing gives *m*-aminoacetophenone.

35.(a)
(i) Couplings of arenediazonium cations and phenols take place most rapidly in slightly alkaline medium because acidic medium (pH < 7) will suppress the ionisation of C_6H_5OH to the more reactive $C_6H_5O^-$, while the alkaline medium (pH > 7) will enhance ionisation of phenol to phenoxide ion.

(ii) strongly alkaline medium (pH > 10) causes the arenediazonium salt to react with the OH^- ion to form a relatively unreactive diazohydroxide or diazoate ion.

$$ArN^+\equiv\ddot{N} \xrightarrow{OH^-} Ar-\ddot{N}=\ddot{N}-\ddot{O}H \xrightarrow{OH^-} Ar-\ddot{N}=\ddot{N}-\ddot{O}\colon^-$$

Diazohydroxide   Diazoate ion

36. (c) Only primary aromatic amines undergo diazotisation followed by coupling.

EXERCISE 20.2

	1	(a,b,d)	2	(a,c,d)	3	(a,c,d)	4	(b,c,d)	5	(a,b,d)	6	(b,c)
>1 CORRECT OPTION	7	(a,b,d)	8	(a,b,d)	9	(a, b, c)	10	(a,b,d)	11	(a, d)	12	(a, b, c, d)
	13	(a, d)	14	(b,d)	15	(a, b, c, d)						
PASSAGE 1	16	(a)	17	(b)	18	(c)						
PASSAGE 2	19	(c)	20	(b)	21	(b)	22	(a)	23	(d)		
PASSAGE 3	24	(d)	25	(c)	26	(b)						
MATCH THE FOLLOWING	27	(A) - b ; (B) - d ; (C) - e ; (D) - a ; (E) - C										
	28	(A) – (c); (B) – (a); (C) – (d); (D) – (b)										
	29	(A) - (b), (B) - (a), (C) - (d), (D) - (c)										
A/R	30	(a)	31	(b)	32	(d)	33	(d)	34	(a)	35	(c)
	36	(a)	37	(a)	38	(d)	39	(c)	40	(d)	41	(b)
	42	(d)										
INTEGER	43	5	44	5	45	4						

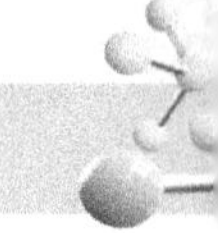

1. Isonitriles (C_6H_5NC) on reduction give 2° amines ($C_6H_5NHCH_3$). All other three methods give aniline.

2. Nitrogen (N) has no d orbital, hence it can't have more than 8 electorns in the outermost shell. All other three options are false.

3. In p-$NH_2C_6H_4COOH$, —COOH group is very weak so it can't transfer H^+ to the weakly basic amino group. All other three form zwitterions.

4. In $C_6H_5OCH_3$, —OCH_3 does not sufficiently increase electron density on the ring. Recall that C_6H_5OH undergoes coupling in weakly alkaline medium which converts C_6H_5OH to the more reactive $C_6H_5O^-$. In options (b) and (c), presence of electron-withdrawing —NO_2 groups increases electrophilic character to such an extent that these diazonium cations can couple even with the compounds having weak electron-releasing groups. Option (d) undergoes coupling reaction easily because –NMe_2 is sufficiently electron-releasing.

5. Recall that the —Cl group present in the o- and p- positions to the electron-withdrawing group is activated toward nucleophilic substitution, hence only —Cl present on the o- and/or p-position to the —NO_2 group will be replaced.

6. In Libermann's nitroso test 2° amine and phenol are used as reagents.

7. In p-aminophenol all the four positions (2, 3, 5 and 6) can be coupled (positions 2 and 6 in presence of H^+ and positions 3 and 5 in presence of OH^-).

8.

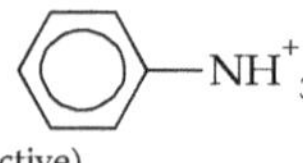

p-Chloroaniline
(—Cl is non-reactive)

(—Cl is present as reactive)

It reacts with $AgNO_3$. The three other options (a, b and d) are not proper reagents to distinguish.

12. (a,b,c,d)

x has maximum electron density hence it is most basic. Lone pair of z is delocalised. All nitrogen atoms x, y and z are sp^2 hybridised.
The compound has stereoisomerism along N = N.

13. (a, d) (a) ....K_a is correct.

(b) is incorrect

(c) is incorrect.

(d) ...... K_b is correct. Steric inhibition of resonance.

14. (b,d) (a) not feasible.
(b) is feasible.

(c) not feasible

more basic amidine type;
electron pair not a part of sextet

(d) is feasible by-product in Wurtz reaction.

40. (d) Statement-1 false, statement-2 true.

41. (b) In presence of acid, –NH_2 group forms –NH_3^+, i.e. anilinium ion and shows m-directing nature. Thus, ring is deactivated for electrophilic substitution reaction.

42. (d) Electron donating tendency to a double bond is called +M effect and the transfer of electrons take place towards the attacking reagent due to +E effect.
In strongly acidic conditions, aniline becomes protonated with the result lone pair of electrons is not available to produce +E and +M effects. Thus here aniline becomes less reactive towards electrophilic substitution. On the other hand, the $-\overset{\oplus}{N}H_3$ group exerts strong –I effect causing deactivation of the ring.

43. 5;

44. 5;

$$Ph - NH_2 \xrightarrow[0-5°C]{NaNO_2 / HCl} Ph - \overset{\oplus}{N_2} \overset{\ominus}{Cl}$$

No. of N-atoms in X is 3.
No. of stereoisomers = 2 (syn/anti).

45. 4;

$$Ph\text{-CH=N-OH} \xrightarrow[\text{rearrangement}]{Beckmann} Ph - NH - CHO \xrightarrow{Hydrolysis} PhNH_2 + HCOOH \text{ (B)}$$

EXERCISE 20.3

1.

(a) [structure: benzene ring with NH_2 at top and CH_3 at bottom — p-toluidine]

(b) [structure: benzene ring with $NH_3^+ Cl^-$]

(c) [structure: benzene ring with NMe_2]

(d) [structure: benzene ring with NH_2, CH_3 and CH_3]

(e) [structure: benzene ring with CH_2NH_2]

(f) $C_6H_5NHC_6H_5$

(g) H_2N-[biphenyl]$-NH_3$

(h) [structure: benzene ring with $NHC_3H_7\text{-}n$]

2.

(a) All the three produce soluble ammonium salts.

$C_6H_5NH_2.HCl$, $C_6H_5N^+H_2CH_3Cl^-$, and $C_6H_5N^+H(CH_3)_2Cl^-$

(b) All the three produce same quaternary ammonium salt, $C_6H_5N^+Me_3I^-$, of course by taking different amount of CH_3I.

(c) $C_6H_5NH_2 \xrightarrow[\text{Pyridine}]{C_6H_5COCl} C_6H_5\overset{H}{\underset{\cdot\cdot}{N}}-\overset{O}{\overset{||}{C}}-C_6H_5$ **Neutral** (due to delocalization of e on N to $-C=O$ group), insoluble in dil acid or base

$\overset{CH_3}{\underset{|}{C_6H_5NH}} \xrightarrow{C_6H_5COCl} C_6H_5\overset{CH_3}{\underset{\cdot\cdot}{N}}-\overset{O}{\overset{||}{C}}-C_6H_5$ **Neutral,** insoluble in acid or base

$\overset{CH_3}{\underset{|}{C_6H_5\underset{\cdot\cdot}{N}}}-CH_3 \longrightarrow$ No reaction. **Basic,** soluble in acid, insoluble in base

(d) $C_6H_5NH_2 \xrightarrow{C_6H_5SO_2Cl} \underset{\text{Acidic (Soluble in base)}}{C_6H_5NHSO_2C_6H_5} \xrightarrow[\text{KOH}]{\text{aq.}} \underset{\text{Soluble}}{C_6H_5N^-SO_2C_6H_5}$

$\overset{CH_3}{\underset{|}{C_6H_5NH}} \longrightarrow \underset{\underset{\text{(Insoluble in acid or base)}}{\textbf{Neutral}}}{\overset{CH_3}{\underset{|}{C_6H_5NSO_2C_6H_5}}} \xrightarrow[\text{KOH}]{\text{aq.}}$ No reaction *i.e.,* insoluble

$\overset{CH_3}{\underset{|}{C_6H_5N}}-CH_3 \longrightarrow$ No reaction ; **Basic** (insoluble in base, soluble in acid)

(e) All the three undergo very fast ring bromination to give corresponding tribromo products.

3.

(a) [structure: benzene ring with $N_2^+Cl^-$ and CH_3]

(b) [structure: benzene ring with $\overset{CH_3}{\underset{|}{N}}-N=O$]

(c) [structure: benzene ring with $N(CH_3)_2$]

(d) $^-Cl^+N_2-$[biphenyl]$-N_2^+Cl^-$

(e) [structure: benzene ring with CH_2OH]

(f) [structure: benzene ring with $N_2^+Cl^-$ at top and SO_3^- at bottom]

4.

(a) $C_6H_5NHCOC_6H_5 + NaOH \xrightarrow{\text{boil}} C_6H_5NH_2 + C_6H_5COO^-Na^+$

(b) $C_6H_5NH_2$ + $H_3CO\overset{\overset{O}{\|}}{-}C-H$ $\longrightarrow$ $C_6H_5NH-\overset{\overset{O}{\|}}{C}-H$ + CH_3OH

    Aniline   Methyl formate

(c) [NHCH₃ ring with NO₂] + HONO $\longrightarrow$ [N(NO)CH₃ ring with NO₂] + H_2O

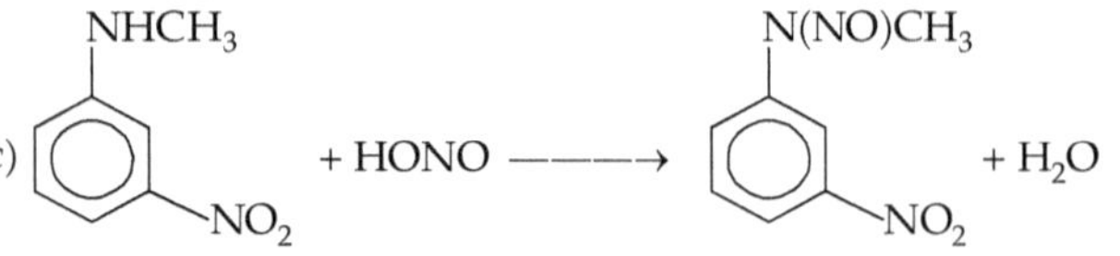

(d) [NH₂ ring with CH₃] + $3Br_2\,(aq.)$ $\longrightarrow$ [tribromo NH₂/CH₃ ring] + 3HBr

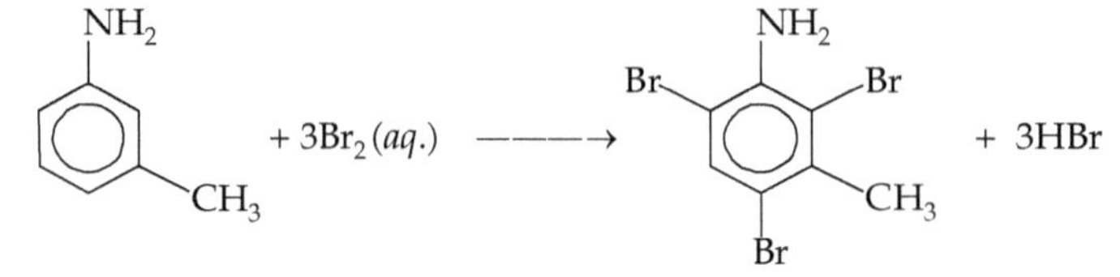

    (—NH_2 is more activating than —CH_3)

(e) [NH₂ ring with CH₃] + $2Br_2\,(aq.)$ $\longrightarrow$ [dibromo NH₂/CH₃ ring] + 2HBr

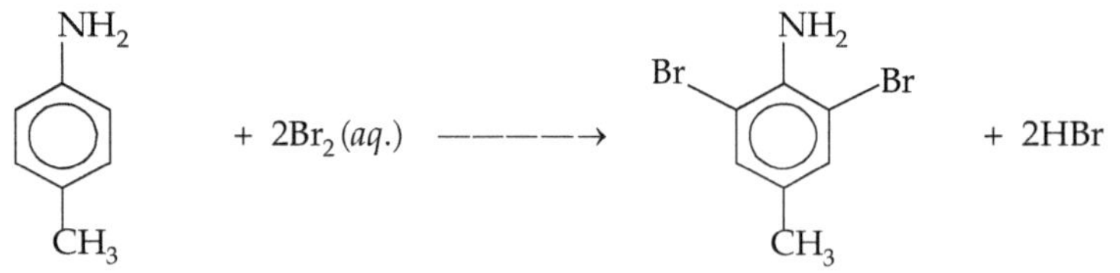

(f) [NHCOCH₃ ring with CH₃] $\xrightarrow[H_2SO_4]{Conc.\ HNO_3}$ [NHCOCH₃ ring with NO₂ and CH₃]

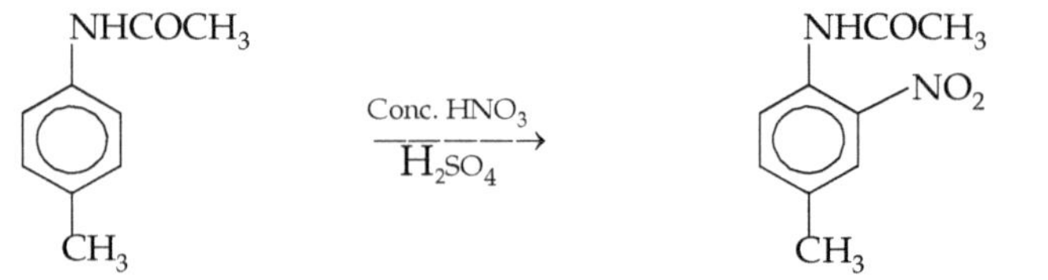

    (—$NHCOCH_3$ is more   (Second —NO_2 is not introduced
    electron-releasing than —CH_3)   because the ring is deactivated
                        due to —NO_2 group, already present)

(g) Activated ring / Deactivated ring — Benzanilide $\xrightarrow{Br_2/Fe}$ Br—[ring]—NH—CO—[ring] + *o*-Isomer

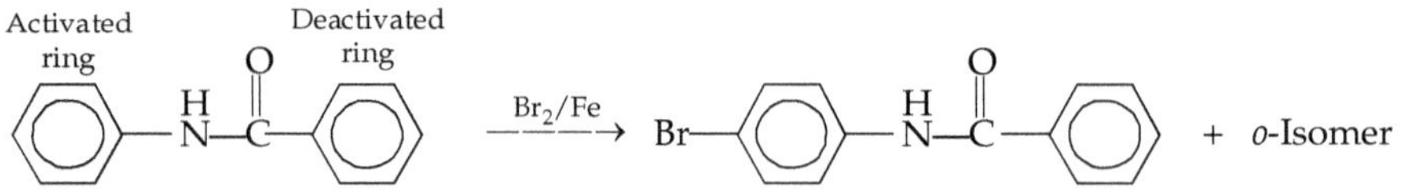

    Benzanilide
    (Ring having —NH—part is
    activated while other having
    —CO— is deactivated

5. (a) C_6H_5COCl $C_6H_5CONH_2$ C_6H_5CN C_6H_5COOH
       [A]   [B]   [C]   [D]

(b) $COCl_2 + C_6H_5NH_2$ (c) [diazonium chloride ring with NO₂, NO₂: G] and [azo ring —N=N—C₆H₄—OCH₃ with NO₂, NO₂: H]
    [E] and [F]

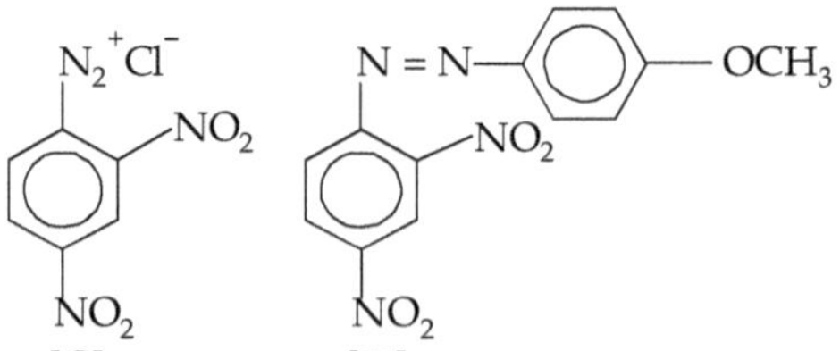

                                           [G]   [H]

(d) [tribromoaniline: I]   [tribromobenzene: J]   (e) [NHCOCH₃ ring with Br: K] + *p*-Isomer
     [I]   [J]   [K]   [L]

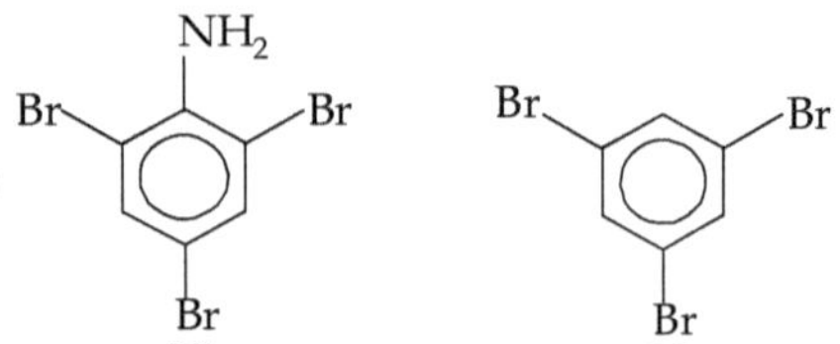

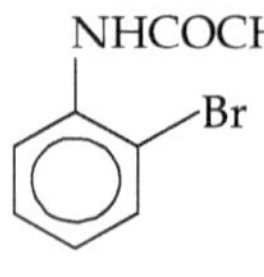

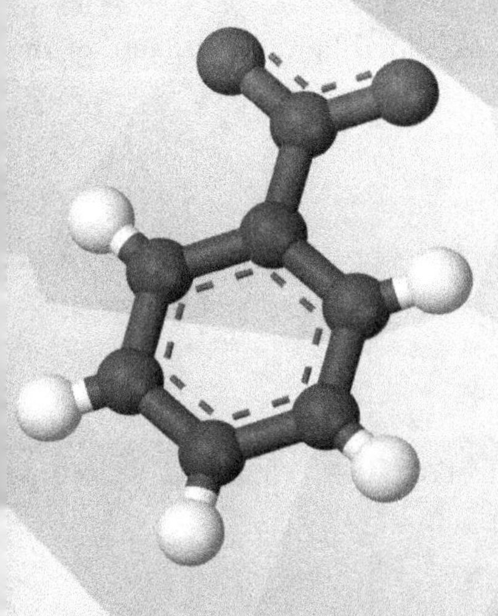

Other Nitrogen Containing Compounds

CHAPTER HIGHLIGHTS

21.1   Nitriles and Isonitriles

21.2   Alkyl Nitrites and Nitro Compounds

21.3   Aromatic Nitro Compounds

21.4   Illustrative Examples

EXERCISES

SOLUTIONS

 **Nitriles and Isonitriles**

A nitrile has the formula $R—C \equiv N:$ (or R—CN). The carbon and the nitrogen of a nitrile are *sp* hybridised. In IUPAC systematic nomenclature, acyclic nitriles are named by adding the suffix *nitrile* to the name of the corresponding hydrocarbon, the carbon atom of the $—C \equiv N$ group is assigned number 1.

$$\overset{2}{C}H_3 —\overset{1}{C} \equiv N: \qquad \overset{3}{C}H_2 = \overset{2}{C}H—\overset{1}{C} \equiv N: \qquad \overset{5}{C}H_2 = \overset{4}{C}H\overset{3}{C}H_2\overset{2}{C}H_2 —\overset{1}{C} \equiv N:$$

Ethanenitrile   Propenenitrile   4-Pentenenitrile
(acetonitrile)   (acrylonitrile)

Cyclic nitriles are named by adding the suffix *carbonitrile* to the name of the ring system to which the —CN group is attached.

Benzenecarbonitrile   Cyclohexanecarbonitrile
(benzonitrile)

Common name of nitriles (given in parentheses) are derived by replacing the *-ic acid* or *-oic acid* ending of the corresponding carboxylic acid by *-onitrile*. Alternatively, nitriles are sometimes given **radicofunctional names** as *alkyl cyanides*.

Isonitriles are functional isomers of nitriles ; the latter being more stable than the former.

$$R—\overset{\oplus}{N} \equiv \overset{\ominus}{C:} \xrightarrow{\text{heat}} R—C \equiv N$$

Isonitriles   Nitriles

These are commonly called by their common names, in which the prefix *iso* is added before the name of the isomeric nitrile. In IUPAC nomenclature, these are named as alkylcarbylamines.

$$CH_3—\overset{\oplus}{N}\equiv\overset{\ominus}{C} \qquad\qquad CH_3CH_2—\overset{\oplus}{N}\equiv\overset{\ominus}{C}$$

Methylcarbylamine   Ethylcarbylamine
Methyl isocyanide   Ethyl isocyanide
Methyl isonitrile   Ethyl isonitrile
Acetoisonitrile   Propionoisonitrile

TEST YOUR UNDERSTANDING - 21.1

1. Give IUPAC names for the following :

$$\underset{\text{(a)}}{} \quad CH_3\overset{\overset{\displaystyle CN}{|}}{C}HCH_3 \qquad\qquad (b)\ CH_3CH_2NC \qquad\qquad (c)\ \text{C}_6\text{H}_5—\overset{\overset{\displaystyle CH_2CH_3}{|}}{C}HCN$$

21.1.1 Preparation of Nitriles and Isonitriles

1. **From alkyl halides.** Aliphatic nitriles are prepared by treating alkyl halides with sodium cyanide in a solvent that dissolves both reactants ; in dimethyl sulphoxide (DMSO), reaction occurs rapidly and exothermically at room temperature.

$$\underset{\text{1° or 2° alkyl halide}}{R—X} \quad + \quad CN^- \longrightarrow R—CN \quad + \quad X^-$$

Remember that this reaction is of the S_{N^2} type and is limited to 1° and 2° alkyl halides ; 3° alkyl halides undergo exclusively elimination reaction because CN^- is a strong base (recall that HCN, conjugate acid of CN^- is a very weak acid).

C_6H_5—CH$_2$Cl $\xrightarrow[\text{DMSO}]{\text{NaCN}}$ C_6H_5—CH$_2$CN

Benzyl chloride   Benzyl cyanide

Cyclopentyl—Cl $\xrightarrow[\text{DMSO}]{\text{NaCN}}$ Cyclopentyl—CN

Cyclopentyl chloride   Cyclopenyl cyanide

In case silver cyanide is used in place of potassium cyanide, isonitrile is the main product, while nitrile is formed only in small amount.

$$CH_3I + AgCN \longrightarrow CH_3NC + AgI$$

Methylcarbylamine

Remember that aryl and vinyl halides are unreactive toward nucleophilic substitution reaction, hence aryl nitriles and vinyl nitriles can't be prepared by this method.

$$C_6H_5Cl \quad \text{or} \quad CH_2=CHCl \xrightarrow[\text{DMSO}]{\text{NaCN}} \text{No reaction}$$

2. **From arenediazonium salts.** Aryl nitriles are prepared from diazonium salts by **Sandmeyer reaction** which involves the reaction of aryl diazonium salt with cuprous cyanide.

$$\underset{\text{Aryl diazonium halide}}{Ar—N_2{}^+X^-} \xrightarrow{\text{CuCN}} Ar—CN + N_2$$

3. **By dehydration of amides.** Amides react with P_4O_{10} (a compound that is often called phosphorus pentoxide and written P_2O_5) or with boiling acetic anhydride to form nitriles.

$$RCONH_2 \xrightarrow[\text{heat,} \quad (-H_2O)]{P_4O_{10} \text{ or } (CH_3CO)_2O} RCN + H_3PO_4 \quad \text{or} \quad CH_3COOH$$

(R = alkyl or aryl group)

This method is useful for preparing nitriles which can't be prepared by nucleophilic substitution reaction between alkyl halides and cyanide ions.

4. **By the dehydration of aldoximes** with acetic anhydride or P_4O_{10}

$$RCH = NOH \xrightarrow{(CH_3CO)_2O} RC \equiv N + H_2O$$

$$\text{Aldoxime} \qquad\qquad \text{Nitrile}$$

(R may be alkyl or aryl)

5. **From Grignard reagents.**

$$RMgX \quad + \quad ClCN \quad \longrightarrow RCN + Mg(Cl)X$$

$$\text{Cyanogen chloride}$$

6. **Carbylamine reaction (*only for isonitriles*).**

$$C_2H_5NH_2 + CHCl_3 + 3KOH \longrightarrow C_2H_5NC + 3KCl + 3H_2O$$

TEST YOUR UNDERSTANDING - 21.2

1.   (a) Try to convert ethanol to (*i*) CH_3CN, and (*ii*) CH_3CH_2CN

     (b) Give steps involved in the synthesis of Me_3CCN from Me_3CCOOH.

21.1.2 Properties of Nitriles and Isonitriles

1. **Nitriles** are more polar than isonitriles, hence they have high dipole moment, high b.p. and are more soluble in water. Recall that carbylamines (isonitriles) are extremely unpleasant, while nitriles are pleasant smelling.

2. **Hydrolysis.** Since nitriles are converted to carboxylic acids on hydrolysis, *these are classified as carboxylic acid derivatives.*

    Like amides, nitriles when heated in aqueous acid or base for several hours give carboxylic acids. Further like amide hydrolysis, nitrile hydrolysis is irreversible.

$$R—C \equiv N \ + \ H_2O \ + \ H_3O^+ \longrightarrow RCOOH \ + \ NH_4^+$$

$$R—C \equiv N \ + \ H_2O \ + \ OH^- \longrightarrow RCOO^- \ + \ NH_3$$

Mechanism for acidic hydrolysis of nitriles

$$R—C \equiv N: + \ H_3O^+ \ \rightleftharpoons \ R—C \equiv \overset{+}{N}H \ \leftrightarrow \ R—\overset{+}{C} = \ddot{N}H \ \rightleftharpoons \ R—C = NH$$

Protonation of the nitrile   Protonated nitrile

(+ve change on N makes C more electron-deficient)

$$R—C = NH \ \rightleftharpoons \ \left[R—C = \overset{+}{N}H_2 \ \leftrightarrow \ R—C—\ddot{N}H_2 \right] \ \rightleftharpoons \ R—C—\ddot{N}H_2 \ + \ H_3O^+$$

Imino acid   Protonated amide   Amide

(Amide tautomer)

In presence of concentrated H_2SO_4, the reaction stops at the protonated amide which constitutes a useful way for preparing amides from nitriles. In presence of dilute acids, amides undergo further hydrolysis to form carboxylic acids as the final product.

$$R-\overset{\overset{\ddot{O}:}{\|}}{C}-\ddot{N}H_2 \xrightarrow{H_3O^+} R-\overset{\overset{+\ddot{O}H}{\|}}{C}-\ddot{N}H_2 \xrightarrow{H_2\ddot{O}:} R-\overset{\overset{:\ddot{O}H}{|}}{\underset{\underset{\ddot{N}H_2}{|}}{C}}-\overset{+}{O}H_2 \rightleftharpoons R-\overset{\overset{:\ddot{O}H}{|}}{\underset{\underset{+NH_3}{|}}{C}}-\ddot{O}H$$

Amide   Protonated amide   Oxonium ion   Ammonium ion
(a proton is lost from O and gained at N)

$$\rightleftharpoons R-\overset{\overset{+\ddot{O}H}{\|}}{C}-\ddot{O}H + :NH_3 \dashrightarrow R-\overset{\overset{\ddot{O}:}{\|}}{C}-\ddot{O}H + NH_4^+$$

Protonated carboxylic acid

Mechanism for basic hydrolysis of nitriles

$$R-\overset{\overset{OH}{|}}{C}=\ddot{N}H \xrightarrow[\text{zation}]{\text{isomeri-}} R-\overset{\overset{O}{\|}}{C}-NH_2 \xrightarrow{OH^-} R\overset{\overset{:\ddot{O}:^-}{|}}{\underset{\underset{NH_2}{}}{C}}-OH \xrightarrow{OH^-} R\overset{\overset{:\ddot{O}:^-}{|}}{\underset{\underset{NH_2}{}}{C}}-\ddot{O}:^- \longrightarrow \overset{\overset{O}{\|}}{\underset{R}{C}}\diagdown O_- + NH_2^-$$

Hydroxy imine Amide

Here also, amides can be isolated under appropriate (milder) conditions.

3. **Addition of Grignard reagents.** Although the carbon-nitrogen triple bond of nitriles is much less reactive toward nucleophilic addition than is the carbon-oxygen double bond of aldehydes and ketones, strongly basic nucleophiles such as Grignard reagents and organolithium compounds easily add on nitriles to form ketones

$$R-C\equiv N + R'MgX \xrightarrow[\text{(ii) } H_2O]{\text{(i) diethyl ether}} R-\overset{\overset{R'}{|}}{C}=NH \xrightarrow[\text{heat}]{H_3O^+} R-\overset{\overset{R'}{|}}{C}=O$$

$$R-C\equiv N + R'Li \longrightarrow R-\overset{\overset{R'}{|}}{C}=N^-Li^+ \xrightarrow{H_3O^+} R-\overset{\overset{R'}{|}}{C}=O + NH_4^+ + Li^+$$

Since nitriles are more reactive than ketones, the next molecule of R'MgX will add to fresh molecule of $RC\equiv N$ to form ketone rather than with ketone to form a 3° alcohol. Although a nitrile has a triple bond, addition of the Grignard or lithium reagent takes place only once because if the addition takes place twice, nitrogen will get a double negative charge which is not possible.

$$R-C\equiv N \xrightarrow{R'Li} R-\overset{\overset{R'}{|}}{C}=N^-Li^+ \xrightarrow{R'Li} \underset{\underset{R'}{|}}{\overset{\overset{R'}{|}}{R-C}}-N^{2-}\,2Li^+$$

(The dianion does not form)

1. Compare the reaction of Grignard reagent with an ester and a nitrile, explain the difference between the intermediates formed in two cases when one molecule of the reagent adds on the compound (ester or nitrile).

4. **Reduction of nitriles.** Nitriles can be reduced to 1° amines by catalytic hydrogenation or $LiAlH_4$.

$$R\!-\!C \equiv N \xrightarrow{\quad 2H_2,\, Raney\ Ni,\, 140°C \quad} R\!-\!CH_2NH_2$$

Nitriles can also be reduced to aldehydes by means disobutylaluminium hydride (DIBAL–H). This reaction is also known as **Stephen reduction.**

$$R\!-\!C \equiv N \xrightarrow{\ (iso\text{–}Bu)_2\ AlH\ } R\!-\!CH = NH \xrightarrow{\ H_2O\ } R\!-\!CHO + NH_3$$

5. **Condensation with aldehydes.** The α-hydrogens of nitriles are appreciably acidic, but less than those of aldehydes and ketones. The acidity constant for acetonitrile (CH_3CN) is about 10^{-25} ($pK_a \approx 25$). Other nitriles with α-hydrogens show comparable acidities, and consequently these nitriles undergo aldol type of condensations.

The note-worthy properties of alkyl isonitriles are hydrolysis, reduction and addition reactions.

(a) Alkyl isonitriles are hydrolysed only by dilute mineral acid (H_2SO_4 or HCl) to form **1° amines**

$$R\!-\!N \overset{+}{\underset{-}{\rightleftharpoons}} C \xrightarrow[\ (+\,2H_2O)\ ]{\ H^+\ } R\!-\!NH_2 + HCOOH$$

Isonitriles do not undergo basic hydrolysis because of their inability to undergo the attack by OH^- ions.

(b) Catalytic hydrogenation or reduction with lithiumaluminium hydride gives 2° amines.

$$R\!-\!N \overset{+}{\underset{-}{\rightleftharpoons}} C \xrightarrow{\ LiAlH_4\ } RNHCH_3$$

(c) Isonitriles undergo certain addition reactions in which addition takes place only on carbon.

$$RN = C = O \xleftarrow[\ or\ O_3\ ]{\ 2HgO\ } \mathbf{RN \overset{+}{\underset{-}{\rightleftharpoons}} C} \xrightarrow{\ 1/8\,S_8\ } RN = C = S$$

Alkyl isocyanate*   **Alkyl isonitrile**   **Alkyl isothiocyanate**

21.2   Alkyl Nitrites and Nitro Compounds

These are functional isomers, *e.g.*

Alkyl nitrite   Nitroalkane

Nitromethane, used as a high-energy fuel for race cars, is a liquid with a b.p. of 101°C, while methyl nitrite is a gas (b.p. –12°C) which causes dilation of blood vessels, on inhalation, hence it is used for the treatment of angina pectoris (a heart disease).

However, remember that alkyl nitrites are esters of nitrous acid (HONO) while nitro compounds are not esters because these can neither be prepared by the interaction of alcohol with an acid (HONO) nor they undergo hydrolysis to form alcohol and acid (nitrous acid). Actually, nitro compounds are regarded as nitro derivatives of the hydrocarbons.

---

*   Recall that methyl isocyanate, MIC was responsible for Bhopal tragedy in Dec. 1984.

21.2.1   Preparation and Properties of Alkyl Nitrites

1.   By the action of nitrous acid on alcohol.

$$C_2H_5OH \xrightarrow[\text{(+ HONO)}]{\text{NaNO}_2,\,\text{H}^+} C_2H_5ONO + H_2O$$

2.   By the action of nitrogen trioxide (N_2O_3) on alcohols.

$$2C_2H_5OH + N_2O_3 \longrightarrow 2C_2H_5ONO + H_2O$$

Nitrogen trioxide is generated *in situ i.e.* it is prepared by the action of conc. HNO_3 on a mixture of conc. H_2SO_4 and alcohol and then adding copper turnings.

3.   By the action of alkyl iodide and potassium nitrite.

$$C_2H_5I + KNO_2 \longrightarrow C_2H_5ONO + KI$$

Properties. Its two worth-mentioning properties are hydrolysis and reduction.

$$C_2H_5\text{—}O\text{—}N = O \xrightarrow{\text{H}^+,\,\text{OH}^-,\,\text{or, neutral medium}} C_2H_5\text{—}OH + HONO$$

$$C_2H_5\text{—}O\text{—}N = O \xrightarrow{\text{Sn + HCl}} C_2H_5OH + H_2NOH \text{ (or } NH_3 + H_2O)$$

21.2.2   Preparation and Properties of Nitroalkanes

Nitro group is found to be a resonance hybrid of the following two structures as evidenced by its equivalent bond length of the two N—O bonds.

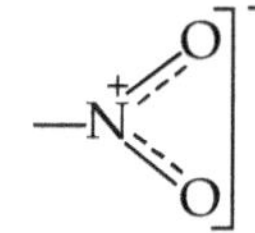

Resonating structures of the – NO$_2$ group   Resonance hybrid of the —NO$_2$ group

Preparation.

1.   By heating an alkyl halide with of solution of silver nitrite.

$$C_2H_5Br + AgNO_2 \longrightarrow C_2H_5NO_2 + AgBr$$

Some alkyl nitrite is also formed as a side-product ; however, the two compounds can be separated easily by fractional distillation.

2.   By the vapour phase nitration of alkanes.

$$CH_3CH_3 + HNO_3 \text{ (fuming)} \xrightarrow{400°C} CH_3CH_2NO_2 + CH_3NO_2$$

The mixture of nitralkanes can be separated by fractional distillation.

3. 3° Nitroalkanes can be prepared by the oxidation of the corresponding 3° amine with $KMnO_4$.

$$R_3CNH_2 \xrightarrow{\text{KMnO}_4} R_3CNO_2 + H_2O$$

Properties. Presence of positive charge on N makes —NO$_2$ a powerful electron-withdrawing group which makes α-hydrogen atom acidic, much more than those of aldehydes and ketones. Further, the carbanion formed by the removal of α-H is stabilized due to resonance (see acidic character). Hence 1° and 2° nitroalkanes are very reactive as compared to 3° nitroalkanes having no α-hydrogen.

1° Nitroalkane   2° Nitroalkane   3° Nitroalkane

1. **Properties of nitroalkanes due to α-H**

(a) **Acidic nature.** Primary and secondary nitroalkanes dissolve in aq. NaOH to form salts.

$$RCH_2-\overset{+}{N}\underset{O_-}{\overset{O}{<}} \xrightarrow[(-H_2O)]{aq.\ NaOH} \overset{-}{RCH}-\overset{+}{N}\underset{O_-}{\overset{O}{<}} \longleftrightarrow RCH=\overset{+}{N}\underset{O_-}{\overset{O^-}{<}}$$

(b) Action of alkaline halogen (X_2 + NaOH)

$$H_3CNO_2 \xrightarrow{Cl_2,\ NaOH} Cl_3CNO_2$$

Nitromethane   Nitrochloroform (Chloropicrin),
a lachrymatory substance

(c) Action of nitrous acid.

(i) $RCH_2NO_2 \xrightarrow{HONO} R\overset{\overset{\textstyle NOH}{\|}}{C}NO_2 \xrightarrow{NaOH} R\overset{\overset{\textstyle NO^-Na^+}{\|}}{C}NO_2$

    A 1° nitroalkane   Nitrolic acid   Sodium nitrolate (**red**)

(ii) $R_2CHNO_2 \xrightarrow{HONO} R_2\overset{\overset{\textstyle N=O}{|}}{C}NO_2 \xrightarrow{NaOH}$ No reaction

    A 2° nitroalkane   Pseudonitrol (**blue**)

(iii) $R_3CNO_2 \xrightarrow{NaOH}$ No reaction due to absence of α-H

    A 3° nitroalkane

Recall that this difference of nitroalkanes toward nitrous acid forms the basis of the **Victor Meyer test** for the distinction of 1°, 2° and 3° alcohols.

(d) *Condensation with aldehydes and ketones.* Nitroalkanes having α-H undergo base catalyzed condensation with aldehydes and ketones.

$$C_6H_5CHO + CH_3NO_2 \xrightarrow{OH^-} C_6H_5CH=CHNO_2$$

TEST YOUR UNDERSTANDING - 21.4

1. Give the starting aldehyde/ketone, and nitroalkane used for synthesizing each of the following compounds.

(a) $C_6H_5CH=\overset{\overset{\textstyle CH_3}{|}}{C}NO_2$ (b) $HOCH_2CH_2NO_2.$

(e) **Mannich reaction.** This is the condensation between formaldehyde and compound having active hydrogen and ammonia or a 1° or a 2° amine to form Mannich base.

$$R_2CHNO_2 + HCHO + R'NH_2 \xrightarrow{HCl} R_2\overset{\overset{\textstyle NO_2}{|}}{C}\overset{\overset{\textstyle R'}{|}}{CH_2NH} + H_2O$$

2. **Reduction**

(a) Reduction in acidic medium, like Sn + HCl, Fe + CH_3COOH ; $LiAlH_4$; or H_2—Ni, gives amines.

$$C_2H_5NO_2 + 6H \xrightarrow{Sn+HCl} C_2H_5NH_2 + 2H_2O$$

(b) Reduction in neutral medium, like Zn dust + NH_4Cl gives hydroxylamines.

$$C_2H_5NO_2 + 4H \xrightarrow{Zn\ dust + NH_4Cl} C_2H_5NHOH$$

3.   **Hydrolysis.** Primary nitroalkanes are hydrolysed to hydroxylamine and carboxylic acid, while secondary nitroalkanes are hydrolysed to ketones.

$$CH_3CH_2NO_2 \xrightarrow{\ HCl\ } CH_3COOH + NH_2OH$$

$$2\,(CH_3)_2CHNO_2 \xrightarrow{\ HCl\ } 2(CH_3)_2CO + N_2O + H_2O$$

Tertiary amines do not undergo hydrolysis.

21.3   Aromatic Nitro Compounds

21.3.1   Preparation

1.   **Direct nitration.** This is the most important method for preparing aromatic nitro compounds. Nitration can be done by variety of reagents, like a mixture of conc. HNO_3 and conc. H_2SO_4, acetyl nitrate (N_2O_5 in acetic anhydride), fuming HNO_3 etc. Since $—NO_2$ group is deactivating, it is very difficult to introduce the second and third $—NO_2$ group, however this can be done by carrying out the reaction, at high temperature and with strong nitrating agent like fuming HNO_3. For example,

(i)

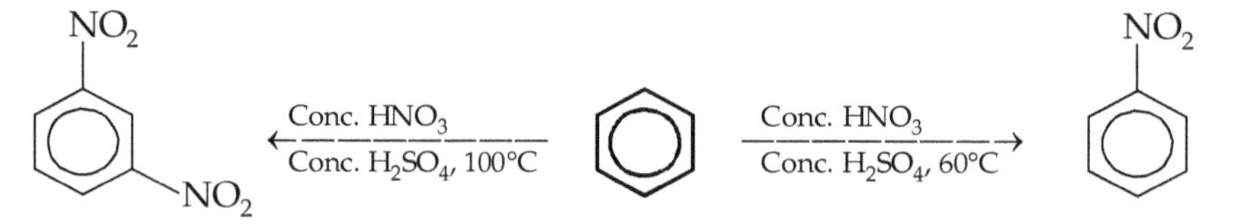

m-Dinitrobenzene   **Benzene**   Nitrobenzene

(ii)

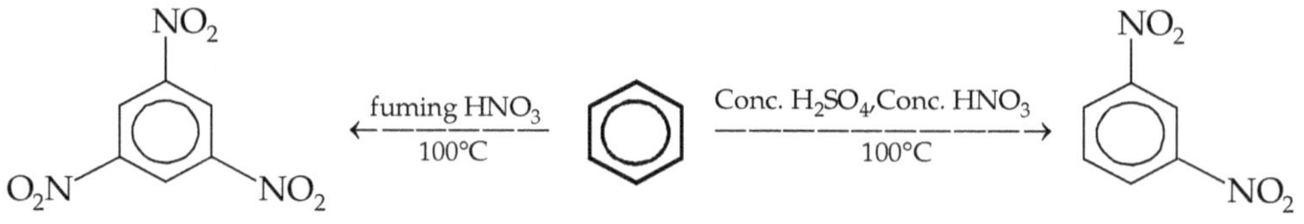

1, 3, 5-Trinitrobenzene   **Benzene**   m-Dinitrobenzene

Recall that nitration is an electrophilic substitution hence presence of electron-releasing group like $—OH$, $—NH_2$, $—CH_3$, $—OR$ etc., in the nucleus facilitates nitration. Thus aromatic compounds bearing these groups (*e.g.* toluene, aniline, phenol etc.) can be nitrated easily as compared to benzene.

2.   **From diazonium salts (indirect method).** Since diazonium ion can be easily replaced by $—NO_2$ group, arenediazonium salts are used for preparing the aromatic nitro compounds which cannot be prepared by direct method.

(i)

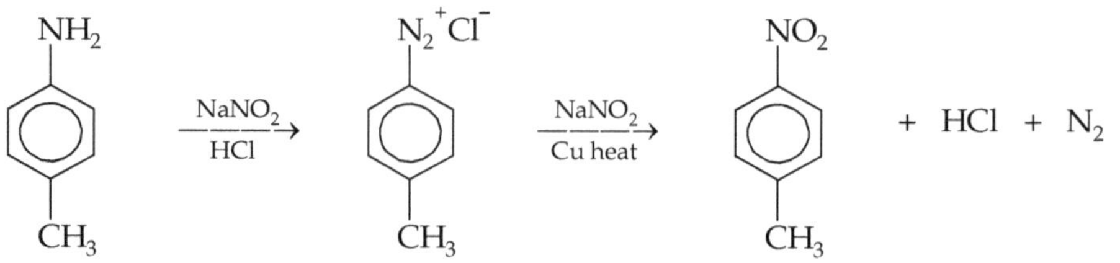

$+ \; HCl \; + \; N_2$

(ii)

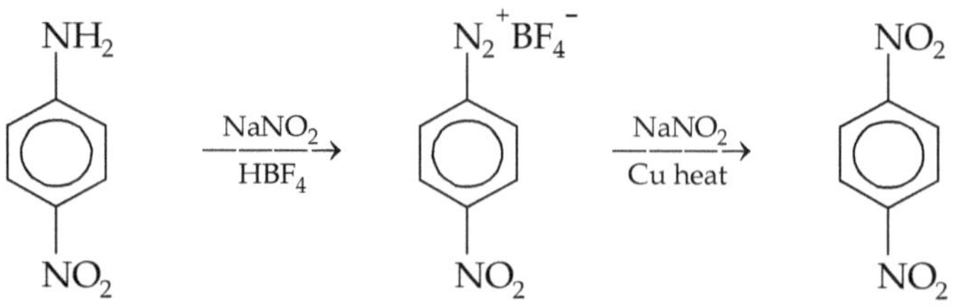

p-Nitroaniline   p-Dinitrobenzene

TEST YOUR UNDERSTANDING - 21.5

1. Give steps involved in the conversion of aniline to *o*-dinitrobenzene.

21.3.2   Properties of Aromatic Nitro Compounds

Nitro compounds are highly coloured (*yellow*, orange, red etc.), insoluble in water. Its three worth-mentioning properties are reduction, electrophilic substitution and nucleophilic substitution.

1. **Reduction.** Aromatic nitro compounds can be reduced to a variety of products through the following sequence.

$$H_2N\!-\!\!\bigcirc\!\!-\!OH$$

p-Aminophenol

$$C_6H_5NO_2 \longrightarrow C_6H_5NO \longrightarrow C_6H_5NHOH \longrightarrow C_6H_5NH_2$$

Nitrobenzene   Nitrosobenzene   Phenylhydroxylamine   Aniline

$$\begin{array}{ccc} C_6H_5N\!\to\!O & C_6H_5N & C_6H_5NH \\ \| & \| & | \\ C_6H_5N & C_6H_5N & C_6H_5NH \end{array}$$

Azoxybenzene   Azobenzene   Hydrazobenzene

Each of the above product can be isolated depending upon the nature of the reducing agent. Following table lists the important products along with the corresponding reducing agent for that very particular compound.

Reduction of $C_6H_5NO_2$ under different conditions

	Reagent	Product
1.	**Reduction in acidic medium**	
	$Sn + HCl$, $Zn + HCl$, $SnCl_2 + HCl$, $Fe + H_2O + HCl$	Aniline
2.	**Reduction in neutral medium**	
	Zn dust $+ NH_4Cl$, Al-Hg couple $+ H_2O$	Phenylhydroxylamine
3.	**Reduction in alkaline medium**	
	(*a*) $Na_3AsO_3 + NaOH$	Azoxybenzene
	(*b*) $Zn + NaOH$, CH_3OH	Azobenzene
	(*c*) $Zn + NaOH$; C_2H_5OH	Hydrazobenzene
4.	**Reduction by metal hydrides and cata —H_2**	
	$H_2 + Pt$ or Raney Ni ; or $LiAlH_4$	Aniline
5.	**Electrolytic reduction** in presence of dil.H_2SO_4	*p*-Aminophenol

In case the compound contains two —NO_2 groups, selective reduction (reduction of only one —NO_2 group) can be achieved by using $(NH_4)_2S$ or Na_2S.

m-Dinitrobenzene $\xrightarrow[\text{or } Na_2S]{(NH_4)_2S}$ m-Nitroaniline

$\xleftarrow[\text{HCl}]{\text{1 mol } SnCl_2}$ $\xrightarrow[\text{warm}]{\text{polysulphide}}$

2.   **Substitution is benzene nucleus of nitrobenzene.** Resonance in nitrobenzene imparts following characteristic features.

Resonating structures of nitrobenzene   Resonance hybrid of nitrobenzene

(*i*)   It imparts partial double bond character to carbon-nitrogen bond causing replacement of —NO_2 a difficult task. However, if second —NO_2 group in present in the *ortho-* and *para* positions, one of them can be replaced **by a nucleophile.**

$+$ aq. KOH, NH_3 or C_2H_5OK $\longrightarrow$

(Where, Nu = OH, NH_2, or OC_2H_5)

(*ii*)   It imparts partial positive (especially *o-* and *p-*positions) charge on the ortho and para positions deactivating benzene nucleus for electrophiles and making the *ortho-* and *para-* positions reactive for nucleophiles. Thus nitrobenzene undergoes electrophilic substitution with difficulty and at *m-*position, however it undergoes nucleophilic substitution at *ortho-* and *para-*positions easily.

(*a*)   **Electrophilic substitution.** As mentioned above, nitrobenzene undergoes electrophilic substitution only *under drastic conditions,* and at *meta* position. However, nitrobenzene having activating group like —R, —OR, —NH_2, etc. undergoes electrophilic substitutions relatively easily and at the position governed by the activating group rather than the nitro group.

$\xrightarrow[H_2SO_4]{HNO_3}$ $\xrightarrow[H_2SO_4]{HNO_3}$

2, 4, 6-Trinitrotoluene
(TNT)

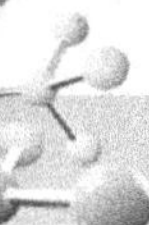

(*b*) **Nucleophilic substitution.** Recall that benzene is inert to nucleophiles ; however nitrobenzene undergoes nucleophilic substitution in *o*- and and *p*-positions, when fused with KOH.

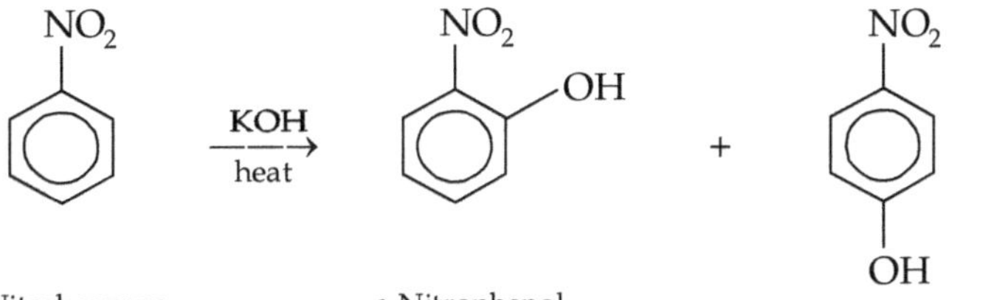

Nitrobenzene *o*-Nitrophenol *p*-Nitrophenol

When nitrobenzene having electron-withdrawing group in *o*- or *p*-position is heated with ethanolic KCN—the —NO_2 group is eliminated and a —COOH group is introduced in the *ortho* position to the leaving —NO_2 group (**Von Richter reaction**).

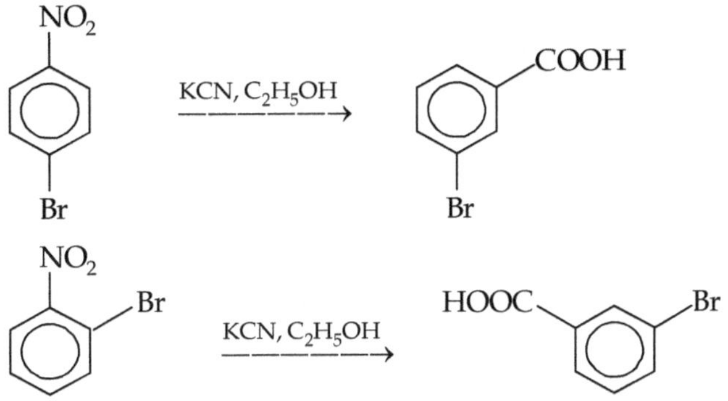

21.4 ILLUSTRATIVE EXAMPLES

Example 1 :

Supply structures to the bracketed compounds [A] to [L].

(*a*) $C_6H_5NO_2 \xrightarrow{\text{Zn, aq. } NH_4Cl} [A] \xrightarrow[NH_4OH]{AgNO_3} [B] \xrightarrow{CH_3MgI} [C]$

$[B] \xrightarrow{Pd/H_2} [D]$

(*b*) $C_6H_5NO_2 \xrightarrow[\text{in presence of dil. } H_2SO_4]{\text{electrolysis}} [E] \xrightarrow[\text{(iii) heat, under pressure}]{\text{(i) NaOH, (ii) } CO_2} [F]$

(*c*)

$\xrightarrow[C_2H_5OH]{\text{KOH, heat}} [\ ] \longrightarrow [G]$

(*d*) $TNT + C_6H_5CHO \longrightarrow [H] + [I]$

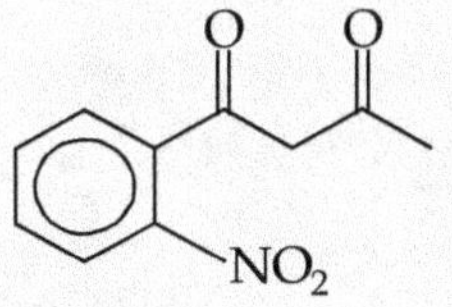

(*e*)

$\xrightarrow{Br_2 . Fe} [J] \xrightarrow{KCN, C_2H_5OH} [K]$

(*f*)

$+ \begin{array}{l} COOC_2H_5 \\ | \\ COOC_2H_5 \end{array} \xrightarrow{C_2H_5ONa} [L]$

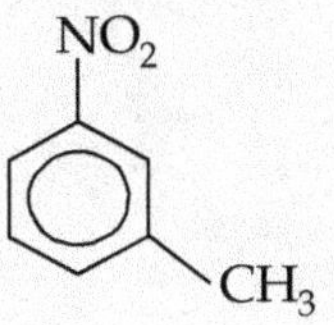

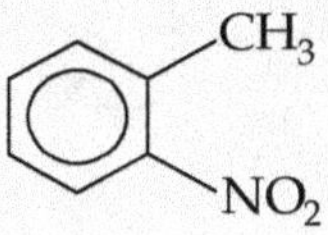

Solution :

(a)

C_6H_5NHOH C_6H_5NO $\underset{\text{CH}_3}{C_6H_5N}\!-\!OH$ $C_6H_5N = NC_6H_5$

[A] formed by   [B] formed   [C] Remember that N = O group   [D] Reduction of

neutral reduction   by oxi. of hydroxylamine   behaves like C = O group   nitrosobenzene

(b)

$H_2N\!-\!\bigcirc\!-\!OH$ $H_2N\!-\!\bigcirc\!\overset{\text{COOH}}{-}\!OH$

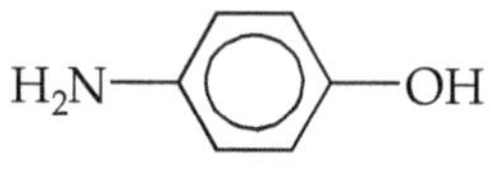

[E], Formed by electrolytic reduction 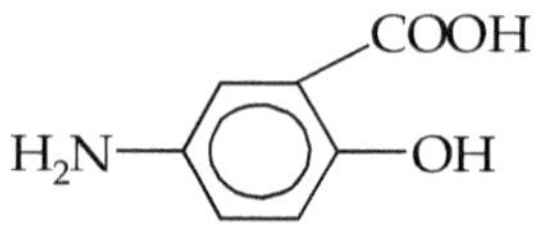   [F], Formed by Kolbe's reaction

(c)

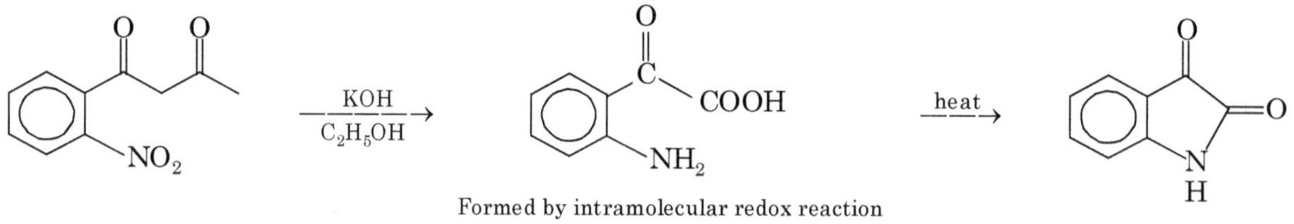

Formed by intramolecular redox reaction

(d)

Three —NO_2 groups in *o*-and *p*-positions make —CH_3 group reactive (acidic)

[H] and [I] *cis*- and *trans*-isomers

(e)

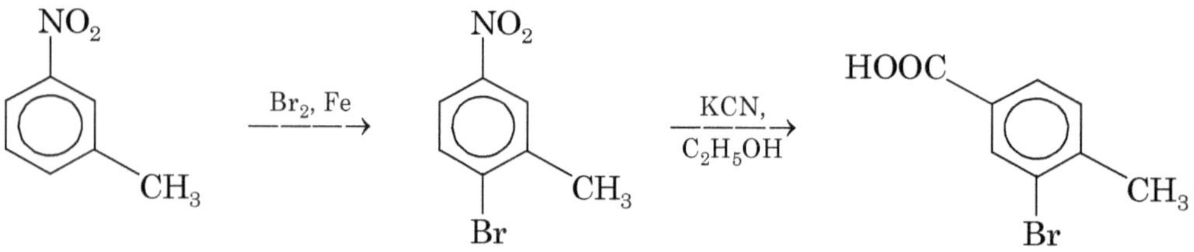

—CH_3 is activating group   [j]   [k], Formed by Von Richter reaction

(f)

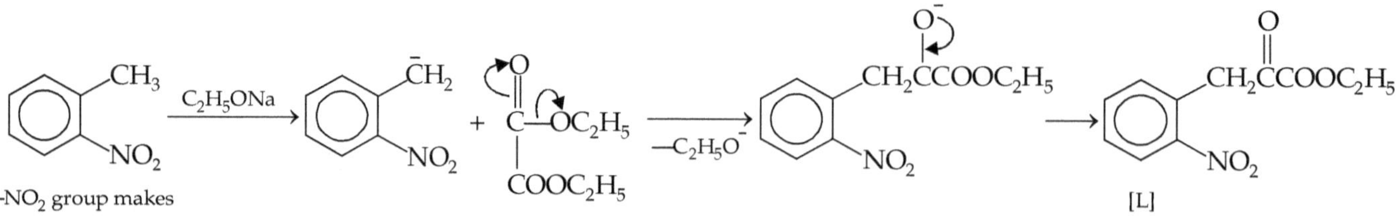

—NO_2 group makes —CH_3 reactive   [L]

Example 2 :

Give steps involved in the following conversions :

(a)   Nitrobenzene to *m*-nitrobenzoic acid   **(b)**   *p*-Nitrotoluene to *m*-nitrotoluene

(c)   Nitrobenzene into *sym*-tribromabenzene.

Solution :

(a)

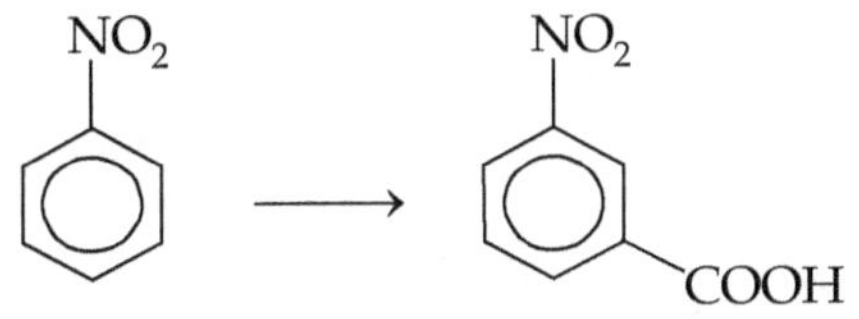

Although *m*-nitrobenzoic acid can be prepared easily by oxidising *m*-nitrotoluene, but it is very difficult to convert nitrobenzene to *m*-nitrotoluene because nitrobenzene does not undergo Friedel-Craft reaction. Hence indirect route is adopted, it is advisable to proceed backward for getting different steps.

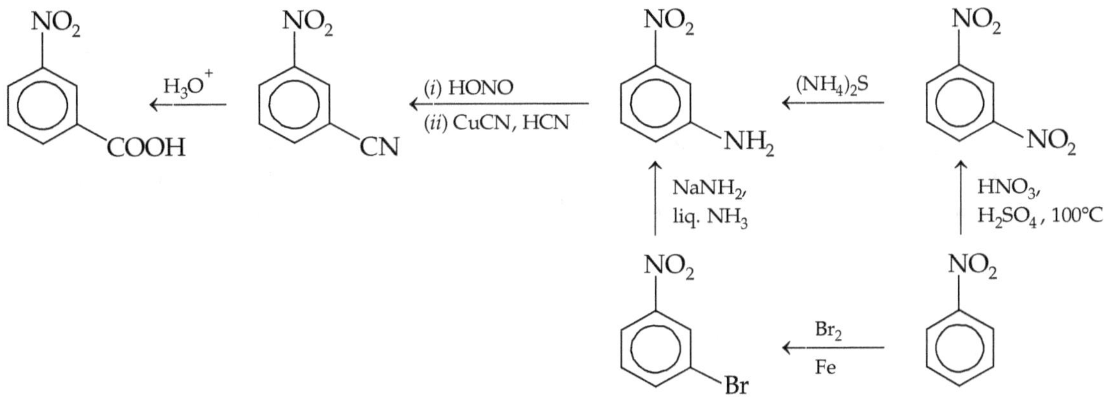

(b)

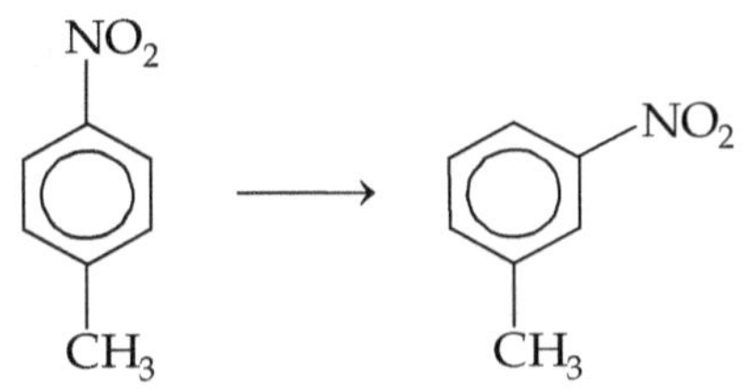

—NO_2 group in the *m*-position to —CH_3 *i.e.* in the *o*-position to the existing —NO_2 group can be introduced easily by converting existing —NO_2 group (*m*-directing) to the —NH_2 group (*o, p*-directing).

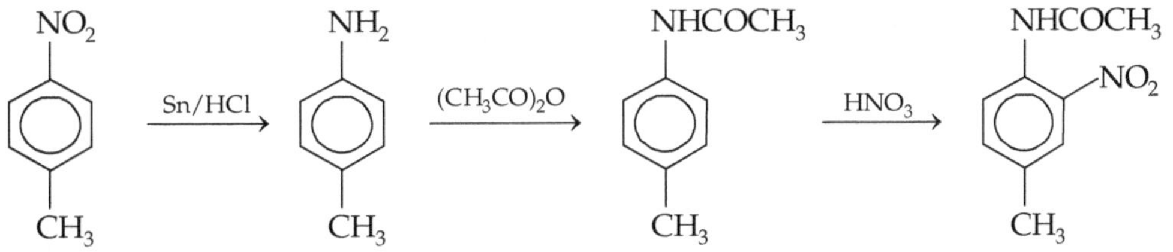

Now the —$NHCOCH_3$ group can be easily removed via diazotisation.

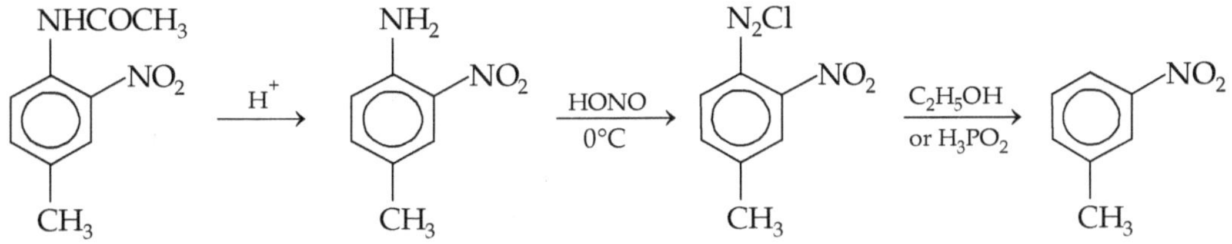

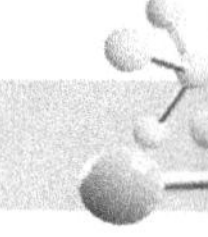

(c)

Remove —NO_2 group already present in the molecule (as in the above example) through diazotisation but by first introducing three Br.

$$\text{(Nitrobenzene)} \xrightarrow{H_2/Pt} \text{(Aniline)} \xrightarrow[\text{Water}]{Br_2} \text{(2,4,6-tribromoaniline)} \xrightarrow[(ii)\ H_3PO_2]{(i)\ HONO} \text{(1,3,5-tribromobenzene)}$$

Example 3 :

An organic compound A of the formula $C_2H_5NO_2$ on reduction gives compound B which undergoes haloform reaction to form compound C. The compound C when treated with nitric acid forms compound D of the formula CCl_3NO_2 ; compound D can also be obtained directly by the action of Cl_2 and NaOH on the compound E of the formula CH_3NO_2. Identify compounds A to D and explain the reactions involved.

Solution :

Let us summarise the given reactions.

$$A \xrightarrow{\text{reduction}} B \xrightarrow[\text{(haloform reaction)}]{Cl_2,\, OH^-} C \xrightarrow{HNO_3} D \xleftarrow[\text{NaOH}]{Cl_2} E$$

$$(C_2H_5NO_2) \qquad\qquad (CCl_3NO_2) \qquad (CH_3NO_2)$$

Formation of D from E indicates that E (CH_3NO_2) is a nitromethane and hence D is trichloronitromethane, nitrochloroform or chloropicrin. Hence compound C should be chloroform, $CHCl_3$ consequently compound B should be CH_3CH_2OH and A as ethyl nitrite.

$$C_2H_5ON = O \xrightarrow{\text{reduction}} C_2H_5OH \xrightarrow{Cl_2,\, OH^-} CHCl_3 \xrightarrow{HNO_3} NO_2CCl_3 \xleftarrow[\text{NaOH}]{Cl_2} CH_3NO_2$$

$$\text{(A)} \qquad\qquad \text{(B)} \qquad\quad \text{(C)} \qquad\quad \text{(D)} \qquad\quad \text{(E)}$$

EXERCISE 21.1 (MCQ - ONE option correct)

1. Which of the following is not the correct name for (cyclohexane)—CN

   (a) Cyclohexanecarbonitrile   (b) Cyclohexanenitrile

   (c) Cyclohexanonitrile   (d) None of the three.

2. Protonation of acid amides ($RCONH_2$) is likely to give

   (a) $R-\overset{\overset{+OH}{\|}}{C}-NH_2$ (b) $R-\overset{\overset{O}{\|}}{C}-\overset{+}{N}H_3$

   (c) Both   (d) None.

3. Methyl nitrite shows tautomerism

$$H_3C-\overset{+}{N}\overset{O}{\underset{O^-}{\diagdown}} \rightleftharpoons H_2C=\overset{+}{N}\overset{OH}{\underset{O^-}{\diagdown}}$$

         I   II

Predict their relative acidity.

   (a) Both are equal in acidic character

   (b) I is more acidic than II

   (c) II is more acidic than I

   (d) None of then is acidic.

4. The order of increasing boiling points among the three compounds is

   $C_2H_5ONO(I)$, $C_2H_5NO_2(II)$ $C_2H_6(III)$

EXERCISE 21.1 (MCQ - ONE option correct)

1. Which of the following is not the correct name for

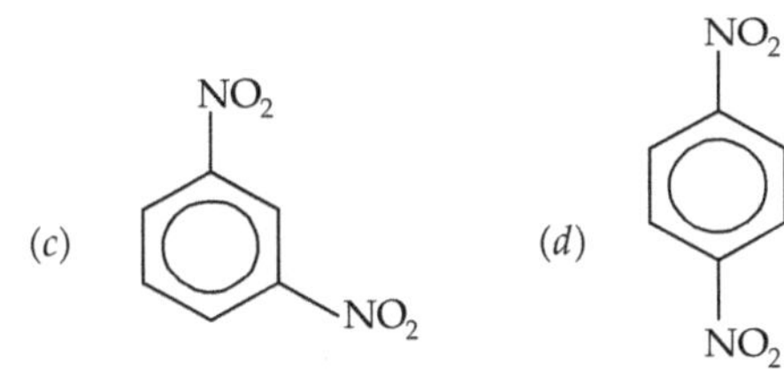

(a) Cyclohexanecarbonitrile   (b) Cyclohexanenitrile
(c) Cyclohexanonitrile   (d) None of the three.

2. Protonation of acid amides ($RCONH_2$) is likely to give

(a) $R-\overset{\overset{+}{O}H}{\underset{}{\overset{\|}{C}}}-NH_2$ (b) $R-\overset{O}{\underset{}{\overset{\|}{C}}}-\overset{+}{N}H_3$

(c) Both   (d) None.

3. Methyl nitrite shows tautomerism

$$H_3C-\overset{+}{N}\overset{\nearrow O}{\underset{\searrow O_-}{}} \rightleftharpoons H_2C=\overset{+}{N}\overset{\nearrow OH}{\underset{\searrow O_-}{}}$$

     I   II

Predict their relative acidity.
(a) Both are equal in acidic character
(b) I is more acidic than II
(c) II is more acidic than I
(d) None of then is acidic.

4. The order of increasing boiling points among the three compounds is
$C_2H_5ONO(I), \quad C_2H_5NO_2(II) \quad C_2H_6(III)$
(a) III < II < I   (b) I < II < III
(c) III < I < II   (d) III < I ≈ II.

5. Which of the following gives a primary alcohol on reduction ?
(a) Alkyl carbylamine   (b) Alkyl nitrite
(c) Nitroalkane   (d) None of the three.

6. When a nitrogenous substance X is treated with nitrous acid, a blue colour is obtained. The compound X can be
(a) $CH_3CH_2NO_2$ (b) $(CH_3)_2CHNO_2$
(c) CH_3CH_2ONO (d) $(CH_3CH)_2ONO$.

7. The compounds X and Y in the following reaction respectively are

$$O_2N-\underset{}{\bigcirc}\xrightarrow[C_2H_5OH]{Zn/NaOH}[X]\xrightarrow[Conc.\,HCl]{Cold}[Y]$$

(a) ⬡—NH_2 and ⬡—$\overset{+}{N}H_3\,\overset{-}{C}l$

(b) ⬡—$NHOH$ and HO—⬡—NH_2

(c) ⬡—$NH-HN$—⬡
   and H_2N—⬡—⬡—NH_2

(d) ⬡—$NH-HN$—⬡
   and   ⬡—$\overset{HCl\;\;HCl}{NH-HN}$—⬡

8. Which of the following method gives good yield for 1, 3, 5-trinitrobenzene, commonly known as TNB ?

(a) ⬡ $\xrightarrow[Conc.\,H_2SO_4]{fuming\,HNO_3}$ TNB

(b) *o*-nitrotoluene $\xrightarrow[Conc.\,H_2SO_4]{Conc.\,HNO_3}$ trinitrotoluene $\xrightarrow[(ii)\,Soda\,lime]{(i)\,Na_2Cr_2O_7/\overset{+}{H}}$ TNB

(c) Both are equally good
(d) None is suitable.

9. A neutral benzenoid nitrogenous organic compound has zero dipole moment, its probable structure is

(a) ⬡—$NHCOCH_3$ (b) ⬡—$CONH_2$

(c) *m*-dinitrobenzene   (d) *p*-dinitrobenzene

10. Predict the product for the following reaction

$$\underset{NO_2}{\bigcirc}\xrightarrow{Sn/HCl}A\xrightarrow{NaNO_2/HCl}B\xrightarrow{NaNO_2-Cu/\Delta}$$

(a) nitrobenzene   (b) *p*-nitroaniline

(c) *o*-dinitrobenzene   (d) *p*-nitrobenzenediazonium chloride

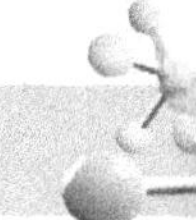

11. 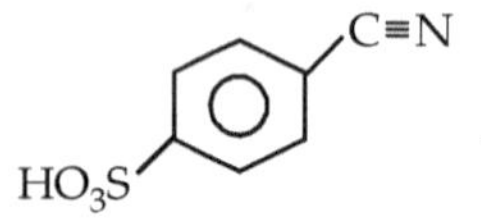 $\xrightarrow{\text{dilute NaOH}/\Delta}$ $(C_7H_7NSO_4)$

$\xrightarrow{KOBr/\Delta}$ Product $\xrightarrow{Br_2/H_2O}$ end product.

The end product is

(a) 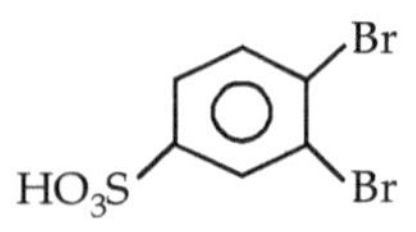 (b) 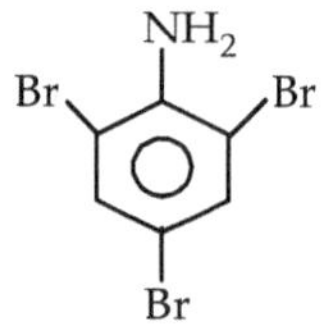

(c) 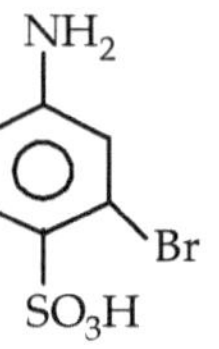 (d) 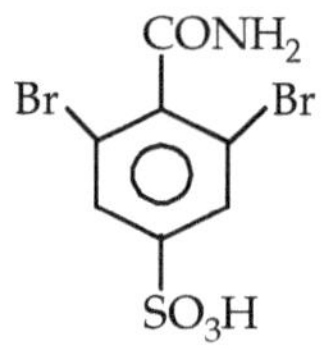

12. 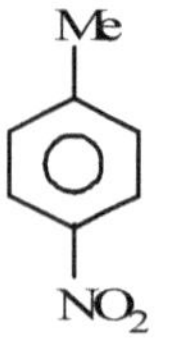 $\xrightarrow{Br_2/Fe}$ $\xrightarrow{Sn/HCl}$ $\xrightarrow{NaNO_2/HCl}$ $\xrightarrow{H_3PO_2}$

$\xrightarrow{KMnO_4/H^+}$ (P) Product.

The product (P) is .... bromobenzoic acid

(a) ortho (b) meta

(c) para (d) ortho and para both

13. The most unlikely representation of resonance structures of *p*-nitrophenoxide ion is

(a) 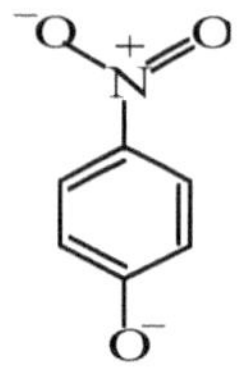 (b) 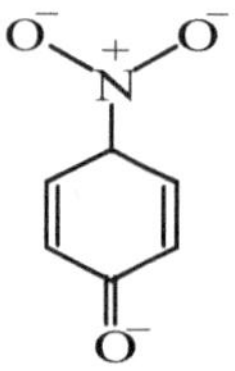

(c) 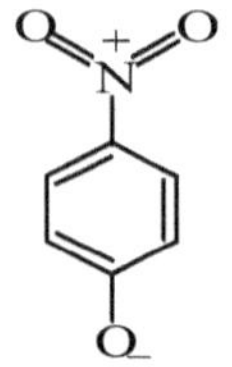 (d) 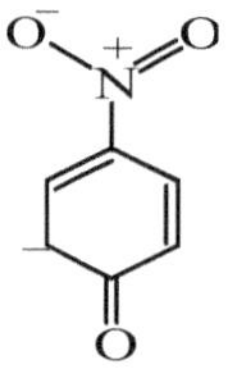

14. Among the following statements on the nitration of aromatic compounds, the false one is

(a) the rate of nitration of benzene is almost the same as that of hexadeutereobenzene.

(b) the rate of nitration of toluene is greater than that of benzene.

(c) the rate of nitration of benzene is greater than that of hexadeutereobenzene

(d) nitration is an electrophilic substitution reaction.

15. Nitrobenzene can be reduced to aniline by

H_2/Ni (I)	Sn/HCl (II)
$Zn/NaOH$ (III)	$LiAlH_4$ (IV)

(a) I, II and III (b) I and II

(c) I, II and IV (d) only II

16. 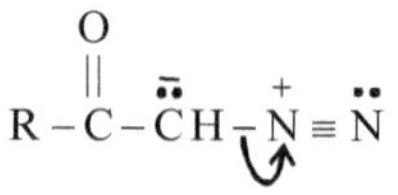 $\longrightarrow$ Intermediate + N_2

What is the nature of intermediate in this reaction ?

(a) Carbonium ion (b) Carbanion

(c) Carbene (d) Free radial

17. In the reaction 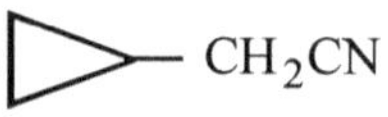 $\xrightarrow[NaNH_2,\ NH_3\ -\ 80°C]{CH_3Br}$ the products obtained are

(a) 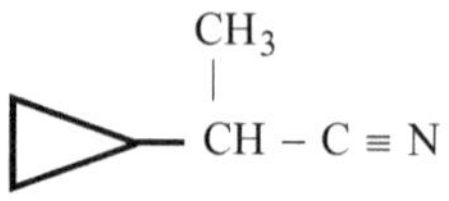 (b) 

(c) 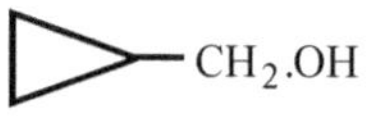 (d) None

18. In the reaction,

$CH_3CN + 2H \longrightarrow X \xrightarrow{\text{Boiling } H_2O} Y$, the term Y is

(a) Acetone (b) Ethanamine

(c) Acetaldehyde (d) Dimethylamine

19. 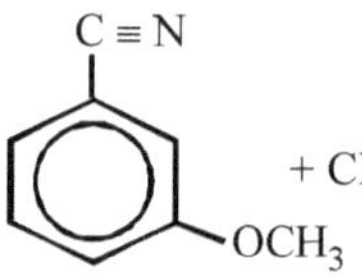 $+ CH_3MgBr \longrightarrow Q \xrightarrow{H_3O^+} P$

The product 'P' in the above reaction is

(a) 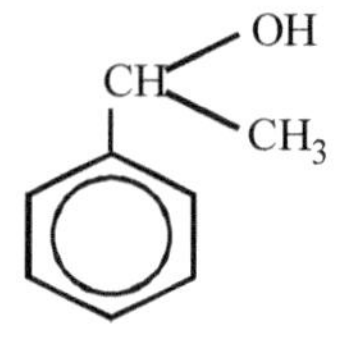 (b) 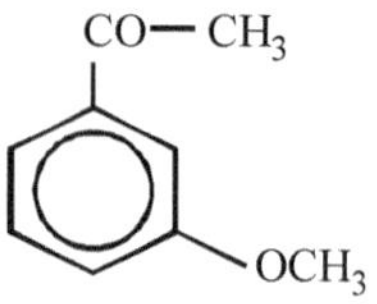

(c) 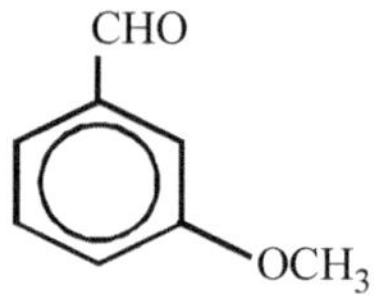 (d) 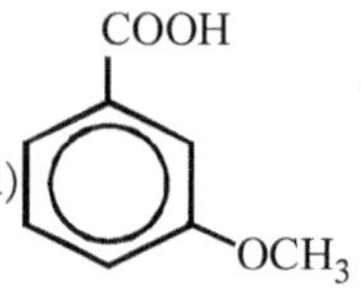

20. In the acidic reduction of nitrobenzene, which of the following is the intermediate?

(a) $C_6H_5-N=O$ (b) $C_6H_5NH-NHC_6H_5$

(c) $C_6H_5-N=N-C_6H_5$ (d) $C_6H_5-N=\overset{\overset{O}{\uparrow}}{N}-C_6H_5$

21. The major product (70% to 80%) of the reaction between m-dinitrobenzene with NH_4HS is

(a) 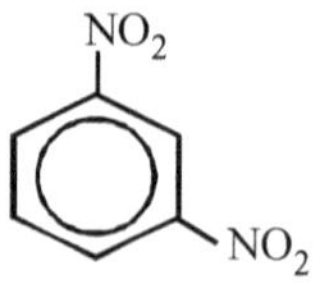 (b) 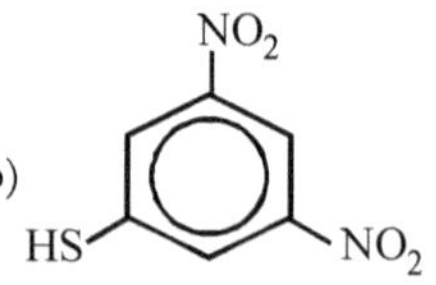

(c) 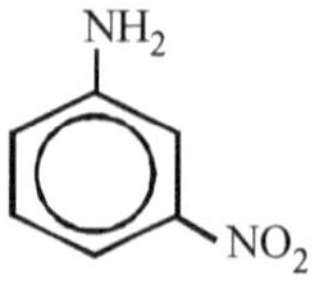 (d) 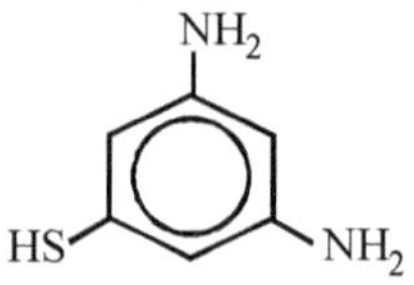

22. The following reaction is

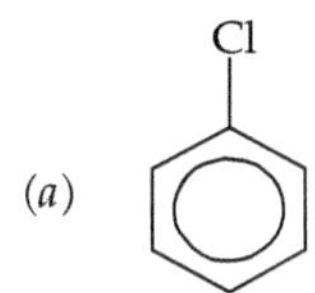

(a) nucleophilic substituton (b) electrophilic substitution
(c) free radical substitution (d) electrophilic addition

23. 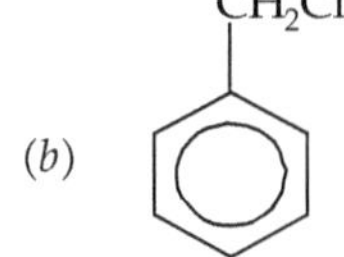

(a) 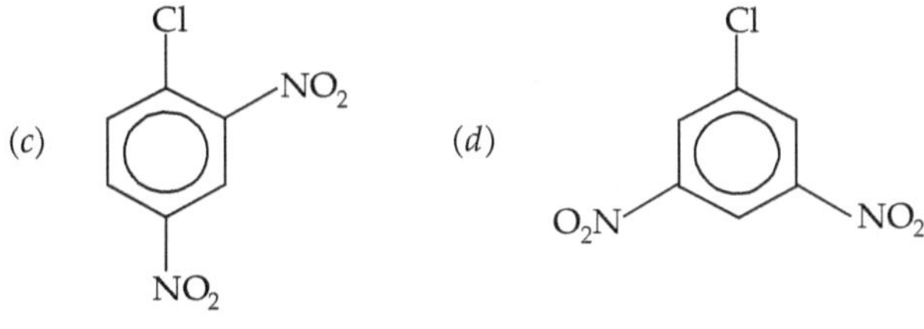

24. A nitro alkane reacts with HONO to give insoluble product in alkali which turns blue on treatment with an alkali. The nitro alkane is

(a) $CH_3CH_2NO_2$

(b) $CH_3-CH-CH_2NO_2$
       $|$
      CH_3

(c) $(CH_3)_2CHNO_2$

(d) $(CH_3)_3CNO_2$

25. Which nitro alkane will give ketone when boiled with HCl?

(a) $(CH_3)_2CHNO_2$

(b) $CH_3CH_2NO_2$

(c) $(CH_3)_3CCH_2NO_2$

(d) $(CH_3)_3CNO_2$

EXERCISE 21.2 (MCQ 1 or >1 option correct, Passage based, Matching, A/R)

DIRECTIONS for Q. 1 to Q. 11 : Multiple choice questions with one or more than one correct option(s).

1. Which of the following reaction can form a nitrile when treated with NaCN in DMSO ?

2. Which of the following shows tautomerism ?
(a) C_6H_5OH
(b) CH_3NO_2
(c) $C_6H_5CH_2NO_2$
(d) $(CH_3)_3CNO_2$

3. Which of the following reacts with nitrous acid ?
(a) Acetamide
(b) 2-Nitrobutane
(c) 2-Methyl-2-nitropropane
(d) Diethylamine.

4. Which of the following compounds can reduce Tollen's reagent?
(a) CH_3CHO
(b) $C_6H_5NO_2$
(c) C_2H_5NHOH
(d) $CH_2OHCOCH_3$

5. *p*-Nitroaniline can be obtained by

6. The products of reaction of alcoholic silver nitrite with ethyl bromide are
(a) ethane
(b) ethene
(c) nitroethane
(d) ethyl nitrite

7. Which gases are poisonous?
(a) Lewisite
(b) Mustard
(c) Phosgene
(d) MIC

8. Butanonitrile may be prepared by heating
(a) Propyl alcohol with KCN
(b) Propyl magnesium chloride with Cyanogen chloride
(c) Butyl chloride with KCN
(d) Propyl chloride with KCN

9. The representations of resonance structures of p-nitrophenoxide ion are

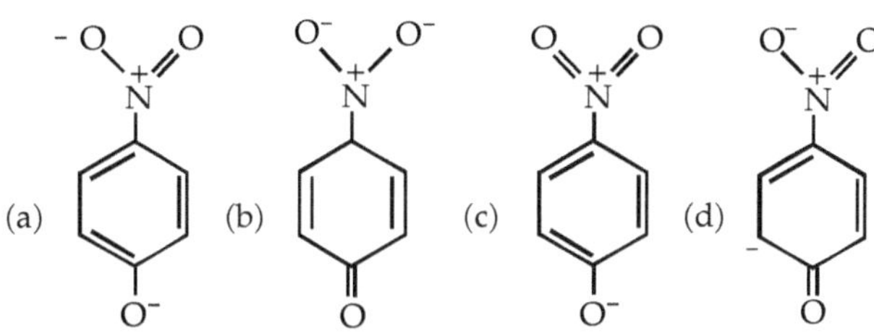

10. When nitrobenzene is treated with Br_2 in presence of $FeBr_3$, the **major product formed is** m-bromonitrobenzene. Statements which are related to obtain the m-isomer are

    (a) The electron density on meta carbon is more than that on ortho and para positions

    (b) The intermediate carbonium ion formed after initial attack of Br^+ at the meta position is least destabilised

    (c) Loss of aromaticity when Br^+ attacks at the ortho and para positions and not at meta position

    (d) Easier loss of H^+ to regain aromaticity from the meta position than from ortho and para positions.

11. Ethyl isocyanide on hydrolysis in acidic medium generates

    (a) propanoic acid and ammonium salt

    (b) ethanoic acid and ammonium salt

    (c) methylamine salt and ethanoic acid

    (d) ethylamine salt and methanoic acid

DIRECTIONS for Q. 12 to Q. 14 : Read the following passages and answer the questions that follows :

PASSAGE 1

The reduction of nitro compounds to primary amines occurs through the intermediate formation of nitroso compounds and hydroxylamines. Catalytic hydrogenation of reduction of a nitro compound with an active metal and concentrated hydrochloric acid always gives the corresponding primary amines. In the neutral medium, the nitro compounds are reduced to the corresponding hydroxylamines. However, in the basic medium, bimolecular reduction products are obtained which result through initial condensation of nitroso and hydroxylamine intermediates followed by its reduction to give different products depending upon the nature of the reducing agent used.

12. In the acidic reduction of nitrobenzene, which of the following is the intermediate?

    (a) $C_6H_5 - N = O$

    (b) $C_6H_5NH - NHC_6H_5$

    (c) $C_6H_5 - N = N - C_6H_5$

    (d) $C_6H_5 - N = \overset{O}{\overset{\uparrow}{N}} - C_6H_5$

13. The reagent that reacts with nitromethane to form methylhydroxylamine is ?

    (a) Zn/HCl   (b) Zn/NH_4Cl

    (c) Zn/NaOH   (d) Sn/HCl

14. Hydrazobenzene is formed when nitrobenzene is reduced with

    (a) Zn/HCl   (b) Zn/NaOH

    (c) $Zn/NaOH-CH_3OH$ (d) Zn/NH_4Cl

Instructions for Q. 15 to 16 : Following questions are Multiple Matching type Questions :

15.

	Column - I		*Column - II*
(A)	Nitriles	(a)	1° amine
(B)	Isonitriles	(b)	2° amine
(C)	Ketones	(c)	Hydrolysis
(D)	Phthalimide	(d)	Reductive amination

16.

	Column - I		*Column - II*
(A)	Bromine water	(a)	Yellow precipitate
(B)	Nitrobenzene	(b)	Acetoacetic ester
(C)	CHI_3	(c)	1-Butyne
(D)	Acidic hydrogens	(d)	Lemon yellow oily liquid

Instructions for Q. 17 to Q. 22 : Following questions are Assertion and Reasoning Type Questions :

Note : Each question contains STATEMENT-1 (Assertion) and STATEMENT-2 (Reason). Each question has 5 choices (a), (b), (c), (d) and (e) out of which ONLY ONE is correct.

(a) Statement-1 is True, Statement-2 is True; Statement-2 is a correct explanation for Statement-1.

(b) Statement-1 is True, Statement-2 is True; Statement-2 is NOT a correct explanation for Statement-1.

(c) Statement -1 is True, Statement-2 is False.

(d) Statement -1 is False, Statement-2 is True.

(e) Statement -1 is False, Statement-2 is False.

17. **Statement-1 :** Alkyl isocyanides with acidified water gives alkyl formamide.

    Statement-2 : In isocyanides, carbon first acts as a nucleophile and then as an electrophile.

18. **Statement-1 :** Methyl isocyanide reacts with ozone to form methyl isocyanate.

    Statement-2 : Methyl isocyanate was responsible for Bhopal tragedy.

19. **Statement-1 :** Alkyl cyanide can be prepared by carbylamine reaction

    Statement-2 : Ethyl amine when heated with chloroform in presence of alcoholic KOH, cyanide is formed.

20 **Statement-1 :** Nitrobenzene does not undergo Friedel Craft alkylation.

    Statement-2 : Nitrobenzene is used as solvent in laboratory and industry.

21. **Statement-1 :** Alkyl isocyanides in acidified water give alkyl formamides.

    Statement-2 : In isocyanides, carbon first acts as a nucleophile and then as an electrophile.

22. **Statement - 1:** Benzonitrile is prepared by the reaction of chlorobenzene with potassium cyanide.

    Statement - 2 : Cyanide (CN^-) is a strong nucleophile.

SOLUTIONS

EXERCISE 21.1

1	(c)	6	(b)	11	(b)	16	(c)	21	(c)
2	(a)	7	(c)	12	(a)	17	(a)	22	(a)
3	(c)	8	(b)	13	(c)	18	(c)	23	(a)
4	(c)	9	(d)	14	(b)	19	(b)	24	(c)
5	(c)	10	(a)	15	(c)	20	(a)	25	(a)

1. Cyclohexanenitrile is the wrong name.

2. The cation produced by the protonation of carbonyl group of amides is stabilized by resonance.

$$R\!-\!\overset{:\overset{..}{O}}{\underset{}{C}}\!-\!\overset{+}{N}H_3 \xleftarrow{\ H^+\ } R\!-\!\overset{:\overset{..}{O}}{\underset{}{C}}\!-\!\overset{..}{N}H_2 \xrightarrow{\ H^+\ } R\!-\!\overset{+\overset{..}{O}H}{\underset{}{C}}\!-\!\overset{..}{N}H_2 \longleftrightarrow R\!-\!\overset{:\overset{..}{O}H}{\underset{}{C}}=\overset{+}{N}H_2$$

An acylammonium ion   Acid amide   o-protonated amide
(the positive charge is   (the positive charge is delocalized)
localized on N)

3. The conjugate base of the *aci*-form (II) is more stable.

4. Nitro compounds, being relatively more polar than nitrites, have higher boiling points than the corresponding nitrites.

5. $R\!-\!O\!-\!N=O \xrightarrow{\text{reduction}} R\!-\!OH + H_2NOH$

7. Reduction of nitrobenzene in alkaline medium gives hydrazobenzene which rearranges in presence of HCl to form **4,4**-diaminodiphenyl, commonly known as benzidine (benzidine rearrangement).

8. Introduction of one —NO_2 group in benzene nucleus deactivates for further nitration. However, in option (*b*), nitration of *o*-nitrotoluene is not difficult because of the presence of activating —CH_3 group. Hence 2, 4, 6-trinitrotoluene is easily prepared from *o*-nitrotoluene. Further, —CH_3 group is easily oxidizable when —NO_2 groups are present in benzene nucleus as compared to oxidation of $C_6H_5CH_3$.

9. Neutral nature of the compound indicates that it should be a nitro compound. Further zero dipole moment indicates its symmetrical structure, *i.e.* it should be a benzene derivative having same group (—NO_2) in positions *p*- to each other.

10. (a)

11. (b)

12. (*a*)

13. (c) N can't have more than 8 electrons in its valence shell as it does not have any *d* orbital. In (c), N has 10 electrons.

14. (c) **Note :** As NO_2^+ is an electrophile so nitration is electrophilic substitution reaction.

Nitration in toluene is greater because of electron repelling (+I) nature of CH_3 group. Nitration of C_6H_6 and C_6D_6 takes place at the same rate because the rate determining step is the formation of carbocation which is same in both cases, in other words cleavage of C – H or C – D bond constitutes the fast step.

15. (*b*) $LiAlH_4$ does not reduce –NO_2 group to – NH_2 group.

16. (c) $R\!-\!\overset{O}{\overset{\|}{C}}\!-\!\overset{..}{\underset{}{C}}H\!-\!\overset{+}{N}\equiv \overset{..}{N} \xrightarrow{\ -N_2\ } R\!-\!\overset{O}{\overset{\|}{C}}\!-\!\overset{..}{C}H \longrightarrow \overset{O}{\overset{\|}{C}}=CHR$

Ketene   Carbene (neutral)

17. (a) Nitriles having α-hydrogen atom form alkyl derivatives with RBr in presence of $NaNH_2 / NH_3$.

18. (c) $CH_3CN + 2H \rightarrow CH_3CH = NH \xrightarrow{H_2O,\ boil} CH_3CHO$

                        X   Y

Note that cyanides are reduced only by 2H atoms, so reduction stops at aldimine stage which on hydrolysis with water gives aldehyde; it is an example of Stephen's reaction

19. (b)

20.(a) Nitrobenzene is reduced in the following manner through various intermediates to form aniline as the final product.

$$C_6H_5NO_2 \xrightarrow{2[H]} C_6H_5NO \xrightarrow{2[H]}$$

nitrobenzene   nitrosobenzene

$$C_6H_5NHOH \xrightarrow{2[H]} C_6H_5NH_2$$

phenylhydroxylamine   aniline

21.(c)

22.(a) Although benzene does not undergo nucleophilic substitution, nitrobenzene undergoes such reaction due to the presence of electron withdrawing – NO_2 group which makes o - and p - carbon electron deficient and hence liable to be attacked by OH^- (a nucleophile)

23.(a)

24.(c) See action of HONO on P, S and T nitro alkanes.

25.(a) 1° nitro alkanes give aldehyde and 2° nitro alkanes give Ketones (See text)

EXERCISE 21.2

	1	(b,c)	2	(a,b,c)	3	(a,b,d)	4	(a,c,d)	5	(c,d)
>1 CORRECT OPTION	6	(c, d)	7	(a, b, c, d)	8	(b, d)	9	(a, b, d)	10	(a, d)
	11	(d)								
PASSAGE 1	12	(a)	13	(b)	14	(b)				
MATCH THE FOLLOWING	15	(A) – (a); (B) – (a,b,c); (C) – (a,b,d); (D) – (a)								
	16	(A) – (b, c); (B) – (d); (C) – (a); (D) – (b, c)								
A/R	17	(a)	18	(b)	19	(e)	20	(b)	21	(a)
	22	(d)								

1. $C_6H_5CH_2Cl$ (b) is arylsubstituted alkyl halide, hence it undergoes nucleophilic substitution ; while in (c) **Cl is activated by the presence of electron-withdrawing —NO_2 groups in** *ortho-* **and** *para-***positions.**

2. *tert*-Nitroalkanes do not have labile H (H in α-position to the —NO_2 group) and hence can't exhibit tautomerism.

3. *tert*-Nitro compounds (Me_3CNO_2) do not react with HONO because they do not have any α-H. The three others reach with HONO as usual.

$$\underset{2°\ \text{Nitroalkane}}{CH_3\overset{\overset{\displaystyle C_2H_5}{|}}{C}HNO_2} \xrightarrow{HONO} \underset{\text{Pseudonitrol (blue)}}{(CH_3)_2\overset{\overset{\displaystyle N=O}{|}}{C}NO_2}$$

4. Aldehydes, α-hydroxyketones and hydroxylamines reduce Tollens' reagent.

5. —SO_3H group present in o- and p-positions are easily replaced.

10. (*a,d*) Nitro group decreases the electron density at the *meta*-position in comparison to ortho and para position due to – I and –M effects.

The above intermediate is a resonance hybrid of three structures, hence is more stable than the corresponding intermediate from *ortho* and *para*-attack.

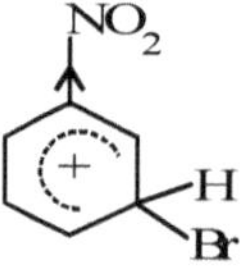

11. (*d*) Ethyl isocyanide on hydrolysis forms primary amines.

$$CH_3CH_2N \equiv C + H_2O \xrightarrow{H^+} CH_3CH_2NH_2 + HCOOH$$

19. (*d*) Chlorobenzene is resonance stabilized. Thus aryl halides (chlorobenzene) do not undergo nucleophilic substitution. Statement-2 is correct.

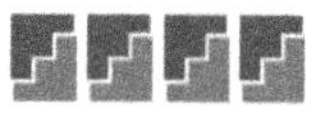

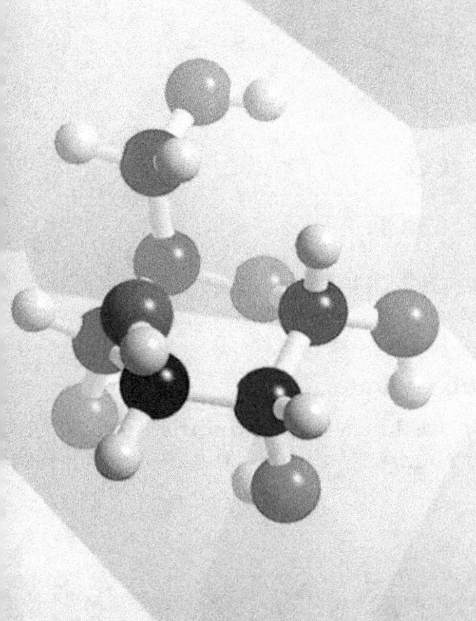

22

Carbohydrates

CHAPTER HIGHLIGHTS

<table>
<tr><td>

22.1   **Definition and Classification**

22.2   **Importance of Carbohydrates**

22.3   **D and L Designations of Monosaccharides**

22.4   **D-(+)-Glucose**

22.5   **(–)-Fructose**

</td><td>

22.6   **(+)-Sucrose**

22.7   **Some Artificial Sweetners**

22.8   **Polysaccharides**

22.9   **Illustrative Examples**

       EXERCISE

       SOLUTIONS

</td></tr>
</table>

 ## Definition and Classification

Historically, carbohydrates were once considered to be "hydrates of carbon" because molecular formulas of many carbohydrates (but not all) correspond to $C_x(H_2O)_y$ see examples (*a*). However, certain carbohydrates do not correspond to this general formula, see examples (*b*). Moreover, several compounds are although not carbohydrates, their molecular formula correspond to the above general formula, see examples (*c*).

(*a*) $C_6H_{12}O_6$ $C_{12}H_{22}O_{11}$ $(C_6H_{10}O_5)_n$
       Glucose and Fructose   Sucrose   Cellulose and starch

(*b*) $C_6H_{12}O_5$ $C_7H_{14}O_6$
       Rhamnose   Rhamnohexose

(*c*) CH_2O $C_2H_4O_2$ or CH_3COOH $C_3H_6O_3$ $C_6H_{12}O_6$
       Formaldehyde   Acetic acid   Lactic acid   Inositol

Simple carbohydrates are also known as *sugars* or *saccharides*, and name of most sugars end in *–ose*.

Carbohydrates are polyhydroxyaldehydes, polyhydroxyketones or compounds that can be hydrolyzed to them. A carbohydrate that cannot be hydrolyzed to simpler compounds is called a **monosaccharide**. A carbohydrate that can be hydrolyzed to, two, three and indefinite monosaccharide molecules is called a **disaccharide,** a **trisaccharide,** and a **polysaccharide** respectively.

A monosaccharide may be further classified ; if it contains an aldehydic group it is called an **aldose,** and if it contains a ketonic group it is called a **ketose.** Alternatively, a monosaccharide may be classified on the basis of the number of carbon atoms present it it, *viz.* **triose, tetrose, pentose, hexose, heptose,** and so on. Most naturally occurring monosaccharides are pentoses or hexoses. These two classifications are frequently combined. A C_4 aldose, for example, is called on *aldotetrose*, a C_5 ketose is called a *ketopentose.*

CH₂OH	CH₂OH		CH₂OH

$$
\begin{array}{cccc}
\text{CHO} & \overset{\displaystyle CH_2OH}{\underset{|}{CO}} & \text{CHO} & \overset{\displaystyle CH_2OH}{\underset{|}{CO}} \\
| & | & | & | \\
(CHOH)_n & (CHOH)_n & CHOH & CHOH \\
| & | & | & | \\
CH_2OH & CH_2OH & CH_2OH & CH_2OH
\end{array}
$$

      An aldose   A ketose   An aldotriose   A ketotetrose

Glyceraldehyde (an aldotriose) is considered to be the simplest chiral carbohydrate.

Carbohydrates that reduce Fehling's or Benedict's or Tollens' reagent are known as **reducing sugars.** All monosaccharides, whether aldose or ketose, and *most* disaccharides are reducing sugars. However, the most common disaccharide, sucrose (also known as table sugar) is a **non-reducing sugar.**

TEST YOUR UNDERSTANDING - 22.1

1. What are oligosaccharides ? Classify the following carbohydrates as mono–, di–, tri–, or poly-saccharide. Which of the following can be considered as oligosaccharide.

    (a) $C_{12}H_{22}O_{11}$ (b) $C_{18}H_{32}O_{16}$ (c) $C_{16}H_{26}O_{13}$ (d) $(C_5H_8O_4)_n$ (e) $C_6H_{12}O_6$.

2. Give the hydrolysis products for each of the above carbohydrate.

3.   (a)   Write a structural formula for (*i*) an aldotriose, and a (*ii*) ketohexose

    (b)   Classify the following monosaccharides

      (*i*) $HOCH_2CHOHCOCH_2OH$ (*ii*) $HOCH_2(CHOH)_3CHO$ (*iii*) $HOCH_2(CHOH)_2CH_2CHO$.

4. Write molecular formula for (*i*) a hexose trisaccharide, (*ii*) a tetrose tetrasaccharide, and (*iii*) a pentose polysaccharide also known as polypentoside or pentosan.

 **22.2**   **Importance of Carbohydrates**

Carbohydrates are the most abundant organic constituents of plants. They are the important source of chemical energy for living organisms (*e.g.* sugars and starches). Certain carbohydrates support the plant tissues, *e.g.* cellulose in wood, cotton, and flax ; carbohydrate, like chitin, forms the major constituent of the shells of crabs and lobsters. In addition to this, we encounter carbohydrate at almost every turn of our daily lives, *viz.* (*i*) sugars make fruits, sweet and yield alcohol on fermentation ; (*ii*) cellulose materials like cotton, linen, grass, wood, etc. supply clothes, paper, plastics, lacquers, paints and explosives, (*iii*) some glucose is converted into fatty acids and amino acids, (*iv*) ribose and deoxyribose (aldopentoses) are components of nucleic acids which determine human heredity.

Carbohydrates are synthesized in green plants by *photosynthesis*, a process that uses solar energy to reduce, or "fix", carbon dioxide.

$$x CO_2 + y\,H_2O + \text{Solar energy} \xrightarrow{\text{chlorophyll}} \underset{\text{Carbohydrate}}{C_x(H_2O)_y} + x O_2$$

This stored solar energy is released when animals or plants metabolize carbohydrates to carbon dioxide and water.

$$C_x(H_2O)_y + x\,O_2 \longrightarrow x\,CO_2 + y\,H_2O + \text{Energy}$$

Although some of the energy released in the oxidation of carbohydrates is converted into heat, much of it is conserved in the form of chemical compound mainly adenosine triphosphate (ATP) which is synthesized from adenosine diphosphate (ADP) and inorganic phosphate (P*i*). Plants and animals can use the conserved energy of ATP (or very similar substances) to carry out all of their energy-requiring processes like contraction of a muscle, the synthesis of a macromolecule, and so on.

$$\text{ATP} + H_2O \longrightarrow \text{ADP} + P\textit{i} + \text{Energy}$$

22.3 D and L Designations of Monosaccharides

The simplest monosaccharides are glyceraldehyde and dihydroxyacetone. Of these two compounds, only glyceraldehyde contains a **stereocenter** (a chiral carbon), hence it exists in two enantiomeric forms.

Glyceraldehyde (an aldotriose)   Dihydroxyacetone (a ketotriose)   (+)-Glyceraldehyde   and   (–)-Glyceraldehyde

Earlier in the 20th century, when the absolute configuration of any organic compound was not known, configuration of organic compounds were related to glyceraldehyde. (+)-Glyceraldehyde is designated as D-(+)-glyceraldehyde and (–)-glyceraldehyde is designated as L-(–)-glyceraldehyde. These two compounds serve as configurational standards for all monosaccharides. A monosaccharide whose highest numbered stereocenter (the penultimate carbon) has the same configuration as D-(+)-glyceraldehyde is designated as a D sugar, and similarly L sugar is related to L-(–)-glyceraldehyde.

A D-aldotetrose
(The highest stereocenter, C_3 has –OH on right, and hence D–)   An L-ketopentose
(The highest stereocenter, C_4 has –OH on left, hence L-)

Although the D, L-nomenclature is not unambiguous, while the modern R, S-nomenclature (Ch. 3) is unambiguous, this stereochemical designations is highly entrenched in the literature of carbohydrate and amino acid chemistry and hence its use in carbohydrate chemistry is not replaced by the modern Cahn-Ingold–Prelog system (R, S- nomenclature). This system has the disadvantage of specifying the configuration of only one stereocenter (the penultimate carbon).

Like R, S-designations, the D, L-designations are not necessarily related to the optical rotations of the sugars. Thus, one may encounter D-(+)-, (D)-(–)-, L-(+)- , or L-(–)-sugar.

TEST YOUR UNDERSTANDING - 22.2

1. Designate the following Fischer projections of glyceraldehyde as D or L

   (a) (b) (c)

2. How many chiral carbon's are present in an aldotetrose ? Draw the Fischer formulas for all the possible stereoisomers of an aldotetrose and classify them as D and L sugars.

3. Assign the specification, R or S, to the following :

   (a) D-(+)-Glyceraldehyde   (b) D-(–)-Glyceric acid

   (c) D-(–)-3-Bromo-2-hydroxypropionic acid   (d) D-(–)-Lactic acid

   (e) L-(+)-Lactic acid.

4. (a) How many stereoisomers does an aldopentose have ?

   (b) Is there any aldopentose, which can have only 4 stereoisomers ?

Epimers : When the two sugars differ in the configuration of only one carbon atom, other than C-1, these are called **epimers**, and the carbon atom where they differ is generally mentioned. In case, the number of carbon atom is not specified, it is assumed to be C-2. Thus glucose and mannose are C-2 epimers, while glucose and D-allose are C-3 epimers.

C-2 epimers   C-3 epimers

	CHO			^{1}CHO			^{1}CHO	
HO—		—H	H—^{2}		—OH	H—^{2}		—OH
HO—		—H	HO—^{3}		—H	H—^{3}		—OH
H—		—OH	H—^{4}		—OH	H—^{4}		—OH
H—		—OH	H—^{5}		—OH	H—^{5}		—OH
	CH_2OH			$^6CH_2OH$			$^6CH_2OH$	
	D-Mannose			D-Glucose			D-Allose	

22.4 D-(+)-Glucose

(+)-Glucose is the most important monosaccharide because it is a monomer of many important polysaccharides like starch, cellulose and glycogen and since it plays a vital role in biological processes. Glucose occurs in free as well as combined state, *viz.* disaccharide (sucrose), polysaccharides (*e.g.* cellulose, starch, glycogen) and glycosides. Important sources of free glucose are ripe grapes (hence it is also called **grape sugar**), honey, human blood, urine of diabetic patient, etc. In laboratory, glucose is prepared by the hydrolysis of sucrose, while commercially it is prepared by the hydrolysis of starch.

$$C_{12}H_{12}O_{11} \xrightarrow[\text{heat for 2 hrs.}]{\substack{\text{(i) alcohol}\\\text{(ii) dil. HCl, 50°C}}} C_6H_{12}O_6 \quad + \quad C_6H_{12}O_6$$

Sucrose   Glucose   Fructose
(insoluble in alcohol)   (soluble in alcohol)

$$(C_6H_{10}O_5)_n \xrightarrow[\text{heat}]{\text{dil. } H^+} nC_6H_{12}O_6$$

Starch   Glucose

Glucose is a white crystalline substance (m.p. 160°C), soluble in water, sparingly soluble in alcohol. It is dextrorotatory, hence also called *dextrose*. It shows **mutarotation** (change in specific rotation in aqueous solution of the compound).

Chemical properties. (+)-Glucose is a typical monosaccharide, hence study on the structure and reactions of monosaccharides is mainly due to (+)-glucose. Following chemical reactions of glucose reveal that (+)-glucose is a six-carbon, straight-chain, pentahydroxyaldehyde, *i.e.* it is an aldohexose.

(i)

$$
\begin{array}{c}
CN \\
| \\
CHOH \\
| \\
(CHOH)_4 \\
| \\
CH_2OH
\end{array}
\xleftarrow{\text{HCN}}
\begin{array}{c}
CHO \\
| \\
(CHOH)_4 \\
| \\
CH_2OH
\end{array}
\xrightarrow{(CH_3CO)_2O}
\text{Penta-O-acetylglucose}
$$

Glucose cyanohydrin   **(+)-Glucose**   Glucose pentaacetate
(indicates presence of —CHO group)   (indicates presence of 5 –OH groups)

(ii)

$$
Cu_2O\downarrow +
\begin{array}{c}
COONa \\
| \\
(CHOH)_4 \\
| \\
CH_2OH
\end{array}
\xleftarrow[\text{Cu(OH)}_2 + \text{NaOH}]{\text{Fehling's solution}}
\begin{array}{c}
CHO \\
| \\
(CHOH)_4 \\
| \\
CH_2OH
\end{array}
\xrightarrow[\text{[Ag (NH}_3)_2\text{]OH}]{\text{Tollens' reagent}}
\begin{array}{c}
COONH_4 \\
| \\
(CHOH)_4 \\
| \\
CH_2OH
\end{array}
+ 2Ag\downarrow
$$

Red ppt.   **(+)-Glucose**   Silver mirror

(iii) $\underset{\text{(strong oxi. agent)}}{\overset{\text{Conc. HNO}_3}{\longleftarrow}}$

$$\begin{matrix} \text{COOH} \\ | \\ (\text{CHOH})_4 \\ | \\ \text{COOH} \end{matrix} \qquad \begin{matrix} \text{CHO} \\ | \\ (\text{CHOH})_4 \\ | \\ \text{CH}_2\text{OH} \end{matrix} \qquad \begin{matrix} \text{COOH} \\ | \\ (\text{CHOH})_4 \\ | \\ \text{CH}_2\text{OH} \end{matrix}$$

Glucaric acid   **(+)-Glucose**   Gluconic acid
(Saccharic acid)

Reaction of glucose with Conc. HNO₃ (strong oxi. agent) gives Glucaric acid (Saccharic acid); with Br₂ Water (mild oxidising agent) gives Gluconic acid.

(iv) $\underset{\text{heat}}{\overset{\text{P/HI}}{\longleftarrow}}$

$$\begin{matrix} \text{CH}_3 \\ | \\ (\text{CH}_2)_4 \\ | \\ \text{CH}_3 \end{matrix} \qquad \begin{matrix} \text{CHO} \\ | \\ (\text{CHOH})_4 \\ | \\ \text{CH}_2\text{OH} \end{matrix} \qquad \begin{matrix} \text{CH}_2\text{OH} \\ | \\ (\text{CHOH})_4 \\ | \\ \text{CH}_2\text{OH} \end{matrix}$$

n-Hexane   **(+)-Glucose**   Glucitol
(indicates presence of   (Sorbitol)
a striaght chain of 6 C's)

Glucose with NaBH₄, H₂/Ni, or Na (Hg) + water gives Glucitol (Sorbitol).

(v) $\overset{\text{5 HIO}_4}{\longleftarrow}$

$$\begin{matrix} \text{HCOOH} \\ + \\ \text{4 HCOOH} \\ + \\ \text{CH}_2\text{O} \end{matrix} \qquad \begin{matrix} \text{CHO} \\ | \\ (\text{CHOH})_4 \\ | \\ \text{CH}_2\text{OH} \end{matrix} \qquad \begin{matrix} \text{CH}=\text{NNHC}_6\text{H}_5 \\ | \\ (\text{CHOH})_4 \\ | \\ \text{CH}_2\text{OH} \end{matrix}$$

5 moles of formic acid   **(+)-Glucose**   Glucose phenylhydrazone
1 mole of formaldehyde

Glucose with C₆H₅NHNH₂ (1 mole) gives Glucose phenylhydrazone.

Reaction of carbohydrates with phenylhydrazine requires special attention. At first stage, carbohydrates react with phenylhydrazine to form phenylhydrazones. However, if an excess of phenylhydrazine is used, the reaction proceeds further to yield products known as **osazone,** which contain two phenylhydrazine residues per molecule.

$$\begin{matrix} \text{CHO} \\ | \\ \text{CHOH} \\ \vdots \end{matrix} \xrightarrow[\text{(1st mole)}]{\text{C}_6\text{H}_5\text{NHNH}_2} \begin{matrix} \text{CH}=\text{NNHC}_6\text{H}_5 \\ | \\ \text{CHOH} \\ \vdots \end{matrix} \xrightarrow[\text{(2nd mole)}]{\text{C}_6\text{H}_5\text{NHNH}_2} \begin{matrix} \text{CH}=\text{NNHC}_6\text{H}_5 \\ | \\ \text{CO} \\ \vdots \end{matrix} + \text{C}_6\text{H}_5\text{NH}_2 + \text{NH}_3$$

$$\begin{matrix} \text{CH}=\text{NNHC}_6\text{H}_5 \\ | \\ \text{CO} \\ \vdots \end{matrix} \xrightarrow[\text{(3rd mole)}]{\text{C}_6\text{H}_5\text{NHNH}_2} \underset{\textbf{Osazone}}{\begin{matrix} \text{CH}=\text{NNHC}_6\text{H}_5 \\ | \\ \text{C}=\text{NNHC}_6\text{H}_5 \\ \vdots \end{matrix}} \xrightarrow[(-\,2\,\text{C}_6\text{H}_5\text{NHNH}_2)]{\text{H}^+} \underset{\text{Osone}}{\begin{matrix} \text{CHO} \\ | \\ \text{CO} \\ \vdots \end{matrix}}$$

Both of the phenylhydrazine residues of osazone can be removed to form dicarbonyl compounds, known as **osones.**

Osazones are highly coloured, crystalline compounds and can be readily identified, isolated and purified. Hence formation of osazone is used in the identification of carbohydrates. Osazone formation is not limited to carbohydrates, but in general it is a typical reaction of α-hydroxyaldehydes and α-hydroxyketones (*e.g.* benzoin, although not a carbohydrate, C₆H₅CHOHCOC₆H₅, it forms osazone). Further osazone formation involves only the first two carbon atoms, *i.e.* CHOCHOH— in aldoses and CH₂OHCO— in ketoses, of a compound without affecting the configuration of the rest of the molecule. Thus hexoses having similar configuration on C₃, C₄ and C₅ will form same osazone, *e.g.* glucose, mannose and fructose.

$$\begin{matrix} {}^1\text{CHO} \\ \text{H} - {}^2\text{OH} \\ \text{HO} - {}^3\text{H} \\ \text{H} - {}^4\text{OH} \\ \text{H} - {}^5\text{OH} \\ {}^6\text{CH}_2\text{OH} \end{matrix} \quad ; \quad \begin{matrix} {}^1\text{CHO} \\ \text{HO} - {}^2\text{H} \\ \text{HO} - {}^3\text{H} \\ \text{H} - {}^4\text{OH} \\ \text{H} - {}^5\text{OH} \\ {}^6\text{CH}_2\text{OH} \end{matrix} \quad ; \quad \begin{matrix} {}^1\text{CH}_2\text{OH} \\ {}^2\text{CO} \\ \text{HO} - {}^3\text{H} \\ \text{H} - {}^4\text{OH} \\ \text{H} - {}^5\text{OH} \\ {}^6\text{CH}_2\text{OH} \end{matrix} \xrightarrow{3\,\text{C}_6\text{H}_5\text{NHNH}_2} \text{Same osazone}$$

          Glucose   Mannose   Fructose

22.4.1   Structural relation between glucose, mannose and fructose.

A pair of diastereomeric aldoses that differ only in the configuration about one of its chiral carbon are called epimers, e.g. glucose and mannose are examples of C–2 epimers ; while glucose and fructose, similarly mannose and fructose are simply isomers.

(vi)   When monosaccharides are dissolved in aqueous base, they undergo isomerization. For example, aqueous solution of D-glucose in presence of base undergoes isomerization to form D-mannose and D-fructose. This type of reaction is called the **Lobry de Bruyn van Ekenstein rearrangement.**

This is the reason why D-fructose (not having an —CHO group) reduces Tollens' reagent (ammonical solution of silver nitrate), Fehling's solution (an alkaline solution cupric tartrate) and Benedict's reagent (an alkaline solution of cupric citrate). Actually, in presence of alkaline solution, ketoses (*e.g.* fructose) are converted to aldoses which reduce the above mentioned reagents.

TEST YOUR UNDERSTANDING - 22.3

1.   Give the configuration of (–)-glucose, (–)-mannose, and (+)-fructose.

2.   Compare the reactions of an aldohexose and a 2-ketohexose with (*i*) Tollens' reagent, (*ii*) Fehling solution, (*iii*) Benedict's reagent, and (*iv*) Bromine water.

3.   (*a*)   Give the products of oxidation with periodic acid with each of the following compound :

   (*i*) Glycerol, (*ii*) Glyceraldehyde, (*iii*) Dihydroxyacetone, (*iv*) Propane-1, 3-diol.

   (*b*)   Describe how oxidation with periodate can be used in a simple way to distinguish between an aldohexose and a ketohexose?

4.   Establish the structure of the following glucose derivatives from their periodate oxidation products given against each of them.

   (*a*) $A + 5\ HIO_4 \longrightarrow 2\ HCHO + 4\ HCOOH$ (*b*) $B + 4\ HIO_4 \longrightarrow CHOCOOH + 4\ HCOOH$

   (*c*) $C + 3\ HIO_4 \longrightarrow 2\ CHOCOOH + 2\ HCOOH.$

22.4.2   Structure of (+)-Glucose

Structure of (+)-glucose, an aldohexose, is not so simple as drawn above. An aldohexose with four stereogenic centers will have $2^4 = 16$ stereoisomeric compounds ; 8 belongs to D series and 8 to the L series. All are known, either as naturally occurring substances or as the product of synthesis. Of these 16 stereoisomeric aldohexoses, only one is the (+)-glucose, second is its enantiomer (–)-glucose, and the other 14 isomers are diastereomers of (+)-glucose, namely mannose, galactose, talose, etc. As expected, these other aldohexoses undergo the same set of reactions that has been described for glucose. However, remember that they undergo these reactions at different rates (characteristics of diastereomers). Specific configurations of the four stereogenic carbons of glucose, C_2 to C_5, was assigned by Emil Fischer in 1900, see structure I. In IUPAC nomenclature and with the Cahn-Ingold-Prelog system of designations, the Fischer's open chain structure of D-(+)-glucose is (2R, 3S, 4R, 5R)-2, 3, 4, 5- pentahydroxyhexanal.

D-(+)-Glucose
(Open-chain structure)

Cyclic structure of D-(+)-glucose
Fischer formula   Haworth formula
(Substituents that are to the right in a Fischer projection
are "*down*" in the corresponding Haworth formula)

Drawing Haworth structure for cyclic hemiacetals of sugars :

(i)   Lay down the Fischer projection : right → down and left → up.

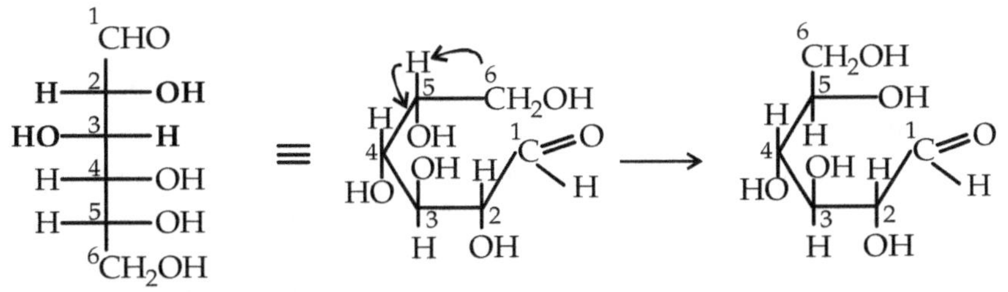

Glucose

(ii)   Rotate the C_4–C_5 bond to put the –OH in place so that it can form a part of the ring. For a sugar of the D series, this rotation puts the terminal –CH_2OH upward.

(iii)   Close the ring and draw the result. The –OH group at C-1 can be either up or down giving two stereomers, henc groups at C-1 are denoted by wavy line, ‿‿‿.

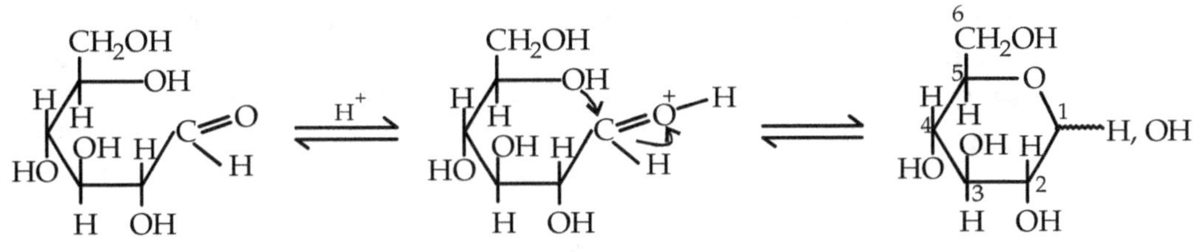

Haworth structure

Since some sugars exist in five-membered rings. Formation of five-membered ring of fructose is shown below.

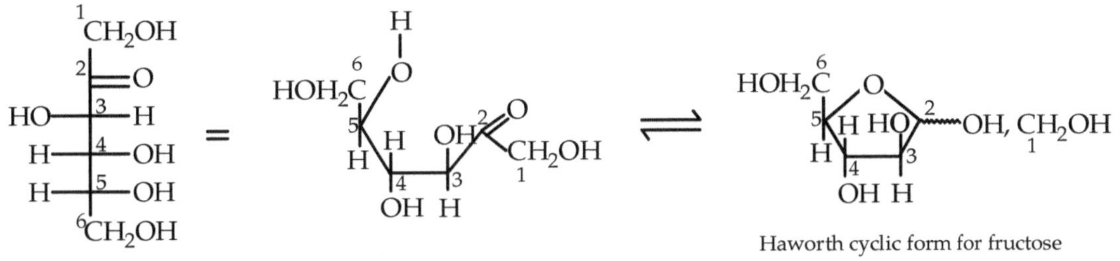

Haworth cyclic form for fructose

Significance of the word pyranose and furanose in carbohydrates. We have observed that the formation of hemiacetal of D-(+)-glucose involves —CHO and the —OH group at C_5 to form a six-membered ring (see structures I and II). However, it is not true for all carbohydrates, some carbohydrates (and even glucose, to a small extent) exist in the five membered ring where the hemiacetal formation involves —CHO group and the —OH group at C_4. Because of this variation, a system of nomenclature has been introduced to allow designation of the ring size. If the monosaccharide ring is 6 membered the compound is called a **pyranose** (derived from the 6-membered heterocyclic compound, *pyran*) ; and if the ring is 5 membered, the compound is designated as a **furanose** (derived from the five-membered heterocyclic compound, *furan*).

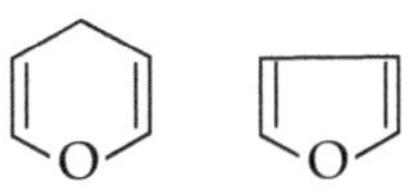

Pyran   Furan

Thus the full name for the two isomeric D-(+)-glucoses is α-D-(+)-glucopyranose and β-D-(+)-glucopyranose. Remember that glucose mainly exists as pyranose (six membered ring). Further although Haworth formulas are widely used in carbohydrates, they do not give an accurate picture of the shape of the six-membered ring for which conformational formula (III) is the best description.

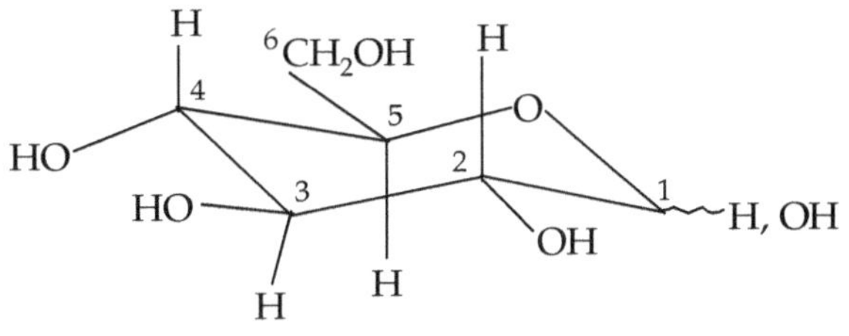

III

D-(+)-Glucopyranose

However, the cyclic structure although explains most of the above mentional reactions, it does not explain following important reactions of D-(+)-glucose.

(*i*)   It neither forms a bisulphite addition product with $NaHSO_3$ nor responds Schiff's test (both are reactions of —CHO group).

(*ii*)   It forms two isomeric methyl D-glucosides when treated with methanol and HCl.

(*iii*)   It exists in two isomeric forms both of which undergo **mutarotation.**

To explain above reactions, tremendous studies was done on the structure of D-(+)-glucose which led to a cyclic structure, II (rather than open chain structure). The cyclic forms of D-(+)-glucose are cyclic hemiacetals* formed by an intramolecular reaction of the —OH group at C_5 with the aldehyde group. Note that cyclization of the open chain structure of D-(+)-glucose has created a new stereocenter at C_1 which explains the existence of two cyclic forms of D-(+)-glucose, namely α– and β–. These two cyclic forms are *diastereomers, such diastereomers which differ only in the configuration of chiral carbon developed on hemiacetal formation* (it is C_1 in glucose and C_2 in fructose) *are called* **anomers** and the hemiacetal carbon (C_1 or C_2) is called the **anomeric carbon.** Remember that the prefixes α and β describe relative configuration. The configuration of the anomeric carbon (C_1) is said to be α when its —OH group is on the same side as the —OH group at the highest numbered stereogenic center (which is C_5 here) of the Fischer projection, in case the —OH group at the anomeric carbon and the highest numbered stereogenic center are on opposite sides of a Fishcer projection, the configuration at the anomeric carbon is β. Existence of two D-(+)-glucose and hence its cyclic hemiacetal structure is proved by isolation of the two D-(+)-glucoses under different conditions. When crystallized from ethanol, D-(+)-glucose yields α–D-(+)-glucose (better to name α–D-(+)-glucopyronose), m.p. 146° C, $[\alpha]_D = 112.2°$. Crystallization from a water-ethanol mixture produces β–D-(+)-glucopyranose, m.p. 150°, $[\alpha]_D = + 18.7°$. In the solid state the two forms do not interconvert and are stable indefinitely. Their structures have been unambiguously confirmed by X-ray crystallography. The optical rotations cited above for each isomer are those measured *immediately* after each one is dissolved in water.

Like hemiacetals, α- and β-D-(+)-glucose are readily hydrolyzed by water. In aqueous solution either anomer is converted, *via* the open chain form, into an equilibrium mixture containing both cyclic isomers.

α–D-(+)-Glucopyranose
m.p. 146°C ; $[\alpha]_D = + 112.2°$
(36% at equilibrium)

Open chain form
of D-(+)-glucose
(negligible % at equbilibrium)

β–D-(+)-Glucopyranose
m.p. 150°C ; $[\alpha]_D = + 18.7°$
(64% at equilibrium)

Thus when an aqueous solution of either form is allowed to stand, its rotation changes from + 112.2° (in case of α-) or + 18.7° (in case of β-) to a constant value of + 52.5°. *This change in rotation toward an equilibrium value is called mutarotation.*

The distribution between the α and β anomeric forms at equilibrium is readily calculated from the optical rotations of the pure isomers and the final optical rotation of the solution ; in case of D-(+)-glucose it is found to be 36 percent α and 64 percent β. The concentration of open chain D-(+)-glucose in solution at equilibrium is very small and

---

*   Acetals are the products formed by the reaction of an aldehyde or ketone with two moles of methanol in the presence of anhydrous HCl.

Aldehyde   Hemiacetal   Acetal

In glucose, both, —CHO as well as —OH group are provided by the same molecule, cyclization takes place leading to the formation of cyclic hemiacetal.

responsible for its reaction with Tollens' reagent, Fehling solution, and phenylhydrazine. Solutions of D-(+)-glucose give a negative test with Schiff's reagent and $NaHSO_3$ because reaction with these reagents are reversible, and the equilibrium favours unreacted hemiacetal form. On the other hand, osazone formation and Fehling reactions are irreversible, equilibrium is shifted to restore the low concentration of the open-chain structure.

22.4.3 Methyl D-Glucosides

Since two isomeric D-(+)-glucoses exist, there may be two isomeric methyl D-glucosides (obtained by reacting D-glucose with methanol in presence of HCl). The glucosides are full acetals, fairly stable in aqueous solution ; hence they do not undergo mutarotation. When heated with aq. acids, they are hydrolysed to yield the original hemiacetals (α- or β-glucose) ; however they are not readily hydrolyzed to hemiacetals and to open-chain aldehyde by alkalies hence they do not reduce Tollens' or Fehling's reagent (alkaline reagents), hence **glucosides are non-reducing sugars.**

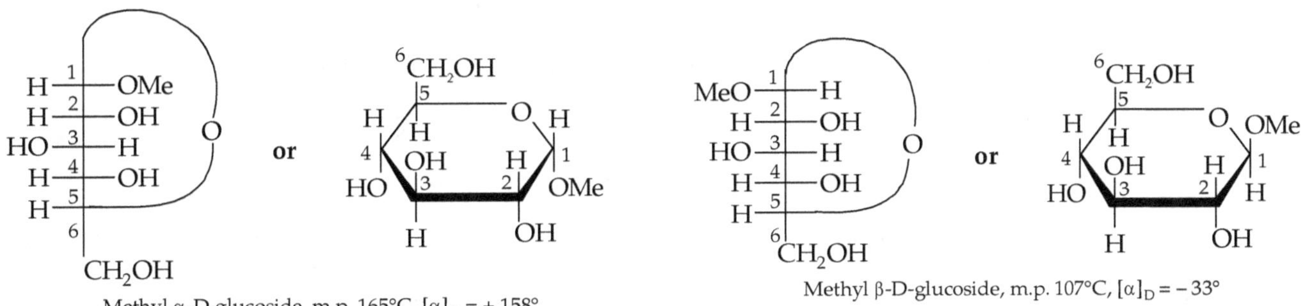

Methyl α-D-glucoside, m.p. 165°C, $[\alpha]_D = +158°$

Methyl β-D-glucoside, m.p. 107°C, $[\alpha]_D = -33°$

TEST YOUR UNDERSTANDING - 22.4

1. Differentiate between epimers and anomers.
2. Name the enantiomer of α-D-(+)-glucose.
3. Do the anomers of D-glucose have specific rotations of the same magnitude but opposite signs ?
4. Can inverting the configuration of C_5 of D-glucose give L–glucose ?
5. Give two products of the reaction of an aldohexose with excess of $(MeO)_2SO_2$, dimethyl sulphate or CH_3I in concentrated NaOH.
6. Explain the following :
   (a) (+)-Glucose reacts with Fehling's solution and phenylhydrazine, but not with $NaHSO_3$.
   (b) Although glucose reacts with Fehling's solution, methyl glucosides do not react.
   (c) (+)-Glucose reacts with acetic anhydride to give two isomeric pentaacetyle derivatives neither of which reduces Fehlings' or Tollens' reagent.
   (d) Glycosides show mutarotation in acidic solution but not in neutral or basic aqueous solution.

22.5 (–)-Fructose

(–)-Fructose is the most important example not only of 2-ketohexoses but of all ketoses. It occurs widely in fruits and, combined with glucose, in the disaccharide sucrose (common table sugar). Commercially, fructose is obtained by the hydrolysis of the polysaccharide, inulin.

$$(C_6H_{10}O_5)_n \;+\; n\,H_2O \xrightarrow[\text{heat}]{H_2SO_4} n\,C_6H_{12}O_6$$

Inulin   Fructose

Fructose is a white crystalline compound (m.p. 104°C), soluble in water and alcohol, but insoluble in ether (remember that nearly all carbohydrates are insoluble in ether). It is sweetest of all sugars and exhibits mutarotation; the $[\alpha]_D$ for α-, β-, and equilibrium mixture of fructose are $-21°$, $+133.5°$ and $-92.3°$ respectively. It responds most of the usual reactions of the ketonic and hydroxyl groups. Its worth-mentioning properties are oxidation, reduction and osazone formation.

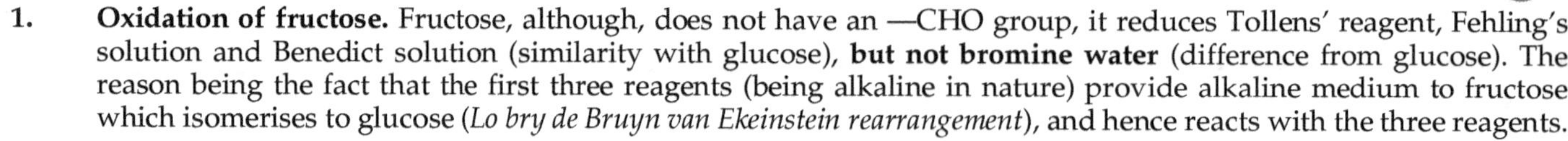

1. **Oxidation of fructose.** Fructose, although, does not have an —CHO group, it reduces Tollens' reagent, Fehling's solution and Benedict solution (similarity with glucose), **but not bromine water** (difference from glucose). The reason being the fact that the first three reagents (being alkaline in nature) provide alkaline medium to fructose which isomerises to glucose (*Lo bry de Bruyn van Ekeinstein rearrangement*), and hence reacts with the three reagents.

$$\text{Fructose} \underset{}{\overset{\text{OH}^-\ \text{from the reagents}}{\rightleftharpoons}} \text{Glucose} \underset{}{\overset{\text{Reagent}}{\rightleftharpoons}} \text{Gluconic acid}$$

(Here reagent means Tollens' reagent, Fehling solution or Benedict reagent.)

Since bromine water does not provide OH⁻ ions, fructose can't change to glucose in presence of bromine water, hence it is not oxidized by aqueous solution of bromine.

2. **Reduction.** Fructose, on reduction with Ni/H_2, Na–Hg and water or $LiAlH_4$ gives two alcohols, *viz.* sorbitol and mannitol (difference from glucose which on reduction gives only one alcohol, sorbitol).

CH_2OH		CH_2OH		CH_2OH
CO	$\xrightarrow[\text{H}_2\text{O}]{\text{Na–Hg}}$	$H—\overset{*}{C}—OH$	$+\ HO—$	$\overset{*}{C}—H$
$(CHOH)_3$		$(CHOH)_3$		$(CHOH)_3$
CH_2OH		CH_2OH		CH_2OH
Fructose		Sorbitol		Mannitol

The reason is very clear : reduction of fructose ($>C=O \longrightarrow —\overset{*}{C}HOH$) develops one more chiral carbon atom leading to two isomers, while reduction of glucose does not develop any additional chiral carbon [—CHO $\longrightarrow$ —CH_2OH)].

3. **Osazone formation.** Fructose reacts with excess of phenylhydrazine [3 moles of the reagent per mole of fructose) to form osazone hich is same as that formed by glucose.

Fructose		Osazone		Glucose
CH_2OH		$CH=NNHC_6H_5$		CHO
CO	$\xrightarrow{3\,C_6H_5NHNH_2}$	$C=NNHC_6H_5$	$\xleftarrow{3\,C_6H_5NHNH_2}$	$H—C—OH$
$(CHOH)_3$		$(CHOH)_3$		$HO—C—H$
CH_2OH		CH_2OH		$H—C—OH$
				$H—C—OH$
				CH_2OH

Now as we know from our previous discussion that osazone formation involves only first two carbon atoms, formation of same osazone from glucose (of known configuration) and fructose indicates that the two sugars have same configuration at C_3, C_4 and C_5 and differ only in the nature of the first two carbon atoms.

Thus by knowing the structure of D-glucose, we can write down the open chain structure of D-fructose as IV. However, like aldoses (*e.g.* glucose), ketoses (*e.g.* fructose) exist mainly as cyclic hemiacetals, better known as cyclic hemiketals (see structures V and VI).

D-Fructose	α-D-Fructofuranose	β-D-Fructofuranose
IV	V	VI

Note that the configuration of the anomeric carbon, which is C_2 in fructose, is said to be α when its OH group is on the same side as the OH group at the highest numbered stereogenic center which is C_5 here.

TEST YOUR UNDERSTANDING - 22.5

1. (*a*)   How many ketotetroses are possible ?

    (*b*)   How many chiral carbon centers are present in (–)– fructose ? Name the number of stereoisomers of fructose.

    (*c*)   Which is the anomeric carbon in fructose ?   (*d*)   What are deoxysugars ?

2. Differentiate between hemiacetal and acetal.

22.6 (+)-Sucrose

Ordinarily table sugar is a disaccharide (carbohydrates that yield two monosaccharide molecules on hydrolysis), called *sucrose. Sucrose*, the most widely occurring disaccharide, is formed in all photosynthetic plants. Commercially, it is obtained from sugarcane or sugar beets. It is colourless, crystalline, water soluble, sweet compound, dextrorotatory $[\alpha]_D$ + 66.5° compound **that does not show mutarotation.** Sucrose, on hydrolysis by dil. aqueous acid, or by the enzyme (*invertase*) gives D-(+)-glucose and D-(–) fructose.

$$C_{12}H_{12}O_{11} \ + \ H_2O \ \xrightarrow[\text{or invertase}]{H^+} \ C_6H_{12}O_6 \ + \ C_6H_{12}O_6$$

$$\text{(+)-Sucrose} \qquad\qquad\qquad \text{D-(+)-Glucose} \qquad \text{D-(–)-Fructose}$$

Structurally, the two monosacchaide units (D-glucose and D-fructose) of sucrose are joined at their anomeric carbons, *i.e.*, C_1 of glucose is joined to C_2 of fructose through their —OH groups. Thus the disaccharide (sucrose) does not have free anomeric hydroxyl group and hence it can't have free —CHO or >C = O group is its structure. Consequently sucrose is found to be **non-reducing sugar,** and neither shows mutarotation nor forms osazone.

Disaccharides in which anomeric hydroxyl group of either of the monosaccharide is free can regenerate its — CHO or >C = O, hence such disaccharides are **reducing,** and exist in α- and β- forms which undergo mutarotation, common examples are lactose, maltose, cellobiose etc.

Specific rotation of (+)-sucrose and its hydrolysate. (+)-Sucrose has a specific rotation of + 66.5°, while its hydrolyate (a mixture of equal amounts of D-(+)-glucose and D-(–)-fructose) has a specific rotation of –19.9°. Since the specific rotation of the hydrolysis product is opposite to that of (+)-sucrose, hydrolysis of sucrose is commonly called as *inversion of sucrose* and the hydrolysis product is called *invert sugar.* The inversion in rotation is due to the presence of equal amount of D-(–)-fructose with a large negative specific rotation of –92.4°.

$$C_{12}H_{12}O_{11} + H_2O \ \xrightarrow[\text{or invertase}]{H^+} \ C_6H_{12}O_6 \ + \ C_6H_{12}O_6$$

$$\begin{array}{ccc} \text{Sucrose} & \text{D-(+)-Glucose} & \text{D-(–)-Fructose} \\ [\alpha]_D = + 66.5° & [\alpha]_D = + 52.7° & [\alpha]_D = - 92.4° \end{array}$$

$$\text{Invert sugar, } [\alpha]_D = - 19.9°$$

Honey mainly contains invert sugar, the bees supply the enzyme invertase.

Remember the following order of sweetness of the common sugars (mono- and oligo- saccharides are called sugars, while polysaccharides are called *non-sugars*)

$$\text{Fructose} \ > \ \text{Invert sugar} \ > \ \text{Sucrose} \ > \ \text{Glucose} \ > \ \text{Maltose} \ > \ \text{Lactose}$$

One of the interesting reactions of sucrose is its reactions with conc. H_2SO_4 to give free carbon (commonly known as **sugar charcoal,** a very pure form of carbon) along with water ; the reaction is known as dehydration. A part of carbon is oxidised by conc. H_2SO_4 to form CO_2 and SO_2, the latter is detected due to its characteristic smell.

$$C_{12}H_{12}O_{11} \ + \ H_2SO_4 \longrightarrow \ 12\,C \ + \ 11\,H_2O$$
$$\text{Sucrose} \qquad\qquad \text{Sugar charcoal}$$

$$C + 2H_2SO_4 \longrightarrow 2\,SO_2 \ + \ CO_2 + 2H_2O$$

TEST YOUR UNDERSTANDING - 22.6

1.   Can you calculate the specific rotation of invert sugar, given $[\alpha]_D = + \ 52.7°$ for D-glucose, and $[\alpha]_D = - 92.4°$ for D-fructose ?

22.7 Some Artificial Sweetners

Sucrose and fructose are the most common natural sweeteners. Since they add to our calorie and promote tooth decay, some artificial sweetening agent were developed. Important artificial sweetening agents are mentioned below.

1. **Aspartame.** It is the most successful and widely used artificial sweetner. It is the methyl ester of a dipetide formed from phenylalanine and aspartic acid. It is roughly 100 times as sweet as sucrose. Its limitations are its slow hydrolysis in solution and decomposition with heat.

2. **Alitame.** It is a compound related to aspartame, but with important properties like more stability and more sweetness. It is nearly 2000 times as sweet as sucrose.

3. **Sucralose.** It is a trichloro derivative of sucrose. It looks and tastes like sugar, it is stable at the temperatures used for cooking and baking, and neither causes tooth decay nor provides calories. It is 600 times sweeter than sucrose.

4. **Cyclamate and Saccharin.** These were popular sweetners at one time, a mixture of 10 part of cyclamate and 1 part of saccharin proved sweetner than either compound individually. However, this mixture produced tumours in animals, hence its use was banned. Saccharin is still used is some products.

5. **Sucronic acid.** It is reported to be 200,000 times as sweet as sucrose.

6. **L-Glucose.** L-Sugars are also artificial sweetners and they provide nearly zero calories because our enzymes selectively metabolize only the D-sugars.

22.8 Polysaccharides

Polysaccharides are naturally occurring polymers of aldoses or ketoses. The most common polysaccharides are the polymers of aldohexoses or ketohexoses, and have the general formula $(C_6H_{10}O_5)_n$. Common examples are cellulose, starch, glycogen, inulin etc. ; all of these on hydrolysis give indefinite number of monosaccharides of the formula $C_6H_{12}O_6$ which may be glucose, fructose or other hexose depending upon the individual polysaccharide.

$$(C_6H_{10}O_5)_n + nH_2O \longrightarrow n\,C_6H_{12}O_6$$

Cellulose, starch and glycogen are the polysaccharides of D-(+)-glucose ; they differ in the point of linkage of the glucose units, of molecular size and shape. Further starch contains two different monosaccharides : (*a*) a water-soluble fraction (20%) called *amylose* and (*b*) a water-insoluble fraction (80%) called *amylopectin*. *Dextrin* is one of the intermediate hydrolysis products of starch.

$$\text{Starch} \xrightarrow{\text{hydrolysis}} \text{Dextrin} \xrightarrow{\text{hydrolysis}} \text{(+)-Maltose} \xrightarrow{\text{hydrolysis}} \text{D-(+)-glucose}$$

Glycogen is the form of a polysaccharide of (+)-glucose which is stored in animals (hence also called *animal starch*). It is released from liver (where it is stored) upon metabolic demand and hydrolysed in the system to (+)-glucose. **Inulin** is a polysaccharide of fructose.

22.9 ILLUSTRATIVE EXAMPLES

Example 1 :

(a) **Draw the Fischer projection formulas for the possible stereoisomer of 2-(methylamino)-1-phenylpropan-1-ol.**

(b) **The erythro stereoisomers of the above compound represent ephedrine (a bronchodilator), while the threo stereoisomers represent pseudoephedrine (a decongestant). Which structure you will give for ephedrine and pseudoephedrine?**

(c) **Label the structure for (–)-ephedrine and (+)-pseudoephedrine?**

Solution :

(a)

```
      C₆H₅              C₆H₅              C₆H₅          C₆H₅
  H——————OH        HO——————H        H——————OH   HO——————H
  H——————NHCH₃  H₃CHN——————H   H₃CHN——————H    H——————NHCH₃
      CH₃              CH₃              CH₃          CH₃
       I                II               III          IV
   \_____________________/      \_____________________/
          erythro-                      threo-
```

(b)   Structures I and II represent enantiomers of ephedrine, while structures III and IV represent enantiomers of pseudoephedrine.

(c)   The direction of optical rotation has no relation with the D or L designation (except for glyceraldehyde) so it is not possible to assign the (–)– or (+)– sign for structures. The optical rotation can only be determined with the help of polarimeter.

Example 2 :

Aldohexoses have four chiral carbon atoms, and hence it exists in eight enantiomeric pairs. Out of the eight D-aldohexoses, how many are expected to yield optically inactive alditols on reduction, write the Fischer projection formulas for such D-aldohexoses?

Solution :

Only those alditols would be optically inactive, whose molecules possess a plane of symmetry. There are two such D-alditols and hence two D-aldohexoses.

```
      CHO                   CH₂OH                        CH₂OH                      CHO
  H——————OH             H——————OH                    H——————OH                 H——————OH
  H——————OH    NaBH₄    H——————OH ······Plane of    HO——————H     NaBH₄       HO——————H
  H——————OH    ———→     H——————OH      symmetry      HO——————H     ←———        HO——————H
  H——————OH             H——————OH                    H——————OH                 H——————OH
      CH₂OH                 CH₂OH                        CH₂OH                      CH₂OH
                       Optically inactive            Optically inactive
```

These two aldohexoses are D-allose and D-galactose.

Example 3 :

Two D-aldohexoses *A* and *B* are oxidised with nitric acid to form optically inactive aldaric acids. Compound *A* is degraded to an D-aldopentose which on oxidation with HNO_3 gives an optically active aldaric acid. However, on similar treatment aldohexose B gives optically inactive aldaric acid. Determine the structures of *A* and *B*.

Solution :

Only following two configurations of aldohexose will give optically inactive acid, on oxidation.

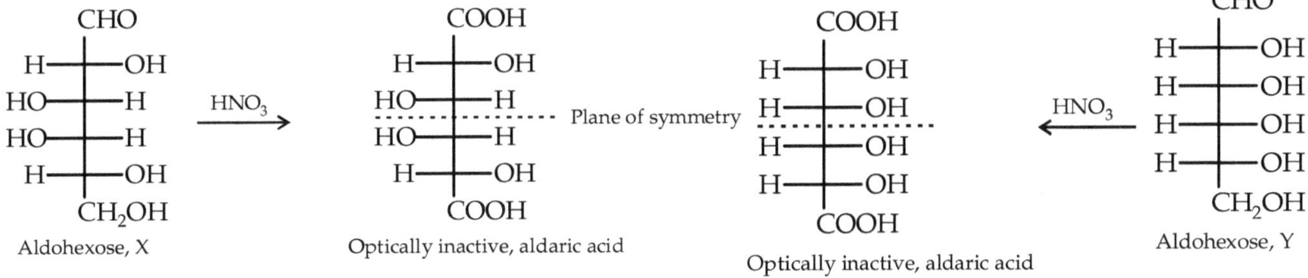

```
      CHO                  COOH                        COOH                       CHO
  H——————OH            H——————OH                   H——————OH                 H——————OH
 HO——————H    HNO₃    HO——————H ·····Plane of      H——————OH     HNO₃        H——————OH
 HO——————H    ———→    HO——————H      symmetry      H——————OH     ←———        H——————OH
  H——————OH            H——————OH                    H——————OH                 H——————OH
      CH₂OH                COOH                        COOH                       CH₂OH
   Aldohexose, X    Optically inactive,        Optically inactive,          Aldohexose, Y
                         aldaric acid               aldaric acid
```

Now let us take the lower homologue of the two aldohexoses and observe the optical activity of their corresponding aldaric acids.

$$
\begin{array}{c}
\text{CHO} \\
\text{HO}-\!\!-\text{H} \\
\text{HO}-\!\!-\text{H} \\
\text{H}-\!\!-\text{OH} \\
\text{CH}_2\text{OH}
\end{array}
\xrightarrow{\ \text{HNO}_3\ }
\begin{array}{c}
\text{COOH} \\
\text{HO}-\!\!-\text{H} \\
\text{HO}-\!\!-\text{H} \\
\text{H}-\!\!-\text{OH} \\
\text{COOH}
\end{array}
\quad ; \quad
\begin{array}{c}
\text{CHO} \\
\text{H}-\!\!-\text{OH} \\
\text{H}-\!\!-\text{OH} \\
\text{H}-\!\!-\text{OH} \\
\text{CH}_2\text{OH}
\end{array}
\xrightarrow{\ \text{HNO}_3\ }
\begin{array}{c}
\text{COOH} \\
\text{H}-\!\!-\text{OH} \\
\text{H}-\!\!-\text{OH} \\
\text{H}-\!\!-\text{OH} \\
\text{COOH}
\end{array}
$$

Aldopentose form X   Optically inactive   Aldopentose form Y   Optically inactive

Hence X is **A** and Y is **B.**

Example 4 :

Observe the following reactions carefully, and answer the question given below :

$$
\begin{array}{c}
\text{CHO} \\
\text{H}-\!\!-\text{OH} \\
\text{HO}-\!\!-\text{H} \\
\text{H}-\!\!-\text{OH} \\
\text{H}-\!\!-\text{OH} \\
\text{CH}_2\text{OH}
\end{array}
\xrightarrow[\ \text{Ni}\ ]{\ \text{H}_2\ }
\begin{array}{c}
\text{CH}_2\text{OH} \\
\text{H}-\!\!-\text{OH} \\
\text{HO}-\!\!-\text{H} \\
\text{H}-\!\!-\text{OH} \\
\text{H}-\!\!-\text{OH} \\
\text{CH}_2\text{OH}
\end{array}
\xrightarrow[\ \text{oxidation}\ ]{\ \text{bacterial}\ }
\begin{array}{c}
\text{CH}_2\text{OH} \\
\text{CO} \\
\text{HO}-\!\!-\text{H} \\
\text{H}-\!\!-\text{OH} \\
\text{HO}-\!\!-\text{H} \\
\text{CH}_2\text{OH}
\end{array}
$$

D-Glucose   D-Glucitol   L-Sorbose

Explain the conversion of D-glucitol to L-sorbose.

Solution :

Bacterial oxidation of D-glucitol is specific, it selectively oxidises the –CHOH group of D-glucitol that corresponds to C-5 of D-glucose.

$$
\begin{array}{c}
\text{CH}_2\text{OH} \\
\text{H}-\!\!-\text{OH} \\
\text{HO}-\!\!-\text{H} \\
\text{H}-\!\!-\text{OH} \\
\text{H}-\!\!-\text{OH} \\
\text{CH}_2\text{OH}
\end{array}
\xrightarrow[\ \text{oxidation}\ ]{\ \text{bacterial}\ }
\begin{array}{c}
\text{CH}_2\text{OH} \\
\text{H}-\!\!-\text{OH} \\
\text{HO}-\!\!-\text{H} \\
\text{H}-\!\!-\text{OH} \\
=\!\text{O} \\
\text{CH}_2\text{OH}
\end{array}
\ \equiv\
\begin{array}{c}
\text{CH}_2\text{OH} \\
\text{CO} \\
\text{HO}-\!\!-\text{H} \\
\text{H}-\!\!-\text{OH} \\
\text{HO}-\!\!-\text{H} \\
\text{CH}_2\text{OH}
\end{array}
$$

bacterial oxidation   L-Sorbose

Example 5 :

Supply structures for A to D in the following series of reactions.

$$
\begin{array}{c}
\text{CHO} \\
\text{H}-\!\!-\text{OH} \\
\text{HO}-\!\!-\text{H} \\
\text{H}-\!\!-\text{OH} \\
\text{H}-\!\!-\text{OH} \\
\text{CH}_2\text{OH}
\end{array}
\xrightarrow{\ \text{aq. Br}_2\ } [\text{A}]
\underset{\substack{\text{Separated} \\ \text{and further treated}}}{\overset{\text{pyridine}}{\rightleftharpoons}} [\text{B}]
\xrightarrow{\ \text{H}^+\ } [\text{C}]
\xrightarrow{\ \text{Na/Hg}\ } [\text{D}]
$$

Solution :

The reaction sequence shows Fischer projections:

Starting compound (CHO, H—OH, HO—H, H—OH, H—OH, CH$_2$OH) — $\xrightarrow{\text{aq. Br}_2}$ — **[A]** (COOH, H—OH, HO—H, H—OH, H—OH, CH$_2$OH) — $\underset{\text{pyridine}}{\rightleftharpoons}$ — **[B]** (COOH, HO—H, HO—H, H—OH, H—OH, CH$_2$OH) — $\xrightarrow{\text{H}^+}$

Epimerisation (in presence of base) — **[C]** (a δ-lactone ring: CO, HO—H, HO—H, H—OH, H—, CH$_2$OH) — $\underset{\text{H}_2\text{O}}{\xrightarrow{\text{Na/Hg}}}$ — **[D]** (CHO, HO—H, HO—H, H—OH, H—OH, CH$_2$OH)

[C] — A δ-lactone, (more stable than γ-lactone)

[D] — A, C–2 epimer of the starting compound

Example 6 :

Identify compounds A, B and C in the following reactions.

$$\text{CHO—(CHOH)}_4\text{—CH}_2\text{OH} \xrightarrow[\text{C}_6\text{H}_5\text{NHNH}_2]{\text{excess of}} \text{[A]} \xrightarrow{\text{C}_6\text{H}_5\text{CHO}} \text{[B]} \xrightarrow[\text{CH}_3\text{COOH}]{\text{Zn}} \text{[C]}$$

Solution :

Starting material (CHO, CHOH, (CHOH)$_3$, CH$_2$OH) $\xrightarrow{3\,\text{C}_6\text{H}_5\text{NHNH}_2}$ **[A]** (CH=NNHC$_6$H$_5$, C=NNHC$_6$H$_5$, (CHOH)$_3$, CH$_2$OH) $\xrightarrow[(-\,2\,\text{C}_6\text{H}_5\text{CH}=\text{NNHC}_6\text{H}_5)]{2\,\text{C}_6\text{H}_5\text{CHO}}$ **[B]** (CHO, CO, (CHOH)$_3$, CH$_2$OH) $\xrightarrow[\text{CH}_3\text{COOH}]{\text{Zn}}$ **[C]** (CH$_2$OH, CO, (CHOH)$_3$, CH$_2$OH)

In the conversion of **[B]** to **[C]**, the more reactive aldehyde group of the osone is reduced.

Example 7 :

Can you imagine a carbohydrate, other than D-(+)-glucose, which on oxidation with HNO$_3$ gives same aldaric acid as D-(+)-glucose ?

Solution :

First of all, write down the reaction involving oxidation of D-(+)-glucose with HNO$_3$. Now write the equivalent structure of the aldaric acid (aldaric acids are dicarboxylic acids obtained by oxidation of the two terminal carbon atoms of the monosaccharide to —COOH groups).

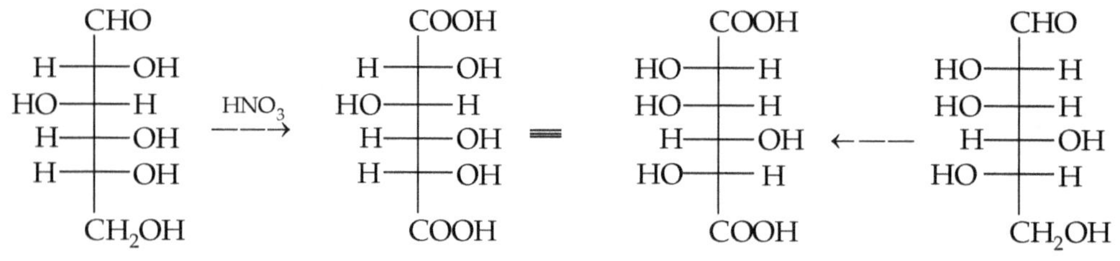

$$\text{(D)-(+)-Glucose} \xrightarrow{HNO_3} \text{Aldaric acid}$$

Example 8 :

A monosaccharide is treated with HCN, the product hydrolyzed and reduced to 2-methylhexanoic acid by heating with HI and P. Establish the structure of the monosaccharide.

Solution :

Summarise the given facts in the form of equation

$$\text{Monosaccharide} \xrightarrow{HCN} [\ ] \xrightarrow{\text{hydrolysis}} [\ ] \xrightarrow{HI/P} HOOCCH(CH_2)_3CH_3$$
$$\text{2-Methylhexanoic acid}$$

Above reactions lead to following conclusions.

(*i*)   Since the starting compound is a monosaccharide, it must have a —CHO   or   >C = O group.

(*ii*)   Formation of carboxylic acid, having a branched alkyl chain indicates that the monosaccharide is a ketose. Position of ketonic group is indicated by the nature of alkyl group, which is —CH_3, here.

Hence the above reactions can be explained by taking 2-ketohexose as the monosaccharide.

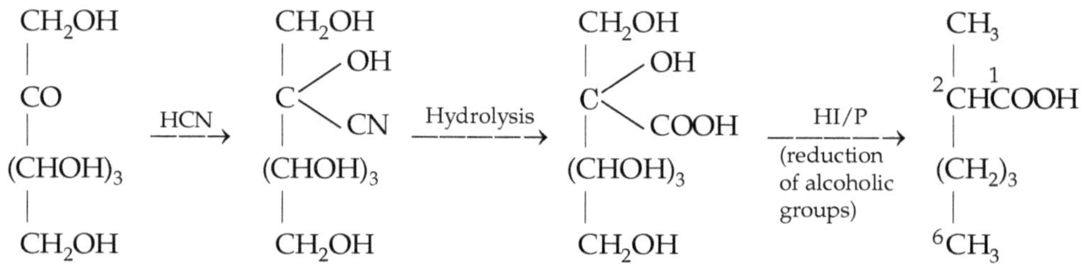

A 2-ketohexose (*e.g.* fructose) $\xrightarrow{HCN}$ $\xrightarrow{\text{Hydrolysis}}$ $\xrightarrow[\substack{\text{(reduction} \\ \text{of alcoholic} \\ \text{groups)}}]{HI/P}$ 2-Methylhexanoic acid

Had the keto group been on C_3 wrt to the upper CH_2OH group, the final product would have been 2-ethylpentanoic acid.

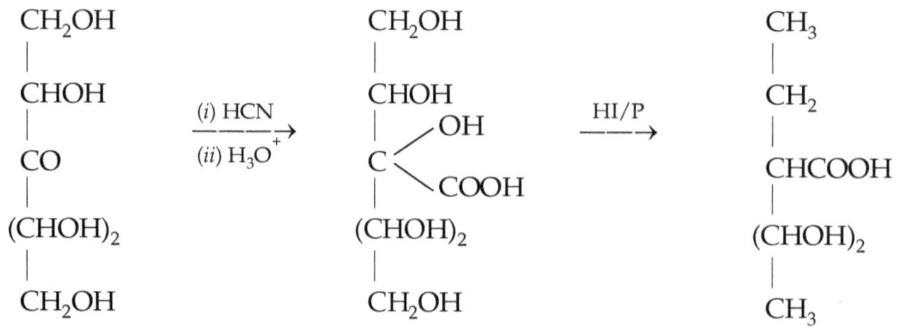

A 3-ketohexose $\xrightarrow[\text{(ii) } H_3O^+]{\text{(i) HCN}}$ $\xrightarrow{HI/P}$ 2-Ethylpentanoic acid

Example 9 :

The specific optical rotations of pure α- and β-D-mannopyranose are + 29.3° and –17.0, respectively. When either form is dissolved in water, specific optical rotation of the equilibrium mixture is found to be + 14.2°. Calculate the percentage of each isomer at equilibrium.

Solution :

Let fraction of α-anomer $= x$

∴　　Fraction of β-anomer $= (1 - x)$

Hence $x (+ 29.3°) + (1 - x) (- 17.0°) = + 14.2°$

$$29.3° \, x + (- 17° + 17°x) = + 14.2°$$

$$29.3°x + 17°x = 14.2° + 17°$$

$$46.3°x = 31.2°$$

$$x = 0.67$$

∴　Fraction of α-anomer = 0.67 or 67%

and　fraction of β-anomer　= 0.33 or 33%.

Example 10 :

Interconversion of the open chain and cyclic hemiacetal forms of glucose is catalysed by either acid or base.

(a)　Propose a mechanism for the cyclization, in presence of a trace of acid.

(b)　The cyclic hemiacetal form of glucose is more stable than the open chain form, so at equilibrium very little of the open chain form is present. When Tollens reagent is added to glucose solution, what do you expect about the amount of the cyclic form of glucose with time.

Solution :

(a)

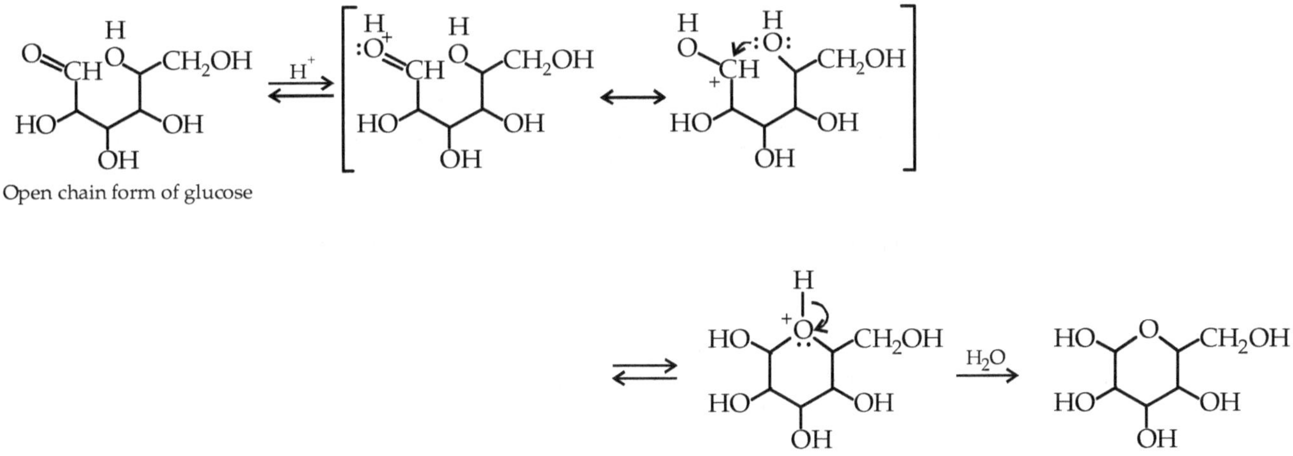

Open chain form of glucose

Cyclic form (hemiacetal)

(b)　In the basic solution of the Tollens reagent, an equilibrium exists between the hemiacetal (cyclic) form and open chain form, of course the former is present in larger concentration. However, the Tollen's reagent oxidises the open chain form to a carboxylate ion causing conversion of further amount of cyclic form to open chain which is again oxidised to carboxylate, thus more and more amount of cyclic form is converted to carboxylate with the time and ultimately all the cyclic form is converted to the carboxylate (**Le Chatelier principle**).

$$\text{Cyclic form} \rightleftharpoons \text{Open chain form} \xrightarrow[\text{(irreversible)}]{\text{Ag}^+} \text{Oxidised to carboxylate}$$

Example 11 :

When glucose is treated with a base, a mixture of glucose, mannose and fructose is obtained. Explain by giving proper mechanism.

$$
\begin{array}{ccc}
\text{D-Glucose} & \text{D-Mannose} & \text{D-Fructose}
\end{array}
$$

Solution :

Under basic conditions, the proton alpha to the aldehyde (or ketone) carbonyl group is reversibly removed to form corresponding enolate.

Enolate

The enolate so formed may undergo two different reactions forming two different compounds.

(a)   **Reprotonation of enol at C_2 :** Since C_2 of enolate is no longer asymmetric, reprotonation can occur on either face of the enolate, giving a mixture of the original sugar and its C_2 epimer.

D-Glucose   D-Mannose

Since this reaction leads to a mixture of epimers, it is called **epimerization**.

(b)   **Reprotonation of enol on the C_1 oxygen :** This leads to an **enediol** intermediate which is easily converted into a ketose (fructose) by a series of reactions.

enolate   enediol   D-Fructose

Since this reaction leads to isomer, it is known as **isomerization**.

EXERCISE 22.1 (MCQ - ONE option correct)

1. The general formula for most of carbohydrates is $C_n(H_2O)_m$; in this formula the value of n and m may be

(a) $n > m$ (b) $n < m$

(c) Both   (d) None.

2. The molecular formula for a pentose tetrasaccharide should be

(a) $C_{24}H_{42}O_{21}$ (b) $C_{20}H_{32}O_{16}$

(c) $C_{20}H_{36}O_{18}$ (d) $C_{20}H_{34}O_{17}$.

3. (+)-Glucose is oxidised in the tissues to CO_2 and H_2O with the release of energy. This energy is

(a) first formed and then stored inside the tissue

(b) originally supplied by enzymes present in the tissues

(c) originally supplied by sun

(d) None of the above is true.

4. (+)-Glucose and (–)-fructose can be differentiated by

(a) Tollen's reagent   (b) Fehling solution

(c) Bromine water   (d) None of the three.

5. $\text{D-(+)-Glucose} \xrightarrow{5\,(CH_3CO)_2O} \text{D-(+)-Glucose pentaacetate}$

Which statement is true about glucose pentaacetate ?

(a) It will react with phenylhydrazine but not with Tollens' reagent.

(b) It will react with Tollens' reagent but not with phenylhydrazine.

(c) It will react with both of the above mentioned reagents.

(d) It will react neither with phenylhydrazine nor with Tollens' reagent.

6. Which of the following is not possible in glucose ?

(a) (+)-form   (b) (–)-form

(c) *rac*-form   (d) *meso* form.

7. Which of the following statement is true ?

(a) Epimers are also anomers

(b) Anomers are also epimers

(c) Both of the above statements are true

(d) Neither of the two statement is true

8. The enantiomer of α-D-(+)-glucose is

(a) β-D-(+)-glucose   (b) α-D-(–)-glucose

(c) α-L-(–)-glucose   (d) β-L-(–)-glucose.

9. A D-ketotetrose is reduced to give two products

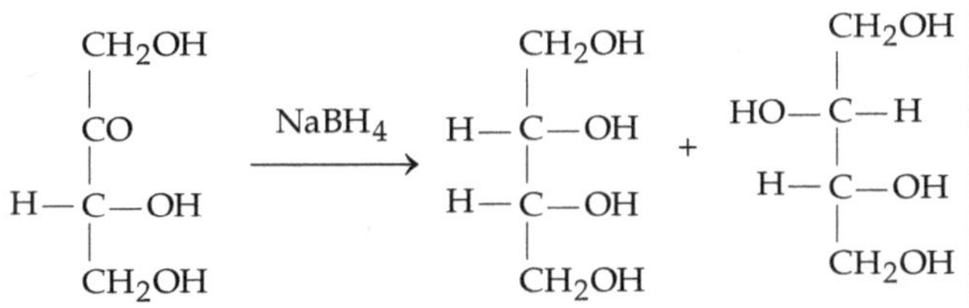

$$\begin{array}{ccc}
CH_2OH & & CH_2OH \\
| & & | \\
CO & \xrightarrow{NaBH_4} & H-C-OH \\
| & & | \\
H-C-OH & & H-C-OH \\
| & & | \\
CH_2OH & & CH_2OH \\
\end{array}$$

$$+\;\begin{array}{c}
CH_2OH \\
| \\
HO-C-H \\
| \\
H-C-OH \\
| \\
CH_2OH \\
\end{array}$$

I   II

The two products I and II are

(a) enantiomers   (b) diastereomers

(c) anomers   (d) none of the three.

10.

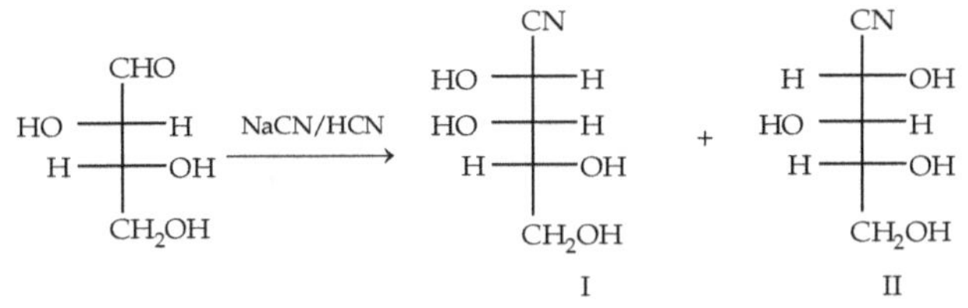

$$\begin{array}{c}
CHO \\
| \\
HO-C-H \\
| \\
HO-C-H \\
| \\
H-C-OH \\
| \\
CH_2OH \\
\end{array} \xrightarrow{NaCN/HCN}
\begin{array}{c}
CN \\
| \\
HO-C-H \\
| \\
HO-C-H \\
| \\
H-C-OH \\
| \\
CH_2OH \\
\end{array}\;(I)
\;+\;
\begin{array}{c}
CN \\
| \\
H-C-OH \\
| \\
HO-C-H \\
| \\
H-C-OH \\
| \\
CH_2OH \\
\end{array}\;(II)$$

Compounds I and II may be grouped as

(a) diastereomers   (b) epimers

(c) C–2 epimers   (d) all of the three.

11. Which one is the absolutely specific term ?

(a) A diastereomer   (b) An epimer

(c) An anomer   (d) None of the three.

12. Pick up the correct statement.

(a) α- and β-D-glucoses are diastereomers

(b) α- and β-D-glucoses are anomers

(c) α- and β-D-glucoses are epimers

(d) All the above statements are correct.

13. When an aqueous solution of D-glucose is treated with a base, it is converted into D-fructose and D-mannose, this conversion (isomerisation) involves

(a) enolization   (b) tautomerization

(c) both (a) and (b)   (d) none of the two.

14. The anomeric carbon atom in glucose and fructose is

(a) C_1 (b) C_2 (c) C_5

(d) C_1 in glucose and C_2 in fructose.

15. Fructose on reduction gives a mixture of two alcohols which are related as

(a) diastereomers   (b) epimers

(c) both (a) and (b)   (d) anomers.

16. Predict the nature of the products Z and Z′ in the following series of reactions

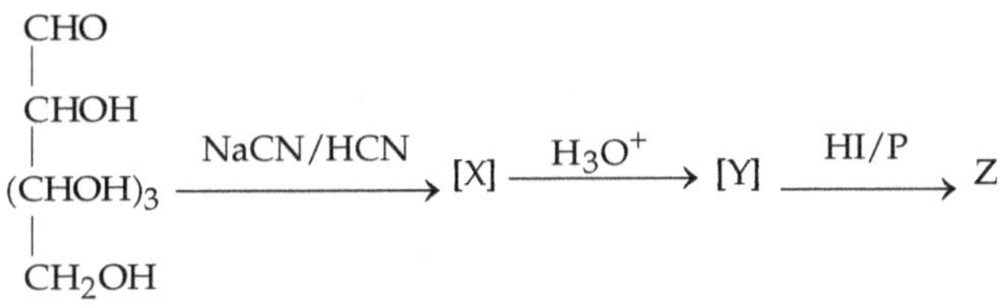

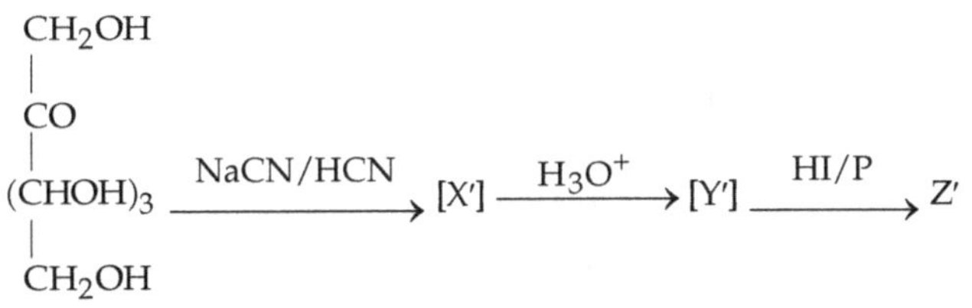

$$\begin{array}{c}
CHO \\
| \\
CHOH \\
| \\
(CHOH)_3 \\
| \\
CH_2OH \\
\end{array} \xrightarrow{NaCN/HCN} [X] \xrightarrow{H_3O^+} [Y] \xrightarrow{HI/P} Z$$

$$\begin{array}{c}
CH_2OH \\
| \\
CO \\
| \\
(CHOH)_3 \\
| \\
CH_2OH \\
\end{array} \xrightarrow{NaCN/HCN} [X'] \xrightarrow{H_3O^+} [Y'] \xrightarrow{HI/P} Z'$$

(a) Both are *n*-heptane

(b) Both are *n*-heptanoic acid

(c) Both are 7-iodoheptanoic acid

(d) Z is *n*-heptanoic acid, and Z′ is a substituted hexanoic acid.

17. Which of the following evolves carbon dioxide, on oxidation with periodate ?

(a)
$$\begin{array}{c} CHO \\ | \\ CHOH \\ | \\ CHOH \\ | \\ CH_2OH \end{array}$$

(b)
$$\begin{array}{c} CH_2OH \\ | \\ CO \\ | \\ CHOH \\ | \\ CH_2OH \end{array}$$

(c)   Both (d)   None.

18. Which of the following pairs can be distinguished by Fehling's solution ?

(a)   Glucose and fructose

(b)   Glucose and sucrose

(c)   Methanal and ethanal

(d)   Hydroxypropanone and benzaldehyde.

19. Benedict's reagent is reduced by which type of carbohydrates?

(a)   Acetals (b)   Hemiacetals

(c)   Glucose pentacetate (d)   None of the three.

20. What will happen when D-(+)-glucose is treated with methanolic —HCl followed by Tollens' reagent ?

(a)   A black ppt. will be formed

(b)   A red ppt. will be formed

(c)   A green colour will appear

(d)   No characteristic colour or ppt. will be formed.

21. Pick the up the false statement.

(a)   Ketoses show the phenomenon of mutarotation.

(b)   Glycosides show the phenomenon of mutarotation

(c)   There is a relationship between the ability of a sugar to mutarotate and reduce Tollens' reagent.

(d)   None of the above statement is false.

22. Which is true about the acidic character of hydroxyl groups of sugars and hydroxyl group of an alcohol ?

(a)   The OH's of sugars are more acidic than that of a typical alcohol.

(b)   The OH's of sugars are less acidic than that of a typical alcohol.

(c)   Both have similar acidic character.

(d)   The OH's of sugars are neutral while that of an alcohol is acidic.

23. Honey is more sweet than glucose because it has

(a)   pure glucose

(b)   sucrose which is sweeter than glucose

(c)   invert sugar

(d)   none of the above three is correct.

24. Which of the following carbohydrate in not related to (+)glucose?

(a)   Amylopectin (b)   Amylose

(c)   Inulin (d)   Glycogen.

25. Which of the following is (are) not polysaccharide(s)?

(a)   Amylose (b)   Amylopectin

(c)   Inulin (d)   Sucrose

26. Cellulose upon acetylation with excess acetic anhydride/H_2SO_4 (catalytic) gives cellulose triacetate whose structure is

(A)

(B)

(C)

(D)

27. Which compound will not give the Tollen's test

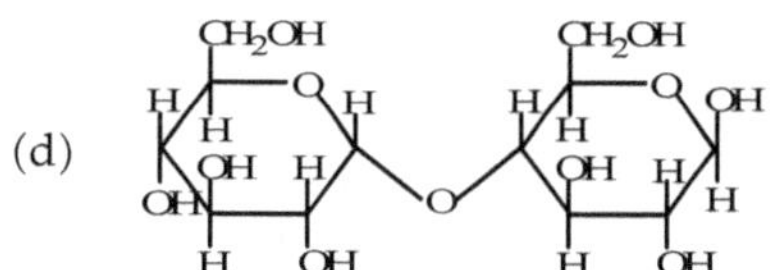

28. Glucose reduces
(a) Tollen's reagent   (b) Fehling's solution
(c) Benedict's solution   (d) All

29. S_1 : Sucrose has $C_1 - C_2$ glycosidic linkage between β-D-glucose & α-D-fructose.
S_2 : Glucose does not give positive test with 2, 4-DNP.
S_3 : Pentacetate of glucose does not form oxime.

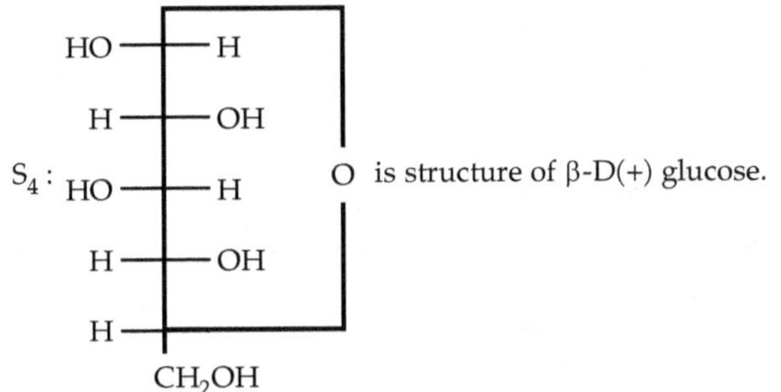

S_4 :   O is structure of β-D(+) glucose.

Which of the following is correct statements (F = False, T = True)
(a) FFTT   (b) FFTF
(c) FFFT   (d) TTTT

30. Methyl-α-D-glucoside and methyl-β-D-glucoside are
(a) Epimers
(b) Anomers
(c) Enantiomers
(d) Conformational diastereomers

31. The term anomers of glucose refers to
(a) A mixture of (D)-glucose and (L)-glucose
(b) Enantiomers of glucose
(c) Isomers of glucose that differ in configuration at carbon one (C-1)
(d) Isomers of glucose that differ in configurations at carbons one and four (C-1 and C-4)

32. Which of the following pairs are enantiomers ?
(i) D-Glucose and L-glucose.
(ii) R-Tartaric acid and S-tartaric acid
(iii)

(iv) 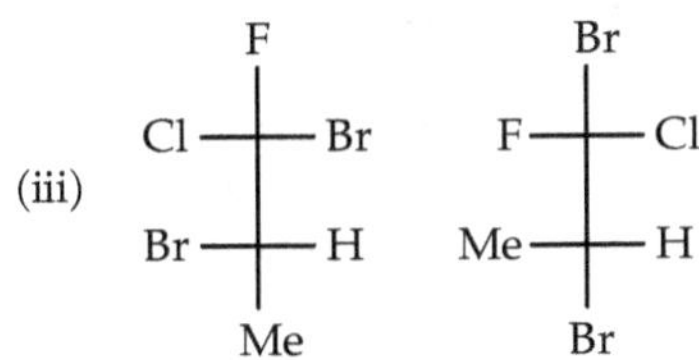 $+ D_2 \xrightarrow[\Delta]{Ni} A + B$; Product A and B.

(a) I, II   (b) I, II, III
(c) I, II, III, IV   (d) II, IV

33. If C-5 carbon of D-glucose is inverted, the new compound is related with parent compound as
(I) Diastereomer
(II) Enantiomer
(III) Epimer
(IV) Anomer
(a) I and III   (b) II and III
(c) IV and I   (d) I only

34. The pair of compounds in which both the compounds give positive test with Tollen's reagent is
(a) Glucose and Sucrose
(b) Fructose and Sucrose
(c) Acetophenone and Hexanal
(d) Glucose and Fructose

35. The two forms of D-glucopyranose obtained from the solution of D-glucose are called
(a) Isomers   (b) Anomers
(c) Epimers   (d) Enantiomers

36. Among cellulose, poly (vinyl chloride), nylon and natural rubber, the polymer in which the intermolecular force of attraction is weakest is
(a) Nylon   (b) Poly (vinyl chloride)
(c) Cellulose   (d) Natural rubber

37. The two functional groups present in a typical carbohydrate are:
(a) – CHO and – COOH
(b) > C = O and – OH
(c) – OH and – CHO
(d) – OH and – COOH

38.

Compounds I and II may be grouped as
(a) diastereomers   (b) epimers
(c) C–2 epimers   (d) all of the three.

39. When an aqueous solution of D-glucose is treated with a base, it is converted into D-fructose and D-mannose, this conversion (isomerisation) involves
(a) enolization   (b) tautomerization
(c) both (a) and (b)   (d) none of the two.

40. Bombardment of aluminium by α-particle leads to its artificial disintegration in two ways, (i) and (ii) as shown. Products X, Y and Z respectively are,

$$^{27}_{13}\text{Al} \xrightarrow{\text{(ii)}} {}^{30}_{15}\text{P} + \text{Y}$$
(i) ↓   ↓
$$^{30}_{14}\text{Si} + \text{X} \qquad {}^{30}_{14}\text{Si} + \text{Z}$$

(A) proton, neutron, positron
(B) neutron, positron, proton
(C) proton, positron, neutron
(D) positron, proton, neutron

41. The following carbohydrate is

(a) a ketohexose   (b) an aldohexose
(c) an α-furanose   (d) an α-pyranose

EXERCISE 22.2 (MCQ 1 or >1 option correct, Passage based, Matching, A/R)

DIRECTIONS for Q. 1 to Q. 9 : Multiple choice questions with one or more than one correct option(s).

1. Which of the following statement is correct ?
- (a) Fruit mainly contains glucose as carbohydrate
- (b) Honey mainly contains invert sugar
- (c) Blood sugar and grape sugar mainly contain glucose
- (d) Sucrose is an oligosaccharide.

2. Which of the following can form osazone ?

(a)
$$CHO - CHOH - CHOH - CH_2OH$$

(b)
$$CHO - CH_2 - CHOH - CH_2OH$$

(c)
$$CHO - CHOH - CH_2 - CH_2OH$$

(d)
$$C_6H_5 - CHOH - CO - C_6H_5$$

3. Which of the following statement(s) is(are)
- (a) Glucose and fructose forms same compound on heating with P and hydriodic acid
- (b) Glucose and fructose differ in the configuration only at C_1 and C_2
- (c) Both form two isomeric cyanohydrins
- (d) The two are epimers

4. Which of the following are correct statements?
- (a) Invert sugar is the sweetest sugar
- (b) Fructose is a reducing sugar
- (c) Fructose is a ketohexose
- (d) Fructose has four chiral centers

5.

I, II, III, IV (Fischer projections with C_6H_5, OH, NHCH$_3$, CH$_3$, H, CH$_3$HN substituents)

- (a) I and III are enantiomers
- (b) II and IV are enantiomers
- (c) I and III are erythro isomers
- (d) II and IV are threo isomers

6.

I, II, III (Fischer projections with CHO, CH$_2$OH)

- (a) I and II are epimers
- (b) II and III are epimers
- (c) all the three are epimers
- (d) No one is epimer to other

7. The correct statement(s) about the following sugars **X** and **Y** is(are)

X, **Y** (disaccharide structures)

- (a) **X** is a reducing sugar and **Y** is a non-reducing sugar
- (b) **X** is a non-reducing sugar and **Y** is a reducing sugar
- (c) The glucosidic linkages in **X** and **Y** are a and b, respectively
- (d) The glucosidic linkages in **X** and **Y** are b and a, respectively

8. Which of the following statement is (are) correct?
- (a) Glucose requires three moles of phenylhydrazine to give osazone
- (b) Glyceraldehyde on oxidative cleavage with HIO_4 will give three different products
- (c) Through Killiani - Fischer synthesis if we add two more C-atoms in a chain of (D)-glyceraldehyde, total number of possible compounds will be four
- (d) Hydrolysis of lactose gives one unit of β-D-glucose and one unit of α-D-galactose

9. The correct statement(s) about the following sugars **X** and **Y** is(are)

X, **Y** (disaccharide structures)

- (a) **X** is a reducing sugar and **Y** is a non-reducing sugar
- (b) **X** is a non-reducing sugar and **Y** is a reducing sugar
- (c) The glucosidic linkages in **X** and **Y** are α and β, respectively
- (d) The glucosidic linkages in **X** and **Y** are β and α, respectively

INSTRUCTION for Q. 10 to Q. 29 : Read the passages given below and answer the questions that follow.

PASSAGE 1

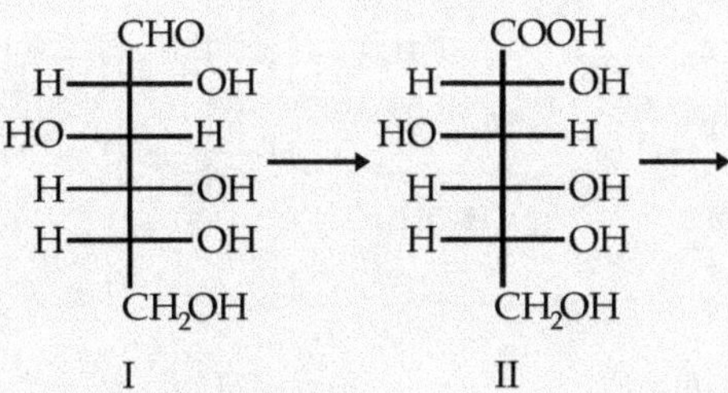

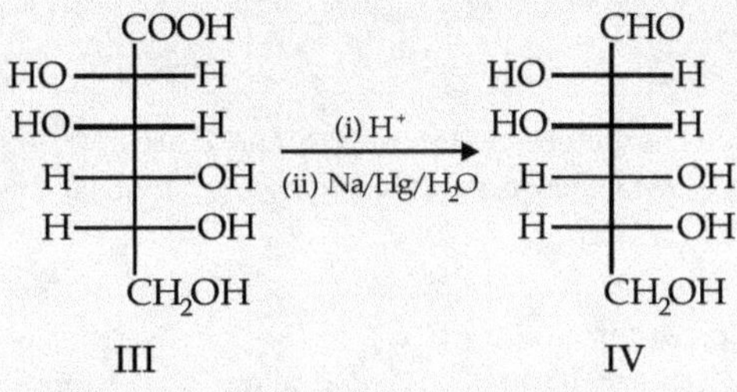

10. Compound I can be converted to II by using
(a) HNO_3 (b) $KMnO_4$
(c) $NaOH -Br_2$ (d) Br_2

11. Conversion of II to III can be affected by
(a) H^+ (b) pyridine
(c) heat (d) irradiation to U V light

12. Which of the following are epimers?
(a) I and IV (b) II and III
(c) Both (d) None

PASSAGE 2

Carbohydrates are polyhydroxyaldehydes or polyhydroxyketones. However, in actuality, the carbonyl groups are often present as hemiacetals and acetals. Below are the structures of some carbohydrates

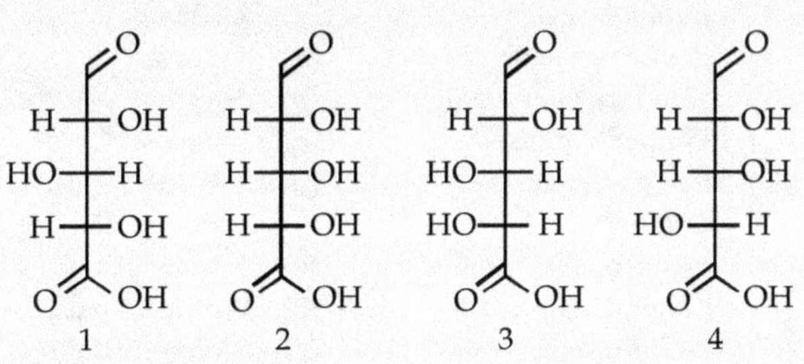

13. The stereochemical relationship of compounds (3) and (4) is that they are
I. diastereomers II. enantiomers III. epimers
(a) III only (b) I and II
(c) I and III (d) II and III

14. The (-) enantiomer of each compound is oxidized by bromine water to yield the corresponding dicarboxylic acid, which will still be optically active. This is possible in
(a) 2 and 3 (b) 3 and 4
(c) 1 and 2 (d) 1 and 4

15. To convert these compounds to riboses (five-carbon sugars), one must
(a) cyclize the chain by forming a hemiacetal with the C-4 hydroxyl and the C-1 aldehyde
(b) oxidize the C-1 aldehyde to a carboxylic acid
(c) reduce the C-5 carboxylic acid to an alcohol
(d) reduce the C-5 carboxylic acid to an aldehyde

PASSAGE 3

Carbohydrates are optically active polyhydroxy aldehydes or ketones or substances which on hydrolysis give such compounds (although there are few exceptions to this definition). Certain carbohydrates can be hydrolysed to simpler carbohydrates, while the others are not hydrolysed to simpler products; the former are called oligo- or poly-saccharides, while the latter are known as monosaccharides. Monosaccharides are further classified as aldoses and ketoses which in turn are classified on the basis of number of carbon atoms like aldopentoses, ketohexoses, etc.

Although major function of carbohydrates is to provide energy to living organisms, certain carbohydrates like cellulose support the plant tissues, while ribose and deoxyribose (aldopentoses), constituents of nucleic acids (RNA and DNA), are responsible for protein synthesis and human heredity.

16. The first member of aldose sugars is
(a) aldodiose (b) aldotriose
(c) aldotetrose (d) glucose

17. The first member of ketose sugars is
(a) ketodiose (b) ketotriose
(c) ketotetrose (d) fructose

18. How many enantiomeric pairs are possible for a carbohydrate of the formula, $CHO(CHOH)_5CH_2OH$?
(a) 8 (b) 16
(c) 32 (d) 64

19. A carbohydrate of five carbon atoms has two asymmetric carbon atoms and found to be constituent of nucleic acids. It is
(a) $C_5H_{10}O_5$ (b) $C_5H_{10}O_4$
(c) both (d) none

20. How many chiral carbon atoms are present in the carbohydrate molecule which is found to be constituent of nucleic acids?
(a) 1 (b) 2
(c) 3 (d) 4

PASSAGE 4

Read the following defintions :
(i) Carbohydrates which differ in configuration at glycosidic carbon (aldehydic or ketonic carbon atom involved in ring formation) are called anomers; when H is on left and OH is on right, the anomer is α-, while when H is on right and OH is on left, the anomer is β-
(ii) Carbohydrates which differ in configuration at any asymmetric carbon atom other than glycosidic carbon are called epimers.
(iii) Optical isomers which are not enantiomers are called diastereomers.

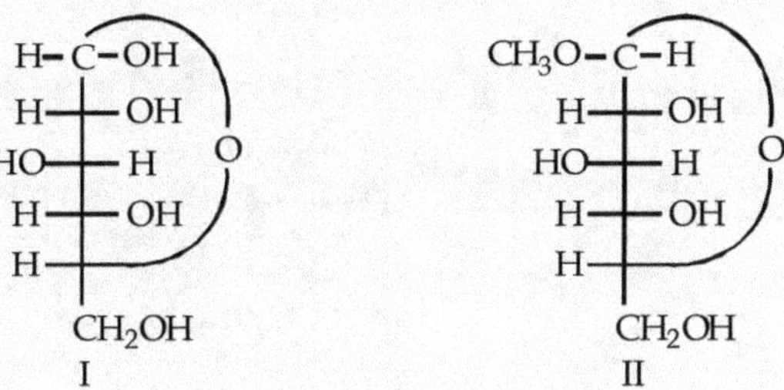

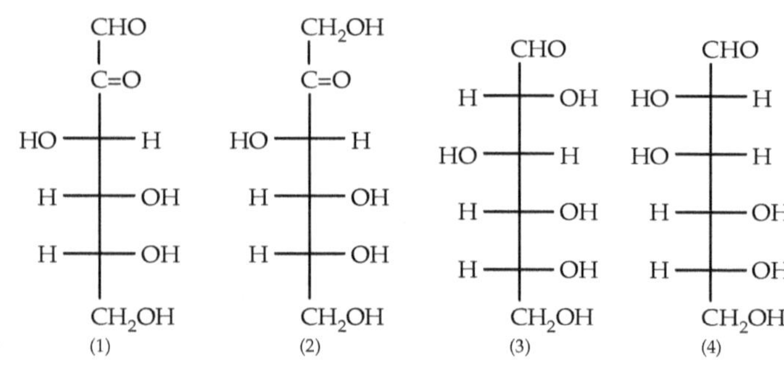

III   **IV**

21. In which of the above structures glycosidic carbon is present at C-2 position?
- (a) II
- (b) III
- (c) IV
- (d) None

22. Which of the following is β-anomer?
- (a) II
- (b) IV
- (c) II and IV
- (d) None

23. Which of the following constitute anomeric pair?
- (a) I and III
- (b) I and IV
- (c) III and IV
- (d) None

24 Which of the following constitute epimeric pair?
- (a) I and III
- (b) I and IV
- (c) III and IV
- (d) None

25. Which of the following constitute diastereomeric pair?
- (a) I and III
- (b) I and IV
- (c) III and IV
- (d) All the three

26. Which of the following has different ring, with respect to size, than others?
- (a) II
- (b) III
- (c) IV
- (d) None

PASSAGE 5

$$[X] \xrightarrow[P\ \text{mole}]{HIO_4} (1\ \text{mole})\ HCOOH$$

$$[X] \xrightarrow{\text{Hydrolysis}} [Y] + [Z]$$

$$[Y\ \text{or}\ Z] \xrightarrow[]{3\,PhNHNH_2/\ H^+} + PhNH_2 + NH_3$$

---

27. Compounds Y and Z can be :

- (a) 1 only
- (b) 2, 3
- (c) 1, 4
- (d) 2, 3, 4

28. The value of P is :
- (a) 2
- (b) 3
- (c) 4
- (d) 5

29. The true characteristics about X, Y and Z are :
- (a) Oligosaccharide - X, Reducing - X, Monosaccharide - Y, Z, Mutarotation - Y, Z
- (b) Oligosaccharide - X, Reducing - Y, Z, Monosaccharide - Y, Z, Mutarotation - Y, Z
- (c) Oligosaccharide - Y, Z, Reducing - Y, Z, Monosaccharide - X, Mutarotation - Y, Z
- (d) Oligosaccharide - Y, Z, Reducing - X, Monosaccharide - X, Mutarotation - X

Instructions for Q. 30 to Q. 37 : Following questions are Multiple Matching type Questions :

30.

Column - I		Column - II	
Reactant		**Product**	
(A)	Glucose + OH⁻	(a)	Fructose
(B)	Fructose + $3C_6H_5NHNH_2$	(b)	Glucosazone
(C)	Mannose + OH⁻	(c)	Mannose
(D)	Glucose + $3C_6H_5NHNH_2$	(d)	Fructosazone

31.

Column - I		Column - II	
(A)	Reducing sugar	(a)	Frutose
(B)	Non-reducing sugar	(b)	Sucrose
(C)	Epimer of glucose	(c)	Mannose
(D)	Isomer of glucose	(d)	Ribose

32.

Column - I		Column - II	
(A)	α-Glucopyranose	(a)	Mutarotation
(B)	β-Methylglucoside	(b)	Artificial sweetner
(C)	L-Glucose	(c)	Non-reducing sugar
(D)	Sucrose	(d)	Natural sweetner

33. Match the chemical substances in **Column I** with type of polymers/type of bonds in **Column II**. Indicate your answer by darkening the appropriate bubbles of the 4 × 4 matrix given in the ORS.

Column I		Column II	
(A)	cellulose	(a)	natural polymer
(B)	nylon-6, 6	(b)	synthetic polymer
(C)	protein	(c)	amide linkage
(D)	sucrose	(d)	glycoside linkage

34.

Column I		*Column II*

(A) 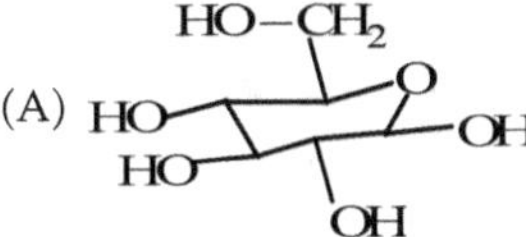

    (a) reacts with Br_2 water

(B) $CH_3 - CH = CH_2$ (b) oxidised by $KMnO_4$

(C) D-Glucose   (c) reacts with $CHCl_3$ / KOH to give cyclo compound

(D) 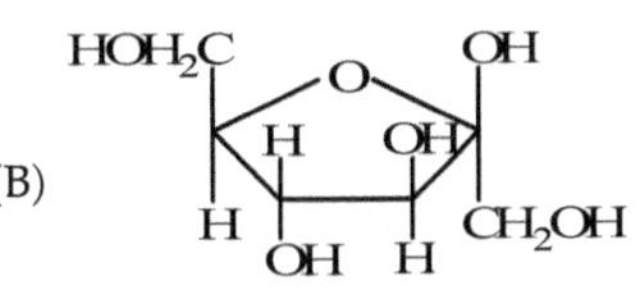

    (d) H_2O soluble in high amount

    (e) reacts with acetic anhydride

35.

Column I   *Column II*

(A) 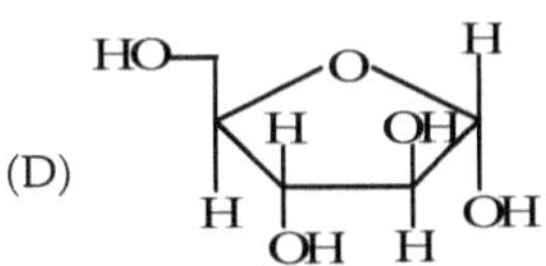

    (a) Aldohexoses

(B)

    (b) Hemiacetals

(C)

    (c) Mutarotates in H_2O

(D)

    (d) Reducing sugars

    (e) Glycosides

36. Match the reaction in **Column I** with corresponding products in column II.

Column I	*Column II*
(A) D-glucose $\xrightarrow{OH^-}$	(a) D-glucose
(B) D-fructose $\xrightarrow{OH^-}$	(b) D-fructose
(C) On reaction with HIO_4, gives 5 moles of HCOOH and 1 mole of HCHO	(c) D-Mannose (C-2-epimer of D-glucose)
(D) On reaction with phenylhydrazine forms same osazone	(d) D-galactose (C-4 epimer of D-glucose)

37. Match the chemical substances in **Column I** with type of polymers/type of bonds in **Column II**.

Column I	*Column II*
(A) Cellulose	(p) Natural polymer
(B) Nylon-6, 6	(q) Synthetic polymer
(C) Protein	(r) Amide linkage
(D) Sucrose	(s) Glycoside linkage

Instructions for Q. 38 to Q. 45 : Following questions are Assertion and Reasoning Type Questions :

Note : Each question contains STATEMENT-1 (Assertion) and STATEMENT-2 (Reason). Each question has 5 choices (a), (b), (c), (d) and (e) out of which ONLY ONE is correct.

(a) Statement-1 is True, Statement-2 is True; Statement-2 is a correct explanation for Statement-1.

(b) Statement-1 is True, Statement-2 is True; Statement-2 is NOT a correct explanation for Statement-1.

(c) Statement -1 is True, Statement-2 is False.

(d) Statement -1 is False, Statement-2 is True.

(e) Statement -1 is False, Statement-2 is False.

38. **Statement 1 :** Reducing sugars undergo mutarotation.

Statement 2 : During mutarotation, one pure anomer is converted into an equilibrium mixture of two anomers.

39. **Statement 1 :** Galactose is the C_4-epimer of glucose.

Statement 2 : Glucose and galactose differ in configuration at C_4.

40. **Statement 1 :** A solution of sucrose in water is dextrorotatory but on hydrolysis in presence of little hydrochloric acid, it becomes laevorotatory.

Statement 2 : Sucrose on hydrolysis gives unequal amounts of glucose and fructose as a result of which change in sign of rotation is observed.

41. **Statement 1 :** Hydrolysis of sucrose is known as inversion of cane sugar.

Statement 2 Sucrose is a disaccharide.

42. **Statement 1 :** Sucrose is a non-reducing sugar.

Statement 2 : It has glycosidic linkage.

43. **Statement 1 :** Maltose is a reducing sugar which gives two moles of D-glucose on hydrolysis.

Statement 2 : Maltose has a 1, 4-β-glycosidic linkage

44. **Statement 1 :** Glucose gives a reddish-brown precipitate with Fehling's solution.

Statement 2 : Reaction of glucose with Fehling's solution give CuO and gluconic acid.

45. **Statement 1 :** Glucose gives a reddish-brown precipitate with Fehling's solution.

Statement 2 : Reaction of glucose with Fehling's solution give CuO and gluconic acid.

EXERCISE 22.3   (Subjective Problems)

1. Write the Fischer projection formula for L-(+)-arabinose, obtained by the hydrolysis of a polysaccharide, found in a natural gum ; configuration of D-(–)-arabinose is given on the right side.

2. (*a*) Establish the optical nature of the reactant and product.

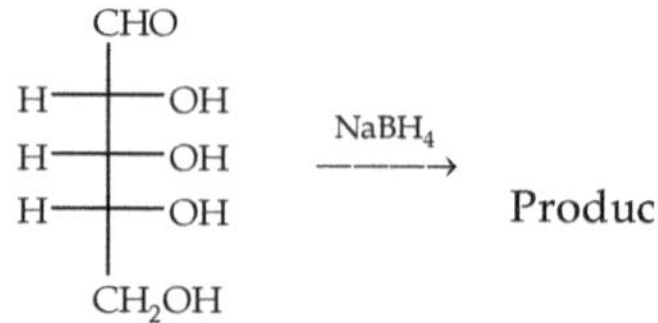

(*b*) Write down the structure of the compound A in the following reaction.

$$\text{D-Glucose} \xrightarrow{\text{HNO}_3} \text{Glucaric acid} \xleftarrow{\text{HNO}_3} \text{A}$$

3. Differentiate between hemiacetals and acetals with reference to carbohydrates.

4. Which of the following can show mutarotation ?
(*a*) L-(–)-Glucose   (*b*) Methyl α-glucopyranoside
(*c*) Glucose penta-acetate   (*d*) Methyl β-glucofuranoside
(*e*) α-Glucopyranose   (*f*) β-Glucofuranose.

5. The rate of oxidation of reducing sugars by cupric ions is found to be proportional to sugar and [OH⁻], but independent of [Cu²⁺]. What does this kinetic suggest about the mechanism of oxidation ?

6. An optically inactive carbohydrate *bio-inonose*, $C_6H_{10}O_6$ shows following reactions.

(*i*) It reduces Benedict's solution but does not react with bromine water.

(*ii*) It reacts with acetic anhydride to form penta-acetate.

(*iii*) On reduction with sodium borohydride, it gives two isomeric compounds of the formula $C_6H_{12}O_6$ which gives six moles of HCOOH on oxidation with periodic acid.

Identify the nature of functional groups present in bio-inonose and explain its conversion to two isomeric compounds. Also explain the given oxidation of isomeric compounds.

7. When galactose is dissolved in water, its specific rotation gradually changes to +80.2°, if the specific rotation of α-anomer is +150.7° and that of β-anomer is +52.8°, determine the percentage of the two anomers at equilibrium.

SOLUTIONS

EXERCISE 22.1

1	(a)	6	(d)	11	(d)	16	(d)	21	(b)	26	(c)	31	(c)	36	(d)	41	(b)
2	(d)	7	(b)	12	(d)	17	(b)	22	(a)	27	(d)	32	(a)	37	(c)		
3	(c)	8	(c)	13	(c)	18	(b)	23	(c)	28	(a)	33	(a)	38	(d)		
4	(c)	9	(b)	14	(d)	19	(b)	24	(c)	29	(b)	34	(d)	39	(c)		
5	(d)	10	(d)	15	(c)	20	(d)	25	(d)	30	(c)	35	(b)	40	(a)		

1. The value of n in $C_n(H_2O)_m$ may be either same as m as in monosaccharides or more than m as in oligosaccharides, but never less than m.
2. The general formula for oligosaccharides is $(C_5H_{10}O_5)_n + (n-1)\,H_2O$.
3. Photosynthesis takes place in presence of sunlight, the light energy is stored in the form of chemical energy in carbohydrates. It is this energy that is released when glucose is oxidised.
4. Bromine, a mild oxidising agent, oxidises only glucose (aldoses, in general) to gluconic acid. Tollens' reagent and Fehling solution, being alkaline in nature, cause isomerization of fructose to glucose hence both of them react with these reagents.
5. During acetylation of (+)-glucose, it is the C_1—OH of the hemiacetal that is acetylated and not the C_5—OH that forms the ring (cyclic structure). Since equilibrium with the open-chain aldehyde is prevented, the penta-acetate does not respond the aldehydic reactions.

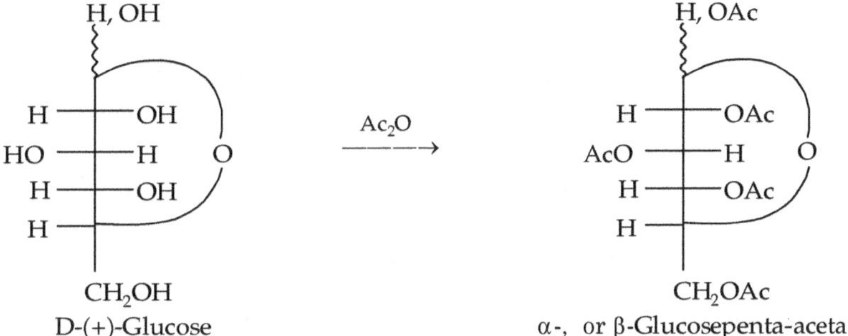

6. Since the two ends of the glucose molecule are dissimilar, *meso* form is not possible.
7. Epimers are those diastereomers which differ in the configuration of only one chiral carbon which may be C_1, C_2, C_3, etc. ; while anomers are diastereomers that differ in the configuration of a specific chiral carbon which is C_1 in aldoses and C_2 in ketoses.
8. In the D family the more dextrorotatory anomer is named α-D-. In the L family the more laevorotatory anomer is named α-L-.
9. Diastereomers are isomers which are not enantiomers. Since structures I and II are not non-superimposable mirror-image of each other, these are not enantiomers.
10. When structures I and II are C–2 epimers, it implies that these are epimers and diastereomers too.
11. Since diastereomers are all those isomers which are not enantiomers, there may be more than one diastereomer of a compound. An epimer differs in the configuration of only one chiral carbon, so an epimer can be C—2, C—3, C—4, etc. An anomer may be α- or β- ; so no term is absolutely specific.
12. Same as for Q. 11.
13. When an aqueous solution of D-glucose, D-mannose or D-fructose is treated with a base, it undergoes enolization and a series of keto-enol tautomerization to form a mixture of the three monosaccharides (*Lobry de Bruyn van Ekenstein transformation*). For reactions, consult text.
14. An anomeric carbon is that which is developed by intramolecular reaction between carbonyl group and —OH group of the same molecule. Thus it should be C_1 in glucose and C_2 in fructose.
15. Ketoses on reduction produce a new chiral carbon leading to the formation of two isomeric alcohols which are diastereomeric as well as C–2 epimers.

16.

$$\begin{array}{ccccc}
\text{CHO} & & \text{COOH} & & \text{COOH} \\
| & & | & & | \\
\text{CHOH} & \xrightarrow[\;(ii)\ H_3O^+\;]{(i)\ NaCN/HCN} & \text{CHOH} & \xrightarrow[\text{(Reduction of —OH)}]{HI/P} & \text{CH}_2 \\
| & & | & & | \\
\text{(CHOH)}_3 & & \text{CHOH} & & \text{CH}_2 \\
| & & | & & | \\
\text{CH}_2\text{OH} & & \text{(CHOH)}_3 & & \text{(CH}_2)_3 \\
 & & | & & | \\
 & & \text{CH}_2\text{OH} & & \text{CH}_3
\end{array}$$

Z (*n*-Heptanoic acid)

$$
\begin{array}{ccccc}
\mathrm{CH_2OH} & & \mathrm{CH_2OH} & & \mathrm{CH_3} \\
| & & | & & | \\
\mathrm{CO} & & \mathrm{C}\!\!<^{\mathrm{OH}}_{\mathrm{COOH}} & & \mathrm{CHCOOH} \\
| & \xrightarrow[\text{(ii) } H_3O^+]{\text{(i) NaCN/HCN}} & | & \xrightarrow{\ HI/P\ } & | \\
\mathrm{(CHOH)_3} & & \mathrm{(CHOH)_3} & & \mathrm{(CH_2)_3} \\
| & & | & & | \\
\mathrm{CH_2OH} & & \mathrm{CH_2OH} & & \mathrm{CH_3}
\end{array}
$$

Z' (2-Methylhexanoic acid)

17. A ketonic group having —OH group on both sides is removed as CO_2 during oxidation with periodate.

18. Glucose is a hemiacetal, so in presence of a base (alkaline medium is provided by Fehling's solution) it can develop —CHO group in the form of open chain structure which responds Fehling's solution. Sucrose is a glycoside, *i.e.* its hemiacetal OH groups (one due to glucose and another due to fructose) are not free, so it can't attain —CHO group. Hence it will not respond Fehling's solution.

19. Same explanation as that of Q. 18. Also see Q. 5.

20. Reaction of D-(+)-glucose with methanolic —HCl leads to formation of methyl glucoside (C_1—OH group is methylated) which, being acetal, is not hydrolysable by base, so it will not respond Tollens' reagent.

21. Carbohydrates having hemiacetal type of structures, which is observed in all monosaccharides, show mutarotation. Further the reduction of Tollens' reagent and mutarotation both depend on the presence of the free carbonyl form. Glycosides do not mutarotate because here the OH group of hemiacetal is blocked.

22. The OH's of sugars are more acidic than that of a typical alcohol because of their mutual electron-withdrawing inductive effect.

23. Honey has mainly invert sugar which is more sweet than ordinary sugar (sucrose), and glucose.

24. Inulin is a polysaccharide of fructose, while all others are polysaccharides of glucose ; although all the four has same molecular formula, $(C_6H_{10}O_5)_n$.

1. Fruit mainly contains fructose, hence the latter is commonly known as fruit sugar.

2. α-Hydroxyaldehydes and α-hydroxyketones form osazone. In compound II, aldehydic and —OH groups are separated by CH_2, *i.e.*, it is β-hydroxyaldehyde hence it will not form osazone.

27. Compound given in option (a), (b) and (d) do not have any hemi-acetal group so can't be oxidised by Tollen's regent and will not give Tollen's test.

31.(*c*) Due to cyclic hemiacetal or cyclic hemiketal structures, all the pentoses and hexoses exist in two stereoisomeric forms i.e., α form in which the OH at C_1 in aldoses and C_2 in ketoses lies towards the right and β form in which it lies towards left. Thus glucose, fructose, ribose etc., all exist in α and β form. Glucose exists in two forms α-D-glucose and β-D-glucose.

$$
\underset{\text{Glucose}}{\alpha-D-(+)} \rightleftharpoons \text{equilibrium mixture} \rightleftharpoons \underset{\text{(+) Glucose}}{\beta-(D)-}
$$

As a result of cyclization, anomeric carbon (C-1) becomes asymmetric and the newly formed –OH group may be either on left or on right in Fischer projection thus resulting in the formation to two isomers (anomers). The isomers having –OH group on the left of the C-1 designated β-D-glucose and the other having –OH group on the right as α-D-glucose.

32. (III) is identical pair; in (IV) products A and B are distereomers.

34. Glucose being an aldose responds to Tollen's test while fructose, although a ketose, undergoes rearrangement in presence of basic medium (provided by Tollen's reagent) to form glucose, which then responds to Tollen's test.

35. The two isomeric forms (α – and β –) of D-glucopyronose differ in configuration only at C–1; hence these are called anomers.

36. Nylon and cellulose, both have intermolecular hydrogen bonding, polyvinyl chloride has dipole-dipole interaction, while natural rubber has van der Waal forces which are weakest.

37. Glucose is considered as a typical carbohydrate which contains –CHO and –OH group.

38. When structures I and II are C–2 epimers, it implies that these are epimers and diastereomers too.

39. When an aqueous solution of D-glucose, D-mannose or D-fructose is treated with a base, it undergoes enolization and a series of keto-enol tautomerization to form a mixture of the three monosaccharides (*Lobry de Bruyn van Ekenstein transformation*). For reactions, consult text.

40. (a)
$$
_{13}A\ell^{27} + {_2}\alpha^4 \longrightarrow {_{14}}Si^{30} + {_1}p^1
$$
$$
(X)
$$

$$
_{13}A\ell^{27} + {_2}\alpha^4 \longrightarrow {_{15}}p^{30} + {_0}n^1
$$
$$
(Y)
$$

$$
_{15}p^{30} \longrightarrow {_{14}}Si^{30} + {_1}\beta^0
$$
$$
(Z)
$$

41. (b)

It is a β-pyranose hence it is an aldohexose.

EXERCISE 22.2

>1 CORRECT	1	(b,c,d)	2	(a,c,d)	3	(a, b, c)	4	(b, c)	5	(c, d)
OPTION	6	(a, b)	7	(b,c)	8	(a, c)	9	(b, c)		
PASSAGE 1	10	(d)	11	(b)	12	(c)				
PASSAGE 2	13	(a)	14	(c)	15	(c)				
PASSAGE 3	16	(b)	17	(b)	18	(b)	19	(b)	20	(b,c)
PASSAGE 4	21	(c)	22	(c)	23	(d)	24	(a)	25	(d)
	26	(d)								
PASSAGE 5	27	(d)	28	(b)	29	(b)				
MATCH THE FOLLOWING	30	(A) –a, c ; (B) – b, d ; (C) – a, c ; (D) –b, d								
	31	(A) – a, c, d; (B) – b; (C) – c; (D) – a, c								
	32	(A)-a, d ; (B)-c ; (C)-a, b ; (D)-c, d								
	33	A-(a) & (d) ; (B)-(b) &(c) ; (C)-(a) & (c); D-(d)								
	34	A-(a, b, e); (B)-(a, b, c); (C)-(a, b, d, e); D-(a, b, e)								
	35	A-(a, b, c) ; (B)-(b, c, d) ; (C)-(b, c, d, e); D-(b, c, d)								
	36	A-(a, b, c) ; (B)-(a, b, c) ; (C)-(a, c, d); D-(a, b, c)								
	37	A-(a, d) ; (B)-(b, c) ; (C)-(a, c); D-(d)								
A/R	38	(b)	39	(b)	40	(d)	41	(a)	42	(a)
	43	(c)	44	(c)	45	(c)				

8. Glucose requires 3 moles of phenylhydrazine to give osazone. Glyceraldehyde on cleavage with HIO_4 gives 2 moles of HCOOH + 1 mole of HCHO
Through Killiani - Fischer synthesis, we will be able to get following four products.

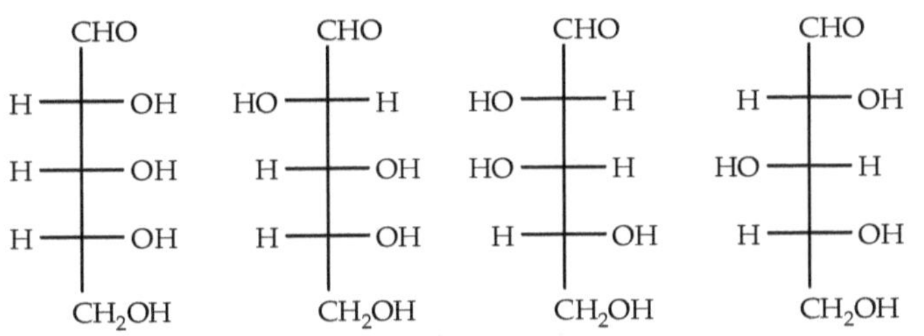

Hydrolysis of lactose gives one unit of β-D-glucose and α-D-glucose.

9. We know that carbohydrates having acetal linkage are non-reducing while that with hemiacetal linkage are reducing. In the given structure,
X has acetal linkage, hence non-reducing.
Y has hemiacetal linkage, hence reducing.
Further **X** is α-anomer, while **Y** is β-anomer of D-(+)- glucose.

Sol. 27-29.

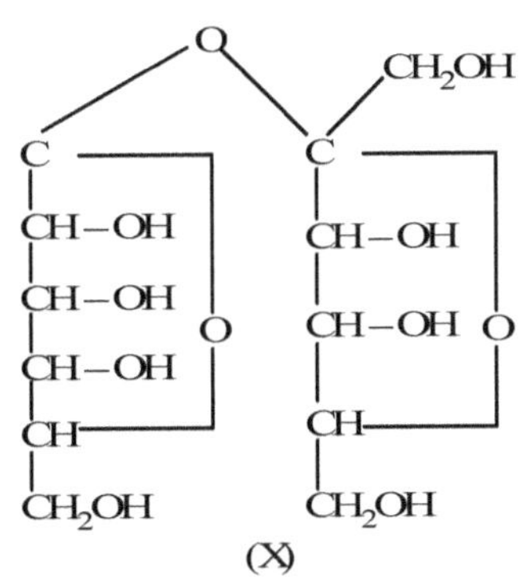

$$[X] \xrightarrow{\text{Hydrolysis}} \underset{(Y)}{\text{Glucose or Mannose}} + \underset{(Z)}{\text{Fructose}}$$

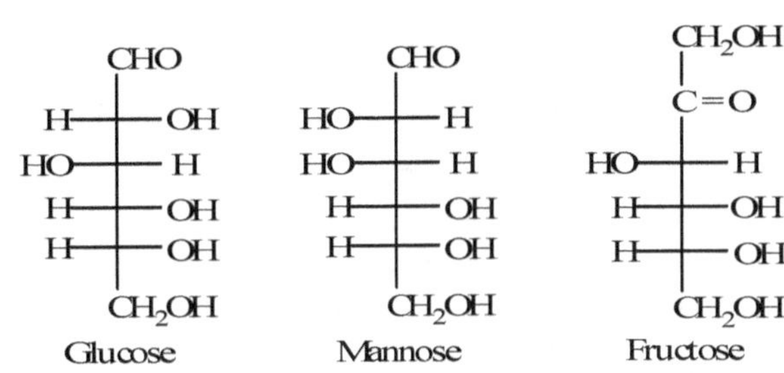

34. (A)-a,b,e; (B)-a,b,c; (C)-a,b,d,e; (D)-a,b,e;
35. (A)-a,b,c, d; (B)-b,c,d; (C)-b,c,d,e; (D)-b,c,d;
36. (A)-a,b,c; (B)-a,b,c; (C)-a,c,d; (D)-a,b,c;
37. (A) : (p, s) Cellulose is a natural polymer and has a $C_1 - C_4$ β-glycosidic linkage.
(B) : (q, r) Nylon-6, 6 is a synthetic polymer of hexamethylenediamine and adipic acid and has amide linkages.
(C) : (p, r) Proteins are natural polymers of α amino acids joined by amide linkages (peptide bonds).
(D) : (s) Sucrose is a disaccharide of α-D glucose and β-D-fructose and has an α, β-glycosidic linkage.
45. Statement-1 is correct, but statement-2 is incorrect because glucose on reaction with Fehling solution gives Cu_2O and not CuO.

EXERCISE 22.3

1.

```
         CHO              Mirror           CHO
    H ——— OH                |         HO ——— H
   HO ——— H                 |          H ——— OH
   HO ——— H                 |          H ——— OH
         CH₂OH              |              CH₂OH
   L-(+)-Arabinose                  D-(–)-Arabinose
```

The two are enantiomers

2. *(a)*

```
         CHO                              CH₂OH
    H ——— OH            NaBH₄        H ——— OH
    H ——— OH           ─────→        H ——— OH
    H ——— OH                         H ——— OH
         CH₂OH                           CH₂OH
   Optically active              Optically inactive (meso)
                                   (cf. meso-tartaric acid)
```

(b)

```
      CHO              COOH               COOH              CHO
  H ——— OH          H ——— OH          HO ——— H          HO ——— H
 HO ——— H          HO ——— H          HO ——— H          HO ——— H
  H ——— OH   HNO₃   H ——— OH    ═     H ——— OH   HNO₃   H ——— OH
  H ——— OH  ─────→  H ——— OH         HO ——— H   ←────  HO ——— H
      CH₂OH            COOH               COOH              CH₂OH
  D-Glucose
```

3. Hemiacetals are the condensation products obtained by the interaction of a carbonyl group and an alcoholic group. In case of carbohydrates both these groups are provided by the same molecule, so here a cyclic hemiacetal is formed. Hemiacetals are easily hydrolysed by aqueous solution and by alkalis. These are reducing in nature and undergo mutarotation. Glucose, fructose, and monosaccharides, in general, are examples of hemiacetals.

Acetals are the products obtained by the reaction of hemiacetal with another molecule of alcohol. Since here the —OH group of hemiacetal has reacted with the alcoholic group of another molecule, it is not free. Hence it can't be converted into open-chain structure, hence it is non-reducing and does not undergo mutarotation. It is stable to alkali but can be hydrolysed by acids. Alkyl glucoside and sucrose are examples of acetals.

4. When the anomeric hydroxyl group of a sugar is free *i.e.,* when the sugar is hemiacetal, one anomer (α- or β-) is converted to another (β- or α-) and thus such sugars show mutarotation.

In the compounds *(a)*, *(e)* and *(f)*, the anomeric —OH group is free, *i.e.,* these are hemiacetals, hence will show mutarotation. In compounds *(b)*, *(c)* and *(d)*, the anomeric —OH group is not free, it is present in the form of —OCH₃, —OAc and —OCH₃ respectively, so α- or β- form can't be converted to another, hence no possibility of mutarotation.

5. The kinetics of the reaction suggest that the rate-determining step involves the reaction with OH⁻ prior to the reaction with Cu²⁺. Reaction of reducing sugars with OH⁻ probably involves abstraction of H⁺ leading to the formation of enediol.

```
      O                        ⎡  O              O⁻   ⎤           OH
      ‖                        ⎢  ‖              |     ⎥           |
      C—H          OH⁻         ⎢  C—H            C—H   ⎥    H⁺     C—H      Cu²⁺
      |           ─────→       ⎢  |      ←──→    ‖     ⎥   ─────→  ‖      ─────→  Oxidation products
   H—C—OH                      ⎢  C—OH           C—OH  ⎥           C—OH
      |                        ⎣                       ⎦           |
                                    Carbanion                    Enediol
```

6. *(i)* Positive reaction with Benedict solution and negative reaction with Br₂ water indicate that bio-inonose has either an —CHO group or an α-hydroxy ketonic group which is converted to —CHO group in presence of OH⁻ ions provided by Benedict solution.

(ii) Molecular formula of the saturated open-chain compound corresponding to the carbonyl compound, $C_6H_{10}O_6$ will be $C_6H_{14}O_6$ which indicates that the compound has 2° of unsaturation, 1° of unsaturation is in the form of carbonyl group, so the 2nd unsaturation must be in the form of one ring (double bond is discarded due to negative reaction with Br₂ water).

Thus the compound bio-inonose should have following structure.

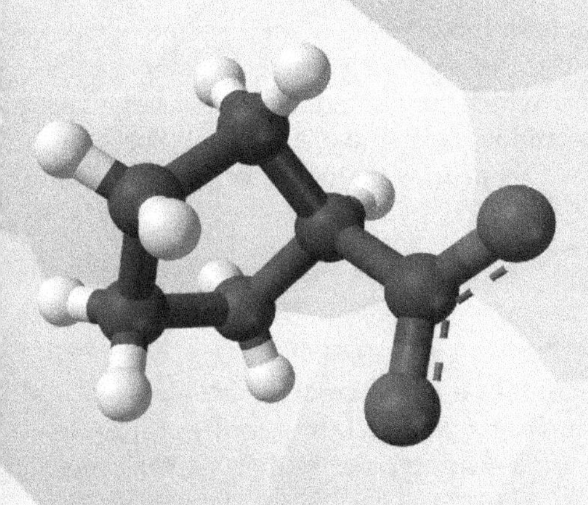

23

Amino Acids & Polymers

 ## 23.1   Introduction

Amino acids are the compounds having amino as well as carboxyl group in the same molecule. These are classified as α, β, γ, and so on, depending the relative position of the two groups.

$$\underset{\alpha}{H_2N}CH_2COOH \qquad \underset{\alpha}{H_2N}\overset{CH_3}{\overset{|}{CH}}COOH \qquad H_2N\overset{\beta}{CH_2}\overset{\alpha}{CH_2}COOH \qquad H_2N\overset{\gamma}{CH_2}\overset{\beta}{CH_2}\overset{\alpha}{CH_2}COOH$$

α-Amino acids   β-Amino acid   γ-Amino acid

Of the different types of amino acids, α-amino acids are most important as they constitute the building blocks of **proteins** (naturally occurring polymers of α-amino acids). A single protein molecule contains indefinite number of amino acid units which can be of 22 different types. It is the number of different combinations of these amino acids which gives rise to infinite number of protein molecules. However, human body is capable of synthesizing *only some of these 22 amino acids,* and hence the remaining amino acids, which our body can't biosynthesize must be supplied from outside in the form of diet, such amino acids are called **essentail amino acids.** On the whole, there are 10 essential amino acids, although this number is eight for adult humans. Thus the other amino acids which are synthesized in the body are known as **non-essential amino acids.** All of the 22 amino acids contain a primary amino group, except two (proline and hydroxyproline) which are secondary amines, and also known as *imino acids.*

Proline

Hydroxyproline

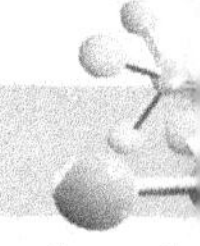

In addition to the carboxyl group and the amino group *alpha* to it, some amino acids contain a second carboxyl group (*e.g.* aspartic acid and glutamic acid) or a potential carboxyl group in the form of a carboxyamide (*e.g.* asparagine) ; these are called **acidic amino acids.** Similarly, there are some **basic amino acids** too, which contain an additional basic group in the form of an amino group (*e.g.* lysine), a guanido group (*e.g.* arginine), or an imidazole ring (*e.g.* histidine). Some of the amino acids contain benzene or heterocyclic ring systems, phenolic or alcoholic —OH groups, halogens or sulphur atoms.

 ## 23.2 Configuration of Natural Amino Acids

With the exception the simplest amino acid, glycine, all amino acids contain a chiral center. Further, *almost* all naturally occurring amino acids have L-configuration at the α-carbon, *i.e.* they have the same relative configuration as L-glyceraldehyde. Since the group R nearly always happens to have lower Cahn-Infold-Prolog priority than COOH, most of these have the S configuration.

$$
\begin{array}{ccc}
\text{An L-}\alpha\text{-amino acid} & \text{L-Glyceraldehyde} & \text{Glycine}
\end{array}
$$

COOH	CHO	CH₂COOH
H₂N—C—H	HO—C—H	NH₂
R	CH₂OH	
An L-α-amino acid	L-Glyceraldehyde	Glycine

TEST YOUR UNDERSTANDING - 23.1

1. Draw the Fischer projection formulas for the following amino acids. Designate these as R or S.

$$
(a)\quad \underset{X}{CH_3}\underset{\substack{|\\NH_2}}{CH}COOH
\qquad
(b)\quad CH_2OH\underset{\substack{|\\NH_2}}{CH}COOH
\qquad
(c)\quad H_2N\underset{\substack{|\\CH_2C_6H_5}}{CH}COOH
$$

2. What is the absolute configuration (R or S) at the α carbon atom in each of the following L amino acids ?

$$
(a)\quad H_2N\!-\!\!\begin{array}{c}COOH\\ \hline\\ CH_2OH\end{array}\!\!-H
\qquad
(b)\quad H_2N\!-\!\!\begin{array}{c}COOH\\ \hline\\ CH_2SH\end{array}\!\!-H
\qquad
(c)\quad H_2N\!-\!\!\begin{array}{c}COOH\\ \hline\\ CH_2CH_2SCH_3\end{array}\!\!-H
$$

3. How many chiral carbon atoms are present in threonine, $\overset{CH(OH)CH_3}{\underset{H_3\overset{+}{N}\,CHCOO^-}{|}}$? Write the Fischer projection formulas for its stereoisomers.

23.3 Preparation of Amino Acids

1. **Direct ammonolysis of α-halo acids.** This is simply a nucleophilic substitution.

$$
\underset{X}{CH_3}\underset{|}{CH}COOH \xrightarrow{\;NH_3\;(excess)\;} \underset{\underset{NH_3}{\overset{+}{|}}}{CH_3}CHCOO^-
$$

$$(X = Cl \quad or \quad Br)$$

The required α-halo acids or esters can be prepared by (*a*) **Hell-Volhard-Zelinsky halogenation** of the unsubstituted acids or by (*b*) a modification of the **malonic ester synthesis.**

(a) $CH_3CH_2COOH \xrightarrow{Cl_2 \text{ or } Br_2/P} CH_3CHCOOH$
  with Br substituent on the α-carbon.

(b) $^+Na^-CH(COOC_2H_5)_2 \xrightarrow{RCl} RCH(COOC_2H_5)_2 \xrightarrow[\text{(ii) HCl}]{\text{(i) KOH}} RCH(COOH)_2$

$\xrightarrow[\text{reflux}]{Br_2, \text{ ether}} RC(COOH)_2 \xrightarrow{\text{heat}} R\,CHCOOH$

with Br substituents.

2. **From potassium phthalimide.** This method is a modification of the *Gabriel synthesis of amines*. The yields are usually high and the products are easily purified. Here α-halo esters are used instead of α-acids, used in the above method.

$$\text{Potassium phthalimide} \quad N^-K^+ \;+\; ClCH_2COOC_2H_5 \longrightarrow NCH_2COOC_2H_5$$

Potassium phthalimide   Ethyl chloroacetate

$$\xrightarrow[\text{or HCl, } H_2O]{(i)\ KOH,\ H_2O\ ;\ (ii)\ HCl}$$

Phthalic acid (with two COOH groups)

$+\ Cl^-H_3N^+CH_2COOH\ +\ C_2H_5OH$

Glycine hydrochloride

A further modification of this method uses potassium phthalimide and diethyl bromomalonate, hence the method is sometimes named as **phthalimidomalonic ester method.**

$$N^-K^+ + BrCH(COOC_2H_5)_2 \longrightarrow NCH(COOC_2H_5)_2 \xrightarrow[\text{(ii) ClCH}_2COOC_2H_5]{\text{(i) C}_2H_5ONa}$$

$$N-\underset{\underset{COOC_2H_5}{|}}{\overset{\overset{CH_2COOC_2H_5}{|}}{C}}-COOC_2H_5 \xrightarrow[\text{(ii) HCl}]{\text{(i) NaOH}}$$

Phthalic acid (with two COOH groups) $+\ H_3N^+\underset{|}{\overset{CH_2COOH}{}}CHCOOH$

3. **The Strecker synthesis.** In the strecker synthesis, an aldehyde is converted to an α-amino acid with one more carbon atom.

$$CH_3CHO \xrightarrow[\text{or NH}_4Cl/NaCN]{NH_3/HCN} CH_3\underset{\underset{NH_2}{|}}{CH}CN \xrightarrow{H_3O^+,\ \text{heat}} CH_3\underset{\underset{NH_3^+}{|}}{CH}COO^-$$

An α-aminonitrile α-Amino acid

4. **Reductive amination of α-keto acids** (*Knoop synthesis*).

$$CH_3\overset{\overset{O}{\|}}{C}COOH + NH_3 \longrightarrow CH_3\overset{\overset{NH}{\|}}{C}COOH \xrightarrow[\text{or NaBH}_4]{H_2/Pd} CH_3\underset{\underset{NH_3^+}{|}}{CH}COO^-$$

All of the above methods give optically inactive amino acids, and hence these must be resolved if the active materials are desired for comparison with the naturally occurring L acids or for synthesis of peptides. An optically active amino acid may directly be obtained, *i.e..* without the use of resolution, such synthesis is better known as **enantioselective synthesis.** Enantioselective synthesis, *i.e.* when one of the enatiomer is in excess amount than the other, may be achieved by using an optically active reagent or catalyst at some point in the process. Remember that amino acids synthesized in living systems are 100 percent enantioselective because of the involvement of enzymes as catalyst.

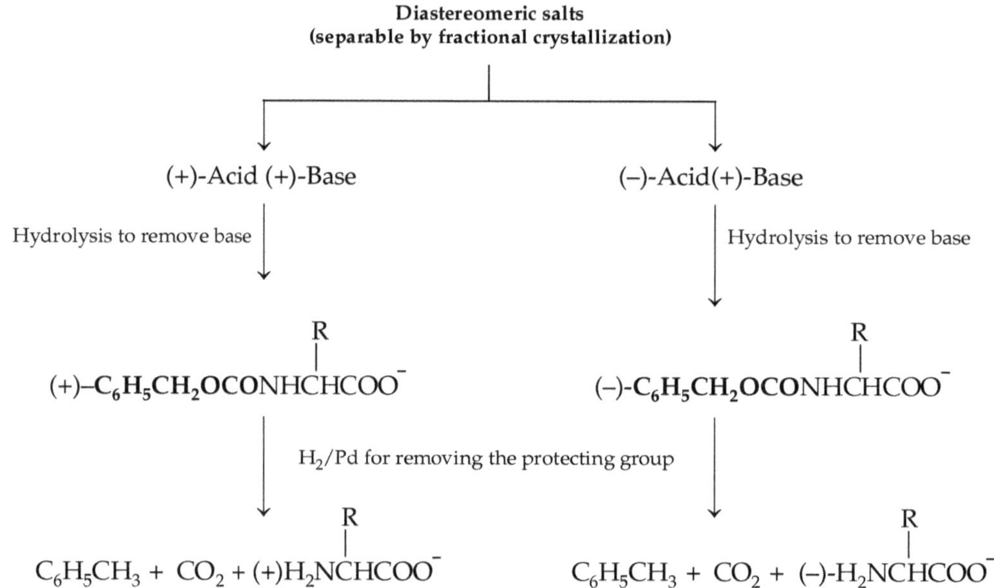

Alternatively, the carboxylic group is protected by esterification and an optically active acid is used as resolving reagent which reacts with the free amino group to form two diasteromeric ammonium salts. Fractional crystallization, hydrolysis of the salt to remove acid, and hydrolysis of the ester to remove protecting group completes resolution.

TEST YOUR UNDERSTANDING - 23.2

1. Give steps involved in the preparation of valine, $Me_2CHCH(NH_2)COOH$ from isobutanol by a Strecker reaction.
2. Prepare valine by (*a*) a HVZ reaction, (*b*) a reductive amination, and (*c*) a Gabriel synthesis.
3. Try to develop a scheme for synthesizing glycine from methyl chloride.
4. Account for the stereochemical specificity of enzymes with chiral substrates.

23.4 Acid-Base Properties

The usual structure of amino acids ($H_2NCH(R)COOH$) shown to contain a free amino and a free cerboxyl group is not in consistent with certain physical and chemical properties.

(*i*) Unlike amines and the lower aliphatic carboxylic acids, all amino acids even the simplest one (glyine) are crystalline solids and **melt with decomposition** at fairly high temperature.

(*ii*) They are **fairly soluble in water,** but insoluble in non-polar solvents like petroleum ether, benzene, or ether.

(*iii*) Amino acids have much **larger dipole moments** than simple amines and simple acids.

$$H_3N^+ - CH_2 - COO^-$$
Glycine, μ=14D

$$CH_3CH_2CH_2NH_2$$
Propylamine, μ=1.4D

$$CH_3CH_2COOH$$
Propanoic acid, μ=1.7D

(*iv*) Amino acids are **less acidic than most carboxylic acids and less basic than most amines.** In fact, the acidic part of the amino acid molecule is the $-NH_3^+$ group, not a –COOH group, while the basic part of the amino acid is the –COO$^-$ group, and not a free –NH$_2$ group.

$$R - COOH \qquad R - NH_2 \qquad H_3\overset{+}{N} - \overset{\overset{\textstyle R}{|}}{C}H - COO^-$$
$$pK_a=5 \qquad\qquad pK_b=4 \qquad\qquad pK_a=10;\ pK_b=12$$

The above properties point out toward the salt like character (dipolar ion structure) to amino acids. Actually, in the dry state, amino acids exist as **dipolar ions** (also known as **zwitterions** or **inner salts**), a form in which the carboxyl group is present as a carboxylate ion, —COO$^-$, and the amino group as an aminium ion, —NH$_3^+$.

$$\overset{\overset{\textstyle R}{|}}{H_2N\,CH\,COOH} \quad\rightleftharpoons\quad H_3\overset{+}{N}\ \overset{\overset{\textstyle R}{|}}{CH\,COO^-}$$
Dipolar ions, I

The dipolar ionic (salt like) structure of amino acids explains all of its above properties.

In aqueous solution, the dipolar ionic structure is not stable and equilibrium exists between the dipolar ionic and the monoionic (cationic and anionic) forms of an amino acid.

$$\overset{\overset{\textstyle R}{|}}{H_3\overset{+}{N}CHCOOH} \quad\underset{}{\overset{H_2O\ (\text{as an acid})}{\rightleftharpoons}}\quad \overset{\overset{\textstyle R}{|}}{H_3\overset{+}{N}CHCOO^-} \quad\underset{}{\overset{H_2O\ (\text{as a base})}{\rightleftharpoons}}\quad \overset{\overset{\textstyle R}{|}}{H_2NCHCOO^-} + H_2O$$

Cationic form — (Dominates in strongly acidic solutions, *e.g.* at pH ≈ 0) | Dipolar ion | **Anionic form** — (Dominates in strongly basic solutions, *e.g.* pH ≈ 14)

The predominant form of the amino acid (cationic, zwitterionic, or anionic) in the solution depends upon the pH of the solution and also on the nature of the side chain (R) of the amino acid. In strongly acidic solutions (pH ≈ 0), all amino acids are present mainly as cations,* while is stronlgy basic solutions (pH ≈ 14), they are present mainly as anions. At some intermediate pH (called the **isoelectric point, pI**), the concentration of the dipolar ion is at its maximum and the concentrations of the anions and cations are low but equal. Isoelectric point is a constant for an amino acid and depends upon the structure of the particular amino acid. Since at the isoelectric point, the cationic and anionic forms of an amino acid are equal, at this point the amino acid practically behaves as a neutral species as indicated by the fact that the amino acid neither migrates to anode nor to cathode when an electric current is passed through its aqeuous solution.

Determination of the isoelectric point. Let us consider the strongly acidic solution of alanine which primarily contains $H_3N^+CH(CH_3)COOH$. As the pH of the solution is raised by adding a base, a proton is removed from the —COOH group of the species to form zwitterion. This dissociation constant of the species is designated as pK_{a1}, and found to be 2.3 for the conjugate acid of alanine.

$$\overset{\overset{\textstyle CH_3}{|}}{H_3\overset{+}{N}CHCOOH} \quad\underset{H^+}{\overset{-H^+}{\rightleftharpoons}}\quad \overset{\overset{\textstyle CH_3}{|}}{H_3\overset{+}{N}CHCOO^-} \quad\underset{}{\overset{-H^+}{\rightleftharpoons}}\quad \overset{\overset{\textstyle CH_3}{|}}{H_2NCHCOO^-}$$

Cationic form (pK_{a_1} ≈ 2.3) | Dipolar ion (pK_{a_2} ≈ 9.7) | Anionic form

If the deprotonation of alanine would have involved the $-\overset{+}{N}H_3$ rather than —COOH, the pK_{a_1} value for the conjugate acid of alanine would have been higher than 5 (pK_a value for a typical RCOOH $\cong$ 5), (a *typical* ammonium ion has $pK_a \cong 9$).

---

* Existence of amino acids as cation ($H_3N^+CH(R)\,COOH$) in strongly acidic medium, and as an anion ($H_2NCH(R)COO^-$) in stronlgy basic medium explains why reactions of amino acids involving acidic group (*e.g.* esterification) and those involving —NH$_2$ group (*e.g.* acetylation) speed up in presence of strong acid and strong base respectively.

When pH is further raised $-\overset{+}{N}H_3$ group of zwitterion is deprotonated (second deprotonation step) to form anionic species. This dissociation constant is designated as pK_{a_2} and found to be 9.7 for the zwitterion of alanine. The isoelectric point (pI) of an amino acid having one $-NH_2$ and one $-COOH$ group is the average of pK_{a_1} and pK_{a_2}. Thus the pI for alanine is 6.0.

$$pI = \frac{2.3 + 9.7}{2} = 6.00$$

pK_{a1} corresponds to ionization of the carboxyl group.

pK_{a2} corresponds to ionization of the ammonium ion.

TEST YOUR UNDERSTANDING - 23.3

1. (a) Write the most stable structural formula for the amino acid, $p\text{-}OHC_6H_4CH_2\overset{\underset{\displaystyle |}{NH_2}}{C}HCOOH$, in its

   (i) zwitterionic form (ii) cationic form (iii) anionic form (iv) dianionic form

   (b) Supply the structure of the species I to IV

   $$^-OOC\overset{\underset{\displaystyle |}{NH_2}}{C}HCH_2COO^- \underset{OH^-}{\overset{H^+}{\rightleftharpoons}} I \underset{OH^-}{\overset{H^+}{\rightleftharpoons}} [II \rightleftharpoons III] \underset{OH^-}{\overset{H^+}{\rightleftharpoons}} IV$$

2. Write structrual formulas for the principal species present in the solution of the amino acid lysine,

   $$H_2N(CH_2)_4\overset{\underset{\displaystyle |}{NH_2}}{C}HCOOH \text{ at pH 1, 9 and 13.}$$

3. Draw the two possible dipolar structures for the amino acid, $H_2N(CH_2)_4CH(NH_2)COOH$. Which one is more likely to be correct ?

4. Explain the following

   (a) *p*-Aminobenzoic acid or *o*-aminobenzoic acid does not exist as the zwitterion, while *p*-aminobenzene-sulphonic acid (sulphanilic acid) exists as zwitterion.

   (b) Sulphanilic acid, a zwitterion dissolves in alkalies but not in acids.

5. To which electrode, an amino acid migrates at a

   (a) pH > pI, (b) pH < pI, and (c) pH = pI.

6. What happens when an electric current is passed through an aqueous solution, buffered at pH = 6.0, containing three amino acids A, B, and C ? The isoelectric points for the three amino acids are 6.0, 3.0 and 10.0 respectively.

Example 1 :

Draw the structure of the predominant form of following amino acids at pH mentioned below them.

(a) $H_2N-\overset{\underset{\displaystyle |}{CH(CH_3)_2}}{C}H-COOH$
Valine at pH 11

(b) 

Proline at pH 2

(c) $H_2N-\overset{\underset{\displaystyle |}{(CH_2)_3-NH-\overset{\overset{\displaystyle NH}{\|}}{C}-NH_2}}{C}H-COOH$
Arginine at pH 7

(d) a mixture of alanine, lysine, and aspartic acid at (i) pH 2, (ii) pH 6, and (iii) pH 11.

$H_2N-\overset{\underset{\displaystyle |}{CH_3}}{C}H-COOH$
Alanine

$H_2N-\overset{\underset{\displaystyle |}{(CH_2)_4NH_2}}{C}H-COOH$
Lysine

$H_2N-\overset{\underset{\displaystyle |}{CH_2COOH}}{C}H-COOH$
Aspartic acid

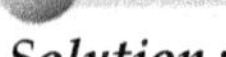

Solution :

The first ionization constant (pK_{a1}) of α-amino acids is nearly 2.3, while the pK_{a2} is about 9.6. Hence in a strongly acidic medium (*pH* below 2), the amino acids exist in cationic form, while in a strongly alkaline medium (*pH* above 10), the amino acids exist in anionic form; the zwitterionic form is predominant at *pH* value ranging between 2 to 9. Thus at the pH below 2, the amino acids exist mainly as the cation, as the pH value exceeds 2.3, the –COOH group starts convering into –COO⁻ and thus zwitterionic form starts appearing. Higher the *pH*, greater number of –COOH will be converted into –COO⁻, and finally as the *pH* increases beyond pK_{a2} (9.6), the $-\overset{+}{N}H_3$ group is converted into –NH₂ and thus the amino acid mainly exists as an anion.

(a)
$$CH(CH_3)_2$$
$$H_2N-\overset{|}{C}H-COO^-$$
Valine at pH 11

(b)
Proline at pH 2

(c)
$$\overset{+}{N}H$$
$$(CH_2)_3-NH-\overset{||}{C}-NH_2$$
$$H_3\overset{+}{N}-\overset{|}{C}H-COO^-$$
Arginine at pH 7

(d)

		Alanine	**Lysine**	**Aspartic acid**
(i)	**pH 2**	CH_3 $H_3\overset{+}{N}-\overset{|}{C}H-COOH$	$(CH_2)_4\overset{+}{N}H_3$ $H_3\overset{+}{N}-\overset{|}{C}H-COOH$	$CH_2\,COOH$ $H_3\overset{+}{N}-\overset{|}{C}H-COOH$
(ii)	**pH 6**	CH_3 $H_3\overset{+}{N}-\overset{|}{C}H-COO^-$	$(CH_2)_4\overset{+}{N}H_3$ $H_3\overset{+}{N}-\overset{|}{C}H-COO^-$	$CH_2\,COO^-$ $H_3\overset{+}{N}-\overset{|}{C}H-COO^-$
(iii)	**pH 11**	CH_3 $H_2N-\overset{|}{C}H-COO^-$	$(CH_2)_4\,NH_2$ $H_2N-\overset{|}{C}H-COO^-$	$CH_2\,COO^-$ $H_2N-\overset{|}{C}H-COO^-$

Example 2 :

Arginine has a strongly basic isoelectric point (10.7), while other amino acids have pI between pK_{a_1} (2.3) and pK_{a_2} (9.7). Explain.

$$NH$$
$$(CH_2)_3-NH-\overset{||}{C}-NH_2$$
$$H_2N-CH-COOH$$

Solution :

The strongly basic isoelectric point (10.7) of arginine is due to unusual basicity of its guanido group which in turn is due to resonance stabilization of its protonated form.

$$R-NH-\overset{NH}{\overset{||}{C}}-NH_2 \xrightarrow{H^+} R-NH-\overset{+NH_2}{\overset{||}{C}}-NH_2 \longleftrightarrow R-NH-\overset{NH_2}{\overset{|}{\underset{+}{C}}}-NH_2$$

guanido group of arginine

$$R-\overset{+}{N}H=C-NH_2 \qquad R-NH-C=\overset{+}{N}H_2$$

Protonation of the $-C=\overset{..}{N}H$ group in preference to $-\overset{..}{N}H_2$ groups is also because of high stability of the corresponding conjugate acid whose three of the resonating structures are identical.

23.5   Reactions of Amino Acids

Amino acids undergo reactions characteristics of both their amino and carboxylic groups. Acylation is a typical reaction of the amino group, while esterification is a typical reaction of the carboxyl group.

$$\overset{R}{\underset{}{\overset{|}{H_3\overset{+}{N}\,CHCOO^-}}} + (CH_3CO)_2O \longrightarrow CH_3\overset{O}{\overset{||}{C}}NH\overset{R}{\overset{|}{CH}}COOH + CH_3COOH$$

$$H_3\overset{+}{N}\,\overset{R}{\overset{|}{CH}}COO^- + CH_3CH_2OH \xrightarrow{\;H^+\;} H_3\overset{+}{N}\,\overset{R}{\overset{|}{CH}}COOC_2H_5$$

Other important reactions of α-amino acids are given below.

(a)   **Reaction with nitrous acid** (*Similarity with 1° amines*).

$$H_3\overset{+}{N}\,\overset{R}{\overset{|}{CH}}COO^- \xrightarrow{\;HONO\;} HO\overset{R}{\overset{|}{CH}}COOH + N_2\uparrow$$

This reaction forms the basis of the **Van Slyke** method for estimation of amino acid or amino group because one mole of N_2 is evolved per —NH_2 group in the amino acid.

(b)   **Reaction with formaldehyde**

$$H_3\overset{+}{N}\,\overset{R}{\overset{|}{CH}}COO^- + CH_2O \longrightarrow CH_2 = N\overset{R}{\overset{|}{CH}}COOH$$

N-Methyleneamino acid

This reaction is used for estimating the —COOH group by titration (**Sorenson titration method**).

(c)   **Reaction with 2, 4-dinitrofluorobenzene** (DNFB, commonly known as Sanger's reagent).

$$O_2N\!\!\bigcirc\!\!\overset{NO_2}{F} + H_3\overset{+}{N}\overset{R}{\overset{|}{CH}}COO^- \xrightarrow{\;Na_2CO_3\;} O_2N\!\!\bigcirc\!\!\overset{NO_2}{-}NH\overset{R}{\overset{|}{CH}}COO^-$$

DNFB   Yellow coloured dinitrophenyl amino acid

(d)   **Reaction with ninhydrin.** This is used as a test for detecting the presence of α-amino acids.

Ninhydrin   Ruhemann's purple (Violet colour)

+ RCHO + CO₂ formed, but not isolated

Note that only N of the amino acid appears in the Ruhemann's purple, the side chain is lost as RCHO and —COO^- part as CO_2. Further, proline and hydroxyproline do not react with ninhydrin because they have secondary amino group.

(e)   Heating of α-amino acids with copper sulphate in presence of dil. NaOH gives *deep blue colour*.

TEST YOUR UNDERSTANDING - 23.4

1.   Give the products of reaction of glycine with

    (a)   aq. KOH   (b)   aq. HCl   (c) C_6H_5COCl + NaOH   (d) $Ba(OH)_2$, heat

2. (*a*) Give the products of the reaction of nitrous acid with $\overset{+}{H_3N}CH(R)COO^-$. What is the special importance of this reaction ?

(*b*) Can you name any amino acid that does not evolve N_2 with nitrous acid ?

(*c*) Determine the volume of N_2 evolved at STP when

    (*i*) 0.01 mole of a mono aminomonocarboxylic acid,

    (*ii*) 0.001 mole of a diaminomonocarboxylic acid is treated with nitrous acid.

3. (*a*) What is the effect of heating on α-amino acids ?

(*b*) When the methyl ester of *rac*-alanine is heated, two diastereomers are obtained, only one of them is resolvable. Explain.

4. Give the reagent used for distinguishing following pairs of α-amino acids.

(*a*) 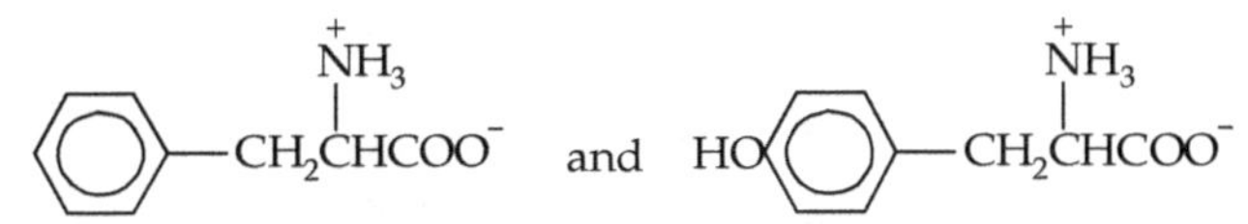   phenyl—$CH_2\overset{\overset{+}{NH_3}}{\underset{|}{C}}HCOO^-$ and   HO—phenyl—$CH_2\overset{\overset{+}{NH_3}}{\underset{|}{C}}HCOO^-$ (*b*) $HOCH_2\overset{\overset{+}{NH_3}}{\underset{|}{C}}HCOO^-$

and $CH_3CHOH\,CHCOO^-$

       Phenylalanine   Tyrosine   Serine   Threonine

Example 3 :

Ninhydrin is the hydrate of indane-1,2,3-trione. Give its reaction with alanine, $CH_3CH(NH_2)COOH$ and draw the important resonating structures of the anion formed.

Solution :

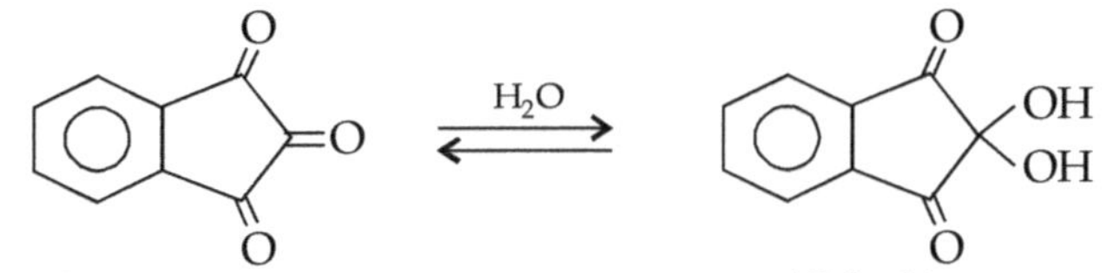

Indane-1,2,3-trione $\xrightarrow{H_2O}$ Ninhydrin

Ninhydrin   + $H_3\overset{+}{N}\overset{\overset{\textstyle CH_3}{|}}{C}HCOO^-$ ⟶ Ruhemann's purple   + $CH_3CHO + CO_2$

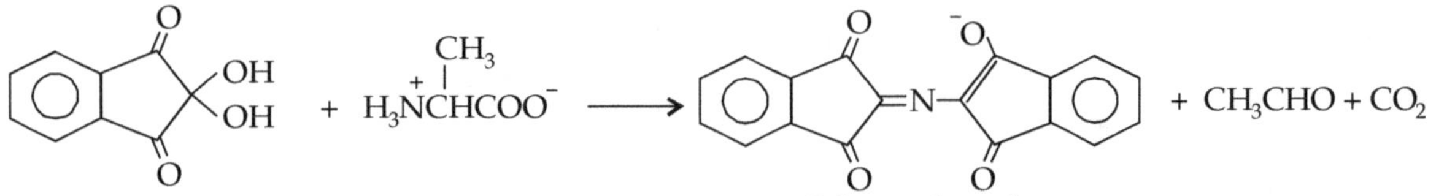

     Alanine

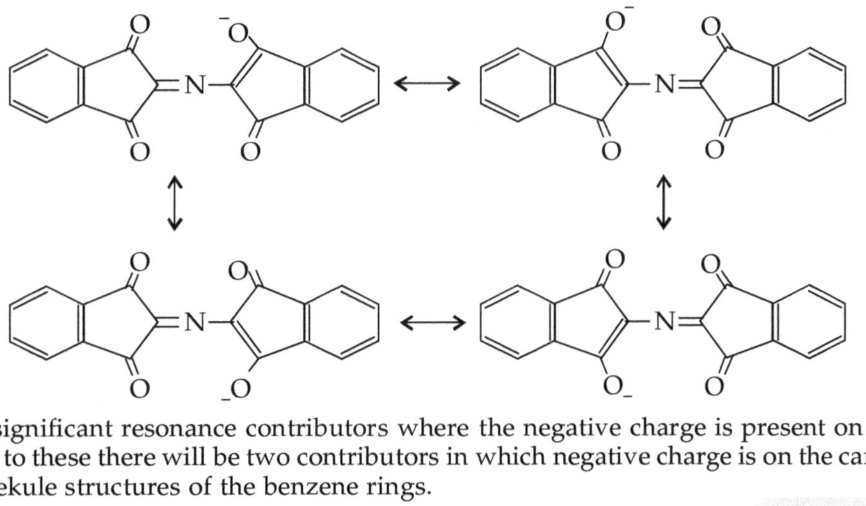

These are the most significant resonance contributors where the negative charge is present on the electronegative oxygens. In addition to these there will be two contributors in which negative charge is on the carbons bonded to the nitrogen, plus the Kekule structures of the benzene rings.

23.6 Peptides

Peptides are polyamides formed by interaction between amino and carboxyl groups of amino acids. The amido group —NHCO—, in such compounds is often referred to as the **peptide linkage.** The peptides are classified into various groups depending upon the number of the amino acid residues in it, *e.g.* a peptide derived from two molecules of the same or different amino acids is known as dipeptide, from three, four or indefinite molecules of amino acids as **tripeptide, tetrapeptide,** and **polypeptide** respectively.

$$\overset{R}{\underset{H_3\overset{+}{N}\,CHCOO^-}{|}} + \overset{R'}{\underset{H_3\overset{+}{N}\,CHCOO^-}{|}} \xrightarrow[(-H_2O)]{} \; H_3\overset{+}{N}\,\overset{R}{\underset{|}{CH}}-\overset{O}{\underset{||}{C}}-NH-\overset{R'}{\underset{|}{CH}}\,OO^-$$

A dipeptide (it has one peptide bond)

Thus the number of peptide bonds in di-, tri-, tera- and penta- peptide is 1, 2, 3 and 4 respectively.

Formula of peptides is written by using the three-letter amino acid abbreviations for the respective amino acids and connecting them by hyphens ; *e.g.* Gly– Gly is a dipepide having 2 molecules of glycine. Further, according to convention, the amino acid written at the left end of a peptide formula is considered to have free amino group hence it is commonly known as **N-terminal amino acid** ; while the amino acid written at the right end is considered to have free carboxyl group, hence it is known as **C-terminal** amino acid.

TEST YOUR UNDERSTANDING - 23.5

1. Write structural formulas for each of the following dipeptides.

    (*a*) Gly–Ala (*b*) Ala–Gly (*c*) Ala–Phe (*d*) D-Ala-D-Ala

    where, Gly = $H_3\overset{+}{N}\,CH_2COO^-$, Ala = $H_3\overset{+}{N}\,\overset{CH_3}{\underset{|}{CH}}\,COO^-$, Phe = $H_3\overset{+}{N}\,\underset{\underset{C_6H_5CH_2}{|}}{CHCOO^-}$

2. Write the structural formula for (*a*) Gly–Ala–Ala, and (*b*) phenylalanylalanylalanine.

3. You are given two α-amino acid molecules, and asked to prepare dipetide. Can you get a specific dipeptide ?

4. (*a*) List and name all the different dipeptides that can be synthesised from glycine and alanine ?

    (*b*) How many tripeptides are possible using three different amino acids ?

The peptide bond is flat : carbonyl carbon, nitrogen, and the four atoms attached to them all lie in a plane. The short (1.32 Å) C—N distance of peptide linkage than the usual C—N single bond (1.47 Å) indicates that the C—N bond in peptides has considerable double bond character which in turn is due to delocalization of nonbonding electrons to the O of C = O. As a result the angles of the bonds to nitrogen are similar to the angles to the trigonal carbon atom.

Due to partial double bond character of the peptide bond, rotation about the amide linkage is not free. Further, the most stable conformation with respect to the peptide bond is that in which the two α carbon atoms are anti to each other.

23.7 Polymers

The macromolecules formed by the union between same or different molecules are known as polymers.

Polymerisation : The process of joining together the simple molecules is known as polymerisation.

MONOMERS : Small molecules which are joined together to form polymers are known as monomers.

DEGREE OF POLYMERISATION : The number of monomolecules (n) which combine to form a given macromolecule is called the degree of polymerisation.

HIGH POLYMERS : Such polymers have high degree of polymerisation.

OLIGOMERS : They have low degree of polymerisation.

DISTINCTION BETWEEN POLYMERS AND MACROMOLECULES : Polymers have repeat units and a macromolecule may or may not have repeat units eg chlorophyll and polythene.

HOMOPOLYMERS : Polymers containing one type of monomer units.

COPOLYMERS : Polymers containing two or more types of monomer units.

CLASSIFICATION : They may be divided into two categories.

(i) *Natural polymers* - They are obtained from natural sources eg **poly saccharides** (starch, cellulose), **Proteins** (polymers of amino acids), gums, resins (cross linked polymers formed by compounds containing double or triple bonds slowly oxidised by atmospheric oxygen). **natural rubber** (polymer of isoprene), **Nucleic acids** (polymers of nucleotides) silk and wool (polymers of amino acids).

(ii) *Synthetic polymers* - Polymers prepared by synthesis (man made), are known as synthetic polymers eg. polystyrene, nylon, PVC etc.

CLASSIFICATION BASED ON STRUCTURE :

(i) *Linear polymers* - Polymers containing the monomeric units linked together to form long straight chains stacked over one another to give packed structure.

Such polymers have high tensile strength, high densities, high m.p. and b.p. Examples - fibres and plastics.

(ii) *Branched polymers* - Long chain of monomer units containing side chains of different length forms branched polymers. The chains are loosely packed, hence polymers have low density, low m.p. and low tensite strength. Examples - Amylopectin and glycogen.

(iii) *Cross - linked* or three dimensional polymers - Such polymers have three dimensional network and are hard, brittle and rigid. Examples - Bakelite, melamine.

STEREOCHEMICAL CLASSIFICATION :

Polymers of propylene can be classified into

(i) *Isotactic* - with all methyl groups on one side of extended chain

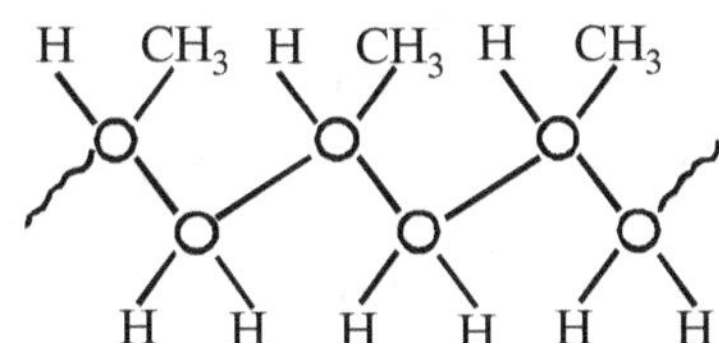

(ii) *Syndiotactic,* with methyl groups alternating regularly side to side

(iii) *Atactic*-with random distribution of methyl groups

(Above polymers are obtained by coordination polymerisation)

CLASSIFICATION BASED UPON MODE OF SYNTHESIS :

(i) *Addition polymers* - Polymers formed without the elimination of any elements and the molecular weight of the polymer is the exact multiple of the monomer unit are known as addition polymers

$$n\left(\begin{array}{c} R \\ | \\ CH = CH_2 \end{array}\right) \rightleftarrows \quad \left(\begin{array}{c} R \\ | \\ CH - CH_2 \end{array}\right)_n$$

Alkene → Polyalkene

(ii) *Condensation polymers* - They are formed with elimination of certain elements in the form of H_2O, C_2H_5OH, NH_3 etc. and molecular weight of polymer is not exact multiple of monomer unit eg. terephthalic acid condenses with ethylene glycol to give polyester

$$n\ HOOC-\langle_\rangle-COOH + n\ HO(CH_2)_2OH \longrightarrow -(OC-\langle_\rangle-\overset{\overset{O}{\|}}{C}-O-(CH_2)_2-O)_n + (n-1)H_2O$$

Terephthalic acid   ethylene glycol   Polyester

CHAIN GROWTH AND STEP GROWTH POLYMERS :

(i) *Chain growth polymers* - In chain growth polymerisation each step consumes a reactive particle and produces another similar particle.

$$\overset{\bullet}{A} + \overset{\overset{R}{|}}{C}H = CH_2 \rightarrow A - \overset{\overset{R}{|}}{C}H - \overset{\bullet}{C}H_2$$

$$A - \overset{\overset{R}{|}}{C}H - \overset{\bullet}{C}H_2 + \overset{\overset{R}{|}}{C}H = CH_2 \rightarrow A - \overset{\overset{R}{|}}{C}H - CH_2 - \overset{\overset{R}{|}}{C}H - \overset{\bullet}{C}H_2$$

(ii) *Step growth polymers* - Polymerisation proceeds through various steps independent of each other and it happens when monomer units contain more than one functional group. For example formation of nylon 66, bakelite etc proceed by step growth polymerisation.

$$n\ H_2N-(CH_2)_6 NH_2 + n\ HOOC(CH_2)_4 COOH \rightarrow -(NH-(CH_2)_6-NH-\overset{\overset{O}{\|}}{C}-(CH_2)_4-\overset{\overset{O}{\|}}{C})_n + (n-1)H_2O$$

Heaxamethylene diamine   Adipic acid   Nylon 66

CLASSIFICATION ON THE BASIS OF PHYSICAL PROPERTIES AND INTERPARTICLE FORCES :

(i) *Elastomers* - They can be easily stretched and can be made rigid to some extent by adding cross linking agents eg vulcanised rubber. They possess weakest intermolecular forces.

(ii) *Thermoplastics* - They become soft on heating and harden on cooling. eg polythene, polystyrene. They can be worked up again and again. Forces between molecules are intermediate of elastomers and fibers.

(iii) *Thermosetting* - Such polymers undergo chemical changes when heated and set to hard mass when cooled eg Bakelite. Such polymers can not be reworked. There is excessive cross linking on heating and three dimensional net work of bonds.

(iv) *Fibres* - Linear polymers containing polymeric units joined by hydrogen bonding. They can be woven into fabrics. Rayons, nylons are the examples.

FORMATION OF ADDITION POLYMERS :

They can be obtained by

(i) Free radical polymerisation

(ii) Cationic polymerisation

(iii) Anionic polymerisation

(iv) Ziegler - Natta polymerisation or coordination polymerisation

VULCANIZATION OF RUBBER :

Heating of rubber with sulphur which causes formation of sulphur bridges between molecules which are then cross linked is known as vulcanization of rubber. The vulcanised rubber is more elastic than natural rubber.

Vulcanization may be brought about by free radical generators (peroxides, azo compounds) and metal oxides (ZnO or MgO) also.

ANTI OXIDANTS :

Natural rubber is very sensitive to oxidation by air and ozone which can be inhibited by adding anti oxidants. They undergo easy oxidation and prevent the oxidative degradation of rubber. Examples are N - phenyl - β - naphthylamine and Di - β - naphthyl - p - phenylenediamine.

MOLECULAR MASS OF POLYMERS :

It is of two types

(i) **Number average molecular mass** $(\overline{Mn})$ given by

$$\overline{Mn} = \frac{N_1M_1 + N_2M_2 + N_3M_3 + \dots\dots}{N_1 + N_2 + N_3 + \dots\dots} = \frac{\sum N_iM_i}{\sum N_i}$$

Where N_1 number of molecules having molecular mass M_1 and so on. It is measured by osmotic pressure measurement.

(ii) **Mass - average molecular mass** $(\overline{Mw})$ given by

$$\overline{Mw} = \frac{N_1M_1^2 + N_2M_2^2 + N_3M_3^2 + \dots\dots}{N_1M_1 + N_2M_2 + N_3M_3 + \dots\dots} = \frac{\sum N_iM_i^2}{\sum N_iM_i}$$

It is determined by ultra centrifugation or sedimentation.

POLYDISPERSITY INDEX :

It is the ratio of mass average molecular mass $\overline{M}_w$ to the number average molecular mass $\overline{M}_n$

$$PDI = \frac{\overline{M}_w}{\overline{M}_n}$$

When PDI = 1 or nearly 1, we have monodisperse system in which all molecules have identical molecular mass. Natural polymers are monodisperse and synthetic polymers are polydisperse i.e. PDI > 1 for such polymers

IMPORTANT ADDITION POLYMERS :

(i) *Polyethylene*

$$n\,CH_2 = CH_2 \xrightarrow[1500\,atm;150-250°C]{\text{Traces of O}_2} (CH_2 - CH_2)_n$$
$$\text{Polythene}$$
$$\text{or Polyethylene}$$

Free radical initiator gives low density polythene and ionic catalyst gives high density polythene. It is white, transluscent, rigid, linear, used for making tubes, pipes, coated wires, insulator parts. etc.

(ii) *Polypropylene*

$$n\,CH_3 - CH = CH_2 \xrightarrow[Al(C_2H_5)_3 + TiCl_3]{\text{Ziegler Natta Catalyst}} \underset{\text{Polypropylene}}{(\overset{\overset{\displaystyle CH_3}{|}}{CH} - CH_2)_n}$$

It has good hardness, stiffness, resistance. Used for making ropes, carpets, washing machine parts etc.

(iii) *Polystyrene*

$$n\,C_6H_5 - CH = CH_2 \xrightarrow{\text{Benzoyl Peroxide}} (\overset{\overset{\displaystyle C_6H_5}{|}}{CH} - CH_2)_n$$

It is transparent, light, moisture resistant used for battery cases, refrigerator parts, electric insulators, combs, buttons TV cabinets. Its trade name is **Styrofoam** or **styron**.

(iv) **Polymethyl methy** acrylate, **Lucite** or **Plexiglass**.

$$n\,CH_2 = \overset{\overset{\displaystyle COOCH_3}{|}}{\underset{\underset{\displaystyle CH_3}{|}}{C}} \xrightarrow[\text{or } H_2O_2]{\text{Acetylperoxide}} (CH_2 - \overset{\overset{\displaystyle COOCH_3}{|}}{\underset{\underset{\displaystyle CH_3}{|}}{C}} -)_n$$

Methylmeth acrylate (MMA)　　　　　　PMMA

It is hard, fairly rigid. It is used for making lenses, artificial eyes, dentures, aircraft windows.

(v) *Polyvinyl chloride (PVC)*

$$n\ CH_2 = CH - Cl \xrightarrow[\text{Under pressure}]{\text{Benzoyl peroxide or } H_2O_2} (CH_2 - \underset{\underset{Cl}{|}}{CH})_n$$

It is resistant to light, atmopheric oxygen, chemically inert. It is used for electrical insulators, floor covering, safety helmets etc.

(vi) *Teflon, Polytetrafluoroethylene (PTFE) of Fluon*

$$\underset{\text{Tetrafluoro ethene}}{n\ CF_2 = CF_2} \xrightarrow[\text{Amm.−peroxosulphate } (NH_4)_2 S_2O_8]{\text{Benzoyl peroxide or}} (\underset{\underset{F}{|}}{\overset{\overset{F}{|}}{C}} - \underset{\underset{F}{|}}{\overset{\overset{F}{|}}{C}})_n$$

It is extremely tough, resistant to heat and chemicals. It is used for making gaskets, pump parts, coating utensils, high frequency insulator

(vii) *Polyacrylonitrile (PAN), acrilon or orlon*

$$\underset{\text{Acrylonitrile}}{n\ CH_2 = \underset{\underset{CN}{|}}{CH}} \longrightarrow \underset{\text{orlon}}{(CH_2 - \underset{\underset{CN}{|}}{CH})_n}$$

It is hard used in preparing cloths, carpets

RUBBERS

(i) *Buna - S or SBR or GSR (Government styrene rubber)*

$$n\ \underset{\underset{\underset{\text{Styrene}}{C_6H_5}}{|}}{CH = CH_2} + n\ \underset{\text{Butadiene}}{CH_2 = CH - CH = CH_2} \xrightarrow[\Delta]{Na} \underset{\underset{\underset{\text{Buna−S}}{C_6H_5}}{|}}{(CH - CH_2 - CH_2 - CH = CH - CH_2 -)_n}$$

It is used for manufacture of tyres, floor tiles, gaskets, cable insulators etc.

(ii) *Nitrile rubber* (GR-A or Buna - N)

$$n\ \underset{\text{Butadiene}}{CH_2 = CH - CH = CH_2} + n\ \underset{\text{Acrylonitrile}}{CH_2 = \underset{\underset{CN}{|}}{CH}} \longrightarrow \underset{\text{Nitrile rubber}}{(CH_2 - CH = CH - CH_2 - CH_2 - \underset{\underset{CN}{|}}{CH})_n}$$

Excellent resistant to heat and chemicals. It is used for making conveyer belts, printing rollers, automobile parts.

(iii) *Neoprene*

$$n\ CH_2 = CH - \underset{\underset{Cl}{|}}{C} = CH_2 \xrightarrow{K_2S_2O_8} \underset{\text{Neoprene}}{(CH_2 - CH = \underset{\underset{Cl}{|}}{C} - CH_2)_n}$$

Chloroprene

It is resistant to heat and chemicals. It is used for making protective clothing, reaction vessels, floor tiles etc.

(iv) *Heavy rubber* - It is cis poly isoprene having length of repeat unit 8.1 A°.

(v) *Gutta percha* - It is trans poly isoprene having length of repeat unit 4.72A°.

IMPORTANT CONDENSATION POLYMERS :

(A) **Nylons** - Synthetic polyamids are known as Nylons

(i) *Nylon 66:* Copolymer of adipic acid (6C) and hexamethylene diamine (6C).

$$n\ \underset{\text{Adipic acid}}{HOOC(CH_2)_4 COOH} + n\ \underset{\text{Hexamethylene diamine}}{H_2N(CH_2)_6 NH_2} \rightarrow \underset{\text{Nylon 66}}{(\overset{\overset{O}{\|}}{C} - (CH_2)_4 - \overset{\overset{O}{\|}}{C} - NH - (CH_2)_6 - NH)_n}$$

It has high tenacity and elasticity. It is resistant to abrasion and not affected by sea water. It is used for reinforcement of rubber tyres, manufacture of parachute, safety belts, carpets and fabrics.

(ii) *Nylon 6:* Homopolymer of caprolactam (6C)

Cyclo hexanone → Oxime → Caprolactam → $H_2N(CH_2)_5COOH$ ε-Amino Caproic acid

(Reagents: NH_2OH; Beckmann rearrangement; H_2O, Δ)

$$\xrightarrow[\text{Polymerise}]{\Delta} \quad -(NH(CH_2)_5-\overset{O}{\overset{||}{C}}-NH-(CH_2)_5-\overset{O}{\overset{||}{C}})_n$$

Nylon-6

(iii) *Nylon 6, 10* - Copolymer of hexamethylene diamine (6C) and sebacoyl chloride (10C)

$$H_2N-(CH_2-)_6NH_2 + Cl-\overset{O}{\overset{||}{C}}-(CH_2)_8-\overset{O}{\overset{||}{C}}-Cl \xrightarrow{\Delta} -HN-(CH_2)_6-(NH-\overset{O}{\overset{||}{C}}-(CH_2)_8-\overset{O}{\overset{||}{C}})_n$$

Hexamethylene diamine　　Sebacoyl chloride　　Nylon 6, 10

It is used for making brush bristlers

(iv) *Kevlar:* It is aromatic polyamide resembling nylons

$$n\ ClOC-\langle\rangle-COCl + n\ H_2N-\langle\rangle-NH_2 \rightarrow (\overset{O}{\overset{||}{C}}-\langle\rangle-\overset{O}{\overset{||}{C}}-NH-\langle\rangle-NH)_n$$

Terephthalic acid-dichloride　　P-phenylenediamine　　Kevlar

It is used in aircraft industries, bullet proof vests, helmets, ropes cables.

(B) **Polyesters:** Condensation polymers of a dibasic acid and a diol

(i) *Terylene* (dacron) / Polyethylene Terephthalate (PET)

$$n\ HO.CH_2CH_2OH + n\ HOOC-\langle\rangle-COOH \xrightarrow{\Delta} (O\ CH_2CH_2-O-\overset{O}{\overset{||}{C}}-\langle\rangle-\overset{O}{\overset{||}{C}})_n$$

Ethylene glycol　　Terephthalic acid　　Terylene

It is resistant to mineral and organic acids. It is used for blending with wool to provide better crease, in safety helmets and aircraft battery boxes.

(ii) *Glyptal or Alkyd resin* (general name) : Condensation polymers of dibasic acids and polyhydroxy alcohols

$$n\ HO.CH_2CH_2OH + n\ \langle\rangle\text{(COOH, COOH)} \longrightarrow -O-(CH_2CH_2-O-\overset{O}{\overset{||}{C}}\langle\rangle\overset{O}{\overset{||}{C}})_n$$

Ethylene glycol　　Pthlalic acid　　Glyptal

Cross linked copolymer; For making good insulators, Sheets, rods switches lacquers and adherant paints.

(C) **Thermo setting resins:**

(i) *Bakelite:* Phenol formaldehyde resin

$$n\ \langle\rangle\text{OH (Phenol)} + n\ HCHO\ \text{(Formaldehyde)} \xrightarrow{\overline{O}H} \text{Bakelite}$$

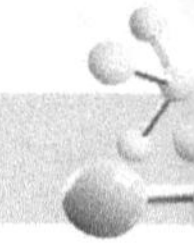

High degree polymerisation leads to rigid, hard, scratch resistant, infusible, attacked by alkalies phenolic resins. They are used for making switches, plugs telephone parts. Sulphonated bakelites are used as ion - exchange resins in water softening.

Low degree polymerisation gives bonding glue, preparation of varnishes and lacquers.

(ii) *Urea formaldehyde resin*

$$H_2N.CO.NH_2 + HCHO \xrightarrow{\text{basic medium}}$$

Urea (2 parts)   form aldehyde (1 part)

$$\begin{array}{c} -N-CH_2-N-CH_2- \\ | \qquad\qquad | \\ CO \qquad\quad CO \\ | \qquad\qquad | \\ -N-CH_2-N-CH_2- \end{array}$$

Urea formaldehde resin (Crosslinked polymer)

It is used for bonding grinding wheels, insulation, cation exchanger and decorative articles.

(iii) *Melamine formaldehyde resins* **(MF resin):**

Malamine   Formaldehyde   Phthalic intermediate

It is better than UF resin and used in making decorative laminates crockery under the trade name melmac, plywood industry as adhesive.

(iv) *Polyuresthanes* - Polymers of diisocyanate and diol eg. : Perlon-U

$$C=N-(CH_2)_6-N=C+HO.(CH_2)_4OH \xrightarrow{\text{Polymerisation}} \{C-NH(CH_2)_6-NH-C-O(CH_2)_4-O\}_n$$

1,6 Hexamethylene diisocyanate   1,4-Butanediol   Polyurethane Perlon-U

It is substitute of leather. They are used as foams, films adhesives, gaskets etc.

SILICON RESINS : Different organo-silicon chlorides can be polymerised by carefully controlled hydrolysis giving silicon resins. They contain alternate silicon oxygen structure.

$$\begin{array}{c} R \qquad\quad R \qquad\quad R \\ | \qquad\qquad | \qquad\qquad | \\ R-Si-\left[O-Si-O\right]-Si-R \\ | \qquad\qquad | \qquad\qquad | \\ R \qquad\quad R \qquad\quad R \end{array}_n$$

where R = alkyl or phenyl radical

Silicones may be (a) liquid silicones or silicone oils (b) silicon greases (c) silicon rubbers (d) solid silicones.

RESIN : Resin is a low molecular weight polymer used as binder, fusible and mouldable. It changes into infusible cross - linked form during moulding in presence of catalyst.

RAYON : It is artificial silk. Actually the term includes all synthetic fibres manufactured from cellulose. The manufacturing can be carried out by

(i)   Acetate process   (ii)   Viscose process.

PLASTICIZERS : The substances added to resins to increase their plasticity and flexibility are known as plasticizers. Examples are, vegetable oils (non drying), phosphates (tributyl phosphate, triphenyl phosphate etc), esters of oleic, stearic or phthalic acids and camphor etc.

RECLAIMED RUBBER: Rubber obtained from waste rubber articles.

REINFORCED RUBBER OR PLASTIC: They are obtained by adding solid fillers. They are also known as filled plastics or rubbers.

23.8 ILLUSTRATIVE EXAMPLES

Example 4 :
Give the product obtained when an α-amino acid is treated with $SOCl_2$.

Solution :
Like carboxylic acids, α-amino acids react with $SOCl_2$ to form acid chlorides. However, acid chlorides are not isolated as the final product, because as soon as these are formed, two or more molecules react with each other to form peptides.

$$2H_2N\overset{R}{\underset{|}{C}}HCOOH \xrightarrow{SOCl_2} \left[H_2N\overset{R}{\underset{|}{C}}HCOCl + H_2N\overset{R}{\underset{|}{C}}HCOCl \right] \longrightarrow H_2N\overset{R}{\underset{|}{C}}H\mathbf{CONH}\overset{R}{\underset{|}{C}}HCOCl$$

$$\xrightarrow{H_2NCHRCOCl} H_2N\overset{R}{\underset{|}{C}}H\mathbf{CONH}\overset{R}{\underset{|}{C}}H\mathbf{CONH}\overset{R}{\underset{|}{C}}HCOCl$$

Higher (*tri-*) peptide

Example 5 :
Identify the products A and B in the following reactions

$$HO-\!\!\bigcirc\!\!-CH_2\overset{NH_2}{\underset{|}{C}}HCOOH \xrightarrow{aq.\,Br_2} [A] \xrightarrow[NaOH]{(CH_3)_2SO_4} [B]$$

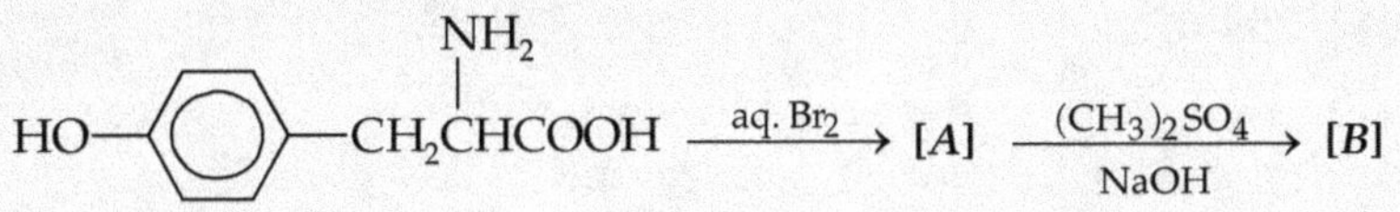

Tyrosine

Solution :
The first step involves electrophilic substitution of the benzene, while in the second step phenolic —OH group is methylated.

$$\underset{Br}{\overset{Br}{HO-\!\!\bigcirc\!\!-}}CH_2\overset{NH_2}{\underset{|}{C}}HCOOH \qquad\qquad \underset{Br}{\overset{Br}{CH_3O-\!\!\bigcirc\!\!-}}CH_2\overset{NH_2}{\underset{|}{C}}HCOO^-Na^+$$

[A] $\qquad\qquad\qquad\qquad\qquad$ [B]

Example 6 :
Identify the bracketed compounds in the following reactions.

(a) $\quad CH_3COOC_2H_5 + \overset{COOC_2H_5}{\underset{COOC_2H_5}{|}} \xrightarrow{NaOC_2H_5} [A] \xrightarrow{dil.\,H_2SO_4} [B] \xrightarrow[H_2/Pt]{NH_3} [C]$

(b) $\quad CH_2 = CHCHO \xrightarrow{CH_3SH} [D] \xrightarrow[(ii)\,H_3O^+]{(i)\,NH_3,\,HCN} [E]$

(c) $\quad C_6H_5N = C = S + Me_2CH\overset{COO^-}{\underset{|}{C}}HNH_3^+ \xrightarrow{OH^-} [F] \xrightarrow{H^+} [G]$

(d) $\quad CH_3CH = CH_2 \xrightarrow{NBS} [H] \xrightarrow[(ii)\,H^+]{(i)\,KCN} [I] \xrightarrow[(ii)\,NH_3]{(i)\,P/Br_2} [J] \xrightarrow{HONO} [K] \xrightarrow{heat} [L]$

Solution :

(a)

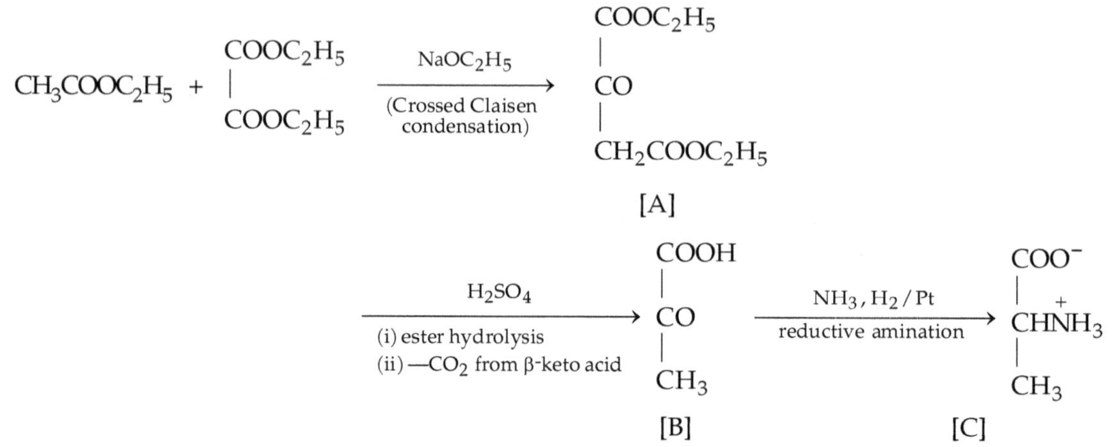

$$CH_3COOC_2H_5 \; + \; \underset{COOC_2H_5}{\overset{COOC_2H_5}{|}} \xrightarrow[\substack{\text{(Crossed Claisen} \\ \text{condensation)}}]{NaOC_2H_5} \quad \underset{CH_2COOC_2H_5}{\overset{COOC_2H_5}{\underset{|}{\overset{|}{CO}}}}$$

[A]

$$\xrightarrow[\substack{\text{(i) ester hydrolysis} \\ \text{(ii)} -CO_2 \text{ from } \beta\text{-keto acid}}]{H_2SO_4} \quad \underset{CH_3}{\overset{COOH}{\underset{|}{\overset{|}{CO}}}} \xrightarrow[\text{reductive amination}]{NH_3, H_2/Pt} \quad \underset{CH_3}{\overset{COO^-}{\underset{|}{\overset{|}{\overset{+}{C}HNH_3}}}}$$

[B]   [C]

(b)

$$CH_2 = CH - CHO \xrightarrow[\text{(Michael addition)}]{CH_3SH} \underset{[D]}{CH_3SCH_2CH_2CHO} \xrightarrow[\text{(ii) } H_3O^+]{\text{(i) } NH_3, HCN} \underset{[E]}{CH_3SCH_2\overset{\overset{+}{N}H_3}{\underset{|}{C}HCOO^-}}$$

(c)

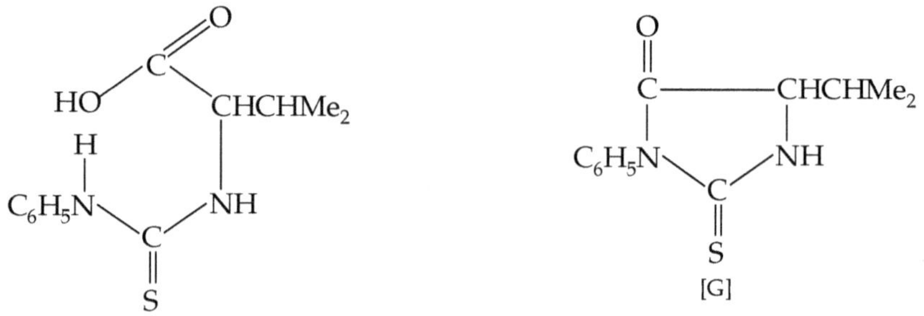

[F]

[G]

(d)

$$\underset{[H]}{BrCH_2CH = CH_2} \, , \quad \underset{[I]}{HOOCCH_2CH = CH_2} \, , \quad \underset{[J]}{HOOC\overset{NH_2}{\underset{|}{C}HCH = CH_2}}$$

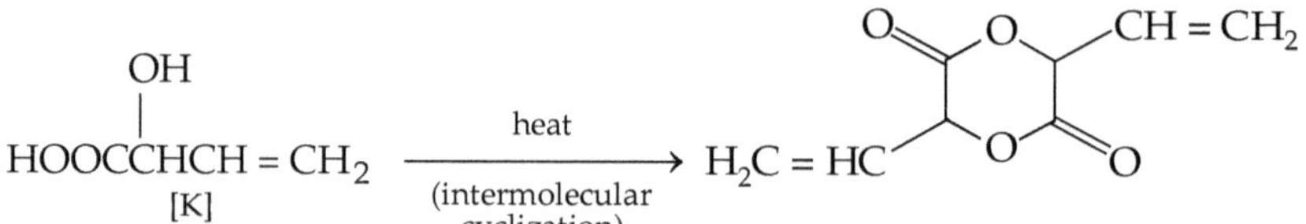

$$\underset{[K]}{HOOC\overset{OH}{\underset{|}{C}HCH = CH_2} } \xrightarrow[\substack{\text{(intermolecular} \\ \text{cyclization)}}]{\text{heat}} \quad \text{Lactone (}cf.\text{ lactams)}$$

Example 7 :

Identify the bracketed compounds in the following reactions.

(a)

$$\overset{+}{H_3}N\,CH_2COO^- \xrightarrow[\text{(ii) HCl}]{\text{(i) } p-CH_3C_6H_4SO_2Cl,\, NaOH} [A] \xrightarrow{Na/NH_3(liq.)} [B] + [B']$$

(b)

$$H_2N\,\overset{CH_3}{\underset{|}{C}HCOO\,C_2H_5} \xrightarrow{p-CH_3C_6H_4SO_2Cl} [C] \xrightarrow{Na/liq.\,NH_3} [D] + [D']$$

$$\overset{\displaystyle CH_3}{\underset{\displaystyle |}{}}$$

(c) $H_2N\,CHCOOH \xrightarrow{C_6H_5CH_2OCOCl} [E] \xrightarrow{H_2/Pd} [F] + [G]$

(d) $[G] \xrightarrow{heat} [H]$

(e) $PhthN–CH(COOC_2H_5)_2 \xrightarrow{OC_2H_5^-} [I] \xrightarrow[\text{(ii) } H_3O^+]{\text{(i) } CH_2=CHCOOC_2H_5} [J] \xrightarrow{H^+} [K]$

(where Phth = Phthalyl group)

(f) $CH_3CH(OH)CCl_3 \xrightarrow{NaN_3/OH^-} [L] \xrightarrow{H_2O} [M] \xrightarrow{H_2/Pd} [N]$

Solution :

(a) $p\text{-}CH_3C_6H_4SO_2NHCH_2COOH$ [A] ; $p\text{-}CH_3C_6H_4SO_2OH$ [B] $+ H_2NCH_2COOH$ [B']

(Na in liq. NH_3 reduces preferentially aromatic sulphonyl group, leaving —COOH as such)

(b) $p\text{-}CH_3C_6H_4SO_2NH\,CHCOOC_2H_5$ [C] (with CH_3 on the CH) $p\text{-}CH_3C_6H_4SO_2OH$ [D] $+ H_2NCHCH_2OH$ [D'] (with CH_3)

(Na in liq. NH_3 reduces both —SO_2Cl as well as —COOR group)

(c) $C_6H_5CH_2OCONH\,CHCOOH$ [E] (with CH_3), $C_6H_5CH_3 + CO_2 + H_2NCHCOOH$ [F] [G] (with CH_3)

(H_2/catalyst does not reduce —COOH although it reduces —COOR)

(d)

A diketopiperazine ring with two CH_3 groups, O, NH, HN, O.

[H]

(e) $Phth\,N\overset{..}{C}(COOC_2H_5)_2$ [I] $\xrightarrow[\text{Michael addition}]{\text{(i) } CH_2=CHCOOC_2H_5,\ \text{(ii) } H_3O^+}$ $PhthN—CCH_2CH_2COOC_2H_5$ with two $COOC_2H_5$ groups [J]

$\xrightarrow{H^+} H_3\overset{+}{N}\,CHCH_2CH_2COOH$ (with COO^-) + Phthalic acid

[K], Glutamic acid

(f) $CH_3\!-\!\overset{O^-}{\underset{H}{C}}\!-\!\overset{Cl}{\underset{Cl}{C}}\!-\!Cl \xrightarrow[(-Cl^-)]{OH^-} CH_3\!-\!C\overset{O}{\diagdown}\!C\!-\!Cl$ (epoxide, with H and Cl) $\xrightarrow[(-Cl^-)]{N_3^-} CH_3\!-\!\overset{H}{\underset{N_3}{C}}\!-\!\overset{O}{\overset{\|}{C}}Cl \xrightarrow{H_2O} CH_3\!-\!\overset{H}{\underset{N_3}{C}}\!-\!\overset{O}{\overset{\|}{C}}OH \xrightarrow{H_2/pd} CH_3\!-\!\overset{H}{\underset{NH_3^+}{C}}\!-\!COO^-$

[L]   [M]   [N]

Example 8 :

Give steps involved in the following conversions.

(a) Adipic acid → proline

Adipic acid   proline

(b)   Acrylic acid ⟶ β-Aminopropanoic acid (Pantothenic acid)

(c)   Acrylic acid ⟶ γ-Aminobutyric acid (GABA)

(d) Vanillin → 3,4-Dihydroxyphenylalanine

Vanillin   3, 4-Dihydroxyphenylalanine

Solution :

(a)   The required compound has 5 C's with an amino group, while the starting compound has 6 C's without any amino group ; so this required set can be obtained by converting one of the —COOH groups of adipic acid to NH_2 via a Hofmann rearrangement. The remaining —COOH group is brominated by HVZ reaction.

Adipic acid $\xrightarrow[\text{(ii) } NH_3]{\text{(i) 1 } SOCl_2}$ (amide) $\xrightarrow[\substack{\text{(Hofmann broma-}\\ \text{mide reaction)}}]{Br_2/KOH}$ (pyrrolidine-COOH)

$\xrightarrow[\text{(HVZ reaction)}]{Br_2/P}$ (N–Br, COOH) $\xrightarrow{\text{Intramolecular } S_N{}^2}$ Proline

Remember that adipic acid can be easily obtained by the ozonolysis of cyclohexene.

(b) $CH_2 = CHCOOH \xrightarrow[\text{(ii) } H^+]{\text{(i) : } NH_3 \text{ (Michael addition)}} H_2NCH_2CH_2COOH$

      Acrylic acid   β-Alanine

(c) $CH_2 = CHCOOH \xrightarrow[\text{(Michael addition)}]{CN^-} NCCH_2\overset{-}{C}HCOOH \xrightarrow{H^+} NCCH_2CH_2COOH \xrightarrow{H_2/Pd} H_2NCH_2CH_2CH_2COOH$

GABA (a neurotransmitter)

(d) Vanillin

$$\text{Vanillin} \xrightarrow[\text{OH}^-]{(CH_3)_2SO_4} \text{(3,4-dimethoxybenzaldehyde)} \xrightarrow[\text{(Perkin reaction)}]{Ac_2O/AcONa} \text{(CH=CHCOOH)}$$

$$\xrightarrow{H_2/Pt} \text{(CH}_2\text{CH}_2\text{COOH)} \xrightarrow[\text{(ii) NH}_3]{(i)\ Br_2/P} \text{(CH}_2\text{CHCOO}^-\ \text{NH}_3^+) \xrightarrow{HI} \text{(CH}_2\text{CHCOO}^-\ \text{NH}_3^+)$$

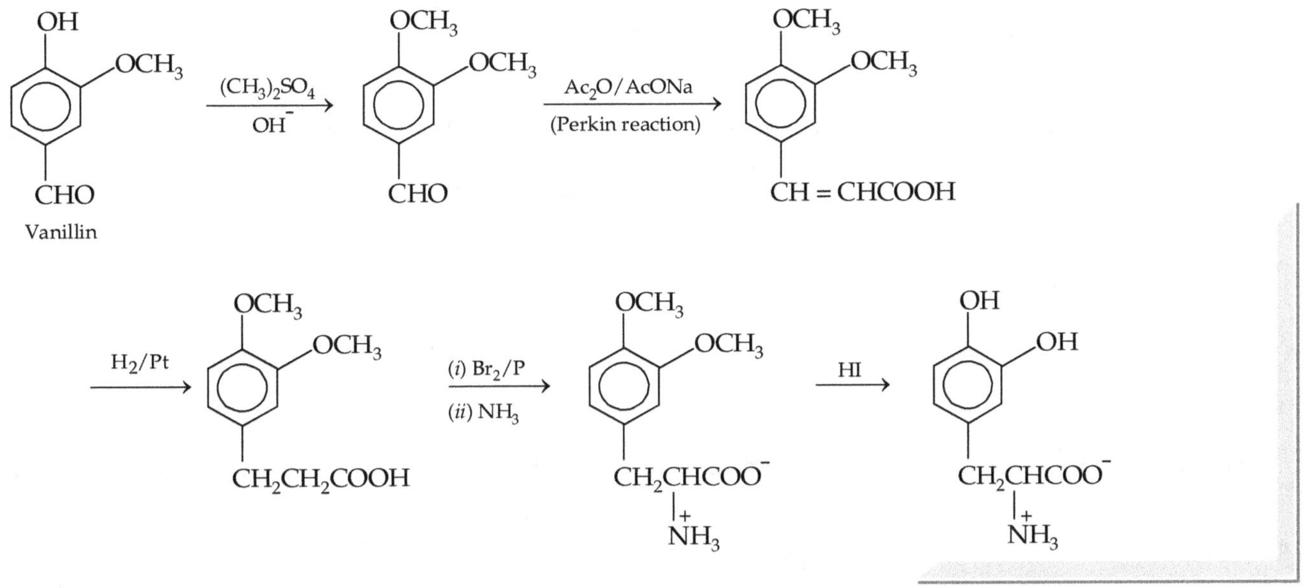

Example 9 :

An organic compound of the molecular formula $C_3H_4O_3$ gives following reactions :

(i)   It evolves carbon dioxide with $NaHCO_3$ solution, and can undergo iodoform reaction.

(ii)   On treatment with hydroxylamine, it gives two isomeric oximes.

(iii)   On treatment with ammonia followed by reduction with $NaBH_4$, it gives an acid B having chiral carbon. The acid B can also be produced by reaction of ethanal with ammonia in presence of potassium cyanide followed by hydrolysis.

Identify compounds A and B and explain the reactions involved.

Solution :

The given reactions of compound A indicate the presence of a —COOH and a —$COCH_3$ group. Thus the compound A should be $CH_3COCOOH$ which explains all the given reactions.

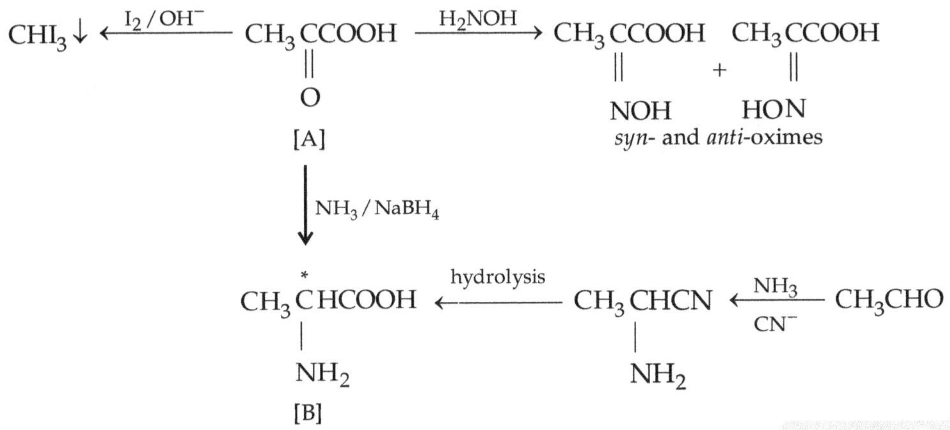

$$CHI_3 \downarrow \xleftarrow{I_2/OH^-} \underset{\substack{\|\\ O\\ [A]}}{CH_3CCOOH} \xrightarrow{H_2NOH} \underset{\substack{\|\\ NOH}}{CH_3CCOOH} + \underset{\substack{\|\\ HON}}{CH_3CCOOH}$$

syn- and *anti-*oximes

$$\downarrow NH_3/NaBH_4$$

$$\underset{\substack{|\\ NH_2\\ [B]}}{CH_3\overset{*}{C}HCOOH} \xleftarrow{\text{hydrolysis}} \underset{\substack{|\\ NH_2}}{CH_3CHCN} \xleftarrow[CN^-]{NH_3} CH_3CHO$$

Example 10 :

An organic compound (A), of the formula $C_5H_{11}O_2N$ found in beet sugar molasses, shows following characteristics. It is water-soluble solid and melts with decomposition. It reacts with HCl to form compound B ($C_5H_{12}O_2NCl$), but it is not affected by base. Compound A can be synthesized easily by the reaction of chloroacetic acid and trimethylamine. Establish the structure of A and suggest another possible method for synthesising it.

Solution :

Synthesis of compound A by the reaction of chloroacetic acid and trimethylamine leads to its following structure.

$$Me_3N + ClCH_2COOH \longrightarrow Me_3N^+CH_2COO^- + HCl$$
$$[A]$$

The above structure of A, being a dipolar explains its solid nature, solubility in water and melting with decomposition. Its reaction with acid involves the —COO$^-$ group.

$$Me_3N^+CH_2COO^- + H^+ \longrightarrow Me_3N^+CH_2COOH$$
$$\text{A (Betaine)}$$

Another synthesis of A.
$$H_3N^+CH_2COO^- \xrightarrow{\text{3MeI}} Me_3N^+CH_2COO^- + 3HI$$
$$\text{Glycine}$$

Example 11 :

Chloramphenicol, commonly known as chloromycetin, is a broad-spectrum antibiotic with the following structure

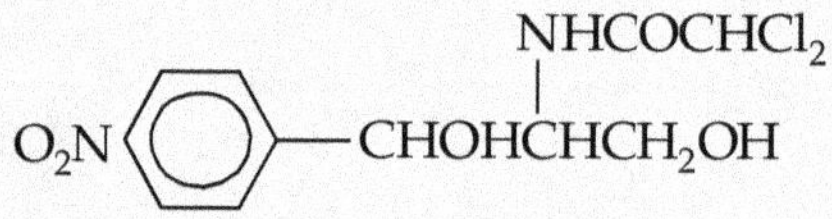

$$O_2N-C_6H_4-\underset{\underset{NHCOCHCl_2}{|}}{CHOHCHCH_2OH}$$

(a)   **Name all the functional groups present in it**

(b)   **How many stereoisomers are possible for this, draw their structures ?**

(c)   **Give the hydrolysis products of chloramphenicol in acidic and basic medium.**

Solution :

(a)   —NO$_2$ (nitro), 2° alcoholic, 1° alcoholic, amide, and halogen.

(b)   It has two chiral carbons, hence can exist in four stereoisomeric forms, i.e. two enantiomeric pairs (drawn below).

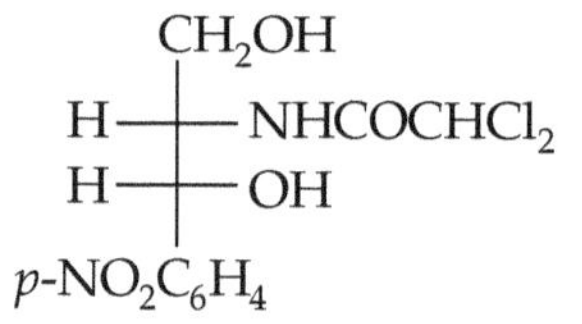

erythro-Chloramphenicol 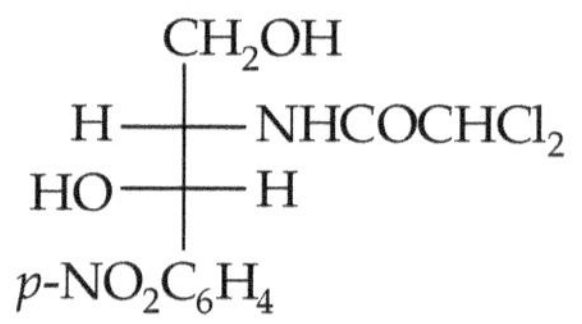   *threo*-Chloramphenicol

(c)

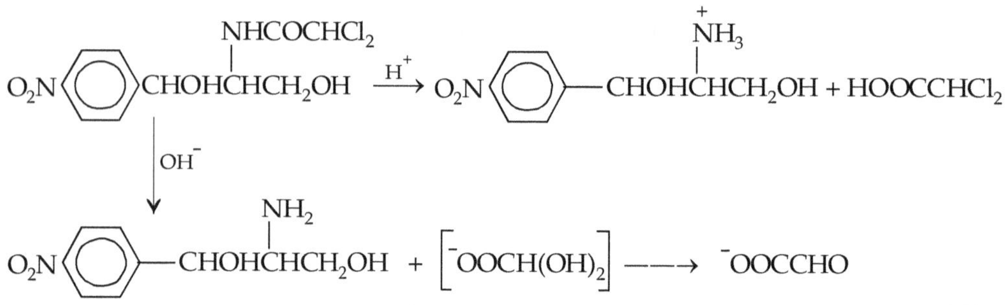

$$O_2N-C_6H_4-\underset{\underset{NHCOCHCl_2}{|}}{CHOHCHCH_2OH} \xrightarrow{H^+} O_2N-C_6H_4-\underset{\underset{NH_3^+}{|}}{CHOHCHCH_2OH} + HOOCCHCl_2$$

with OH^-

$$O_2N-C_6H_4-\underset{\underset{NH_2}{|}}{CHOHCHCH_2OH} + \left[^-OOCH(OH)_2\right] \longrightarrow {}^-OOCCHO$$

Example 12 :

Penicillin, the common antibiotic, has following structure :

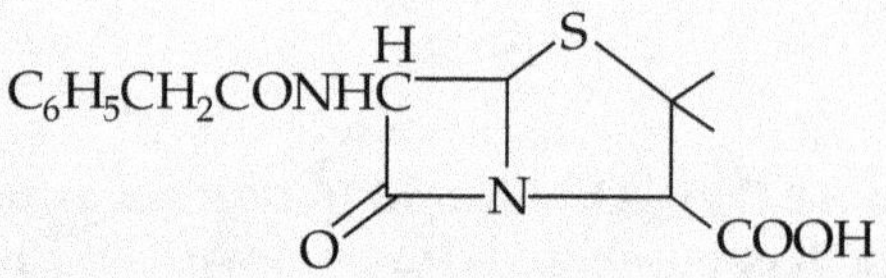

$$C_6H_5CH_2CONHC...$$

(a)   **List the different functional groups present in it.**

(b)   **Write down the hydrolysis products obtained in presence of dil. alkali at room temperature.**

Solution :

(a)   Amide, lactam, carboxylic and thioether linkage.

(b)   When hydrolysed by dilute alkali and at room temperature, lactam group (but not the amide) undergoes hydrolysis.

$$C_6H_5CH_2CONH\overset{H}{C}\cdots \quad \xrightarrow{\text{dil. alkali}} \quad C_6H_5CH_2CONHCH\cdots$$

$$\downarrow \text{Conc. alkali, heat}$$

$$C_6H_5CH_2COOH + H_2NHCH\cdots$$

Example 13 :

The enzyme cytochrome C, involved in oxidation-reduction processes in the living system, has 0.43% Fe and 1.48% S. Determine the minimum molecular weight of the enzyme. Also determine the ratio of Fe : S in the enzyme.

Solution :

The minimum atom of Fe in the enzyme is **one.**

0.43 g of Fe is present in 100 g of enzyme

56 g of Fe is present in $\dfrac{100}{0.43} \times 56 = 1.3 \times 10^4$ g of enzyme

Thus the minimum mol. wt. of the enzyme $= 13000$

Similarly, 32 g of S is present in $\dfrac{100 \times 32}{1.48} = 2.16 \times 10^3$

Thus the minimum mol. wt. corresponding to 1 S atom $= 2160$

$\therefore$ No of S atoms in the enzyme per Fe atom $= \dfrac{13000}{2160} \approx 6$

Example 14 :

Complete the following set of reactions by supplying structures to the compounds A to D.

$$\underset{\text{Acetamidomalonic ester}}{CH_3\overset{O}{\overset{\|}{C}}NHCH(COOC_2H_5)_2} + CH_2=CH-CN \xrightarrow[C_2H_5OH]{C_2H_5ONa} \mathbf{A} \xrightarrow[\text{reflux}]{\text{conc. HCl}} \mathbf{B}$$

$$\downarrow \begin{array}{c} H_2, Ni \\ 70°C, \text{pressure} \end{array}$$

$$\mathbf{D} \xleftarrow[\text{reflux}]{\text{conc. HCl}} \mathbf{C}$$

Solution :

$$CH_3\overset{\overset{\displaystyle O}{\|}}{C}NHCH(COOC_2H_5)_2 + CH_2=CH-C\equiv N \xrightarrow[\;C_2H_5OH\;]{C_2H_5ONa}$$

$$CH_3\overset{\overset{\displaystyle O}{\|}}{C}NH-\underset{\underset{\displaystyle COOC_2H_5}{|}}{\overset{\overset{\displaystyle COOC_2H_5}{|}}{C}}-CH_2CH_2C\equiv N \xrightarrow[\text{with conc. HCl}]{\text{reflux}} H_2NCHCH_2CH_2COOH$$

$$\textbf{A} \qquad\qquad\qquad\qquad \textbf{B } (\text{isolated as zwitterion})$$

$$\Big\downarrow \begin{matrix} H_2,\ Ni \\ 70°C,\ \text{pressure} \end{matrix}$$

$$\left[\; CH_3\overset{\overset{\displaystyle O}{\|}}{C}NH-\underset{\underset{\displaystyle COOC_2H_5}{|}}{\overset{\overset{\displaystyle COOC_2H_5}{|}}{C}}-CH_2CH_2CH_2NH_2 \;\right] \xrightarrow[(-C_2H_5OH)]{} \qquad \textbf{C}$$

$$\xrightarrow[\text{conc. HCl}]{\text{reflux}} H_2N-\underset{\underset{\displaystyle COOH}{|}}{CH}CH_2CH_2CH_2NH_2 \quad or \quad H_3N^+\underset{\underset{\displaystyle COO^-}{|}}{CH}CH_2CH_2CH_2\overset{+}{N}H_3$$

$$\textbf{D}$$

Example 15 :

(a)   **Glutathione is a tripeptide composed of following three amino acids**

$$H_3N^+CH_2COO^- \qquad\qquad H_3\overset{+}{N}\underset{\underset{\displaystyle \text{Glutamic acid}}{}}{\overset{\overset{\displaystyle CH_2CH_2COOH}{|}}{C}}HCOO^- \qquad\qquad H_3\overset{+}{N}\underset{\underset{\displaystyle \text{Cysteine}}{}}{\overset{\overset{\displaystyle CH_2SH}{|}}{C}}HCOO^-$$
$$\text{Glycine}$$

     Partial acid-hydrolysis of glutathione gives two dipeptides: Cys. Gly and Glu. Cys. Determine the possible structure(s) of the tripeptide, glutathione.

(b)   **On the basis of the above established structure explain the function of glutathione as a free radical scavanger in the cells.**

Solution :

(a)   Try to locate the point of overlap from the structures of the two dipeptides

Cys. Gly.

Glu. Cys.

Thus the tripeptide should be :   Glu. Cys. Gly.

This indicates that glutamic acid constitutes N-terminus and glycine constitutes C-termium. Now since glutamic acid has two –COOH groups, each of which may form peptide bond with the –NH$_2$ group of cysteine. Thus on the basis of the above points, glutathione may have either of the two structures.

$$H_3\overset{+}{N}-\underset{}{\overset{\overset{\displaystyle CH_2CH_2COOH}{|}}{C}}H-CO-NH-\overset{\overset{\displaystyle CH_2SH}{|}}{C}H-CO-NH-CH_2-COO^- \qquad or$$

$$H_3\overset{+}{N}-\overset{\overset{\displaystyle COO^-}{|}}{C}H-CH_2-CH_2-CO-NH-\overset{\overset{\displaystyle CH_2SH}{|}}{C}H-CO-NH-CH_2-COO^-$$

(b)   Due to the presence of –CH$_2$SH group in glutathione it reduces the free radicals $\dot{O}H$ and $\dot{O}_2^-$ to H$_2$O and itself oxidised to a disulphide.

$$2R-SH + 2\ \dot{O}H \rightleftharpoons R-S-S-R + HO_2$$

Example 16 :

A nonapeptide of molecular formula, Arg_2, Gly, Phe_2, Ser, Pro_3 has arginine (Arg) residue on both ends. On partial hydrolysis, it gives following peptides.

Phe. Ser + Phe. Arg + Pro. Pro + Arg. Pro + Pro. Gly. Phe + Ser. Pro. Phe

Establish the sequence of amino acids in this nonapeptide.

Solution :

Observe the points of overlap, keeping in mind that you should attach the peptides having Arg at ends.

	Phe. Ser	
		Ser. Pro. Phe
Pro. Gly. Phe		Phe. Arg
Pro. Pro.		
Arg. Pro.		

Complete structure of the nonapeptide

Arg. Pro. Pro. Gly. Phe. Ser. Pro. Phe. Arg.

EXERCISE 23.1 (MCQ - ONE option correct)

1. Which of the following statement(s) is (are) true ?
  (i) All amino acids contain one chiral center.
  (ii) Some amino acids contain one, while some contain more chiral center or even no chiral center.
  (iii) All amino acids found in proteins have L configuration.
  (iv) All amino acids found in proteins have 1° amino group.
  (a) *(ii)*, *(iii)* and *(iv)*   *(b)* *(ii)* and *(iii)*
  (c) *(i)*, *(iii)* and *(iv)*   *(d)* *(i)* and *(iv)*.

2. The nature of carboxylic group in the solid glycine is
  (a) acidic   *(b)* basic
  (c) both   *(d)* none.

3. Which of the following is more acidic ?
  (a) H_2NCH_2COOH *(b)* $H_3\overset{+}{N}CH_2COOH$
  (c) CH_3COOH *(d)* Equal.

4. A strongly alkaline solution of a monoaminodicarboxylic acid contains how many basic groups ?
  (a) 1   *(b)* 2
  (c) 3   *(d)* 4.

5. Which of the following dipolar structure of the amino acid is considered more correct ?

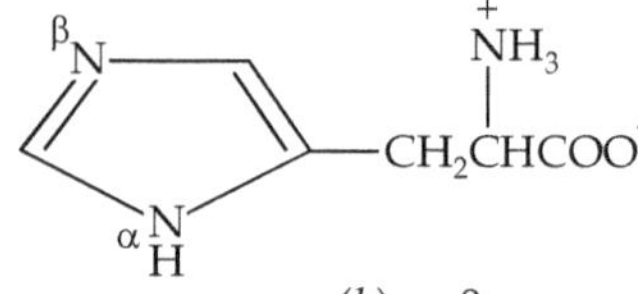

  (a) $H_3\overset{+}{N}CHCOO^-$ (with CH_2COOH)   *(b)* $H_3\overset{+}{N}CHCOOH$ (with CH_2COO^-)
  (c) Both   *(d)* None.

6. Which of the nitrogen of histidine is first protonated ?

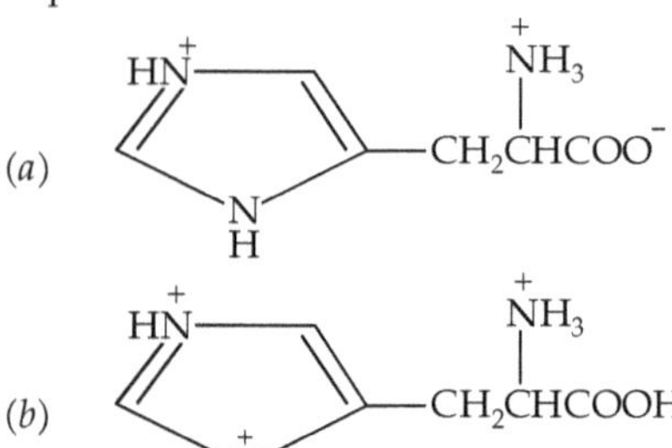

  (a) α   *(b)* β
  (c) both   *(d)* None.

7. Histidine, a heterocyclic amino acid has following structure at pH < 1.82,

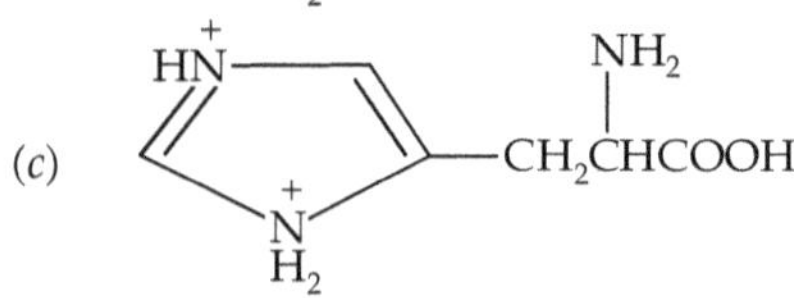

at pH > 1.82 it should have which structure ?

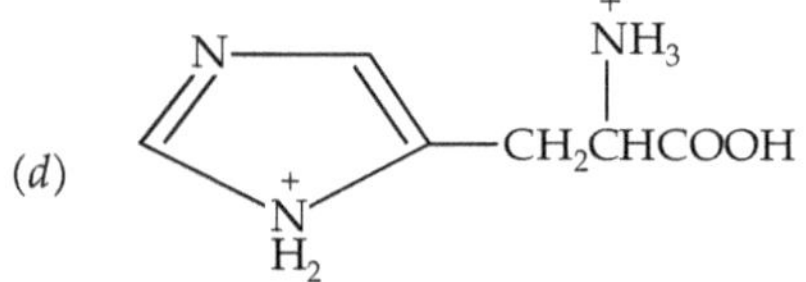

8. Which of the following statement is false ?
  (a) All amino acids, including glycine, are ampholyte.
  (b) An amino acid may be neutral, acidic or basic.
  (c) The basic functional group in amino acids is —COO^-.
  (d) None of the above statement is false.

9. An electric current is passed through an aqueous solution (buffered at pH = 6.0) of alanine (pI = 6.0) and ariginine (pI = 10.2). The two amino acids can be separated because
  (a) alanine migrates to anode, and arginine to cathode.
  (b) alanine migrates to cathode, and arginine to anode.
  (c) alanine does not migrate, while arginine migrates to cathode.
  (d) alanine does not migrate, while arginine migrates to anode.

10. A mixture of two amino acids having pI 9.60 and 5.40 can be separated
  (a) by adjusting the pH of the solution at 9.60
  (b) by adjusting the pH of the solution at 4.20
  (c) by adjusting the pH of the solution at 7.0
  (d) by adjusting the pH of the solution at 7.5.

11. Preparation of glycine by Strecker synthesis involves...... as one of the starting compounds.
  (a) Formaldehyde   *(b)* Acetaldehyde
  (c) Methanol   *(d)* Either *(a)* or *(c)*.

12. In the following series of reactions, compound Z can be

$$Z + NH_3 \xrightarrow{H_2 \text{ (catayst)}} CH_3CH(\overset{+}{N}H_3)COO^-$$

  (a) CH_3CHO *(b)* CH_3COCH_3
  (c) $CH_3COCOOH$ *(d)* None of the three.

13. How many dipeptides are possible from two molecules of a typical α-amino acid ?
  (a) 1   *(b)* 2
  (c) 3   *(d)* 4.

14. Which one of the following statement is false ?
  (a) Gly-Ala and Ala-Gly have same structure.
  (b) A dipeptide bond has two peptide bonds.
  (c) Glycine and alanine form two dipeptides.
  (d) All the above three statements are correct.

15. A molecule of haemoglobin, a protein found in blood, contains four atoms of Fe (56 g-atoms/mol), if the haemoglobin contains 0.35% Fe, the molecules weight of haemoglobin will be
  (a) 64×10^5 *(b)* 128×10^5
  (c) 64×10^3 *(d)* 128×10^3.

16. Select the correct statement(s).

  (a) $HOOC-CH_2-NH-\overset{\overset{O}{\|}}{C}-\underset{\underset{CH_3}{|}}{CH}-NH_2$ is a dipeptide of

  (Glycine & Alanine, whose abbreviated name is GLY-ALA)

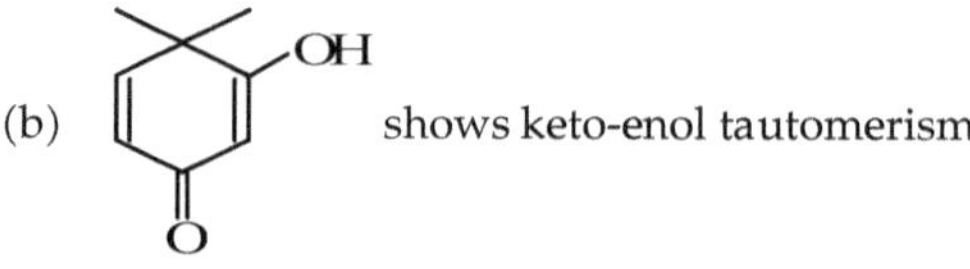

  (b) shows keto-enol tautomerism

  (c) Phenol and benzoic acid can be distinguished by $NaHCO_3$

  (d) [structures] and [structure] can be distinguished by iodoform test

17. Formation of polyethylene from calcium carbide takes place as follows

$$CaC_2 + 2H_2O \longrightarrow Ca(OH)_2 + C_2H_2$$

$$C_2H_2 + H_2 \longrightarrow C_2H_4$$

$$nC_2H_4 \longrightarrow (-CH_2 - CH_2 -)_n$$

The amount of polyethylene obtained from 64.1 kg of CaC_2 is
(a) 7 kg (b) 14 kg
(c) 21 kg (d) 28 kg

18. Which one of the following monomers gives the polymer neoprene on polymerization?

(a) $CCl_2 = CCl_2$ (b) $CH_2 = \overset{\overset{\displaystyle Cl}{|}}{C} - CH = CH_2$

(c) $CF_2 = CF_2$ (d) $CH_2 = CHCl$

19. Plexiglas (PMMA) is a polymer of
(a) Acrylic acid (b) Methyl acrylate
(c) Methyl methacrylate (d) None of these

20. Urethane is

(a) $H_2N - C \equiv N$ (b) $H_2N - \overset{\overset{\displaystyle }{}}{\underset{\underset{\displaystyle O}{||}}{C}} - OH$

(c) $HO - C \equiv N$ (d) $H_2N - \underset{\underset{\displaystyle O}{||}}{C} - OC_2H_5$

21. Which compound/set of compounds is used in the manufacture of nylon-66?
(a) $HOOC(CH_2)_4 COOH + H_2N(CH_2)_6NH_2$
(b) $CH_2 = CH-C(CH) = CH_2$
(c) $CH_2 = CH_2$

(d) $HOOC - \underset{\text{}}{\bigcirc} - COOH$
$+ HOCH_2 - CH_2 OH$

22. Which of the following is not correctly matched?

(a) neoprene; $\left[-CH_2 - \overset{\overset{\displaystyle }{}}{\underset{\underset{\displaystyle Cl}{|}}{C}} = CH - CH_2 - \right]_n$

(b) nylon-66: $\left[-NH-(CH_2)_6 - NH - CO - (CH_2)_4 - \overset{\overset{\displaystyle O}{||}}{C} - O - \right]_n$

(c) terylene; $\left[-OCH_2 - CH_2 - O - \overset{\overset{\displaystyle O}{||}}{C} - \bigcirc - \overset{\overset{\displaystyle O}{||}}{C} - \right]_n$

(d) PMMA : $\left[CH_2 - \overset{\overset{\displaystyle CH_3}{|}}{\underset{\underset{\displaystyle COOCH_3}{|}}{C}} \right]_n$

23. Match List-I (Monomer) with List II (Polymer) and select the correct answer using the codes given below the lists:

List I	List II
I. Hexamethylenediamine	A. Bakelite
II. Phenol	B. Dacron
III. Phthalic acid	C. Glyptal
IV. Terephthalic acid	D. Melamine
	E. Nylon

Codes:
(a) I-E, II-A, III-B, IV-C (b) I-E, II-A, III-C, IV-B
(c) I-D, II-C, III-A, IV-B (d) I-D, II-C, III-A, IV-B

24. Which one of the following is used to make 'non-stick' cookware?
(a) PVC (b) Polystyrene
(c) Poly (ethylene terephthalate)
(d) Polytetrafluoroethylene

25. Synthetic human hair wigs are made from a copolymer of vinyl chloride and acrylonitrile and is called
(a) PVC (b) Polyacrylonitrile
(c) Cellulose (d) Dynel

26. Acrilan is a hard, horny and a high melting material. Which of the following represents its structure?

(a) $\left[CH_2 - \overset{\overset{\displaystyle CH_3}{|}}{\underset{\underset{\displaystyle COOCH_3}{|}}{C}} \right]_n$ (b) $\left(CH_2 - \overset{\overset{\displaystyle }{}}{\underset{\underset{\displaystyle COOC_2H_5}{|}}{CH}} \right)_n$

(c) $\left(CH_2 - \overset{\overset{\displaystyle }{}}{\underset{\underset{\displaystyle Cl}{|}}{CH}} \right)_n$ (d) $\left(CH_2 - \overset{\overset{\displaystyle }{}}{\underset{\underset{\displaystyle CN}{|}}{CH}} \right)_n$

27. Polymer formation from monomers starts by
(a) condensation reaction between monomers
(b) coordinate reaction between monomers
(c) conversion of monomer to monomer ions by protons
(d) hydrolysis of monomers.

28. Nylon threads are made of
(a) polyester polymer (b) polyamide polymer
(c) polyethylene polymer (d) polyvinyl polymer

29. Which of the following is a polyamide?
(a) Bakelite (b) Terylene
(c) Nylon-66 (d) Teflon

30. Which of the following is fully fluorinated polymer ?
(a) PVC (b) Thiokol
(c) Teflon (d) Neoprene

31. Bakelite is obtained from phenol by reacting with)
(a) HCHO (b) CH_3CHO
(c) $CH_3 COCH_3$ (d) $(CH_2OH)_2$

32. Among cellulose, poly (vinyl chloride), nylon and natural rubber, the polymer in which the intermolecular force of attraction is weakest is
(a) Nylon (b) Poly (vinyl chloride)
(c) Cellulose (d) Natural Rubber

33. Among the following substituted silanes the one which will give rise to cross linked silicone polymer on hydrolysis is
(a) R_4Si (b) $RSiCl$
(c) R_2SiCl_2 (d) R_3SiCl

34. Buna-N synthetic rubber is a copolymer of
(a) $H_2C = CH - CH = CH_2$ and $H_5C_6 - CH = CH_2$
(b) $H_2C = CH - CN$ and $H_2C = CH - CHCH_2$

(c) $H_2C = CH - CN$ and $H_2C = CH - \overset{\overset{\displaystyle }{}}{\underset{\underset{\displaystyle CH_3}{|}}{C}} = CH_2$

EXERCISE 23.2   (MCQ 1 or >1 option correct, Passage based, Matching, A/R)

DIRECTIONS for Q. 1 to Q. 9 : Multiple choice questions with one or more than one correct option(s).

1. Which forms *Zwitter* ion ?
- (a) glycine
- (b) sulphanilic acid
- (c) anthranilic acid
- (d) salicyclic acid

2. Peptide linkage is present in :
- (a) protein
- (b) γ-butyrolactam
- (c) Zwitter ion
- (d) phthalimide

3. Alanine forms *Zwitter* ion which exists as :

- (a) $CH_3 - \underset{\underset{\oplus NH_3}{|}}{CH}COO^{\ominus}$ in acidic medium

- (b) $CH_3 - \underset{\underset{\oplus NH_3}{|}}{CH}OOH$ in medium of pH = 4

- (c) $CH_3 - \underset{\underset{NH_3}{|}}{CH} - COO^{\ominus}$ in a medium of pH = 13

- (d) $CH_3 - \underset{\underset{NH_3}{|}}{C}HOO^{\ominus}$ in a medium of pH = 2

4. Which is true about polymers?
- (a) Polymers do not carry any charge
- (b) Polymers have high viscosity
- (c) Polymers scatter light
- (d) Polymers have low molecular weight

5. On the basis of mode of formation, polymers can be classified?
- (a) as addition polymers only
- (b) as condensation polymers only
- (c) as copolymers
- (d) as homopolymers

6. Which of the following polymer(s) involve cross linkages?
- (a) Melmac
- (b) Bakelite
- (c) Polythene
- (d) Vulcanised rubber

7. Which of the following is/are example(s) of addition polymer ?
- (a) Polystyrene
- (b) Nylon
- (c) PVC
- (d) Polypropylene

8. Which of the following is/are example(s) of chain growth polymer?
- (a) Neoprene
- (b) Buna-S
- (c) PMMA
- (d) Glyptal

9. The correct functional group X and the reagent/reaction conditions Y in the following scheme are

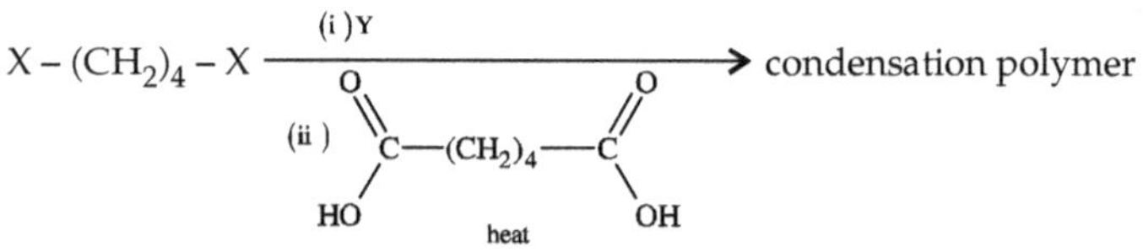

$$X - (CH_2)_4 - X \xrightarrow{(i)\,Y} \text{condensation polymer}$$

(ii) $\underset{HO}{\overset{O}{\underset{\|}{C}}} - (CH_2)_4 - \underset{OH}{\overset{O}{\underset{\|}{C}}}$ heat

- (a) X = $COOCH_3$, Y = $H_2/Ni/heat$
- (b) X = $CONH_2$, Y = $H_2/Ni/heat$
- (c) X = $CONH_2$, Y = $Br_2/NaOH$
- (d) X = CN, Y = $H_2/Ni/heat$

INSTRUCTION for Q. 10 to Q. 17 : Read the passages given below and answer the questions that follow.

PASSAGE 1

With the exception the simplest amino acid, glycine, all amino acids contain a chiral center. Further almost all naturally occurring amino acids have L-configuration at the α-carbon, i.e., they have the same relative configuration as L-glyceraldehyde.

In the dry state, amino acids exist as dipolar ions (also known as zwitterions) or inner salts, a form in which the carboxyl group is present as a carboxylate ion –COO^-, and the amino group as an aminium ion, –NH_3^+.

$$\underset{H_2NCHCOOH}{\overset{\overset{R}{|}}{}} \qquad\qquad \underset{H_3\overset{+}{N}CHCOO^-}{\overset{\overset{R}{|}}{}}$$

The dipolar ionic (salt like) structure of amino acids explains all of its above properties.

10. In aqueous solution, glycine is present as
- (a) $H_3N^+CH_2COO^-$
- (b) $H_3N^+CH_2COOH$
- (c) $H_2NCH_2COO^-$
- (d) All the three

11. In aqueous solution, the basic character of amino acids is due to
- (a) –NH_2 group
- (b) –$\overset{+}{N}H_3$ group
- (c) –COOH group
- (d) –COO^- group

12. Amino acids constitute one of the important class of organic compounds. These are
- (a) Fairly soluble in organic solvents like ether, benzene, etc.
- (b) Fairly soluble in water
- (c) Insoluble in both
- (d) Soluble in both

13. $^-OOC\,\underset{\underset{NH_2}{|}}{C}HCH_2COO^- \overset{H^+}{\rightleftharpoons}$ Product

Product in the above reaction is

- (a) $HOOC\,\underset{\underset{NH_2}{|}}{C}HCH_2COOH$

- (b) $HOOC\,\underset{\underset{NH_2}{|}}{C}HCH_2COO^-$

- (c) $^-OOC\,\underset{\underset{^+NH_3}{|}}{C}HCH_2COO^-$

- (d) Any of the three

14. The principle species present in the solution of lysine,

$$H_2N(CH_2)_4 \overset{\overset{\displaystyle NH_2}{|}}{C}HCOOH \text{ at pH 9 is}$$

(a) $H_3N^+(CH_2)_4 \overset{\overset{\displaystyle +NH_3}{|}}{C}HCOOH$

(b) $H_3N^+(CH_2)_4 \overset{\overset{\displaystyle NH_2}{|}}{C}HCOO^-$

(c) $H_2N(CH_2)_4 \overset{\overset{\displaystyle +NH_3}{|}}{C}HCOO^-$

(d) $H_3N^+(CH_2)_4 \overset{\overset{\displaystyle +NH_3}{|}}{C}HCOO^-$

PASSAGE 2

An α-amino acid 'A' has molecular formula $C_3H_7NO_3$. 'A' on treatment with methanol in presence of HCl yields 'B' $[C_4H_{10}NO_3Cl]$. 'B' on further treatment with PCl_5 yields 'C' $[C_4H_9NO_2Cl_2]$ which on acidic hydrolysis yields 'D' $[C_3H_6NO_2Cl]$. 'D' on reduction with Na(Hg) in dilute acidic medium yields alanine.

15. Compound 'A' has how many functional groups ?
(a) 1   (b) 2
(c) 3   (d) 4

16. Compound 'B' should be

(a) $\overset{\overset{\displaystyle +NH_3Cl^-}{|}}{H-C-COOCH_3}$ with H_2C-OH

(b) $HO-\overset{\overset{\displaystyle +NH_3Cl^-}{|}}{C}\!\!-\!\!\!-\!\!\!-C-O-CH_3$ with H_2C-OH and $\|$ O

(c) $H_3C-CH_2-\overset{\overset{\displaystyle Cl}{|}}{CH}-\overset{\overset{\displaystyle}{|}}{CH}-NH_2$ with OH

(d) $\overset{\overset{\displaystyle +NH_3Cl^-}{|}}{H-C-COOH}$ with H_2C-OCH_3

17. Compound 'D' is

(a) $\overset{\overset{\displaystyle NH_2}{|}}{H-C}\!-\!\overset{\overset{\displaystyle O}{\|}}{C}-Cl$ with H_2C-OH

(b) $H_2C-CH_2-NH-\overset{\overset{\displaystyle O}{\|}}{C}-Cl$ with OH

(c) $\overset{\overset{\displaystyle NH_2}{|}}{H-C}-COOH$ with H_2C-Cl

(d) (a) and (b) both are possible

Instructions for Q. 18 to Q. 20 : Following questions are Multiple Matching type Questions :

18.

	Column - I		Column - II
(A)	Anthranilic acid	(a)	Fuel
(B)	Sulphanilic acid	(b)	Body building
(C)	Amino acids	(c)	Diazotisation
(D)	Carbohydrates	(d)	Zwitterion

19.

	Column - I		Column - II
(A)	Ninhydrin	(a)	CH_2O
(B)	Sanger's reagent	(b)	HONO
(C)	Van Slyke method	(c)	Yellow coloured compound
(D)	Sorensen method	(d)	Violet colour

20. Match the chemical substances in **Column I** with type of polymers/type of bonds in **Column II**.

	Column I		Column II
(A)	cellulose	(p)	Natural polymer
(B)	nylon-6, 6	(q)	Synthetic polymer
(C)	protein	(r)	Amide linkage
(D)	sucrose	(s)	Glycoside linkage

Instructions for Q. 21 to 22 : Following questions are Assertion and Reasoning Type Questions :

Note : Each question contains STATEMENT-1 (Assertion) and STATEMENT-2 (Reason). Each question has 5 choices (a), (b), (c), (d) and (e) out of which ONLY ONE is correct.

(a) Statement-1 is True, Statement-2 is True; Statement-2 is a correct explanation for Statement-1.
(b) Statement-1 is True, Statement-2 is True; Statement-2 is NOT a correct explanation for Statement-1.
(c) Statement -1 is True, Statement-2 is False.
(d) Statement -1 is False, Statement-2 is True.
(e) Statement -1 is False, Statement-2 is False.

21. **Statement-1 :** The melting and solubility of amino acids are generally higher than that of corresponding halo acids.
Statement-2 : The amino acids exist in zwitter ionic forms and behave like salts rather simply as amines of carboxylic acids.

22. **Statement-1 :** At the isoelectric point of an amino acid, it does not migrate under the influence of an electrifield.
Statement-2 : An amino acid at the isoelectric point exists as a zwitter ion.

Instructions for Q. 23 to 24 : Following questions are Integer Type Questions :

23. The total number of basic groups in the following form of lysine is

$$\overset{\oplus}{H_3N}-CH_2-CH_2-CH_2-CH_2-\underset{H_2N}{\overset{}{CH}}-C\overset{O}{\underset{O^{\ominus}}{<}}$$

24. A decapeptide (Mol. Wt. 796) on complete hydrolysis gives glycine (Mol. Wt. 75), alanine and phenylalanine. Glycine contributes 47.0% to the total weight of the hydrolysed products. The number of glycine units present in the decapeptide is

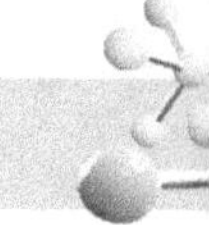

EXERCISE 23.3 (Subjective Problems)

1. Give steps involved in the synthesis of phenylalanine,

$$\overset{\overset{+}{N}H_3}{C_6H_5CH_2\overset{|}{C}HCOO^-},$$ from toluene according to each of the

following methods

(*a*) Malonic ester synthesis (*b*) Gabriel synthesis

(*c*) Strecker synthesis (*d*) Reductive amination.

2. Supply the structures to the compounds A to E in the following reactions.

Bromomalonic ester $\longrightarrow$ [A] $\xrightarrow[\text{C}_2\text{H}_5\text{ONa}]{\text{Br(CH}_2)_3\text{Br}}$ [B]

$\xrightarrow{\text{CH}_3\text{COONa}}$ [C] $\xrightarrow{\text{OH}^-, \text{heat}}$ [D] $\xrightarrow[(-\text{CO}_2)]{\text{OH}^-, \text{heat}}$ [E] $\xrightarrow{\text{HCl}}$

Proline

3. Identify compounds A to F in the following reactions.

$$\text{Ph} \cdots \text{O} \cdots \text{Cl} \; + \; H_2N \cdots \text{OMe} \longrightarrow [A]$$

$\xrightarrow[\text{(ii) HONO}]{\text{(i) NH}_2\text{NH}_2}$ [B] $\xrightarrow{H_3N^+CH_2COO^-}$ [C] $\xrightarrow{H_2/Pt}$ [D] + [E] + [F] .

4. Write down the structures obtained when each of the following amino acids is heated ?

(*a*) An α-Amino acid (*b*) A β-amino acid

(*c*) A γ-amino acid (*d*) A δ-amino acid

(*e*) An ε-amino acid.

5. An organic compound A of the formula $C_5H_{10}N_2O_3$, when hydrolysed gives two compounds B and C. Compound B is optically active while C is optically inactive. However, both B and C give violet colour with nindhydrin and react with sodium nitrite in presence of HCl to give compounds D and E respectively. Assign structures from A to E and give the effect of heating on D and E.

6. Azidothymine, also known as AZT, is the drug used for AIDS patients. It has following structure.

(*a*) Name the different functional groups present in it

(*b*) It can show lactam-lactium type of tautomerism, draw the different possible structures for this.

(*c*) Predict the relative basic/acidic character of the two N's (α- and β).

SOLUTIONS

EXERCISE 23.1

1	(b)	6	(b)	11	(d)	16	(a)	21	(a)	26	(d)	31	(a)
2	(b)	7	(a)	12	(c)	17	(d)	22	(b)	27	(a)	32	(d)
3	(b)	8	(d)	13	(a)	18	(b)	23	(b)	28	(b)	33	(c)
4	(c)	9	(c)	14	(d)	19	(c)	24	(d)	29	(c)	34	(b)
5	(a)	10	(a)	15	(c)	20	(d)	25	(d)	30	(c)		

1. Although D-alanine is a constituent of a bacterial cell walls, it is not found in proteins.

2. In solid state, amino acids exist as zwitterions, which contain $—NH_3^+$ (acidic in nature) and $—COO^-$ (basic in nature).

3. $—\overset{+}{N}H_3$ increases acidity because of its electron-withdrawing inductive effect. Further, the electron-withdrawing nature of $—\overset{+}{N}H_3$ group stabilises the corresponding $—COO^-$.

4. In strongly alkaline solution of an amino acid, all of its $—COOH$ groups are converted into $—COO^-$. Thus a strongly alkaline solution of a monoaminodicarboxylic acid will have one $—NH_2$ and two $—COO^-$ groups, all of which are basic in nature. Further remember that a $—NH_2$ is more basic than a $–COO^-$ group.

5. Consider the parent compound of the species adding H^+ to —COO⁻, and then observe the relative acidic character of the two —COOH groups keeping in mind that — $\overset{+}{N}H_3$ group is electron-withdrawing and hecne acid-strengthening.

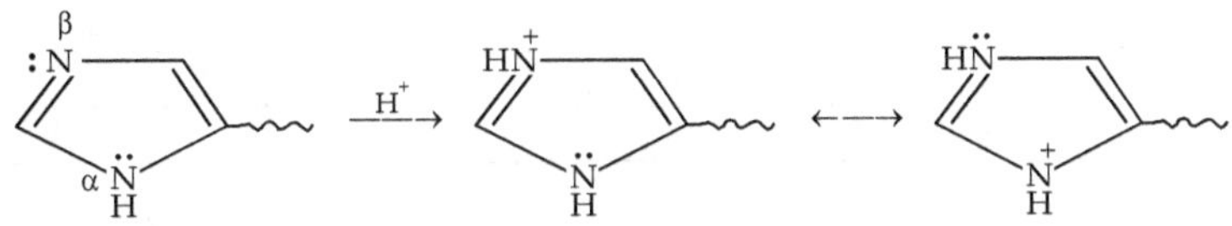

(—COOH on α carbon is more acidic due to – I effect of $\overset{+}{N}H_3$).

6. Protonation at β–N leads to imidazolium ion, which is stabilized by two equivalent resonating structures.

Equivalent resonating structures

7. On increasing the pH by adding an alkali ; H^+ will be lost from —COOH.
8. Every amino acid has at least one basic and one acidic group, so it acts as an amphoteric compound (ampholyte). An amino acid may have one —NH_2 and one —COOH group (neutral amion acids), or two —NH_2 and one —COOH group (basic amino acids), or one —NH_2 and two —COOH groups (acidic amino acids). In amino acids, — $\overset{+}{N}H_3$ acts as an acid while —COO⁻ acts as a basic group.
9. At the given pH (6) of the solution, alanine (pI = 6.0), exists as a dipolar ion while arginine (pH = 10.2) exists as a cation. Hence on passing an electric current, alanine will not migrate to any electrode, while arginine will migrate to cathode.
10. Every amino acid exists exclusively as dipolar ion when the pH of the solution is equal to its isoelectric point (pI), hence at this pH it does not migrate to either electrode, while at other pH, an amino acid migrates either to cathode or to anode depending upon its pI. Thus at pH 9.60, amino acid with pI 5.40 will exist as an anion and migrate to anode ; while that with pI 9.60 will not migrate to any electrode.
11. Glycine has only two C's ; in Strecker synthesis one of which is supplied by CN⁻ so the second must be supplied by an aldehyde having one C only *i.e.* HCHO or its precursor CH_3OH ($CH_3OH \longrightarrow HCHO$).
12. The resulting compound is an α-amino acid and the reagent used for its synthesis are NH_3 and H_2/catalyst, so this is an example of preparation of α-amino acid by reductive amination for which α-keto acids are starting compounds.
13. Two molecules of an α-amino acid will form only one dipeptide, recall that four different dipeptides are formed when two α-amino acids are different.
14. In Gly-Ala, glycine is the N-terminal anino acid and alanine is C-terminal amino acid while opposite is the case with Ala-Gly. A dipeptide (peptide formed from two molecules of an α amino acid) has only one peptide bond. As mentioned above the number of dipeptides formed by two different amino acids is four.
15. Total weight of Fe in a molecule of haemoglobin = 56 × 4 = 224 g
0.35 g of Fe is present in 100 g of haemoglobin

224 g of Fe is present in $\dfrac{100}{0.35}$ × 224 = 6.4 × 10⁴ g haemoglobin.

17. (d) The concerned chemical reactions are

(i) $\underset{64\,kg}{CaC_2} + 2H_2O \rightarrow Ca(OH)_2 + \underset{\text{Ethyne, 26kg}}{C_2H_2}$ (ii) $C_2H_2 + H_2 \rightarrow \underset{\text{Ethylene, 28 kg}}{C_2H_4}$ (iii) $nC_2H_2 \rightarrow \underset{\substack{n\times28\,kg \\ \text{or } 28\,kg}}{[-CH_2-CH_2-]_n}$ $\underset{\substack{n\times28\,kg\,\text{polythene} \\ \text{or } 28\,kg}}{}$

Thus 64 kg of CaC_2 gives 26 kg of acetylene which in turn gives 28 kg of ethylene whose 28 kg gives 28 kg of the polymer, polythene.

22. (b) Nylon-66 is a polyamide, hence it has only –CONH– linkage and no –COO– linkage
27. (a) Polymerisation starts either by condensation or addition reactions between monomers
28. (b) Nylon is a polyamide polymer
29. (c) Nylon is a general name for all synthetic fibres forming polyamides.
30. (c) Teflon is polymer of $CF_2 = CF_2$.
31. (a) Bakelite is formed by the reaction of formaldehyde (HCHO) and phenol so the correct answer is (1).

Bakelite

EXERCISE 23.2

		1	(a, b, c)	2	(a, b, d)	3	(b, c)
>1 CORRECT OPTION		4	(a,b,c)	5	(a,b)	6	(a,b,d)
		7	(a,c,d)	8	(a,b,c)	9	(a, b, c, d)
PASSAGE 1		10	(d)	11	(d)	12	(b)
		13	(c)	14	(b)		
PASSAGE 2		15	(c)	16	(a)	17	(c)
MATCH THE FOLLOWING		18	(A)-c ; (B)-c, d ; (C)-b, c, d ; (D)-a				
		19	(A) - d, (B) - c, (C) - b, (D) - a				
		20	(A) - a, d, (B) - b, c, (C) - a, c, (D) - d				
A/R		21	(a)	22	(a)		
INTEGER		23	2	24	6		

4. (a,b,c)
5. (a,b)
6. (a,b,d) Polythene is a linear polymer
7. (a,c,d) Nylon is a condensation polymer
8. (a,b,c) Glyptal is an example of a step growth polymer
9. (a, b, c, d)

Sol. (10-14) :

(A) $\underset{\underset{H_2C-OH}{|}}{\overset{\overset{NH_2}{|}}{H-C}}-COOH$

(B) $\underset{\underset{H_2C-OH}{|}}{\overset{\overset{\overset{\oplus}{N}H_3Cl^-}{|}}{H-C}}\overset{\overset{O}{\|}}{-C}-O-CH_3$

(C) $\underset{\underset{H_2C-Cl}{|}}{\overset{\overset{\overset{\oplus}{N}H_3Cl^-}{|}}{H-C}}\overset{\overset{O}{\|}}{-C}-O-CH_3$

(D) $\underset{\underset{H_2C-Cl}{|}}{\overset{\overset{NH_2}{|}}{H-C}}-COOH$

20. **(A)-(a, d) :** Cellulose is a natural polymer and has a $C_1 - C_4$ β-glycosidic linkage.
     (B)-(b, c) : Nylon-6, 6 is a synthetic polymer of hexamethylenediamine and adipic acid and has amide linkages.

(C)-(a, c) : Proteins are natural polymers of a amino acids joined by amide linkages (peptide bonds).
(D)-(d) : Sucrose is a disaccharide of α-D glucose and β-D-fructose and has an α, β-glycosidic linkage.

22. (a) Zwitter ion is neutral, so it doesn't migrate under the influence of electric field.

23. 2.
     The basic groups in the given form of lysine is NH_2 (not $\overset{\oplus}{N}H_3$) and CO_2^-.

24. 6
     Molecular weight of decapeptide = 796 g/mol
     Total bonds to be hydrolysed = (10 – 1) = 9 per molecule
     Total weight of H_2O added = 9 × 18 = 162 g/mol
     Total weight of hydrolysis product = 796 + 162 = 958 g
     Total weight % of glycine (given) = 47%

     Total weight of glycine in product $= \dfrac{958 \times 47}{100} g = 450g$

     Molecular weight of glycine = 75 g/mol

     Number of glycine molecule $= \dfrac{450}{75} = 6$

EXERCISE 23.3

1. In such case recall the starting material, required for preparing phenylalanine in each of the method and then apply your mind for preparing that starting material from toluene.
    (*a*) In malonic ester synthesis, the alkyl halide is treated with malonic ester to form α-halogeno acid.

$$C_6H_5CH_3 \xrightarrow{Cl_2,\,light} C_6H_5CH_2Cl \xrightarrow{Na\overset{+}{C}\overset{-}{H}(COOC_2H_5)_2} C_6H_5CH_2CH(COOC_2H_5)_2$$

$$\xrightarrow[\text{(ii) heat}]{\text{(i) hydrolysis}} C_6H_5CH_2CH_2COOH \xrightarrow{Br_2/P} C_6H_5CH_2\overset{\overset{Br}{|}}{C}HCOOH \xrightarrow[NH_3]{excess} C_6H_5CH_2\overset{\overset{\overset{+}{N}H_3}{|}}{C}HCOO^-$$

    (*b*) In Gabriel phthalimide synthesis, α-halogeno ester is treated with phthalimide.

$$C_6H_5CH_3 \xrightarrow{as\ in\ (a)} C_6H_5CH_2\overset{\overset{Br}{|}}{C}HCOOH \xrightarrow{C_2H_5OH,\,H^+} C_6H_5CH_2\overset{\overset{Br}{|}}{C}HCOOC_2H_5$$

$$\xrightarrow{Pot.\ phthalimide} Phth\ N-\overset{\overset{CHCH_2C_6H_5}{|}}{COOC_2H_5} \xrightarrow{hydrolysis} Phthalic\ acid + \overset{}{H_3}\overset{+}{N}\underset{\underset{COO^-}{|}}{CHCH_2C_6H_5}$$

(c) In Strecker synthesis, we require aldehyde ($C_6H_5CH_2CHO$) as the starting compound which can be obtained from toluene as below.

$$C_6H_5CH_3 \xrightarrow{Cl_2,\,light} C_6H_5CH_2Cl \xrightarrow[(ii)\,H_3O^+]{(i)\,NaCN} C_6H_5CH_2COOH \xrightarrow{SOCl_2} C_6H_5CH_2COCl \xrightarrow{LiAlH(OBu\text{-}tert)_3}$$

$$C_6H_5CH_2CHO \xrightarrow[NH_4^+]{CN^-} C_6H_5CH_2\overset{\overset{\displaystyle NH_2}{|}}{C}HCN \xrightarrow{H_3O^+} C_6H_5CH_2\overset{\overset{\displaystyle \overset{+}{N}H_3}{|}}{C}HCOO^-$$

(d) In reductive amination, the starting compound is α-keto acid, $C_6H_5CH_2COCOOH$, which can be obtained from toluene as follows.

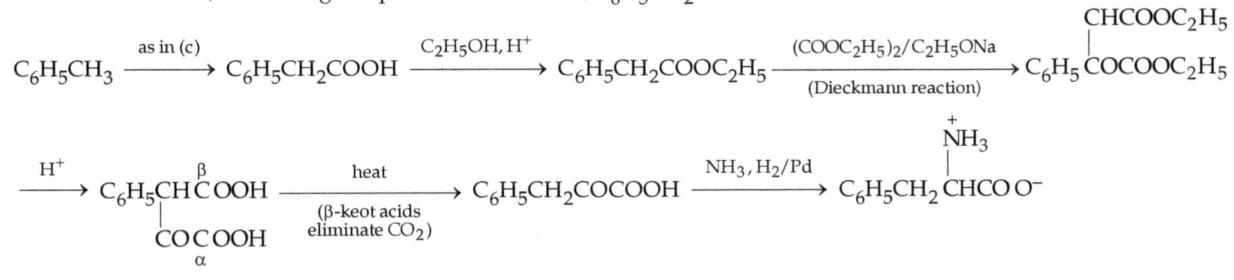

$$C_6H_5CH_3 \xrightarrow{as\ in\ (c)} C_6H_5CH_2COOH \xrightarrow{C_2H_5OH,\,H^+} C_6H_5CH_2COOC_2H_5 \xrightarrow[(Dieckmann\ reaction)]{(COOC_2H_5)_2/C_2H_5ONa} C_6H_5\overset{\overset{\displaystyle CHCOOC_2H_5}{|}}{C}OCOOC_2H_5$$

$$\xrightarrow{H^+} C_6H_5\overset{\beta}{C}H\overset{}{C}OOH \xrightarrow[\substack{(\beta\text{-keot acids}\\ \text{eliminate }CO_2)}]{heat} C_6H_5CH_2COCOOH \xrightarrow{NH_3,\,H_2/Pd} C_6H_5CH_2\overset{\overset{\displaystyle \overset{+}{N}H_3}{|}}{C}HCOO^-$$

with $\underset{\alpha}{\overset{|}{C}OCOOH}$

2.

$$Phth{-}N^-K^+ + Br\,\overset{\overset{\displaystyle COOC_2H_5}{|}}{C}H \xrightarrow{C_2H_5ONa} Phth{-}N\,\overset{\overset{\displaystyle COOC_2H_5}{|}}{C}H$$

with lower $COOC_2H_5$ groups

[A]

$$Phth{-}N\,\overset{\overset{\displaystyle COOC_2H_5}{|}}{\underset{\underset{\displaystyle COOC_2H_5}{|}}{C}}CH_2CH_2CH_2Br\,, \quad Phth{-}N\,\overset{\overset{\displaystyle COOC_2H_5}{|}}{\underset{\underset{\displaystyle COOC_2H_5}{|}}{C}}CH_2CH_2CH_2OCOCH_3\,, \quad Phthalic\ acid + H_2N\,\overset{\overset{\displaystyle COO^-}{|}}{\underset{\underset{\displaystyle COO_-}{|}}{C}}CH_2CH_2CH_2OH$$

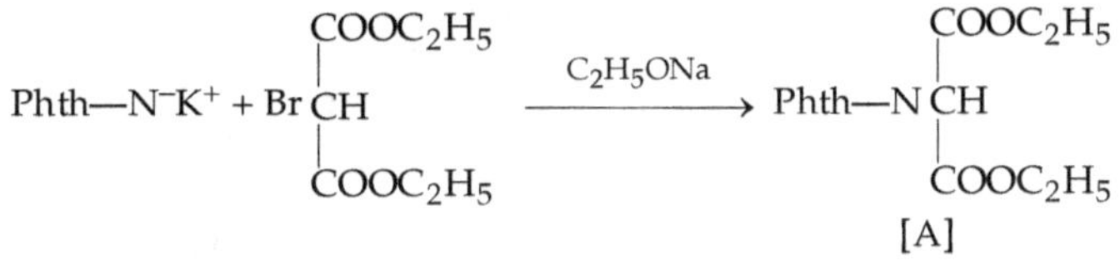

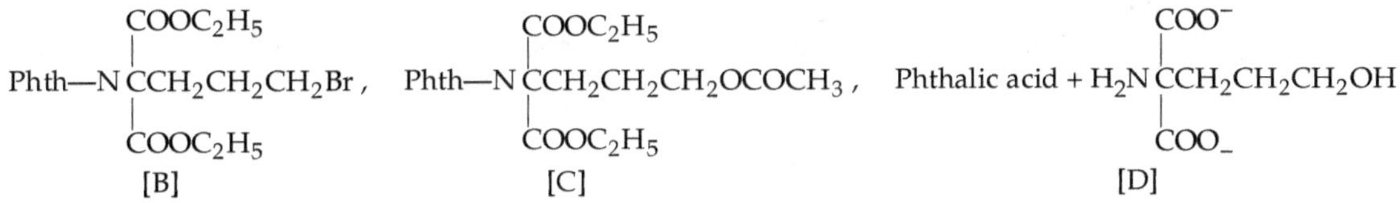

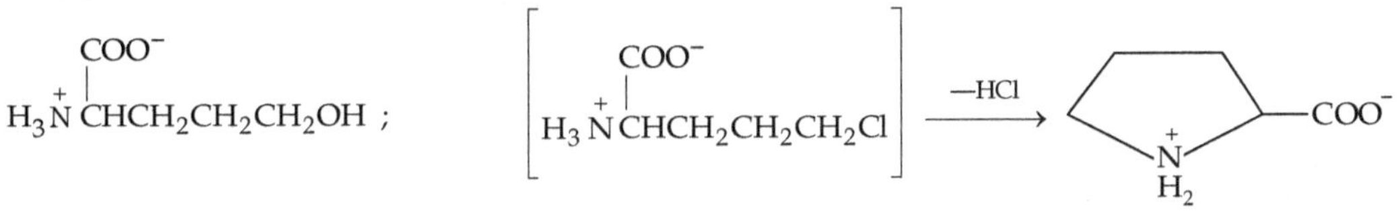

[B]   **[C]**   **[D]**

$$\overset{+}{H_3}\overset{}{N}\,\overset{\overset{\displaystyle COO^-}{|}}{C}HCH_2CH_2CH_2OH\ ; \quad \left[\overset{+}{H_3}\,\overset{}{N}\,\overset{\overset{\displaystyle COO^-}{|}}{C}HCH_2CH_2CH_2Cl\right] \xrightarrow{-HCl}$$

(a cyclic product) $\overset{+}{N}H_2$ ring bearing COO^-

3.

[A] $Ph\text{-}CH_2\text{-}O\text{-}C(=O)\text{-}NH\text{-}CH_2\text{-}C(=O)\text{-}OMe$

[B] $Ph\text{-}CH_2\text{-}O\text{-}C(=O)\text{-}NH\text{-}CH_2\text{-}C(=O)\text{-}N_3$

[C] $Ph\text{-}CH_2\text{-}O\text{-}C(=O)\text{-}NH\text{-}CH_2\text{-}C(=O)\text{-}NH\text{-}CH_2\text{-}COO^-$

[D] $PhCH_3$ + CO_2 + **[E]** $H_3\overset{+}{N}\text{-}CH_2\text{-}C(=O)\text{-}NH\text{-}CH_2\text{-}COO^-$ **[F]**

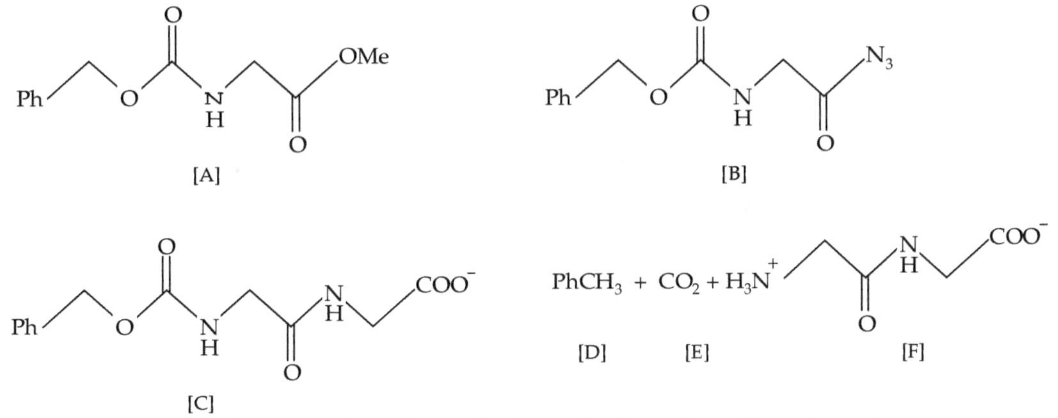

4. (a) α-Amino acids on heating undergo *intermolecular cyclization* to form diketopiperazine :

(b) β-amino acids on heating undergo deamination to form α, β-unsaturated carboxylic acids (in the form of ammonium salt).

(a)

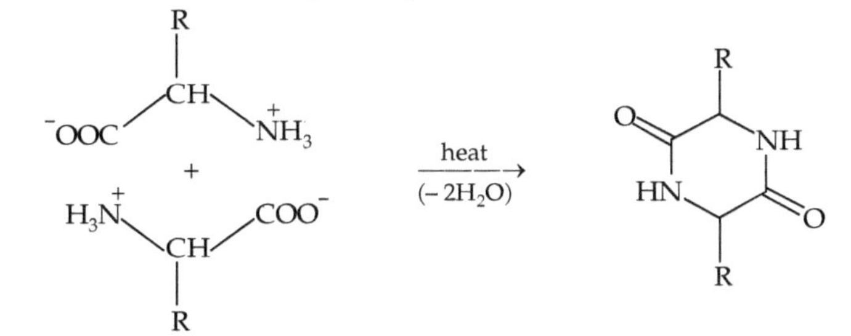

$$2\ \text{Moles of an a-amino acid} \xrightarrow[(-\,2H_2O)]{heat} \text{Diketopiperazine (a cyclic diamide)}$$

(b) $\underset{\text{A }\beta\text{-amino acid}}{\overset{R}{\underset{|}{H_3\overset{+}{N}\,CHCH_2COO^-}}}\xrightarrow[(-NH_3)]{\text{heat}}\overset{R}{\underset{|}{CH}}=CHCOO^-NH_4^+$

(c) A γ-amino acid $\xrightarrow[(-H_2O)]{\text{heat}}$ A γ-lactam (a cyclic amide)

(d) A δ-amino acid $\xrightarrow[(-H_2O)]{\text{heat}}$ A δ-lactam (a cyclic amide)

(e) γ- and δ- amino acids on heating undergo *intramolecular cyclization* to form stable 5- and 6-membered rings respectively. However, intramolecular cyclization of the ε-amino acids would give a seven-memebered ring which is formed with difficulty. Hence the more facile intermolecular reaction occurs, now since the substrate is bifunctional, polymerization occurs.

$$H_3\overset{+}{N}\,\overset{\varepsilon}{CH_2}\overset{\delta}{CH_2}\overset{\gamma}{CH_2}\overset{\beta}{CH_2}\overset{\alpha}{CH_2}COO^- \xrightarrow{\text{heat}} -\underset{H}{N}(CH_2)_5-\underset{\underset{O}{\|}}{C}-\underset{H}{N}-(CH_2)_5-\underset{\underset{O}{\|}}{C}-\underset{H}{N}-(CH_2)_5-\underset{\underset{O}{\|}}{C}-$$

5. Since compounds B and C (hydrolysis products of the compound A) give purple colour with ninhydrin, these must be amino acids and hence the compound A is a dipeptide. Further since the dipeptide A is having 5 C's, its two constituent amino acids should be glycine (having 2 C's) and alanine (having 3 C's). Thus compound A should be Gly-Ala of Ala-Gly both of which explains all the given reactions.

$$\underset{\substack{\text{Gly-Ala (A), } C_5H_{10}N_2O_3}}{\overset{CH_3}{\underset{|}{H_3\overset{+}{N}CH_2CONH\,CHCOO^-}}}\xrightarrow{H_3O^+}\underset{\substack{\text{Achiral, optically inative,}\\\text{hence it is (C)}}}{H_3\overset{+}{N}CH_2COO^-}+\underset{\substack{\text{Chiral, hence}\\\text{it is (B)}}}{\overset{CH_3}{\underset{|}{H_3\overset{+}{N}CHCOO^-}}}$$

$$\overset{CH_3}{\underset{|}{H_3\overset{+}{N}\,CHCOO^-}}\xrightarrow[\text{HCl}]{NaNO_2}\overset{CH_3}{\underset{|}{HO\,CHCOOH}}\xrightarrow{\text{heat}}\ (D)$$

(B)   (D)

$$H_3\overset{+}{N}CH_2COO^-\xrightarrow[\text{HCl}]{NaNO_2}HOCH_2COOH\xrightarrow{\text{heat}}\ (E)$$

(C)   (E)

6. (a) 1° alcoholic, azide, cyclic ether, lactam, ketonic group

(b) [tautomeric equilibrium structures]

(c) α-N is basic, while β-NH having carbonyl group (electronegative group) on both sides is acidic in nature.

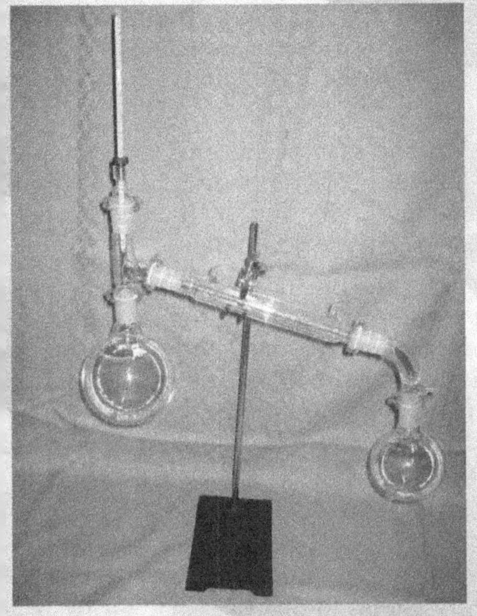

24

Practical Organic Chemistry

 **Purification of Organic Compounds**

In order to study the properties of organic compounds, we require pure compound which in turn can be achieved by any of the following methods.

1. **Crystallisation.** This method is applied for the purification of solid organic compounds. It is based on the fact that certain organic compounds dissolve partly in a solvent (*e.g.* water, alcohol, ether, benzene, acetone, etc.) and their solubility increases with increase in temperature. The filtrate (containing soluble organic compound) in cooled, when organic compound crystallises out ; sometimes crystal formation is initiated by adding a substance from outside, this process is known as **seeding**.

2. **Fractional crystallisation.** This method is used for the purification of a mixture of two components which are soluble in the same solvent but to different extents, *i.e.* one is more soluble than the other. When the hot saturated solution of such mixture is cooled, the less soluble component crystallises out earlier than the more soluble component. The two components are separated and process is repeated several times to get the two components in their respective pure form.

3. **Sublimation.** Certain organic substances change directly from solid to vapour state without passing through the liquid state and vice versa. This process, known as sublimation, is one of the important methods for purifying and separating *organic substances which sublime on heating* (like camphor, naphthalene, anthracene, benzoic acid, phthalic anhydride, ammonium chloride, iodine etc.) *from nonvolatile impurities.*

   Sublimation is based upon the fact that vapour pressure of substances which sublime becomes equal to the atmospheric pressure much before their respective melting points, hence liquid state escapes.

4.   **Distillation.** This method is based on the principle that at a constant pressure every pure liquid boils at a definite temperature, called its *boiling point.* This process is applied for the purification and separation of (*i*) liquids which boil, without decomposition, at atmospheric pressure from non-volatile impurities ; (*ii*) a mixture of two liquids whose boiling points differ by 30–50 K.

5.   **Fractional distillation.** This method is used for the purification and separation of a mixture of two volatile liquids whose boiling points differ only by 10–15 K. The process involves the use of specially designed columns called *fractionating columns.* Common examples are (*i*) separation of acetone (b.p. 325 K) from methanol (b.p. 338 K), (*ii*) separation of petroleum into various fractions like gasoline, kerosene oil, diesel oil etc.

6.   **Vacuum distillation** (*Distillation under reduced pressure*). This method is used for the purification of those liquids which decompose before their boiling points. We know that boiling point of a liquid is a point (temperature) at which its vapour pressure is equal to the atmospheric pressure, a liquid can thus be made to boil below its boiling point by reducing the pressure in the vicinity of the liquid. This is the principle applied in vacuum distillation. For example, under atmospheric pressure (760 mm) glycerol boils at 260°C with some decomposition, however it may be boiled at 180°C, without any decomposition, under reduced pressure (12 mm). Since boiling under reduced pressure, *i.e.* at lower temperature than usual, saves a lot of fuel, it is of great importance in industries, *e.g.* for the concentration of juice in sugar factories.

7.   **Steam distillation** (*Co-distillation with water*). This method is used for the purification and separation of the organic solid or liquid compounds which are *immiscible with water, volatile in steam, contain non-volatile impurities and have high vapour pressure at 373 K* (boiling point of water). It is especially useful to purify essential oils and turpentine oil obtained from plants.

Theory of steam distillation. We know that at the boiling point,

$$\text{Vapour pressure of the liquid} = \text{Atmospheric pressure (P)}.$$

Let p_1 and p_2 be the vapour pressuer of water vapour (steam) and the liquid respectively at the distillation temperature, then at the boiling point,

$$p_1 + p_2 = P \quad \text{or} \quad p_2 = P - p_1$$

From the above relation, it is evident that when a liquid boils in the presence of steam, the vapour pressure of the liquid (p_2) is less than the atmospheric pressure (P), *i.e.* the substance is boiling under somewhat reduced pressure. Hence it will be boiling at a temperature lower than its usual boiling point and also below 373 K. For example, aniline which normally boils at 457 K boils in steam at 371.5 K. *Hence this process can be regarded as analogous to distillation under reduced pressure (here steam reduces the atmospheric pressure).*

The relative amounts of the organic substance and water in the distillate depend upon their molecular weights and vapour pressures at the boiling point. In general,

$$\frac{\text{Wt. of water distilled}}{\text{Wt. of susbtance distilled}} = \frac{\text{Mol. wt. of } H_2O \times p_1}{\text{Mol. wt. of substance} \times p_2}.$$

The process of steam distillation can also be used to separate a mixture of two organic substances one of which is steam volatile while the other is not, *e.g.* when steam is passed through a mixture of *o–* and *p–* nitrophenols, vapours of *o*-nitrophenol are carried by steam leaving behind *p*-nitrophenol in the distillation flask.

8.   **Azeotropic distillation.** Azeotropes are constant boiling mixtures, *i.e.* they distil off at a fixed temperature and without any change in composition. The most familiar example of azeotropic mixture is rectified spirit which contains 95.87 % ethanol and 4.13% water by weight and boils at 351.1 K. Since azeotropes distil off without change in composition, their components can't be separated by fractional distillation, hence these are separated by a special type of distillation called **azeotropic distillation.** Let us illustrate azeotropic distillation by taking example of separation of ethyl alcohol and water from rectified spirit. A suitable amount of benzene is added to the rectified spirit. Benzene forms two different azeotropes with the constituents of rectified spirit.

(*a*)   First of all it takes up all water present and some alcohol to form a ternary azeotrope. This azeotrope consists of 7.4% water, 74.1% benzene, and 18.5% alcohol. It distils at 337.8 K.

(*b*)   Remaining benzene takes up remaining alcohol and forms a binary azeotrope. This azeotrope consists of 67.6 % benzene and 32.4% alcohol. It distils at 341.2 K.

Thus the mixture of rectified spirit and benzene consists of mainly three parts : (*i*) a ternary azeotrope, (*ii*) a binary azeotrope, and (*iii*) remaining pure ethyl alcohol. Since each part distils at different temperatures, these are separated by fractional distillation. The first fraction, *i.e.* ternary azeotrope, distils at 337.8 K, the second fraction, *i.e.* binary azeotrope at 341.2 K and the last fraction, *i.e.* pure ethyl alcohol at 351 K.

9.   **Chromatography.** It is a modern and fast developing technique employed for the separation and purification of a complex *mixture of organic compounds especially carbohydrates, amino acids, plant pigments, terpenoids, vitamins, hormones, etc.* It was discovered by a *Russian botanist, Tswett* in 1906 and later developed by Kuhn, Winterstein and Karrer.

Chromatography is based on the principle of selective adsorption or distribution of the various components of a mixture between *two phases, one fixed and the other moving.* In general, the mixture to be separated is dissolved in a moving phase (liquid or gas) and passed over the fixed phase (solid or liquid). Different components are adsorbed (or distributed) at different levels of the fixed phase. When the fixed phase is solid, the basis of separation is *adsorption,** while when the fixed phase is liquid the basis of separation is *partition.*

Thus *chromatography is the technique of separating the components of a mixture in which separation is done by the differential movement of individual components through a stationary phase under the influence of a mobile phase.*

Classification of chromatography. On the basis of the principle operating in the technique, chromatography can broadly be classified into following two classes.

(*i*)   *Adsorption or column chromatography.* In this technique, the stationary phase is solid while the mobile phase is liquid or gas. Thus this can further be divided into two types depending upon the nature of the mobile phase, *i.e. liquid-solid chromatography* (when mobile phase is liquid) and *gas-solid chromatography* (when mobile phase is gas). *Ion exchange chromatography,* using ion-exchange resins as the stationary phase, is also a type of adsorption chromatography. *Thin layer chromatography* (TLC) is a special case of absorption chromatography in which a glass strip coated with a thin layer of the adsorbent is used as a stationary phase.

(*ii*)   *Partition chromatography.* In this technique, the stationary phase is a liquid supported on an inert solid while the mobile phase may be a liquid (*liquid-liquid partition chromatography*) or a gas (*gas-liquid partition chromatography*). Paper chromatography is the most important example of partition chromatography.

10.   **Chemical methods.** Chemical methods of separation depend upon the nature of the functional group present in the components. Hence these can be applied to solid as well as liquid compounds. A chemical method can be applied only when one of the components of the mixture is soluble in a particular solvent while the other is insoluble in the same solvent. Few such examples are given below.

(*a*)   *Caboxylic acids,* being soluble in $NaHCO_3$, can be separated from compounds which do not react with sodium bicarbonate solution like amines, nitro compounds, aldehydes, ketones, hydrocarbons, certain phenols etc.

(*b*)   *Phenols,* being soluble in strong alkalies like NaOH or KOH, can be separated from compounds which do not react with NaOH or KOH like amines, nitro compounds, aldehydes, ketones, hydrocarbons etc.

(*c*)   *Amines,* being basic, are soluble in dil HCl. Hence these can be separated from compounds which do not react with HCl like carboxylic acids, phenols, aldehydes, ketones, hydrocarbons etc.

(*d*)   *Carbohydrates,* being insoluble in ether, can be separated from most of other organic compounds which are soluble in ether.

Schemes for separation of some binary mixtures are sketched below.

1.   *Separation with water.* (Applied when one of the components is water soluble like phenols, certain carboxylic acids, alcohols etc.)

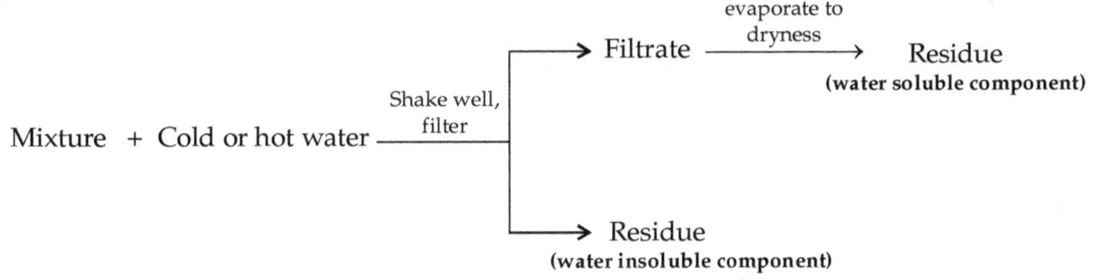

2.   *Separation with sodium bicarbonate.* (Applied when one of the components is a carboxylic acid).

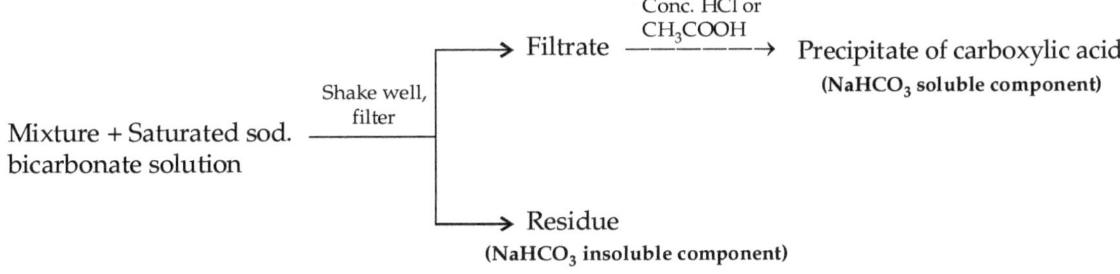

3. *Separation with sodium hydroxide.* (Applied when one of the components is a phenol)

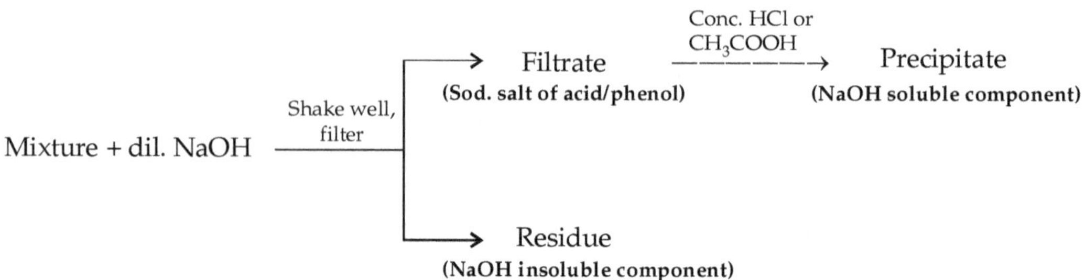

4. *Separation with hydrochloric acid.* (Applied when one of the components is an amine).

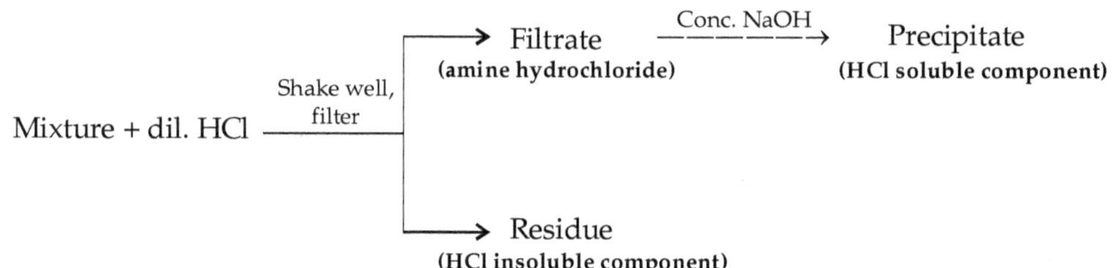

5. *Separation with organic solvents* like ether, benzene, alcohol, etc. (Applied when only one of the components is soluble in a particular solvent)

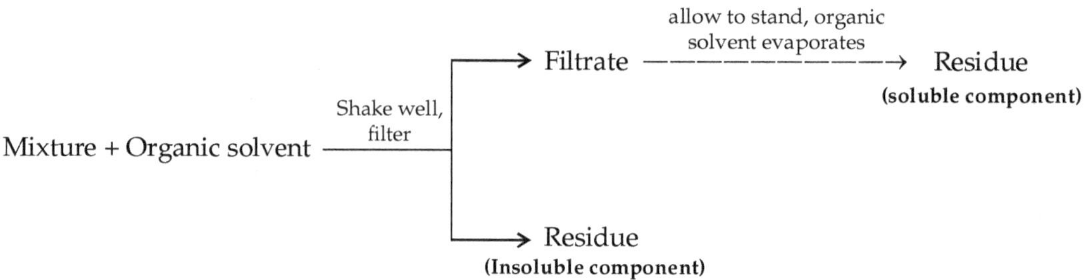

TEST YOUR UNDERSTANDING - 24.1

1. Which method should be used for the purification of a liquid having non-volatile impurities ?

2. How will you separate a mixture of two organic compounds having different solubilities in the same solvent ?

3. What type of compounds are purified by sublimation ?

4. Suggest a method to purify

    (*a*) kerosene containing water.   (*b*) iodine containing traces of common salt.

    (*c*) a mixture of *o*– and *p*–nitrophenols.   (*d*) a substance which starts decomposing much below its b.p.

    (*e*) a mixture of two liquids whose boiling points differ very much.

    (*f*) a mixture of two liquids whose boiling points differ nearly by 10°C.

5. How will you purify an impure sample of (*i*) camphor, and (*ii*) aniline.

6. Define the terms chromatogram and elution.

7. Mention the reagent which can be used for separating each of the following mixtures.

    (*a*) Diphenyl and phenylacetic acid   (*b*) Naphthalene and *p*-bromobenzoic acid

    (*c*) Anthracene and *p*-anisidine   (*d*) Mandelic acid and glucose

    (*e*) α-Nitronaphthalene and lactose   (*f*) *p*-Hydroxybenzoic acid and *p*-aminobenzoic acid

ILLUSTRATIVE EXAMPLES

Example 1 :

Give a roadmap figure showing the separation of *p*-cresol, benzoic acid and cyclohexanone.

Solution :

H_3C—⬡—OH + ⬡=O + ⬡—COOH

Shake with ether, then add aq. $NaHCO_3$

ether layer　　　　　　　　　　　　　　　aqueous $(NaHCO)_3$ layer

H_3C—⬡—OH + ⬡=O　　　　　⬡—COO$^-$Na$^+$

Shake with aq. NaOH

ether layer　　　　　　　　aq. layer

⬡=O　　　H_3C—⬡—O$^-$Na$^+$

evaporate ether　　　　add HCl

⬡=O　　　H_3C—⬡—OH

Example 2 :

Give a schematic diagram for the separation of the following water insoluble compounds present in a mixture.

$$C_6H_5Cl,\ C_6H_5CHO,\ C_6H_5COOH,\ p\text{-}CH_3C_6H_4.OH\ \text{and}\ C_6H_5N(CH_3)_2$$

Solution :

The components can be separated on the basis of their specific reactivity with certain reagents, e.g. only $C_6H_5N(CH_3)_2$ reacts with dil. aq. HCl, only C_6H_5CHO reacts with $NaHSO_3$, phenols and –COOH react with aq. NaOH, only –COOH react with $NaHCO_3$.

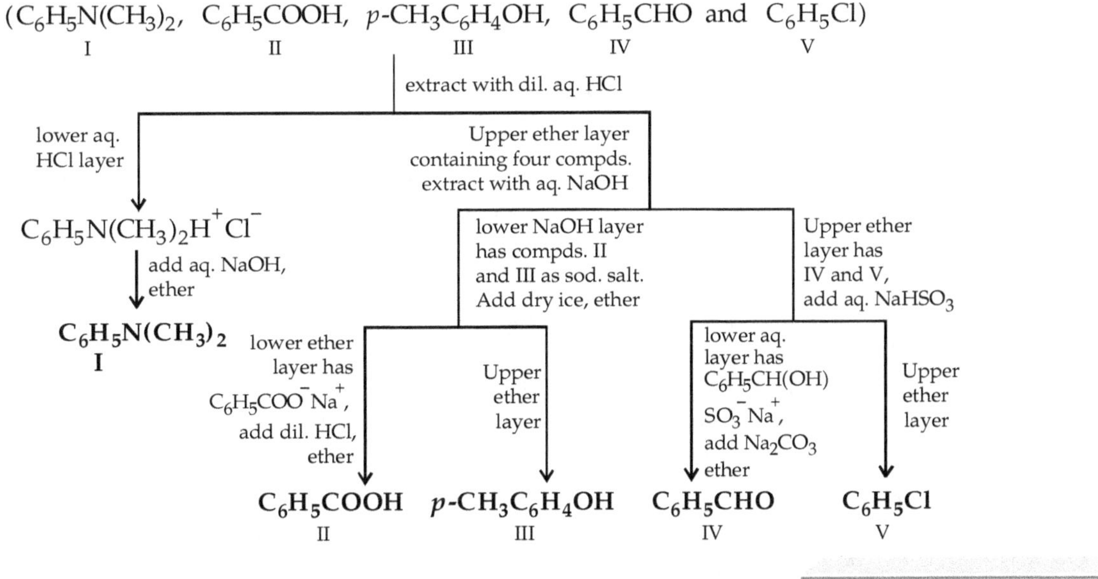

Example 3 :

1-Pentanol is oxidised by PCC mainly to 1-pentanal. However, some overoxidation product, 1-pentanoic acid, although in very small amount is also formed. Give a scheme for separating the three organic compounds by acid-base extractions from each other.

Solution :

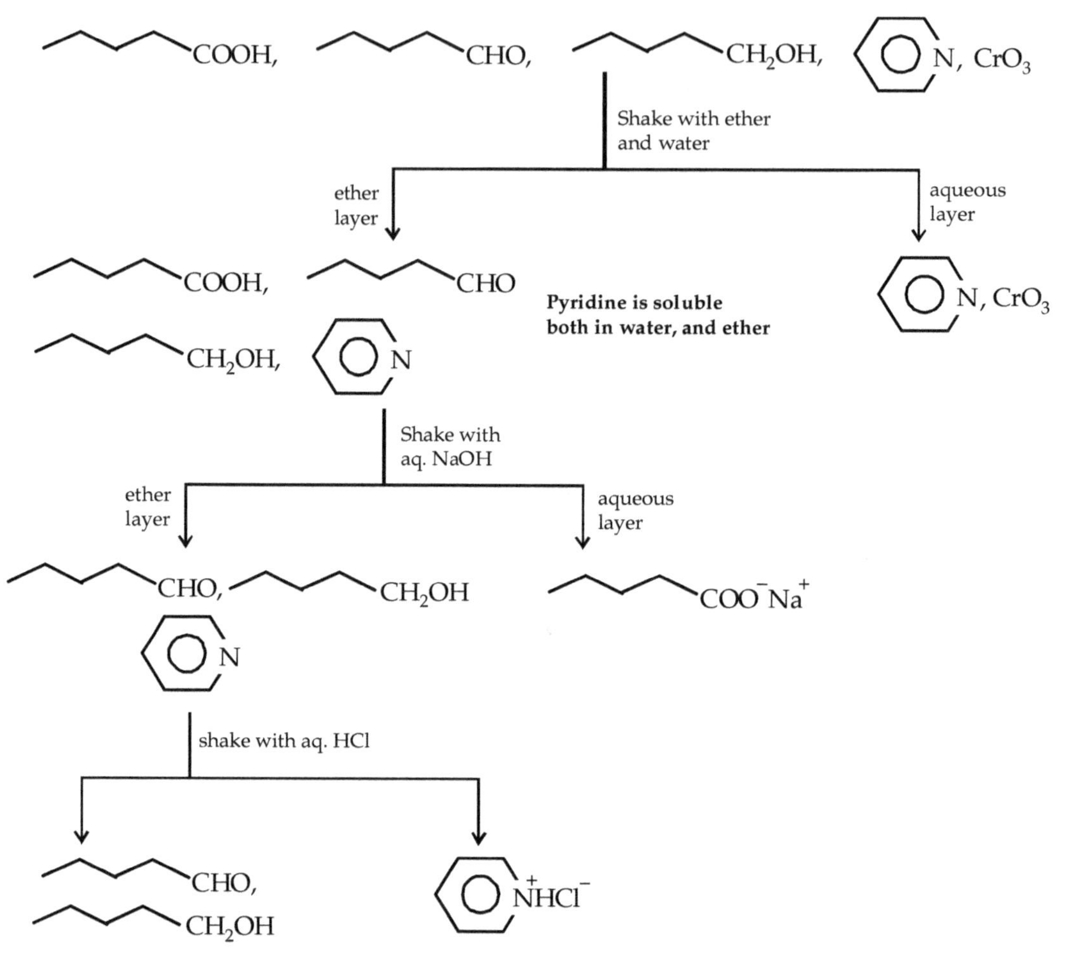

24.2   Qualitative Analysis of Elements

1.   **Detection of carbon and hydrogen.** Since all organic compounds contain carbon, and majority of them also contain hydrogen, in practice carbon and hydrogen are never detected (tested). However, if necessary these can be detected by heating a small quantity of the given *dry* organic compound with *dry* cupric oxide. Carbon and hydrogen, present in the compound,

$$2\,CuO + C \xrightarrow{\text{heat}} 2\,Cu + CO_2 \;;\; CuO + 2H \xrightarrow{\text{heat}} Cu + H_2O$$

are oxidised to CO_2 and H_2O respectively which in turn can be tested by their following reactions.

(*a*)   Carbon dioxide turns lime water milky

$$\underset{\textbf{(Colourless)}}{Ca(OH)_2} + \underset{\textbf{(From C)}}{CO_2} \longrightarrow \underset{\textbf{(Milky)}}{CaCO_3\downarrow} + H_2O$$

(*b*)   Water turns anhydrous copper sulphate (white in colour) to hydrated copper sulphate (blue in colour)

$$\underset{\textbf{(White)}}{CuSO_4} + \underset{\textbf{(From H)}}{5H_2O} \longrightarrow \underset{\textbf{(Blue)}}{CuSO_4.5H_2O}$$

2. **Detection of nitrogen, sulphur and halogens.** Nitrogen, sulphur and halogens are tested from the sodium fusion extract of the organic compound, which is more commonly known as **Lassaigne's extract.** For preparing Lassaigne's extract, a small quantity of the organic compound is fused with sodium metal in a fusion tube. The red hot tube is broken in distilled water, boiled and filtered. The filtrate is known as *Lassaigne's extract* or *sodium extract.*

Chemical reactions involved in the formation of Lassaigne's extract.

(i)   When only N is present $\qquad$ $Na + C + N \longrightarrow NaCN$

(ii)   When only S is present $\qquad$ $2\,Na + S \longrightarrow Na_2S$

(iii)   When both N and S are present $\qquad$ $Na + C + N + S \longrightarrow NaCNS$

(iv)   When halogen is present $\qquad$ $Na + X \longrightarrow NaX$

Lassaigne's extract, so prepared, is used for testing the presence of N, S and halogens.

(a)   *Detection of nitrogen.* Generally, the Lassaigne's extract is alkaline in nature due to reaction of unreacted sodium with water ($2Na + 2H_2O \rightarrow 2NaOH + H_2$). If it is not so, it is made alkaline by adding sodium hydroxide. Now the extract is boiled with ferrous sulphate solution, and then acidified with dil. H_2SO_4 and dil. HCl, appearance of **green** or **blue colour** confirms the presence of nitrogen.

$$FeSO_4 + 2NaOH \longrightarrow Fe(OH)_2 + Na_2SO_4$$

$$Fe(OH)_2 + 6NaCN \longrightarrow \underset{\text{Sodium ferrocyanide}}{Na_4[Fe(CN)_6]} + 2NaOH$$

$$\underset{\substack{\text{(Formed by oxid. of } Fe^{2+} \text{ on} \\ \textbf{boiling in presence of } O_2)}}{4Fe^{3+}} + 3Na_4[Fe(CN)_6] \longrightarrow \underset{\substack{\text{Ferric ferrocyanide} \\ \textbf{(Prussian blue)}}}{Fe_4[Fe(CN)_6]_3} + 12\,Na^+$$

Sometimes, Fe^{3+} ions are provided by adding ferric chloride solution.

A less important test for nitrogen given by certain nitrogenous compounds is evolution of NH_3 by *heating of the compound with soda lime* (NaOH + CaO).

$$CH_3CONH_2 + NaOH \longrightarrow CH_3COONa + NH_3 \uparrow$$

However, this test is not given by compounds containing $—NH_2$, $—NO_2$ and $—N = N—$ groups.

(b)   *Lassaigen's test for sulphur.* Sodium sulphide, if present in Lassaigne's extract can be detected by following tests.

(i)   It gives purple colour with sodium nitroprusside solution.

$$Na_2S + \underset{\text{Sodium nitroprusside}}{Na_2[Fe(NO)(CN)_5]} \longrightarrow \underset{\substack{\text{Sodium thionitroprusside} \\ \textbf{(purple colour)}}}{Na_4[Fe(CN)_5NOS]}$$

(ii)   It gives black precipitate with lead acetate solution.

$$Na_2S + (CH_3COO)_2Pb \longrightarrow 2\,CH_3COONa + \underset{\textbf{Black ppt}}{PbS \downarrow}$$

(c)   *Lassaigen's test for nitrogen and sulphur, when present together.* In case the compound contains both N and S, sodium thiocyanate formed during fusion of organic compound with metallic sodium reacts with Fe^{3+} ions to form blood red coloured, ferric thiocyanate.

$$Fe^{3+} + \underset{\text{Sod. thiocyanate}}{3NaCNS} \longrightarrow \underset{\text{Ferric thiocyanate}}{Fe(CNS)_3} + 3Na^+$$

However, note that the absence of blood red colouration does not necessarily mean that sulphur is absent because in presence of excess of sodium, sodium thiocyanate decomposes to form sodium cyanide and sodium sulphide.

$$NaCNS + 2Na \longrightarrow NaCN + Na_2S$$

(d)   *Lassaigne's test for halogens.* A small portion of the sodium fusion extract[*] is acidified with dil. nitric acid and then treated with silver nitrate solution. If a precipitate is formed, it indicates the presence of a halogen ; the colour of precipitate, in turn, indicates the nature of halogen, *viz.*

(i)   white colour soluble in NH_4OH indicates chlorine.

(ii)   pale yellow colour sparingly soluble in NH_4OH indicates bromine and

(iii)   yellow colour insoluble in ammonia indicates iodine.

$$\underset{\substack{\text{Sod. halide} \\ \text{(Formed in Lassaigne's filtrate)}}}{NaX} + AgNO_3 \longrightarrow \underset{\text{Silver halide}}{AgX \downarrow} + NaNO_3$$

---

[*]   In the preparation of sodium fusion extract used for the detection of halogens, fusion with sodium may be replaced by quicklime CaO, or a mixture of Na_2CO_3 and Zn dust or a mixture of Na_2CO_3 and sugar. These will avoid the formation of NaCN or Na_2S (in case N or S are present) hence step involving boiling with conc. HNO_3 (for the decomposition of NaCN or Na_2S) will be avoided.

Note. Function of nitric acid. In case the compound under investigation is found to contain nitrogen and/or sulphur, the latter two must be destroyed, prior to treatment with $AgNO_3$, by boiling the extract with concentrated nitric acid which decomposes sodium cyanide and sodium sulphide (formed during sodium fusion) as volatile HCN and H_2S.

$$NaCN + HNO_3 \xrightarrow{\text{boil}} NaNO_3 + HCN \uparrow$$

$$Na_2S + 2HNO_3 \xrightarrow{\text{boil}} 2NaNO_3 + H_2S \uparrow$$

If NaCN and Na_2S are not removed, they will be forming precipitate on the addition of silver nitrate. The precipitate of AgCN (white) and Ag_2S (black) will make hindrance in the judgement of silver halide precipitate.

$$NaCN\ (Na_2S) + AgNO_3 \longrightarrow AgCN \downarrow + (Ag_2S\downarrow)$$

Copper wire test or Beilstein's test. A small quantity of the organic compound is taken on the flattened end of the pre-cleaned* copper wire. This end is now inserted in the Bunsen flame—if a *green colour* is developed (due to the formation of volatile cupric halides) in the flame, it indicates the presence of halogen in the compound. This test, although very sensitive, is not always reliable because some compounds containing no halogen (*e.g.* urea, thiourea, organic acids, pyridine, etc.) also respond this test due to the formation of volatile cupric cyanide. Therefore, we can say that a *negative Beilstein's test is the surety for the absence of halogens.*

Chloroform layer test for halogens. In case more than one halogen is present, these may be detected as in inorganic qualitative analysis with the help of chloroform (or carbon disulphide) and chlorine water. Moreover, this test is not interferred even in presence of N and/or S in the compound.

In practice, a small portion (about 2 ml.) of the sodium fusion extract is acidified with dilute HNO_3 or H_2SO_4 ; 1 c.c. of chloroform, carbon disulphide or carbon tetrachloride is added to it and the contents are now shaken with excess of chlorine water. On settling, if the carbon tetrachloride layer becomes : (*i*) *yellow or light brown*–bromine is indicated ; (*ii*) *violet*-iodine is indicated although in such case the compound may have both bromine as well as iodine. So in case, violet colour is obtained the contents are shaken with more chlorine, if violet colour disappears and yellow or brown colour is obtained bromine is also indicated in the compound.

Chemistry of the test. Chlorine oxidises NaI (formed in the fusion extract) to free iodine (*violet*) which when treated with excess of chlorine is further oxidised to iodic acid (*colourless*). Now excess of chlorine oxidises NaBr (formed in the fusion extract, if bromine is present in the compound) to fee bromine (*orange or brown*) which comes in the organic solvent (CS_2, CCl_4 or $CHCl_3$) layer.

$$\underset{\text{From fusion extract}}{2NaI} + Cl_2 \longrightarrow 2NaCl + \underset{\textbf{Violet}}{I_2}$$

$$I_2 + 5Cl_2 + 6H_2O \longrightarrow \underset{\text{Iodic acid (\textbf{colourless})}}{2HIO_3} + 10HCl$$

$$2NaBr + Cl_2 \longrightarrow 2NaCl + \underset{\textbf{(Orange or brown)}}{Br_2}$$

In case chlorine is present along with other halogen (Br and/or I), the Lassaigne's extract is boiled with concentrated nitric acid till the evolution of brown coloured vapours ceases. It is now diluted and treated with silver nitrate; a *curdy white precipitate* soluble in excess of ammonium hydroxide and insoluble in nitric acid cofirms the presence of chlorine.

TEST YOUR UNDERSTANDING - 24.2

1. Can you expect any organic compound (*a*) without carbon, (*b*) without hydrogen ?
2. Can Na be replaced by K or Li for preparing Lassaigne's extract ?
3. Is it necessary to add H_2SO_4 or HCl in the test of nitrogen ? Explain.
4. It is proferred to add conc. H_2SO_4 rather than HCl during the test of nitrogen. Explain.
5. Urea, H_2NCONH_2, although contains nitrogen, *sometimes* it does not respond test for nitrogen.
6. Can you imagine any nitrogenous compound that does not respond Lassaigne's test for nitrogen ?
7. Beilestein's test is not given by which halogen ? Name it.

---

*   Cleaning of copper wire. The copper wire is heated strongly in an oxidisng flame till it gives no colour to the flame.

24.3　Quantitative Analysis of Elements (*Estimation of Elements*)

After detecting various elements in an organic compound, the next step is to estimate the percentage composition of these elements. This is called *quantitative analysis* or *estimation of elements.* Accurate methods are known for the estimation of C, H, N and other elements but not for oxygen which is always determined by difference.

1.　**Estimation of carbon and hydrogen** (*Liebig's method*). Carbon and hydrogen are always estimated simultaneously. The method is based upon the fact that when an organic compound is heated strongly with dry copper oxide in presence of oxygen or air, its carbon and hydrogen are oxidised to carbon dioxide and water vapours respectively.

$$C \text{ (from org. compound)} + 2CuO \xrightarrow{\text{heat}} CO_2 + 2Cu$$

$$2H \text{ (from org. compound)} + CuO \xrightarrow{\text{heat}} H_2O + Cu$$

The resultant CO_2 and H_2O vapours are absorbed separately in potash or ascarite (NaOH + CaO) a nd calcium chloride or magnesium perchlorate solutions respectively and hence the weights of absorbed gases (CO_2 and H_2O) is determined. From the weights of CO_2 and H_2O vapour formed, the weights of carbon and hydrogen in the known weight of the compound are obtained.

$$\textbf{Percentage of carbon} = \frac{\text{Wt. of } CO_2}{\text{Wt. of compound}} \times \frac{12}{44} \times 100$$

Similarly,

$$\textbf{Percentage of hydrogen} = \frac{\text{Wt. of } H_2O}{\text{Wt. of compound}} \times \frac{2}{18} \times 100$$

Example 4 :

0.25 gm of an organic compound containing C, H and oxygen was analysed by the combustion method. The increase in weights of calcium chloride tube and potash bulbs at the end of the operation was found to be 0.15 gm and 0.1873 gm respectively. Calculate the percentage composition of the compound.

Solution :

Wt. of organic compound　　　　　　　　　　　= 0.25 gm

Wt. of H_2O formed (increase in wt. of $CaCl_2$ tube)　= 0.15 gm

Wt. of CO_2 (increase in wt. of potash bulbs)　　= 0.1873 gm

Now from our previous discussion we know that

$$\% \text{ of C} = \frac{12}{44} \times \frac{\text{wt. of } CO_2 \times 100}{\text{wt. of compound}}$$

$$= \frac{12}{44} \times \frac{0.1873 \times 100}{0.25} = \textbf{20.04\%}$$

Similarly,　　　　　　　　$$\% \text{ of H} = \frac{2}{18} \times \frac{0.15 \times 100}{0.25} = \textbf{6.66\%}$$

Hence percentage of oxygen $= 100 - (20.04 + 6.66) = \textbf{73.30}$

Example 5 :

0.36 gm of an organic compound on combustion gave 0.01 mole of CO_2 and 0.005 mole of water. Calculate the percentage of carbon and hydrogen in the compound.

Solution :

First convert the given moles of CO_2 and H_2O into their respective weights, the rest of the procedure is same as usual.

Calculation of wt. of CO_2 and H_2O formed

Since 1 mole of CO_2 weighs　　　　　　= 44 gm

0.01 mole of CO_2 weighs　　　　　　　$$= \frac{44}{1} \times 0.01 = 0.44 \text{ gm.}$$

Similarly, as 1 mole of H_2O weighs $= 18$ gm

0.005 mole of H_2O weighs $= \dfrac{18}{1} \times 0.005 = 0.09$ gm

$\therefore$ Percentage of C $= \dfrac{12}{44} \times \dfrac{0.44 \times 100}{0.36} = \mathbf{33.33\%}$

and Percentage of H $= \dfrac{2}{18} \times \dfrac{0.09 \times 100}{0.36} = \mathbf{2.77\%}$

2. **Estimation of nitrogen.** Nitrogen is generally estimated by two methods : *(A) Duma's method* and *(B) Kjeldahl's method.*

(A) **Duma's method.** This method can be applied to all nitrogenous organic compounds.

Principle. The method is based on the fact that when an organic compound is heated with copper oxide, its carbon, hydrogen, sulphur and nitrogen contents are converted into CO_2, H_2O, SO_2 and N_2 respectively. In case any traces of nitrogen oxides are formed, these are reduced back to free nitrogen by passing it over bright reduced copper gauze. Carbon dioxide, water vapour and sulphur dioxide are absorbed in caustic potash solution and free nitrogen is collected over KOH in a nitrometer. From the volume of nitrogen collected over caustic potash, percentage of nitrogen can be calculated.

$$C + 2CuO \xrightarrow{\text{heat}} CO_2 + 2Cu$$

$$2H + CuO \xrightarrow{\text{heat}} H_2O + Cu$$

$$2N + CuO \xrightarrow{\text{heat}} N_2 + \text{Oxides of N}$$

$$\text{Oxides N} + Cu \xrightarrow{\text{heat}} N_2 + CuO$$

Room temperature and atmospheric pressure are also recorded in order to convert the volume of nitrogen collected under given conditions to volume of N_2 at N.T.P.

$$\therefore \quad \text{Percentage of nitrogen} = \frac{28 \times \text{Vol. of } N_2 \text{ collected at N.T.P.} \times 100}{22400 \times \text{Wt. of organic compound}}$$

$$= \frac{\text{Wt. of nitrogen} \times 100}{\text{Wt. of organic compound}}.$$

Example 6 :

0.290 gm of an organic compound containing nitrogen gave 50.00 ml of nitrogen at N.T.P. What is the percentage of nitrogen in the compound ?

Solution :

Wt. of organic substance $= 0.290$ gm.

Vol. of collected nitrogen at N.T.P. $= 50$ ml.

Now we know that percentage of nitrogen $= \dfrac{28 \times \text{Vol. of } N_2 \text{ collected at N.T.P.} \times 100}{22400 \times \text{Wt. of organic compound}}$

$$= \frac{28 \times 50 \times 100}{22400 \times 0.290} = \mathbf{21.55}$$

Example 7 :

In the determination of nitrogen by Duma's method, 0.200 gm of compound gave 20.7 ml of moist nitrogen at 15°C and 776 mm pressure. Calculate the percentage of nitrogen in the compound (Aq. tension at 15°C = 16 mm ; 1 litre of nitrogen of N.T.P. weighs 1.25 gm).

Solution :

Conversion of volume of N_2 collected to N.T.P. conditions

At given conditions $\qquad P_1 = 776 - 16 = 760$ mm $\qquad V_1 = 20.7$ ml $\qquad T_1 = 15 + 273 = 288$ A

At N.T.P. conditions $\qquad P_2 = 760$ mm $\qquad\qquad\qquad V_2 = ?$ $\qquad\qquad T_2 = 273$ A

Applying the general gas equation

$$\frac{P_1 V_1}{T_1} = \frac{P_2 V_2}{T_2} \quad \text{or} \quad V_2 = \frac{P_1 V_1 \times T_2}{T_1 \times P_2}$$

$$\therefore \qquad V_2 = \frac{760 \times 20.7 \times 273}{288 \times 760} = 19.62 \text{ ml.}$$

Calculation of percentage of nitrogen

Since one litre (1000 ml) of nitrogen at N.T.P. weighs $\quad = 1.25$ gm

$$\therefore \qquad 19.62 \text{ ml. of nitrogen at N.T.P. weigh} \quad = \frac{1.25}{1000} \times 19.62 \text{ gm}$$

Hence $\qquad$ Percentage of nitrogen in the compound $\quad = \dfrac{1.25}{1000} \times 19.62 \times \dfrac{100}{0.200} = \mathbf{12.26\ \%.}$

(B) **Kjeldahl's method.** This method is simpler and convenient, and can be used in compounds in which nitrogen is directly linked to carbon and hydrogen. Therefore, this method is largely used for the estimation of nitrogen in food, fertilizers and drugs. However, the method fails in compounds containing nitrogen joined either to other nitrogen or to oxygen as in nitro, nitroso, azo ($N = N$), azoxy, diazo, hydrazones, oximes, etc. The method is not applicable to compounds containing nitrogen in ring (*e.g.* pyridine, quinoline etc.)

Principle. This method is based on the fact that most of the nitrogenous compounds when heated with concentrated sulphuric acid in a long-necked flask called *Kjedahl's flask* in the presence of potassium sulphate* and a little copper sulphate **(Kjeldahlisation or digestion),** its nitrogen is quantitatively converted into ammonium sulphate. The ammonium sulphate so obtained is decomposed with excess of NaOH solution to give ammonia which is absorbed in an excess of a standard HCl or H_2SO_4 solution. The residual mineral acid is now titrated against a standard sodium hydroxide solution and thus the amount of HCl consumed for the neutralisation of ammonia, and hence the amount of ammonia produced from the known weight of the organic compound is determined.

$$\text{Organic compound containing N} + H_2SO_4 \xrightarrow{\text{heat}} (NH_4)_2SO_4$$

$$(NH_4)_2SO_4 + 2NaOH \xrightarrow{\text{heat}} Na_2SO_4 + 2NH_3 + 2H_2O$$

$$2NH_3 + H_2SO_4 \longrightarrow (NH_4)_2SO_4$$

Hence percentage of nitrogen in the compound $= \dfrac{14 \times \text{Vol. of acid used} \times \text{Normality of acid}}{1000 \times \text{Wt. of organic compound}} \times 100$

Type I. *When the ammonia evolved completely neutralises the standard acid taken.*

Example 8 :

If the ammonia obtained from 0.2160 gm of an organic compound by Kjeldahl method of analysis neuralises 23.85 ml of 0.1150 N acid, what is percentage of nitrogen in the compound?

Solution :

$\qquad$ Wt. of substance taken $\qquad\qquad\qquad = 0.2160$ gm

$\qquad$ Vol. of acid neutralised by NH_3 $\qquad\quad = 23.85$ ml

$\qquad$ Normality of the acid $\qquad\qquad\qquad = 0.1150$ N

$\therefore \quad$ Percentage of nitrogen $\qquad\qquad = \dfrac{1.4 \times N \times V}{\text{Wt. of substance}} = \dfrac{1.4 \times 0.1150 \times 23.85}{0.2160} \text{ gm} = \mathbf{17.77}$

---

* $\quad$ Potassium sulphate raises the boiling point of H_2SO_4 and thus ensures complete reaction.

Type II. *When the ammonia evolved neutralises part of the standard acid and the acid left unused is titrated against standard NaOH.*

Example 9 :

0.445 gm of an organic compound was treated according to Kjeldahl method. The ammonia evolved was absorbed in 100 ml of N/2 sulphuric acid. The excess of the acid required 65.5 ml. N/2 alkali solution for neutralisation. Find the percentage of nitrogen in the compound.

Solution :

$$\text{Wt. of organic compound} = 0.445 \text{ nm}$$
$$\text{Vol. of N/2 } H_2SO_4 \text{ taken} = 100 \text{ ml.}$$

Vol. of N/2 alkali required for the neutralisation of the excess of the acid $= 65.6$ ml.

$$\text{Let the vol. of N/2 unused acid} = V_1 \text{ ml.}$$

Calculation of the volume of $N/2\,H_2SO_4$ *used*

	(For acid)		*(For alkali)*

$$\frac{N_1}{2} \times V_1 = \frac{N_2}{2} \times 65.5$$

$$\therefore \quad V_1 \text{ (vol. of unused acid)} = \frac{1}{2} \times 65.5 \times \frac{2}{1} = 65.5 \text{ ml}$$

$$\therefore \quad \text{Vol. of N/2 acid used for neutralising } NH_3 = 100 - 65.5 \text{ ml.} = 34.5 \text{ ml.}$$

$$\text{Hence, percentage of nitrogen in the compound} = \frac{1.4 \times N \times V}{\text{Wt. of substance}} = \frac{1.4 \times 1 \times 34.5}{2 \times 0.445} = \textbf{54.33\%}$$

Type III. *When the residual acid in the conical flask is diluted to a known volume with water and then titrated against standard alkali solution.*

Example 10 :

0.6 gm of an organic compound was Kjeldahlised and the ammonia evolved was passed into 100 ml of seminormal H_2SO_4. The residual acid was diluted to 500 ml with distilled water ; 25 ml. of diluted acid required 20.4 ml decinormal caustic soda solution for complete neutralisation. Calculate the percentage of nitrogen in the compound.

Solution :

$$\text{Weight of substance taken} = 0.6 \text{ gm}$$
$$\text{Vol. of N/2 } H_2SO_4 \text{ taken} = 100 \text{ ml}$$
$$\text{Let the vol. of N/2 } H_2SO_4 \text{ unused} = V_1 \text{ ml}$$
$$\text{Now 25 ml of the diluted acid solution} = 20.4 \text{ ml N/10 NaOH}$$

$$\therefore \quad \text{Normality of the diluted acid} = 20.4 \times \frac{1}{10} \times \frac{1}{25} = \frac{51}{625} N$$

$$500 \text{ ml. of } \frac{51}{625} N \text{ of diluted acid} \equiv V_1 \text{ ml of N/2 } H_2SO_4 \text{ (unused)}$$

Applying the normality formula

	(For unused acid)		*(For diluted acid)*

$$\frac{N}{2} \times V_1 = \frac{51}{625} N \times 500$$

$$\therefore \quad V_1 = \frac{51}{625} \times 500 \times \frac{2}{1} = 81.6 \text{ ml.}$$

$$\therefore \quad \text{Vol. of N/2 acid used for ammonia} = 100 - 81.6 \text{ ml} = 18.4 \text{ ml.}$$

$$\text{Hence percentage of nitrogen} = \frac{1.4 \times N \times V}{w} = \frac{1.4 \times 1 \times 18.4}{2 \times 0.6} = \textbf{21.46}$$

3. **Estimation of halogens (Carius method). Principle.** Carius method is based on the fact that when an organic compound containing halogen is heated in a sealed tube with fuming nitric acid in presence of silver nitrate ; C, H and S of the compound are oxidised to their respective volatile oxides, while halogen is converted to the silver halide. From the weight of the silver halide formed, percentage of halogen in the organic compound can be calculated.

$$\text{In general, } \% \text{ of halogen} = \frac{\text{At. wt. of halogen} \times \text{Wt. of AgX} \times 100}{\text{Mol. wt. of AgX} \times w}.$$

Note (*i*) The method does not give satisfactory results with iodine because silver iodide is slightly soluble in nitric acid and some molecular iodine is also produced even in presence of excess of silver nitrate.

(*ii*) The method does not give correct result for highly halogenated aromatic compounds.

4. **Estimation of sulphur** (*Carius method*). Sulphur is estimated like halogens but with a slight modification (*here $AgNO_3$ crystals used in halogen estimation are not used*). A weighed amount of organic substance (let it be w gm) is heated with conc. HNO_3 when its C, H and S are oxidised CO_2, H_2O (steam) and H_2SO_4 respectively. The contents of the Carius tube are transferred to a beaker and then treated with excess of barium chloride solution when whole of the sulphuric acid is precipitated as barium sulphate. From the weight of $BaSO_4$ (say x gm), percentage of S canbe calculated.

$$C + 2O \text{ (from } HNO_3) \xrightarrow{\text{heat}} CO_2 \; ; \; 2H + O \text{ (from } HNO_3) \xrightarrow{\text{heat}} H_2O$$

$$S + H_2O + 3O \text{ (from } HNO_3) \xrightarrow{\text{heat}} H_2SO_4$$
$$H_2SO_4 + BaCl_2 \longrightarrow BaSO_4 \downarrow + 2HCl$$

$$\therefore \quad \text{Percentage of S in the compound} = \frac{32 \times x \times 100}{233 \times w}.$$

Example 11 :

0.2595 gm of an organic compound containing sulphur was heated in a Carius tube with fuming nitric acid and the sulphuric acid formed was precipitated as $BaSO_4$ with $BaCl_2$. The weight of dry $BaSO_4$ was 0.350. Find the percentage of sulphur in the substance.

Solution :

$$\% \text{ of sulphur} = \frac{32}{233} \times \frac{\text{Wt. of } BaSO_4 \times 100}{\text{Wt. of compound}} = \frac{32}{233} \times \frac{0.350 \times 100}{0.2595} = \mathbf{18.52}$$

5. **Estimation of oxygen.** There is no satisfactory method for the direct estimation of oxygen in an organic compound. Hence, it is usually calculated by difference. In case, the sum of percentages of all other elements present in the organic compound is less than 100, the remainder gives the percentage of oxygen, *i.e.*,

$$\% \text{ of oxygen} = 100 - \text{Sum of percentages of all other elements}$$

24.4 Determination of Molecular Formula

Knowing the percentage composition of a substance we proceed further for knowing the actual number of constituent atoms present in one molecule of the compound, *i.e.* the molecular formula of the compound. Determination of molecular formula of a compound involves the following three important steps.

(*i*) Calculation of empirical formula. (*ii*) Determination of molecular weight.

(*iii*) Calculation of molecular formula.

1. **Calculation of empirical formula.** *The empirical formula of a compound is the simplest formula which expresses the relative number of atoms present in the molecule.* It is calculated from the percentage composition of the compound by the following steps.

(*i*) *Determination of relative number of atoms.* For this, the percentage composition of each element is divided by its atomic weight. The different numbers so obtained are the relative numbers of different atoms present in the molecule.

(ii) *Determination of simplest ratio.* The relative numbers of different atoms obtained in the above step are divided by the lowest one among them.

(iii) *Whole number.* The numbers expressing the simplest atomic ratio may or may not be whole numbers. In case any of the number is not nearly whole number then all the numbers are multiplied by a suitable common factor to get the smallest possible whole numbers. Minor fractions are neglected.

(iv) *Empirical formula.* The symbols of each element present in the compound are written in a line side by side. The whole numbers of each element obtained in step (iii) are put as subscripts to the lower right hand corner of each respective element. This gives the *empirical* or *simplest formula* of the compound.

2. **Determination of molecular weight.** *The molecular weight of a compound is the relative mass of one molecule of it as compared with the mass of atom of carbon* (^{12}C isotope) *taken as 12 amu.* It is only a number. If we say that molecular weight of a substance is 48, it means that the molecule of this substance is $48/12 = 4$ times as heavy as an atom of carbon.

Gram-molecular weight. *When molecular weight is expressed in grams, it is known as gram molecular weight.* For example, the molecular weight of carbon dioxide is 44, but it gram molecular weight is 44 grams.

Gram-molecular volume. *The volume occupied by the vapour of a gram-molecular weight of substance at N.T.P. is called the gram molecular volume.* Its volume at N.T.P. is 22.4 litres or 22400 ml.

The methods employed for the determination of molecular weights can be divided into two groups.

(i) *Physical methods for volatile compounds.* In these methods a known weight of the organic compound is vaporised and the volume so obtained is reduced to N.T.P. From the volume of the vapours of the compound at N.T.P. from a given amount of the compound, weight of 22.4 litres of vapours is calculated. This weight will be the molecular weight of the compound. In short, these methods are based on the fact that 22.4 *litres of every gas or vapours at N.T.P. weigh equal to its molecular weight in gm.* (gram molecule). The important physical method is Victor Meyer's method.

(ii) *Physical methods for non-volatile compounds.* (a) Freezing point depression method and (b) boiling point elevation method.

(iii) *Chemical methods.* (a) Silver salt method for acids, (b) platinichloride method for bases, and (c) volumetric method for acids as well as bases.

(A)   **Victor Meyer's method.**   Mol. wt $= \dfrac{\text{Weight of compound} \times RT}{PV}$

Where V is the volume in litres collected at pressure P atmosphere and temperature T (in Kelvin) from w g of solute, $R = 0.082$ L atom mol^{-1} K^{-1}.

(B)   **Cryosopic or depression of freezing point method.** This method is based on the fact that freezing point of a solvent is lowered on the addition of a soluble non-electrolyte. Depression in freezing point is found to be proportional to the amount of the solute added to a known weight of the solvent. In other words, freezing point of a solvent is depressed to the same extent when equimolecular quantities of different non-electrolytes are added to a fixed weight of the solvent.

The molecular weight of a non-volatile organic compound can be easily determined by dissolving a definite weight of the substance in a known weight of the solvent. Mathematically,

$$m \;=\; \frac{100\,K_f w}{\Delta T W}$$

where, m = Mol. wt. of the solute W = Weight of the solvent
         w = Weight of the solute K_f = Molecular depression constant
         ΔT = Depression of freezing point.

The **molecular depression constant or the freezing point constant** *is defined as the depression of freezing point which would be produced by dissolving one gram-molecule of the solute in 100 gm. of the solvent.* The molar depression constants for some common solvents are given below.

Water	18.6°C or 1.86	Acetic acid	38.2°C or 3.82
Benzene	51.2°C or 5.12	Phenol	73°C or 7.3

On the other hand, depression of freezing point may be determined experimentally.

(C)   **Ebullioscopic or Elevation of boiling point method.** This method is similar to cryoscopic method and based on the fact that the normal boiling point of a solvent increases (elevates) on the addition of a soluble non-electrolyte. The elevation of boiling point is found to be proportional to the amount of the solute (and not the nature of the solute) added to a known weight of the solvent. The elevation of boiling point produced by adding a known amount of the solute (w) to a known amount of the solvent (W) can be used for determining the molecular weight of the solute (m).

$$m = \frac{100 \, K_b w}{\Delta T W}$$

where, K_b = Molecular elevation constant ΔT = Elevation of boiling point.

Molecular elevation constant or boiling point constant *is defined as the elevation of boiling point which would be produced by dissolving one gram molecule of the solute in 100 gm. of the solvent.* The molecular elevation constants for some common solvents are given below.

Water	5.2°C or 0.52	Acetone	16.7°C or 1.67
Benzene	26.7°C or 2.67	Acetic acid	25.3°C or 2.53
Ether	21.0°C or 2.10	Ethyl alcohol	11.5°C or 1.15

Again, elevation of boiling point is determined experimentally.

(D)   **Silver salt method** (*For organic acids, RCOOH*). This method is based on the fact that most of the organic acids form insoluble silver salts which on ignition decompose to give residue of pure metallic silver.

$$RCOOH \xrightarrow{NH_4OH} RCOONH_4 \xrightarrow{AgNO_3} RCOOAg\downarrow \xrightarrow{ignite} Ag\downarrow$$

From the known weight of the silver salt of the acid taken for ignition and from the weight of metallic silver obtained, the equivalent weight of the silver salt of the acid (let it be E) can be calculated with the help of following relation.

$$RCOOAg \xrightarrow{ignite} Ag$$

Eq. wt.	E	108
or Weight	w g	x g

Mathematically, $\dfrac{\text{Eq. wt. of the silver salt (say } E)}{\text{Eq. wt. of silver (108)}} = \dfrac{\text{Wt. of silver salt taken } (w)}{\text{Wt. of silver obtained } (x)}$

$\therefore$ $E = \dfrac{w}{x} \times 108$

Relation between formulae of RCOOH and RCOOAg

	RCOOH	=	$RCOOAg - Ag + H$

Thus   Eq. wt. of RCOOH = $E - 108 + 1$

or   Eq. wt of RCOOH = $E - 107$

Thus   Eq. wt. of RCOOH = $\left(\dfrac{w}{x} \times 108\right) - 107$

and hence   Mol. wt. of RCOOH = Eq. wt. of the acid × Basicity

$$= \left[\left(\frac{w}{x} \times 108\right) - 107\right] \times n$$

(E)   **Platinum salt method** (*For organic bases, RNH₂*). This method is based on the fact the platinichlorides, also known as chloroplatinates, of organic bases $(B_2H_2PtCl_6)$ when ignited strongly give a residue of platinum.

$$2B \xrightarrow{HCl} 2BHCl \xrightarrow{PtCl_4} B_2H_2PtCl_6 \xrightarrow{heat} Pt$$

From the weight of the platinum salt taken (say w g) for ignition and from the weight of platinum obtained on ignition (say x g), equivalent weight of the base can be calculated.

$B_2H_2PtCl_6$	$\longrightarrow$	Pt
$2B + 2 + 195 + 213 = 2B + 410$		195
w g		x g

Thus $\dfrac{\text{Mol. wt. of chloroplatinate}}{\text{At. wt. of platinum}} = \dfrac{\text{Wt. of chloroplatinate}}{\text{Wt. of platinum}}$

$$\frac{2B + 410}{195} = \frac{w}{x}$$

$$B = \frac{1}{2}\left[\frac{w}{x} \times 195 - 410\right] \quad \text{where B is the equivalent weight of the base}$$

$\therefore$ Mol. wt. of the base   =   Eq. wt. of the base × Acidity

                           = $B \times n$

(F)   **Volumetric method for acids and bases**

This method is based on the following two facts.

(i)   Acids and bases always react with each other (*i.e.* neutralise) in equivalent proportions. Thus 1 litre on N-acid is equivalent to 1 litre of N-alkali.

(ii)   Since one litre of N solution of a substance contained 1 gm. equivalent of the substance, the amount of acid (or base) neutralised by one litre of N-alkali (or N-acid) would be the equivalent weight of the acid (base).

A known weight of the acid (or base) (say w g) is dissolved in water or alcohol and titrated against a standard alkali (or acid) solution (say N/10) using phenolphthalein as indicator. From the amount of the alkali (or acid) required to neutralise the acid (or base), the equivalent weight and hence molecular weight of the acid (or base) is calculated.

$$E = \frac{1000\,w}{NV}$$

Example 12 :

0.25 gm of a dibasic organic acid was dissolved in water and the volume was made to 100 ml., 10 ml. of this solution required 24.6 ml. of N/60 NaOH for neutralisation. Calculate the molecular weight of the acid.

Solution :

$$24.6 \text{ ml. of N/60 NaOH} \equiv 10 \text{ ml. of acid}$$

$$\therefore \quad 246 \text{ ml. of N/60 NaOH} \equiv 100 \text{ ml. of acid} \equiv 0.25 \text{ gm of acid}$$

$$\therefore \quad 1000 \text{ ml. of N/NaOH} = \frac{0.25}{246} \times \frac{60}{1} \times 1000$$

$$\therefore \quad \text{Eq. wt. of the acid} = \frac{0.25 \times 60 \times 1000}{246} = 60.97$$

$$\text{Hence} \quad \text{mol. wt. of the acid} = 60.97 \times 2 \text{ (basicity)} = \mathbf{121.94}$$

Example 13 :

0.184 gm of a diacid organic base required 25.6 ml. of N/8 sulphuric acid for complete neutralisation. Calculate the molecular weight of the base.

Solution :

$$25.6 \text{ ml. of N/8 H}_2\text{SO}_4 \equiv 0.184 \text{ gm of the base}$$

$$\therefore \quad 1000 \text{ ml. of N–H}_2\text{SO}_4 \equiv \frac{0.184}{25.6} \times \frac{8}{1} \times 1000 \text{ gm} = 57.5 \text{ gm.}$$

$$\therefore \quad \text{Eq. wt. of the base} = 57.5$$

$$\text{Hence,} \quad \text{Mol. wt. of the base} = 57.5 \times 2 \text{ (acidity)} = \mathbf{115.0}$$

---

3.   **Calculation of molecular formula.** *The formula which represents the actual number of atoms of various elements present in one molecule of the substance is termed as molecular formula.* It is either the same as the empirical formula of the substance or a simple multiple of it, *i.e.*

$$\text{Molecular formula} = (\text{Empirical formula})_n$$

Where n is a whole number and is the ratio between the molecular weight and the empirical formula weight of the substance, *i.e.*

$$n = \frac{\text{Molecular mass}}{\text{Empirical formula mass}}.$$

Example 14 :

Determine the empirical and molecular formula of dibasic acid from the following data.

(a)   **0.3192 gm of the acid gave on combustion 0.4224 gm of CO_2 and 0.512 gm of H_2O.**

(b)   **It contained 10.52% nitrogen.**

(c)   **The V.D. of its dimethyl ester is 80.50.**

Solution :

(a)   *Calculation of percentage composition*

$$\text{Percentage of C} = \frac{12}{44} \times \frac{0.4224}{0.3192} \times 100 = 36.09$$

$$\text{Percentage of H} = \frac{2}{18} \times \frac{0.512}{0.3192} \times 100 = 5.26$$

$$\text{Percentage of N (given)} = 10.52$$

$$\text{Percentage of O (by difference)} = 100 - (36.09 + 5.26 + 10.52) = 48.13$$

(b)   *Calculation of empirical formula*

Element	Percentage	At.wt.	Relative No. at atoms	Simplest ratio
C	36.09	12	36.09/12 = 3.008	3.008/0.751 = 4
H	5.26	1	5.26/1 = 5.26	5.26/0.751 = 7
N	10.52	14	10.52/14 = 0.751	0.751/0.751 = 1
O	48.13	16	48.13/16 = 3.008	3.008/0.751 = 4

Hence the empirical formula of the acid = $C_4H_7NO_4$

(c)   *Calculation of the molecular formula*

$$\text{Empirical formula wt. of the acid} = 48 + 7 + 14 + 64 = 133$$

$$\text{Mol.wt. of the dimethyl ester} = 2 \times \text{V.D.} = 2 \times 80.50 = 161$$

$$\text{Now let the dibasic acid in question} = R\,(COOH)_2$$

$$\therefore \text{ Its dimethyl ester is} = R(COOCH_3)_2$$

$$\text{Mol. wt. of the acid} = \text{Mol. wt. of ester} - \text{Wt. of two methyl } (CH_3) \text{ groups}$$
$$+ \text{ Wt. of two hydrogen (H) atoms}$$
$$= 161 - 2(3 + 12) + 2 = 133$$

$$\therefore \quad n \text{ (of acid)} = \frac{\text{Mol. wt.}}{\text{Empirical formula wt.}} = \frac{133}{133} = 1$$

$$\therefore \quad \text{Molecular formula of the acid} = \text{Empirical formula} \times n$$
$$= C_4H_7NO_4 \times 1 = \mathbf{C_4H_7NO_4}$$

TEST YOUR UNDERSTANDING - 24.3

1.   An 11.75 g sample of a hydrocarbon is volatilized at 1 atm pressure and 100°C to a gas that occupies 5.0 L. What is its molecular weight ? (R = 0.0821 L atm/mol K).

2.   Complete combustion of 0.858 g of compound X gives 2.63g of CO_2 and 1.28 g of H_2O. Find the percentage composition of X. What is the lowest molecular weight it can have ?

EXERCISE 24.1 (MCQ - ONE option correct)

1. In steam distillation of aniline, function of steam is
  (*a*) to increase the vapour pressure of the liquid to be distilled
  (*b*) to decrease the vapour pressure of the liquid to be distilled
  (*c*) to carry vapours of the liquid with it, it has nothing to do with the vapour pressure of the liquid
  (*d*) to dissolve the liquid due to high temperature

2. In steam distillation
  (*a*) the liquid to be distilled starts boiling at 373 K
  (*b*) the liquid to be distilled starts boiling above 373 K
  (*c*) the liquid to be distilled starts boiling below 373 K
  (*d*) any of the three temperatures.

3. Which of the following is not used for the purification of solid impurities ?
  (*a*) Distillation   (*b*) Sublimation
  (*c*) Crystallisation   (*d*) None of these.

4. Steam distillation is used for the extraction of
  (*a*) fatty acids   (*b*) mineral oils
  (*c*) essential oils   (*d*) higher alkanes.

5. A mixture of *o*-nitrophenol and *p*-nitrophenol can be separated by
  (*a*) sublimation   (*b*) steam distillation
  (*c*) fractional distillation   (*d*) fractional crystallisation.

6. Which of the following technique is most suitable for the purification of cyclohexanone from its mixture containing cyclohexane, benzoic acid and isoamyl alcohol as other components?
  (*a*) Crystallisation   (*b*) Sublimation
  (*c*) Chromatography   (*d*) None of the three

7. Gas chromatography is suitable for types of compounds which are
  (*a*) liquids
  (*b*) highly volatile
  (*c*) vaporised without decomposition
  (*d*) soluble in water

8. Diazo compounds, sometimes do not respond Lassaigne's test for nitrogen because
  (*a*) these are quite stable compounds and do not decompose to elemental nitrogen
  (*b*) these contain very little carbon
  (*c*) these form organometallic compounds with sodium
  (*d*) their nitrogen contents is removed, during heating, in the form of nitrogen gas

9. Sometimes, the colour observed in Lassaigne's test for nitrogen is green. It is because
  (*a*) of green colour of ferrous sulphate
  (*b*) ferric ferrocyanide is also green
  (*c*) of green colour of copper sulphate
  (*d*) of excess of Fe^{3+} ions whose yellow colour makes the blue colour of ferric ferrocyanide to appear green.

10. Which of the following compound will give white precipitate on heating with HNO_3 followed by addition of silver nitrate ?
  (*a*) $(C_2H_5)_3NHCl$ (*b*) 2, 4, 6-Trinitrochlorobenzene
  (*c*) Both (*a*) and (*b*)   (*d*) None.

11. Lassaigne's extract of thiourea, $SC(NH_2)_2$ is boiled with ferrous sulphate and then acidified with HCl, the colour of the resulting solution will be
  (*a*) prussian blue   (*b*) green
  (*c*) black   (*d*) red.

12. In an organic compound, sulphur can be estimated by
  (*a*) Carius method   (*b*) Messenger method
  (*c*) both   (*d*) Lasaisgne's method.

13. The best criteria for testing the purity of a solid organic compound is
  (*a*) melting point   (*b*) mixed melting point
  (*c*) both   (*d*) mixed boiling point.

14. The function of sodium during preparation of Lassaigne's extract is to
  (*a*) decrease the melting point of the compound
  (*b*) increase the ionisation of the compound
  (*c*) convert the covalent compound into ionic compounds
  (*d*) increase the reactivity of the compound.

15. Positive Beilstein test for halogens shows that
  (*a*) halogen is definitely present
  (*b*) a halogen may be present
  (*c*) a halogen is absent
  (*d*) none of these.

16. There is no direct test for the detection of which element in an organic compound ?
  (*a*) N   (*b*) S   (*c*) Cl   (*d*) O

17. One g of an organic nitrogen-containing compound, on heating, decomposes to give 0.2 g of nitrogen. What should be nature of the compound ?
  (*a*) $C_3H_7N_2Cl$ (*b*) $C_6H_5N_2Cl$
  (*c*) $(CH_3)_3N$ (*d*) Datas are insufficient.

18. It percentage of selenium (at. wt. = 78.4) in peroxidase anhydrase enzyme is 0.5% by weight, then the minimum molecular weight of the enzyme should be
  (*a*) 1.568×10^3 (*b*) 2.136×10^4
  (*c*) 1.568×10^4 (*d*) 2.136×10^3.

19. If two compounds have the same empirical formula but different molecular formulae, they must have
  (*a*) different percentage composition
  (*b*) different molecular mass
  (*c*) same vapour density
  (*d*) same viscosity.

20. Empirical formula of hydrocarbon containing 80% C and 20% H is
  (*a*) CH_4 (*b*) CH_3 (*c*) CH_2 (*d*) C_2H.

21. A hydrocarbon has 4 g carbon per g of hydrogen, it can be
  (*a*) CH_4 (*b*) C_2H_6 (*c*) C_2H_2 (*d*) C_2H_4.

22. The simplest ratio of number of C and H atoms in a hydrocarbon is found to be 1 and 2.37 respectively. The molecular weight for the hydrocarbon should be
  (*a*) 42   (*b*) 43   (*c*) 84   (*d*) 86

23. The empirical formula of a carboxylic acid is CH_2O_2, the probable molecular formula of the simplest acid may be
  (*a*) CH_2O (*b*) CH_2O_2 (*c*) $C_2H_4O_4$ (*d*) $C_3H_6O_6$.

24. *p*-Chloroaniline and anilinium hydrochloride can be distinguished by
  (*a*) Sandmeyer reaction   (*b*) $NaHCO_3$
  (*c*) $AgNO_3$ (*d*) Carbylamine test

25. If two compounds have the same empirical formula but different molecular fomulae they must have
  (a) different percentage composition
  (b) different molecular weight
  (c) same viscosity
  (d) same vapour density

EXERCISE 24.2 (MCQ 1 or >1 option correct, Passage based, Matching, A/R)

DIRECTIONS for Q. 1 to Q. 15 : Multiple choice questions with one or more than one correct option(s).

1. The boiling point of a compound depend upon
   (a) hydrogen bonding   (b) polarity of the molecule
   (c) size of the molecule   (d) its solubility in water.

2. Which of the following is true?
   (a) A liquid has same boiling point at all conditions
   (b) A liquid can be made to boil at a temperature lower than its usual boiling point
   (c) A liquid can be made to boil at a temperature higher than its usual boiling point
   (d) Steam distillation means distillation under reduced pressure

3. During steam distillation of a mixture of o-nitrophenol and p-nitrophenol, which of the statement is false
   (a) vapours of o-nitrophenol are carried by steam because of its lower boiling point due to chelation.
   (b) vapours of o-nitrophenols are carried by steam because of its lower boiling point and solubility in steam.
   (c) vapours of o-nitrophenol are carried by steam because its boiling point is reduced by steam.
   (d) vapours of p-nitrophenol are carried by steam because of its lower boiling point.

4. Simple distillation can't be used to separate
   (a) a mixture of ether (b.p. 308 K) & toluene (b.p. 383 K)
   (b) a mixture of benzene (b.p. 353 K) & thiophene (b.p. 357 K)
   (c) a mixture of ethyl alcohol (b.p. 351 K) & water (b.p. 373 K)
   (d) essential oils

5. A mixture of sugar and common salt can't be separated by
   (a) water   (b) alcohol
   (c) petroleum ether   (d) sublimation

6. Lassaigne's test for nitrogen is negative for which compound ?
   (a) NH_2OH (b) NH_2NH_2
   (c) H_2NCONH_2 (d) H_2NCSNH_2

7. Lassaigne's extract of p-nitrochlorobenzene is acidified with dil.HNO_3 and then treated with silver nitrate solution, the white precipitate formed is due to
   (a) AgCl   (b) AgCN
   (c) both (a) and (b)   (d) no white ppt. is obtained.

8. Carius method is reliable for the estimation of
   (a) Cl   (b) Br   (c) I   (d) S.

9. An organic compound is boiled with HNO_3, cooled and then treated with $AgNO_3$, a white precipitate is obtained. The compound can be

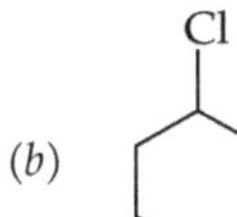

(d) $CH_3 - \overset{\overset{\displaystyle O}{\|}}{C} - Cl$

10. Which of the organic compound will give red colour in Lassaigne test :

(a) NaCNS   (b) $NH_2 - \overset{\overset{\displaystyle S}{\|}}{C} - NH_2$

(c) $NH_2 - \overset{\overset{\displaystyle O}{\|}}{C} - NH_2$ (d) H_2N-⟨○⟩$-SO_3Na$

11. Organic compound A $\xrightarrow{HNO_3 \,/\, AgNO_3}$ white ppt. A can be :
    (a) NH_4Cl
    (b) cyclohexene–Cl
    (c) ⟨○⟩–Cl
    (d) ⟨○⟩–CH_2Cl

12. Detection of the chlorine is possible without preparing sodium extract in :
    (a) O_2N-⟨○⟩$-Cl$ with NO_2 groups   (b) $CHCl_3$
    (c) ⟨○⟩$-CH_2Cl$ (d) $CH_2 = CH - CH_2Cl$

13. Which will give colour with $FeCl_3$?
    (a) cyclohexene–OH
    (b) $CH_3 - \overset{\overset{\displaystyle OH}{|}}{C} = CH - \overset{\overset{\displaystyle O}{\|}}{C} - OC_2H_5$
    (c) ⟨○⟩$-OH$
    (d) ⟨○⟩$-NH_2$

14. p-Chloroaniline and anilinium hydrochloride can be distinguished by
    (a) Sandmeyer reaction   (b) $NaHCO_3$
    (c) $AgNO_3$ (d) Carbylamine test

15. An organic compound is boiled with HNO_3, cooled and then treated with $AgNO_3$, a white precipitate is obtained. The compound can be

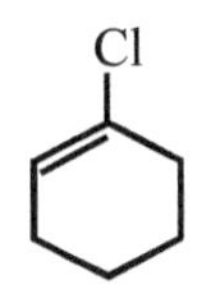 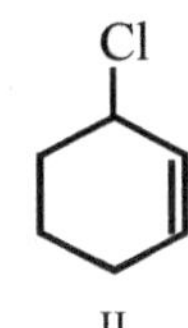 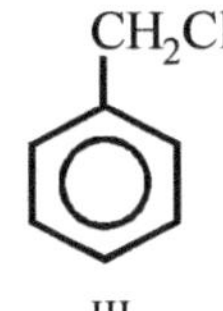

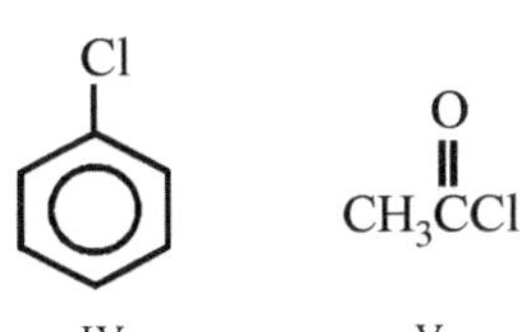

    (a) I, II, III or IV   (b) II, III or V
    (c) only V   (d) Any of the five

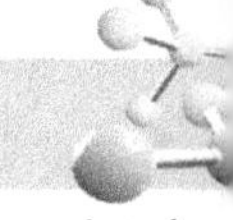

INSTRUCTION for Q. 16 to 27 : Read the passages given below and answer the questions that follow.

PASSAGE 1

In various scientific pursuits, it is important to be able to purify substances so that they can be better studied or better used. Common methods of separating substances are extraction, recrystalization, distillation, and chromatography. A mixture contains the three compounds shown in the table below

Solubility (g/100 mL)

		in H_2O	in ether
(i)	COOH ... NO_2	0.31	25.0
(ii)	NH_2 ... NO_2	0.11	5.5
(iii)	OH ... NO_2	3.02	106

16. The mixture is dissolved in a small amount of ether. To this is added an equal volume of 0.01 M HCl(aq). After shaking, two layers are formed: an aqueous layer and an ether layer. The layers are then separated. Which of the compounds will be found in the aqueous layer?
(a)   (i) only   (b)   (ii) only
(c)   (iii) only   (d)   (ii) and (iii)

17. To the ether layer is added an equal volume of 0.01 M NaOH(aq). Again, two layers are formed. After separating them, which of the compounds will be found in the aqueous layer?
(a)   (i) only   (b)   (iii) only
(c)   (i) and (iii)   (d)   (ii) and (iii)

18. This aqueous layer is evaporated to dryness leaving a solid residue of mass 0.31 g. Ten milliliters of aqueous acid of pH 3 are added. After stirring, the residue is smaller. What is the identity of the residue?
(a)   (i) only   (b)   (ii) only
(c)   (iii) only   (d)   (i) and (iii)

PASSAGE 2

Nitrogen, sulphur and halogens are tested from the sodium fusion extract of the organic compound, which is more commonly known as Lassaigne's extract. For preparing Lassaigne's extract, a small quantity of the organic compound is fused with sodium metal in a fusion tube. The red hot tube is broken in distilled water, boiled and filtered. The filtrate is known as Lassaigne's extract or sodium extract.

Generally, the Lassaigne's extract is alkaline in nature due to reaction of unreacted sodium with water

$$(2Na + 2H_2O \longrightarrow 2NaOH + H_2).$$

If it is not so, it is made alkaline by adding sodium hydroxide. Now the extract is boiled with ferrous sulphate solution, and the acidified with dil. H_2SO_4 or dil. HCl, appearance of green or blue colour confirms the presence of nitrogen.

Lassaigne's test for halogens. A small portion of the sodium fusion extract is acidified with dil. nitric acid and then treated with silver nitrate solution. If a precipitate is formed, it indicates the presence of a halogen; the colour of precipitate, in turn, indicates the nature of halogen.

19. Which of the following compound does not undergo Lassaigne's test for nitrogen?
(a)   Urea   (b)   Hydrazine
(c)   Methylamine   (d) p-Nitroaniline

20. Lassaigne's extract of an organic compound containing C, N, S and Cl is for tested for chlorine with $AgNO_3$, the precipitate formed will be of
(a)   AgCl   (b) Ag_2S
(c)   AgCN   (d)   All the three

21. The colour of precipitate in the above case will be
(a)   White   (b)   Black
(c)   Yellow   (d)   No precipitate

22. For testing chlorine in the Lassaigne's extract containing NaCN, Na_2S, and NaCl; the extract is first boiled with conc. HNO_3 and then treated with $AgNO_3$. What is the function of conc. HNO_3?
(a)   It dissolves the precipitate of Ag_2S and AgCN
(b)   It dissolves the white precipitate of AgCN
(c)   It dissolves the precipitate of AgCl
(d)   It decomposes NaCN and Na_2S

23. Lassaigne's extract, containing NaCN and Na_2S, when treated with ferric chloride generally gives blood red colour, indicating the presence of N and S (both) in the compound. However, sometimes the blood red colour does not appear, the reason being that
(a)   Sodium thiocyanate is not formed
(b)   The sodium thiocyanate is decomposed by means of sodium
(c)   The Fe^{3+} ions are deactivated
(d)   The ferric thiocyanate decomposes

PASSAGE 3

Characteristic reactions of some of the important groups are given below :

I.   Phenols and carboxylic acids are soluble in dil. NaOH, however only carboxylic acids are soluble in very diute (5%) aqueous $NaHCO_3$ solution with the evolution of CO_2 gas.

II.   Lower alcohols containing five or less carbon atoms react with Lucas reagent, while the higher alcohols do not react with the reagent.

III.   Aldehydes and ketones react with 2, 4 dinitrophenylhydrazine to give orange coloured crystals, however only aldehydes reduce Fehling solution.

IV.   Acetaldehyde gives yellow precipitate with alkaline iodine

$$CH_3 - \overset{\overset{\displaystyle O}{\|}}{C} - H \xrightarrow{\ I_2/OH^-\ } CHI_3\downarrow + HCOO^-$$

The following flow-sheet diagram was prepared on the basis of the above reactions.

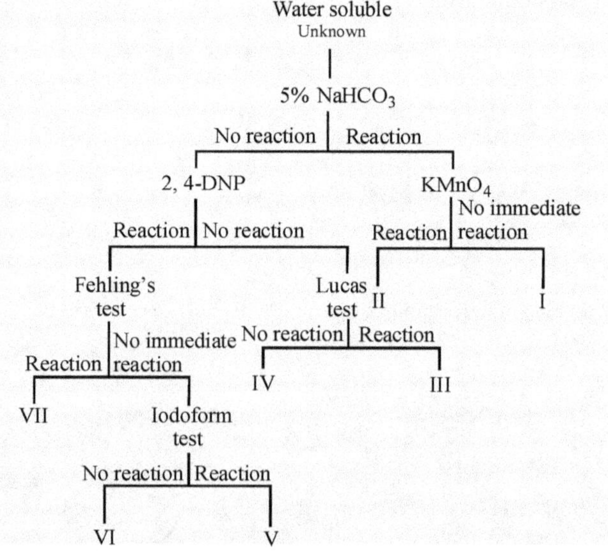

24. Compound II should have

   (a) $-COOH$ group   (b) an alcoholic group

   (c) Both (a) and (b)   (d) A phenolic $-OH$ group

25. Compound III is

   (a) C_6H_5OH (b) $C_6H_{11}OH$

   (c) C_2H_5OH (d) Any of the three

26. Which of the following compound can be an aldehyde?

   (a) V   (b) VI

   (c) VII   (d) IV

27. Compound V can be

   (a) CH_3CHO (b) CH_3COCH_3

   (c) $CH_2ICOC_2H_5$ (d) Any of the three

Instructions for Q. 28 to 34 : Following questions are Multiple Matching type Questions :

28.

Column - I	*Column - II*
(A) Acetoacetic ester	(a) Blue litmus test
(B) 2, 4, 6- trinitrophenol	(b) Evolves CO_2 with $NaHCO_3$ solution
(C) Fructose	(c) Reduces Tollen's reagent
(D) Acetone	(d) Forms 2, 4-DNP derivatives

29.

Column - I	*Column - II*
(A) Molisch test	(a) Glucose
(B) Tollen's reagent	(b) CH_3CHO
(C) Carbylamine test	(c) $C_6H_5NH_2$
(D) Reaction with $I_2 + NaOH$	(d) $CHCl_3$

30.

Column - I	*Column - II*
(A) Lassaigne's extract	(a) N-atom
(B) Sodium carbonate extract	(b) Halogen atom
(C) Beilstein's test	(c) Halide ion
(D) Chloroform test	(d) Sulphur atom

31.

Column - I	*Column - II*
(A) Lassaigne's test for detection	(a) C_6H_6
(B) Dumas method for estimation	(b) $C_6H_5NO_2$
(C) Kjeldahl's method for estimation	(c) Urea
(D) Liebig's method for estimation	(d) Pyridine

32.

Column - I	*Column - II*
(A) Baeyer's reagent	(a) Milkiness
(B) Lucas reagent	(b) Alk. $KMnO_4$
(C) Tollen's reagent	(c) Aldehydes
(D) Phenylhydrazine hydrochloride	(d) Fructose

33.

Column - I Mixture	*Column - II* Method applied for separation
(A) Glucose + Fructose	(a) Sodium bicarbonate solute
(B) Glucose + Benzoic acid	(b) Fractional distillation
(C) Iodine + Chlorine	(c) Sublimation
(D) Kerosene oil + Diesel oil	(d) Chromatography

34.

Column I	**Column II**
(A) $H_2\overset{\oplus}{N}-N\overset{\ominus}{H_3}\,Cl$	(p) sodium fusion extract of the compound gives Prussian blue colour with $FeSO_4$
(B) [structure: $HO-C_6H_4-CH(\overset{\oplus}{N}H_3\overset{\ominus}{I})-COOH$]	(q) gives positive $FeCl_3$ test
(C) [structure: $HO-C_6H_4-\overset{\oplus}{N}H_3\overset{\ominus}{Cl}$]	(r) gives white precipitate with $AgNO_3$
(D) [structure: $O_2N-C_6H_3(NO_2)-NH-\overset{\oplus}{N}H_3\overset{\ominus}{Br}$]	(s) reacts with aldehydes to form the corresponding hydrazone derivative

---

Instructions for Q. 35 to 37 : Following questions are Assertion and Reasoning Type Questions :

Note : Each question contains STATEMENT-1 (Assertion) and STATEMENT-2 (Reason). Each question has 5 choices (a), (b), (c), (d) and (e) out of which ONLY ONE is correct.

   (a) Statement-1 is True, Statement-2 is True; Statement-2 is a correct explanation for Statement-1.

   (b) Statement-1 is True, Statement-2 is True; Statement-2 is NOT a correct explanation for Statement-1.

   (c) Statement -1 is True, Statement-2 is False.

   (d) Statement -1 is False, Statement-2 is True.

   (e) Statement -1 is False, Statement-2 is False.

35. **Statement - 1 :** Aniline on reaction with $NaNO_2$ / HCl at $0^\circ C$ followed by coupling with β-naphthol gives a dark blue precipitate.

   and

   Statement - 2 : The colour of the compound formed in the reaction of aniline with $NaNO_2$/HCl at $0^\circ C$ followed by coupling with β-naphthol is due to the extended conjugation.

36. **Statement-1** : Duma's method is more applicable to nitrogen containing organic compounds than Kjeldahl's method.

   Statement-2 : Kjeldahl's method does not give satisfactory results for compounds in which nitrogen is linked to oxygen.

37. **Statement-1** : Diazonium salts do not respond Lassaigne's test for nitrogen.

   Statement-2 : Diazonium compounds lose N_2 on heating before they combine with sodium.

EXERCISE 24.3 (Subjective Problems)

1. How will you differentiate each of the following pair on the basis of their solubility?

  (a) 4-Chlorophenol and 4-chloro-1-methylbenzene

  (b) 4-Methylphenol and 2,4,6-trinitrophenol.

  (c) Phenol and 2,4-dinitrophenol.

  (d) $C_6H_5SO_2NHCH_3$ and $C_6H_5CONHCH_3$

  (e) 2-Hexanone and hexane

  (f) $CH_3CH_2NH_2$ and CH_3CONH_2

  (g) 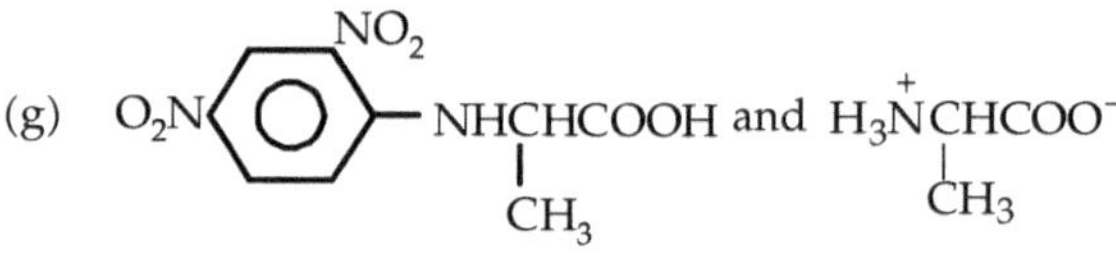

2. How will you distinguish between

  (a) toluene and cyclohexene with bromine

  (b) $(CH_3)_2CHOH$ and $(CH_3)_2CHSH$ by a chemical test

  (c) $(CH_3)_2C(OH)CH_2CH_3$ and $CH_3CH_2CH(OH)CH_2CH_3$ by a chemical test.

  (d) Cyclopentyl chloride and cyclopentanol by solubility test.

  (e) $CH_2=CHCH_2OH$ and $CH_3CH_2CH_2OH$ by Lucas test.

  (f) $(COOH)_2$ and $CH_2(COOH)_2$ by a chemical test.

  (g) $RCOCl$ and $RCOOH$ by aq. $AgNO_3$ test.

  (h) $(CH_3CO)_2O$ and $CH_3COOC_2H_5$ by a chemical test.

  (i) $C_6H_5SO_2NHCH_3$ and $C_6H_5CONHCH_3$ by NaOH.

  (j) 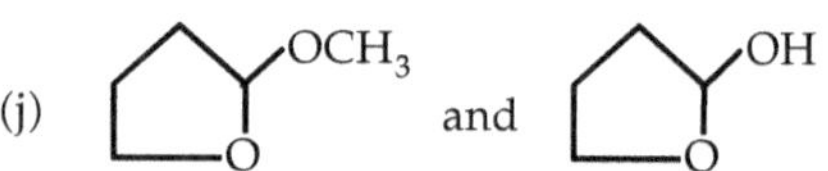

  (k) 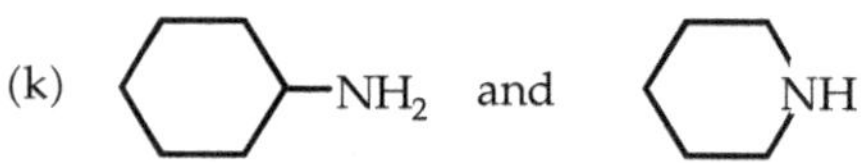

  (l) $(C_2H_5)_3N$ and $(C_2H_5)_2NH$

  (m) $(C_2H_5)_3N^+HCl$ and $(C_2H_5)_4N^+Cl^-$

  (n) $(C_2H_5)_4N^+Cl$ and $(C_2H_5)_4N^+OH^-$

3. What is hydroxamic acid test for esters?

4. Show the scheme to separate a mixture of organic compounds containing following components; benzyl alcohol, phenol, aniline and benzoic acid.

Hint: Treat the ether extract in the following sequence (i) with aq. HCl (for removing aniline), (ii) with aq. $NaHCO_3$ (for removing benzoic acid), and (iii) with aq. NaOH (for removing phenol). Finally benzyl alcohol will remain in ether.

5. 1.325 g sample of a fertilizer is treated in Kjeldahl's apparatus and the evolved ammonia gas is passed into 50 mL of 0.203 NH_2SO_4. The unused acid required 25.32 mL of 0.198 N NaOH. Calculate the percentage of nitrogen in the fertilizer.

6. Determine the molecular weight of the two given compounds from the following datas :

  (*a*) 0.369 g of a bromo derivative when vaporised occupied 67.2 mL at NTP.

  (*b*) 1.49 g of an organic compound gave 448 mL of vapour at STP.

7. An organic compound contains 69.4% C and 5.8% H ; 0.303 g of this compound was analysed for nitrogen, and the ammonia evolved was absorbed in 50 mL of 0.05 M sulphuric acid. The excess of acid required 25 mL of 0.1 M NaOH for neutralisation. Determine the empirical formula for the compound.

8. 0.450 g of an organic compound on ignition gives 0.905 g CO_2 and 0.185 g H_2O. 0.350 g of the same compound on boiling with HNO_3 and adding $AgNO_3$ solution gives 0.574 g of AgCl. If the vapour density of the compound is 87.5, what should be the molecular formula for the compound ?

9. The boiling point of the solution of 5.5 g of an organic compound, containing 42.86% C, 2.40% H, and 16.67% nitrogen, in 45 g of benzene is 1.84°C higher than that of pure benzene. If the molal boiling point elevation constant of benzene is 2.53 K kg mol^{-1}, what will be the molecular formula of the compound?

10. 0.1413 g of a monoacid organic base gave 0.3582 g CO_2 and 0.1904 g water ; 0.1237 g of the substance gave 17.85 mL of dry nitrogen at 27°C and 750 mm pressure. If the chloroplatinate of the base containing 33.4% platinum, determine the molecular formula of the base.

11. A dibasic organic acid gave the following results on analysis. (a) 0.236 g of the acid gave 0.352 g of CO_2 and 0.108 g of H_2O. (b) 0.177 g of acid required 30 mL of 0.1 N NaOH solution for complete neutralisation. Determine the molecular formula of the acid.

12. 0.4 g of a carboxylic acid on combustion gave 0.08 g of water and 0.39 g of CO_2. The silver salt of the acid weighing 1.0 g on ignition gave 0.71 g of silver. Determine the molecular formula of the acid.

13. An acid A contains 40%C, 5.1% H and rest oxygen. Its silver salt contains 65.1% silver. The ethyl ester of A has VD of 87. Determine the molecular formula for A.

14. A monobasic acid contains 68.8% C and 4.9% H. 0.610 g of the acid requires 25 mL of M/10 diacidic base for neutralisation. Determine the molecular formula of the acid.

15. 0.20 g of an organic compound, containing 60% C and 13.3% H, displaced 74.66 mL of air at NTP. Determine its molecular formula.

16. A monobasic acid gave following results.

  (*a*) 0.236 g of it gave 0.528 g CO_2 and 0.324 g water, an combustion.

  (*b*) In nitrogen determination, 0.295 g of it gave 56 mL of N_2 at NTP.

  (*c*) Its platinichloride contains 36.93 % platinum.

  Determine its molecular formula.

SOLUTIONS

EXERCISE 24.1

1	(b)	**6**	(c)	**11**	(d)	**16**	(d)	**21**	(b)
2	(c)	**7**	(c)	**12**	(c)	**17**	(b)	**22**	(d)
3	(d)	**8**	(d)	**13**	(b)	**18**	(c)	**23**	(b)
4	(c)	**9**	(d)	**14**	(c)	**19**	(b)	**24**	(c)
5	(b)	**10**	(c)	**15**	(b)	**20**	(b)	**25**	(b)

1, 2. In steam distillation of aniline, steam decreases vapour pressure of the liquid which in turn starts boiling below its usual boiling point. Hence steam distillation is considered analogous to distillation under reduced pressure.

3. All the three processes can be applied for the removal of solid impurities.

4. Essential oils are volatile, hence carried along with steam during steam distillation.

5. Steam distillation can be applied only when one of the components has b.p. less than bp. of water.

6. A mixture having more than two components can best be separated by chromatography.

7. Gas chromatography is suited for compounds which are not highly volatile and which form vapours without decomposition.

8. Since diazo compounds may lose nitrogen in the form of *nitrogen gas*, they sometimes do not respond Lassaigne's test for nitrogen.

9. Although blue coloured ferric ferrocyanide is formed but due to the presence of yellow coloured Fe^{3+} salts, the blue colour gives the shade of green.

10. $(C_2H_5)_3N^+HCl^-$ is an ionic compound, so it will form precipitate of $AgCl$ on adding $AgNO_3$. In 2, 4, 6-trinitro-chlorobenzene, —Cl is activated due to the presence of three —NO_2 groups in *o*- and *p*-positions, so it will be very reactive leading to formation of $AgCl$ on adding HNO_3 and $AgNO_3$.

11. Compounds having both N and S will form NaCNS leading to red coloured $Fe(CNS)_3$ during Lassaigne's test for nitrogen.

12. Sulphur can be estimated as $BaSO_4$ by Carius as well as Messenger method. In Messenger method, organic compound containing sulphur is heated (oxidised) with alkaline potassium permanganate to form sulphuric acid which is estimated as barium sulphate by adding barium chloride.

$$2KMnO_4 + 2KOH \longrightarrow 2K_2MnO_4 + H_2O + O$$

$$\underset{\text{Thiourea}}{H_2N\overset{\overset{S}{||}}{C}NH_2} + 4O + H_2O \longrightarrow H_2SO_4 + \underset{\text{Urea}}{H_2N\overset{\overset{O}{||}}{C}NH_2}$$

$$H_2SO_4 + BaCl_2 \longrightarrow BaSO_4 \downarrow + 2HCl$$

13. In mixed melting point, the sample whose purity is to be tested is mixed with the pure sample of the compound and the melting point of the mixture is determined, in case the melting point of the mixture is exactly same as the melting point of the pure sample, the compound in question is said to be pure, otherwise impure.

14. Fusion of the organic compound with Na converts organic compound into inorganic compounds.

15. A positive Beilstein's test for halogens does not always indicate the presence of halogen since some halogen free compounds *viz.* urea, thiourea, amides etc. also respond this test. The reason being the fact that these halogen free compounds form cuprous cyanide which is volatile and decomposes to copper which burns with green flame.

16. Oxygen is always detected indirectly, *i.e.* in the form of functional groups like —COOH, —CHO, —NO_2, —$CONH_2$ etc.

17. N-containing compound $\overset{\text{heat}}{\longrightarrow}$ N_2

$\quad$ 2 g $\qquad\qquad$ 0.4 g

0.4 g of N_2 is obtained from 2 g of compound

28 g of N_2 is obtained from $\dfrac{2}{0.4} \times 28 = 140$

Hence molecular weight of the compound is 140 which coincides with $C_6H_5N_2Cl$ (72 + 5 + 28 + 35.5 = 140.5).

18. 0.5 g of Se = 100 g of enzyme

78.4 g of Se = $\dfrac{100}{0.5} \times 78.4 = 1.568 \times 10^4$ g.

19. Molecular mass of a compound depends upon its molecular formula, hence when molecular formulae of the two compounds differ, they will have different molecular weights.

20. Ratio of C : H = $\dfrac{80}{12} : \dfrac{20}{1} = \dfrac{20}{3} : 20 = 1 : 3$

$\therefore$ Expirical formula = CH_3.

21. Ratio of C : H = 4 : 1 = $\dfrac{4}{12} : \dfrac{1}{1} = \dfrac{1}{3} : 1 = 1 : 3$

$\therefore$ Empirical formula = CH_3 or Molecular formula = C_2H_6.

22. Simplest ratio of C : H = 1 : 2.37 or 3 : 7

$\therefore$ Empirical formula = C_3H_7

But C_3H_7 does not coincide to any hydrocarbon ; remember that a hydrocarbon can't have odd number of H atoms. Hence the molecular formula for the hydrocarbon should be C_6H_{14} whose molecular weight will be 72 + 14 = 86.

23. A carboxylic acid should contain —COOH ; hence CH_2O_2 should coincide with H—COOH *i.e.* molecular formula and empirical formula for the simplest carboxylic acid is CH_2O_2.

EXERCISE 24.2

MCQ > 1	**1**	(a,b,c)	**2**	(b,c,d)	**3**	(b,c,d)	**4**	(b,c,d)	**5**	(a,c)
CORRECT	**6**	(a,b)	**7**	(a,b)	**8**	(a,b,d)	**9**	(b,c,d)	**10**	(b, d)
OPTION	**11**	(b, d)	**12**	(a, c, d)	**13**	(a, b, c)	**14**	(c)	**15**	(b)
PASSAGE 1	**16**	(d)	**17**	(a)	**18**	(a)				
PASSAGE 2	**19**	(b)	**20**	(d)	**21**	(b)	**22**	(d)	**23**	(b)
PASSAGE 3	**24**	(c)	**25**	(c)	**26**	(c)	**27**	(d)		
MATCH THE FOLLOWING	**28**	(A)-a, d ; (B)-a, b ; (C)-c, d ; (D) -d								
	29	(A) – a; (B) – a, b; (C) – c, d; (D) – b								
	30	(A) - a,b,c,d; (B) - c; (C) - b,c; (D) - b,c								
	31	(A) – b,d; (B) – b,c,d; (C) – b,c; (D) – a								
	32	(A) – b; (B) – a; (C) – c, d; (D) – c, d								
	33	(A)-d ; (B)-a, c ; (C)-c ; (D)-b								
	34	(A)-c, d ; (B)-a, b ; (C)-a, b, c ; (D)-a, d								
A/R	**35**	(d)	**36**	(b)	**37**	(a)				

1. Boiling point of a liquid has no concern with its solubility; however all the other three factors affect the boiling point of a compound.

2. A liquid has a constant boiling point at atmospheric pressure, however the boiling point of a liquid may be (*a*) decreased by boiling it under reduced pressure, or (*b*) increased by boiling it at pressure higher than atmospheric pressure. Steam reduce atmospheric pressure, hence can be regarded as distillation under reduced pressure.

3. Only *o*-nitrophenol is capable of forming intramolecular H-bonding (chelation) which leads to its lower b.p. (less than 100°C) and also lower solubility in water (steam), all other statements (b, c and d) are false.

4. Simple distillation is applied when boiling points of the two components differ by more than 10°C. Ethanol and water both are capable of forming intermolecular H-bonds with each other, so they distil together. The constituents of essential oils have nearly similar boiling point.

5. Sugar and water, both are soluble in water and both are insoluble in petroleum ether, hence these two solvents can't be used. On the other hand, sugar is soluble in alcohol while sodium chloride is insoluble, hence the two can be separated by alcohol. Sodium chloride undergoes sublimation.

6. Hydroxylamine and hydrazine, both do not have carbon, hence NaCN will not be formed in Lassaigne's extract leading to negative test for nitrogen.

7. Lassaigne's extract for the compound *p*- nitrochlorobenzene contains both NaCN as well as NaCl, so on treatment with $AgNO_3$, the extract gives precipitate of AgCN as well as AgCl unless it is boiled with HNO_3 which will remove NaCN as gaseous HCN.

8. Silver iodide is somewhat soluble in nitric acid.

9. Only compounds containing reactive chlorine, *i.e.* when attached to sp^3 hybrid carbon will react with $AgNO_3$ forming white precipitate of AgCl. Unreactive chlorine (chlorine attached to sp^2 C) can give positive reaction with $AgNO_3$ when the compound is first fused with metallic sodium.

$$CH_3COCl \xrightarrow{H_2O} CH_3COOH + HCl \xrightarrow{AgNO_3} AgCl \downarrow$$

14. **(c)** Anilinium hydrochloride has ionisable chlorine whereas chlorobenze has non ionizable chlorine. Thus anilium hydrochloride gives white precipitate of AgCl with $AgNO_3$.

$$C_6H_5NH_3^+Cl^- + AgNO_3 \rightarrow C_6H_5NH_3^+NO_3^- + AgCl \downarrow$$

In chloroaniline, –Cl is directly attached to benzene ring, hence it is non-reactive.

15. **(b)** Only compounds containing reactive chlorine, i.e. when attached to sp^3 hybrid carbon will react with $AgNO_3$ forming white precipitate of AgCl. Unreactive chlorine (chlorine attached to sp^2 C) can give positive reaction with $AgNO_3$ when the compound is first fused with metallic sodium.

$$CH_3COCl \xrightarrow{H_2O} CH_3COOH + HCl$$
$$\xrightarrow{AgNO_3} AgCl \downarrow$$

24. **(c)** Since the II is soluble in aq. $NaHCO_3$ and oxidised by $KMnO_4$, it should have a $-COOH$ group and an alcoholic group ($1°$ or $2°$).

25. **(c)** Compound III reacts with Lucas reagent, so it should be an alcohol with less than six carbon atoms.

26. **(c)** Among the three given options, Fehling test is given only by VII.

27. **(d)** From the flow-sheet diagram, it is evident that compound V undergoes iodoform reaction. Since all the three compounds can undergo iodoform reaction, all the three options are correct.

$$ICH_2 - \overset{\overset{\displaystyle O}{\|}}{C} - CH_2CH_3 \xrightarrow{I_2} I_3C - \overset{\overset{\displaystyle O}{\|}}{C} - CH_2CH_3$$

$$\xrightarrow{OH^-} CHI_3 \downarrow + CH_3CH_2COO^-$$

34. (A) - r, s; (B) - p, q; (C) - p, q, r;   (D) - p, s
compound (A) does not have carbon, hence does not responds (*p*) test.

35. **(d)** The colour of the azo dye formed will be orange red but not blue. However, the colour of dye can said to be due to extended conjugation due to presence of azo group.

EXERCISE 24.3

1. (a) Only 4-chlorophenol is soluble in aqueous sodium hydroxide

   (b) 2,4,6-Trinitrophenol is exceptionally stronger acid and thus soluble in aq. $NaHCO_3$

   (c) Only 2, 4-dinitrophenol is soluble in aq. $NaHCO_3$

   (d) $C_6H_5SO_2NH\,CH_3$ is soluble in aq. NaOH, while in $C_6H_5CONHCH_3$, N is not acidic enough to dissolve in NaOH. Observe the structure of the conjugate base of the two compounds.

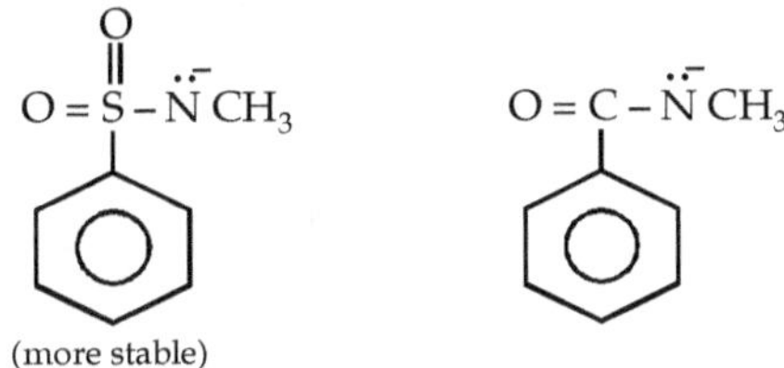

   (more stable)

   (e) Hexane is soluble in conc. H_2SO_4

   (f) $CH_3CH_2NH_2$ is soluble in dil. acids.

   (g)

   Insoluble in aq. HCl
   (2, 4-dinitrophenyl group
   reduces basic character of the –NH group)

   soluble in HCl

2. (a) Toluene reacts with bromine to evolve HBr, while no HBr is evolved in case of cyclohexene. Thus if the reaction is performed in organic solvent, bubbles of HBr can be observed, further the escaping HBr gas will react with moist air forming a cloud. In case, the reaction is performed in water, the HBr (now in the form of acid) can be tested by adding moist litmus paper.

   (b) Thiols give a precipitate with heavy cations like Hg^{2+}, Pb^{2+} and Cu^{2+}.

   (c) The 2° ROH is oxidized by a Cr (VI) reagent, thus changing its colour from orange to green.

   (d) Conc. H_2SO_4 dissolves the alcohol with the evolution of heat. In case of chloride, two different layers will be formed on addition of conc. H_2SO_4.

   (e) Allyl alcohol, although a 1° alcohol, behaves like 3° alcohol because its carbocation (allyl cation) is as stable as 3° cations, hence it will react as fast as 3° alcohols, while propanol will not react with Lucas reagent.

   (f) Oxalic acid is oxidised by acidic $KMnO_4$, thus it discharges $KMnO_4$ solution.

   (g) $RCOCl \xrightarrow{H_2O} RCOOH + HCl$; $HCl \xrightarrow{AgNO_3}$ $AgCl\downarrow$; $RCOOH \xrightarrow{AgNO_3} RCOOAg\downarrow$;
   Insoluble in HNO_3 ; Soluble in HNO_3

   (h) $(CH_3CO)_2O \xrightarrow[\text{warm}]{H_2O}$ CH_3COOH ; $CH_3COOC_2H_5 \xrightarrow[\text{warm}]{H_2O}$ No reaction
   turns blue litmus red

   (i) $C_6H_5SO_2NHCH_3$ is more acidic, hence it dissolves easily in NaOH than $C_6H_5CONHCH_3$.

   (j)

   An acetal ; Hemiacetal (positive test with Tollen's reagent)

   (k) $-NH_2 + C_6H_5SO_2Cl \xrightarrow{KOH} -\overset{\ominus}{N}\overset{K^{\oplus}}{SO_2C_6H_5} \xrightarrow{H_3O^+} -NH\,SO_2\,C_6H_5$
   Hinsberg reagent ; (soluble) ; precipitate

   $>NH + C_6H_5SO_2Cl \xrightarrow{KOH} >N\,SO_2C_6H_5 \xrightarrow{H_3O^+}$ Precipitate
   precipitate

   (l) $(C_2H_5)_2NH$ responds Hinsberg test, while $(C_2H_5)_3N$ does not respond Hinsberg test.

   (m) $(C_2H_5)_3N^+\,HCl + NaOH(aq.) \longrightarrow (C_2H_5)_3N$
   water insoluble

   $\underbrace{(C_2H_5)_4N^+\,Cl^- + NaOH^-(aq.)}_{\text{solution}} \longrightarrow$ No reaction

(n) $(C_2H_5)_4N^+ Cl^- + H_2O \longrightarrow \underbrace{(C_2H_5)_4N^+ OH^- + HCl}_{\text{neutral}}$

$\underbrace{(C_2H_5)_4N^+ OH^- + H_2O}_{\text{basic solution}} \longrightarrow$ No reaction

3. An ester when treated with NH_2OH gives a hydroxamic acid (RCONHOH) which produces a red-violet colour with $FeCl_3$.

$$R-\overset{\overset{\displaystyle O}{\|}}{C}-OR' + H_2NOH \longrightarrow \underset{\text{Hydroxamic acid}}{R-\overset{\overset{\displaystyle O}{\|}}{C}-NHOH} + R'OH$$

Anhydrides also respond this test.

5. Meq of unused acid   = Meq of NaOH = $25.32 \times 0.198 = 5$ meq
No. of meq of acid taken   = $50 \times 0.230 = 10.15$ meq
Meq of acid used   = $10.15 - 5 = 5.15$ meq
or 1.325 g of sample of the fertilizer = 5.15 mL of 1 NH_2SO_4
According to Kjeldahl's method

$$\% \text{ of nitrogen} = \frac{1.4 \times \text{Normality of acid} \times \text{Vol. of acid used (mL)}}{\text{Wt. of compound}} = \frac{1.4 \times 1 \times 5.15}{1.325} = \mathbf{5.44\%}$$

6. (*a*)   67.2 mL of compound at NTP   = 0.369 g

$$22400 \text{ mL of compound} = \frac{0.369 \times 22400}{67.2} = 123 \text{ g}$$

Mol. wt of the bromo derivative   = 123

(*b*)   448 mL of vapour at STP are obtained from 1.49 g

$$22400 \text{ mL of vapour at STP} = \frac{1.49}{448} \times 22400 = \mathbf{74.5 \text{ g}}$$

∴   Mol. wt. of the compound   = 74.5.

7. *Calculation of % of N.*

50 mL of 0.05 M H_2SO_4 = 50 mL of 0.1 NH_2SO_4 ($\because$ $N_{H_2SO_4} = 2 \times M_{H_2SO_4}$)
Excess of acid requires 25 mL of 0.1 M or 0.1 N NaOH   ($\because$ $N_{NaOH} = M_{NaOH}$)
25 mL of 0.1 N NaOH = 25 mL of 0.1 N H_2SO_4
Vol. of 0.1 N H_2SO_4 used for the neutralisation of NH_3 = 50 − 25 = 25 mL

$$\therefore \quad \% \text{ of nitrogen} = \frac{1.4 \times \text{Normality of acid} \times \text{Vol. of acid}}{\text{Wt. of compound}} = \frac{1.4 \times 0.1 \times 25}{0.303} = 11.55\%$$

Hence % of O = 100 − (69.4 + 5.8 + 11.55) = 13.25
Calculation of empirical formula of the compound

Element	Percentage	Relative No. of atoms	Simplest ratio
C	69.4	69.4/12 = 5.8	5.8/0.825 = 7
H	5.8	5.8/1 = 5.8	5.8/0.825 = 7
N	11.55	11.55/14 = 0.825	0.825/0.825 = 1
O	13.25	13.25/16 = 0.825	0.825/0.825 = 1

Thus the empirical formula of the compound = C_7H_7NO.

8. $\% \text{ of C} = \dfrac{12}{44} \times \dfrac{0.905}{0.450} \times 100 = 54.85$

$\% \text{ of H} = \dfrac{2}{18} \times \dfrac{0.185}{0.450} \times 100 = 4.58$

$\% \text{ of Cl} = \dfrac{35.5}{143.5} \times \dfrac{0.574}{0.350} \times 100 = 40.57$

Since the sum of the three % is 100, the compound does not contain any oxygen.
Determination of empirical formula

Element	Percentage	Relative No. of atoms	Simplest ratio
C	54.85	54.85/12 = 4	4/1 = 4
H	4.58	4.58/1 ≈ 4	4/1 = 4
Cl	40.57	40.57/35.5 = 1	1/1 = 1

∴   Empirical formula of the compound = C_4H_4Cl

$$n = \frac{87.5 \times 2}{48 + 4 + 35.5} = \frac{175}{87.5} = 2$$

Thus, molecular formula   = $(C_4H_4Cl)_2 = C_8H_8Cl_2$

9. *Determination of molecular formula*

Element	Percentage	Relative No. of atoms	Simplest ratio
C	42.86	$42.86/12 = 3.57$	$3.57/1.19 = 3$
H	2.40	$2.40/1 = 2.40$	$2.40/1.19 = 2$
N	16.67	$16.67/14 = 1.19$	$1.19/1.19 = 1$
O	38.07	$38.07/16 = 2.38$	$2.38/1.19 = 2$

Thus empirical formula of the compound $= C_3H_2NO_2$

$$\text{Empirical formula weight} = 36 + 2 + 14 + 32 = 84$$

$$\text{Determination of molecular weight} = \frac{K_b \times \omega \times 1000}{\Delta T \times W} = \frac{2.53 \times 5.5 \times 1000}{1.84 \times 45} = 168$$

$$\text{Hence molecular formula} = (C_3H_2NO_2)_2 \qquad (\because \ n = 168/84 = 2)$$
$$= C_6H_4N_2O_4$$

10. Conversion of given volume of N_2 at given conditions to NTP

$$V_2 = \frac{P_1V_1 \times T_2}{T_1 \times P_2} = \frac{17.85 \times 750 \times 273}{300 \times 760} = 16.03 \text{ mL}$$

$$\% \text{ of nitrogen} = \frac{28 \times \text{Vol. of nitorgen at NTP} \times 100}{22400 \times \text{Wt. of compound}} = \frac{28 \times 16.03 \times 100}{22400 \times 0.1237} = 16.198$$

$$\% \text{ of carbon} = \frac{12}{44} \times \frac{0.3582}{0.1413} \times 100$$

$$\% \text{ of hydrogen} = \frac{2}{18} \times \frac{0.1904}{0.1413} \times 100$$

By usual calculations, as above, empirical formula of the compound is found to be $C_5H_{13}N$

Determination of the molecular weight of the organic base.

$$\frac{\text{Mol. Wt. of chloroplatinate } (B_2PtCl_6)}{\text{At. Wt. of platinum}} = \frac{\text{Wt. of chloroplatinate}}{\text{Wt. of platinum}}$$

$$\frac{2B + 410}{195} = \frac{100}{33.4}$$

$$2B = \left(\frac{100}{33.4} \times 195\right) - 410 = 173.8$$

$$B = 86.9 \qquad \text{(where B is the eq. Wt. of the base)}$$

$$\text{Hence Mol. Wt. of the monoacidic base} = 86.9 \times 1 = 86.9$$

$$\therefore \quad \text{Molecular formula} = \frac{\text{Mol. Wt.}}{\text{Emp. formula Wt.}} \times \text{Empirical formula} = \frac{86.9}{86.9} \times C_5H_{13}N = C_5H_{13}N$$

11.
$$\% \text{ of C} = \frac{12}{44} \times \frac{0.352}{0.236} \times 100 = 27.05$$

$$\% \text{ of H} = \frac{2}{18} \times \frac{0.108}{0.236} \times 100 = 5.08$$

$\% \text{ of O} = 100 - (27.05 + 5.08) = 67.87$

As usual and in above examples, empirical formula of the compound $= C_2H_3O_2$

Calculation of molecular weight of the compound

$$30.0 \text{ mL of } 0.1 \text{ N NaOH} = 0.177 \text{ g of acid}$$

$$1000 \text{ mL of } 1 \text{ N NaOH} = \frac{0.177}{30} \times \frac{1000 \times 1}{0.1} = 59 \text{ g}$$

$\therefore \ \text{Eq. Wt. of the acid} = 59$

$\text{Mol. Wt. of the dibasic acid} = \text{Eq. Wt.} \times 2 = 59 \times 2 = 118$

$$\% \text{ Mol formula} = \frac{118}{59} \times C_2H_3O_2 = C_4H_6O_4.$$

12. % of C = $\dfrac{12}{44} \times \dfrac{0.08}{0.40} \times 100 = 2.22$

% of H = $\dfrac{2}{18} \times \dfrac{0.39}{0.40} \times 100 = 27.30$

% of O = $100 - (2.22 + 27.30) = 71.48$

By usual calculations, empirical formula of the acid is found to be CHO_2

Determination of molecular weight

$$\text{Eq. Wt. of acid} = \frac{\text{Wt. of silver salt} \times 108}{\text{Wt. of silver}} - 107 = \left(\frac{1.0}{0.71} \times 108\right) - 107 = 45$$

Mol. Wt. of the diabasic acid $= 45 \times 2 = 90$

$$\text{Mol. formula of the acid} = \frac{\text{Mol. Wt.}}{\text{Empirical formula Wt.}} \times \text{Empirical formula} = \frac{90}{45} \times CHO_2 = C_2H_2O_4$$

13. By usual calculations, empirical formula of the acid $A = C_2H_3O_2$

$$\text{Eq. Wt. of acid A} = \frac{\text{Wt. of Ag salt} \times 108}{\text{Wt. of Ag}} - 107 = \frac{100 \times 108}{65.1} - 107 = 59$$

Molecular weight of the ethyl ester of the acid $= 2 \times 87 = 174$

Determination of molecular weight of the acid

Let the acid is monobasic, RCOOH, then the molecular weight of its ethyl ester ($RCOOC_2H_5$)

$$= RCOOH - H + C_2H_5 = 59 - 1 + 29 = 87$$

Thus the acid is not monobasic, now let it be dibasic, then the molecular weight of its ester

$$= (RCOOH)_2 - 2H + 2\,C_2H_5 = (59)2 - 2 + 2\,(29) = 118 - 2 + 58 = 174$$

Thus the acid is diabasic acid.

Hence its molecular formula $=$ Empirical formula $\times$ Basicity $= C_2H_3O_2 \times 2 = C_4H_6O_4.$

14. Empirical formula of the acid from given percentages $= C_7H_6O_2$

Mol. Wt. of the acid

25 mL of $\dfrac{M}{10}$ diacidic base $=$ 25 mL of $\dfrac{2N}{10}$ or $\dfrac{N}{5}$ or 0.2 N diacidic base

$$\text{Eq. Wt. of acid} = \frac{\text{Wt. of organic acid} \times 1000}{\text{Vol. of base required} \times \text{Normality of base}} = \frac{0.610 \times 1000}{25 \times 0.2} = 122$$

$\therefore$ Mol. Wt. of acid $=$ Eq. wt $\times$ Basicity $= 122 \times 1 = 122$

$\therefore$ Mol. formula of the acid $= \left(\dfrac{122}{84 + 6 + 32}\right) \times C_7H_6O_2 = C_7H_6O_2$

15. By usual calculations, empirical formula of the compound $= C_3H_8O$

Determination of molecular weight

$$\text{Mol. wt. of volatile compound} = \frac{\text{Wt. of compound} \times 22400}{\text{Vol. of air displaced at NTP}} = \frac{0.20 \times 22400}{74.66} = 60$$

$$\text{Molecular formula of the compound} = \frac{60}{36 + 8 + 16} \times C_3H_8O = C_3H_8O$$

16. Empirical formula calculated from percentage of elements $= C_3H_9N$

Determination of molecular weight

$$\frac{\text{Mol. Wt. of chloroplatinate } (B_2H_2PtCl_6)}{\text{At. Wt. of platinum}} = \frac{\text{Wt. of chloroplatinate}}{\text{Wt. of platinum}}$$

$$\frac{2B + 410}{195} = \frac{100}{36.93}$$

$$2B = \left(\frac{100}{36.93} \times 195\right) - 410 = 118.06$$

$$B = 59.03 \text{ (B is eq. Wt. of the base)}$$

$\therefore$ Mol. wt. of the monoacidic base $= 59 \times 1 = 59$

$$\text{Hence, molecular formula of the base} = \frac{59}{36 + 9 + 14} \times C_3H_9N = C_3H_9N$$

AMINES AND BIOMOLECULES

MCQs with One Correct Answer

1. On complete hydrogenation, natural rubber produces
    (a) ethylene–propylene copolymer   **[JEE Adv. 2016]**
    (b) vulcanised rubber
    (c) polypropylene
    (d) polybutylene

2. The major product of the following reaction is

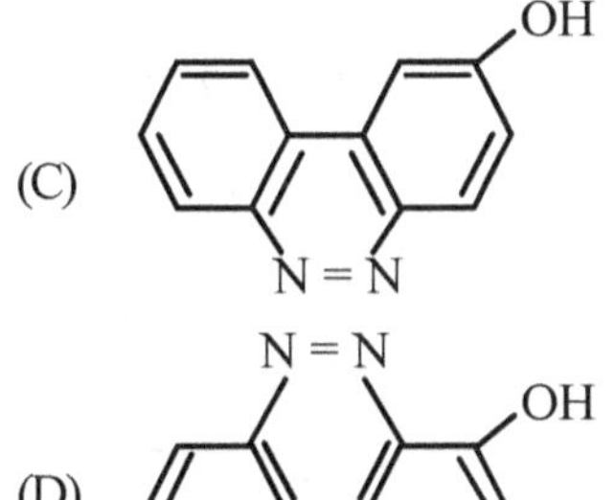

[JEE Adv. 2017]

(A)

(B)

(C)

(D)

3. The order of basicity among the following compounds is
[JEE Adv. 2017]

I   II   III   IV

    (A) II > I > IV > III   (B) IV > II > III > I
    (C) IV > I > II > III   (D) I > IV > III > II

MCQs with One or More Than One Correct

1. Hydrogen bonding plays a central role in the following phenomena   **[JEE Adv. 2014]**
    (a) Ice floats in water
    (b) Higher Lewis basicity of primary amines than tertiary amines in aqueous solutions
    (c) Formic acid is more acidic than acetic acid
    (d) Dimerisation of acetic acid in benzene

2. In the reaction shown below, the major product(s) formed is/are   **[JEE Adv. 2014]**

(a)   + CH$_3$COOH

(b)   + CH$_3$COOH

(c)   + H$_2$O

(d)

3. The major product of the reaction is   **[JEE Adv. 2015]**

(a)   (b)

(c)   (d)

4. In the following reactions, the major product W is

$$\text{C}_6\text{H}_5\text{NH}_2 \xrightarrow[\text{0°C}]{\text{NaNO}_2\,,\;\text{HCl}} \text{V} \xrightarrow{\text{2-naphthol}\,,\;\text{NaOH}} \text{W}$$

[JEE Adv. 2015]

(a) 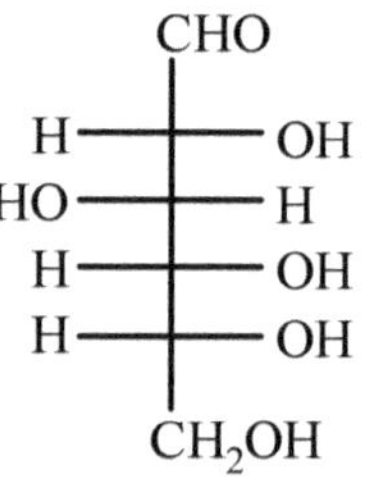

(b)

(c)

(d)

5. In the following reactions, the product S is **[JEE Adv. 2015]**

$$\text{(methylindene)} \xrightarrow[\text{ii. Zn, H}_2\text{O}]{\text{i. O}_3} \text{R} \xrightarrow{\text{NH}_3} \text{S}$$

(a)

(b)

(c)

(d)

6. The product(s) of the following reaction sequence is(are)

[JEE Adv. 2016]

NH_2

(i) Acetic anhydride/pyridine
(ii) KBrO_3/HBr
(iii) H_3O^+, heat
(iv) NaNO_2/HCl, 273-278 K
(v) Cu/HBr

(a) (1,3-dibromobenzene)

(b) (1,4-dibromobenzene)

(c) (1,2,3-tribromobenzene)

(d) (1,2,3,5-tetrabromobenzene)

7. The structure of D-(+)-glucose is **[JEE Adv. 2015]**

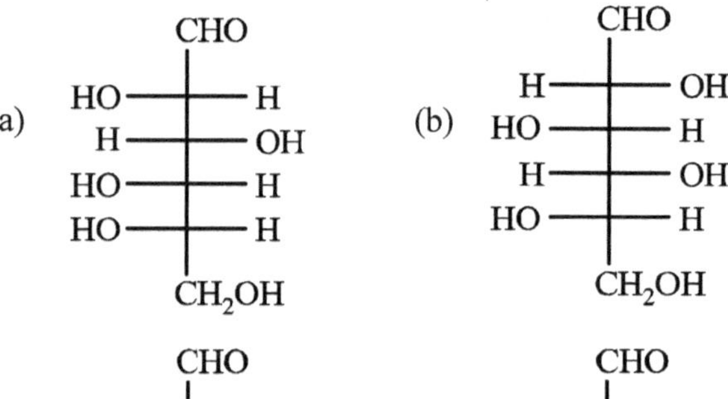

The structure of L-(−)-glucose is

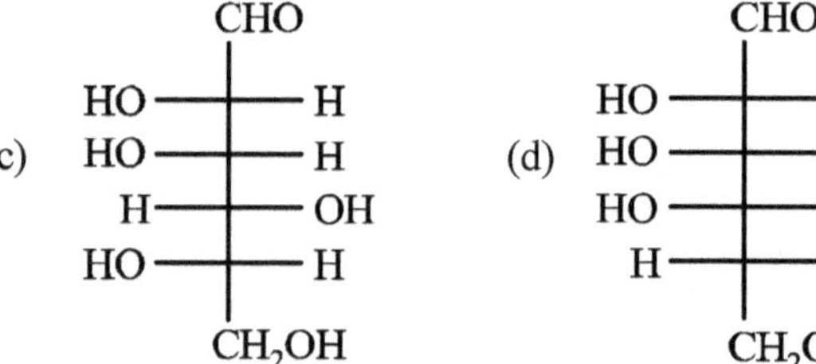

8. For 'invert sugar', the correct statement(s) is(are)
(Given : specific rotations of (+) -sucrose, (+)-maltose, L-(-)-glucose and L-(+) fructose in aqueous solution are + 66°, +140°, −52° and +92°, respectively) **[JEE Adv. 2016]**

(a) 'invert sugar' is prepared by acid catalyzed hydrolysis of maltose

(b) 'invert sugar' is an equimolar mixture of D-(+)-glucose and D-(-)-fructose

(c) specific rotation of 'invert sugar' is −20°

(d) on reaction with Br_2 water, 'invert sugar' forms saccharic acid as one of the products

Match the following

DIRECTIONS (Q. No. 2) : Match the four starting materials **(P, Q, R, S)** given in **List-I** with the corresponding reaction schemes **(I, II, III, IV)** provided in **List-II** and select the correct answer using the code given below the lists.

1.   **List - I**   **List - II**   [JEE Adv. 2014]

P.   H$-\!\!\equiv\!\!-$H   1.   **Scheme I**

(i) $KMnO_4$, $HO^{\ominus}$, heat (ii) $H^{\oplus}$, H_2O
(iii) $SOCl_2$ (iv) NH_3 ? $\longrightarrow C_7H_6N_2O_3$

Q.   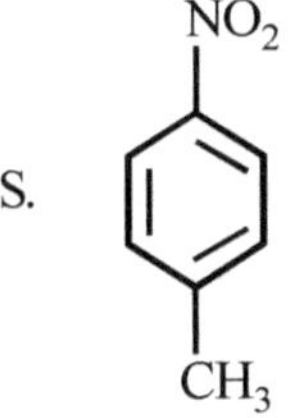   2.   **Scheme II**

(ii) Sn/HCl (ii) CH_3COCl (iii) conc. H_2SO_4 (iv) HNO_3 (v) dil. H_2SO_4,

heat (vi) $HO^{\ominus}$? $\longrightarrow C_6H_6N_2O_2$

R.   3.   **Scheme III**

(i) red hot iron, 873 K (ii) fuming HNO_3, H_2SO_4, heat
(iii) $H_2S.NH_3$ (iv) $NaNO_2$, H_2SO_4 (v) hydrolysis
? $\longrightarrow C_6H_5NO_3$

S.   4.   **Scheme IV**

(i) conc. H_2SO_4, 60°C
(ii) conc. HNO_3, conc. H_2SO_4
(iii) dil. H_2SO_4, heat ? $\longrightarrow C_6H_5NO_4$

Code:

	P	Q	R	S			P	Q	R	S
(a)	1	4	2	3		(b)	3	1	4	2
(c)	3	4	2	1		(d)	4	1	3	2

Comprehension Based Questions

PASSAGE - 1

Treatment of compound O with $KMnO_4/H^+$ gave P, which on heating with ammonia gave Q. The compound Q on treatment with $Br_2/NaOH$ produced R. On strong heating, Q gave S, which on further treatment with ethyl 2-bromopropanoate in the presence of KOH followed by acidification, gave a compound T.

[JEE Adv. 2016]

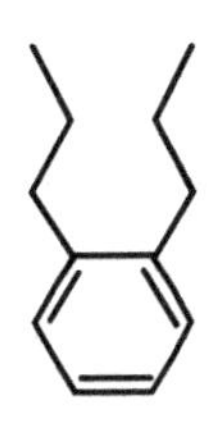

(O)

1.   The compound R is

(a) 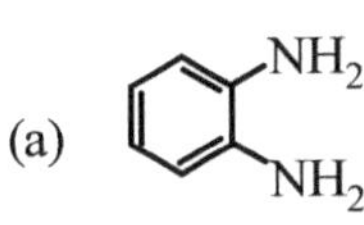   (b) 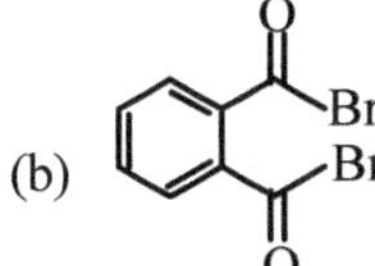

(c) 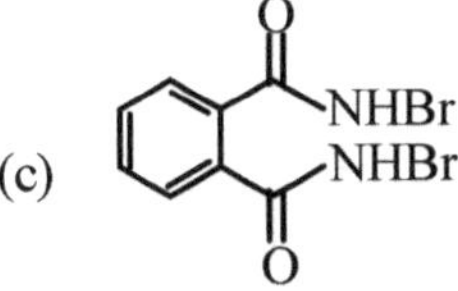   (d) 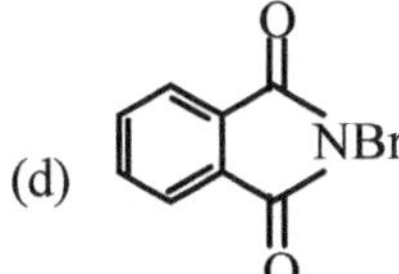

2.   The compound T is
(a)   glycine   (b)   alanine
(c)   valine   (d)   serine

Integer Value Correct Type

1. A tetrapeptide has —COOH group on alanine. This produces glycine (Gly), valine (Val), phenyl alanine (Phe) and alanine (Ala), on complete hydrolysis. For this tetrapeptide, the number of possible sequences (primary structures) with — NH_2 group attached to a chiral center is **[JEE Adv. 2013]**

2. The total number of *distinct naturally occurring amino acids* obtained by complete acidic hydrolysis of the peptide shown below is **[JEE Adv. 2014]**

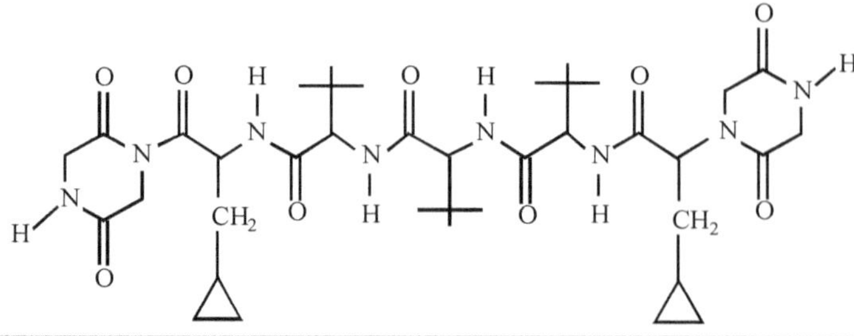

1. A compound with molecular mass 180 is acylated with CH_3COCl to get a compound with molecular mass 390. The number of amino groups present per molecule of the former compound is : **[JEE M 2013]**

  (a) 2

  (b) 5

  (c) 4

  (d) 6

2. An organic compound A upon reacting with NH_3 gives B. On heating B gives C. C in presence of KOH reacts with Br_2 to given $CH_3CH_2NH_2$. A is : **[JEE M 2013]**

  (a) CH_3COOH

  (b) $CH_3CH_2CH_2COOH$

  (c) $CH_3 - \underset{\underset{CH_3}{|}}{CH} - COOH$

  (d) CH_3CH_2COOH

3. The gas leaked from a storage tank of the Union Carbide plant in Bhopal gas tragedy was : **[JEE M 2013]**

  (a) Methyl isocyanate

  (b) Methylamine

  (c) Ammonia

  (d) Phosgene

4. On heating an aliphatic primary amine with chloroform and ethanolic potassium hydroxide, the organic compound formed is: **[JEE M 2014]**

  (a) an alkanol

  (b) an alkanediol

  (c) an alkyl cyanide

  (d) an alkyl isocyanide

5. Considering the basic strength of amines in aqueous solution, which one has the smallest pK_b value? **[JEE M 2014]**

  (a) $(CH_3)_2NH$

  (b) CH_3NH_2

  (c) $(CH_3)_3N$

  (d) $C_6H_5NH_2$

6. In the reaction **[JEE M 2015]**

$$NH_2-C_6H_4-CH_3 \xrightarrow[0-5°C]{NaNO_2/HCl} D \xrightarrow[\Delta]{CuCN/KCN} E + N_2$$

the product E is :

(a) CN — benzene ring with CH_3

(b) CH_3 — benzene ring

(c) COOH — benzene ring with CH_3

(d) H_3C — ring — ring — CH_3

7. In the Hofmann bromamide degradation reaction, the number of moles of NaOH and Br_2 used per mole of amine produced are : **[JEE M 2016]**

  (a) Two moles of NaOH and two moles of Br_2.

  (b) Four moles of NaOH and one mole of Br_2.

  (c) One mole of NaOH and one mole of Br_2.

  (d) Four moles of NaOH and two moles of Br_2.

8. Synthesis of each molecule of glucose in photosynthesis involves : **[JEE M 2013]**

  (a) 18 molecules of ATP

  (b) 10 molecules of ATP

  (c) 8 molecules of ATP

  (d) 6 molecules of ATP

9. Which one is classified as a condensation polymer? **[JEE M 2014]**

  (a) Dacron

  (b) Neoprene

  (c) Teflon

  (d) Acrylonitrile

10. Which one of the following bases is **not** present in DNA? **[JEE M 2014]**

  (a) Quinoline

  (b) Adenine

  (c) Cytosine

  (d) Thymine

11. Which of the vitamins given below is water soluble ? **[JEE M 2015]**

  (a) Vitamin E

  (b) Vitamin K

  (c) Vitamin C

  (d) Vitamin D

12. Which of the following compounds is not an antacid ?

[JEE M 2015]

(a) Phenelzine (b) Ranitidine

(c) Aluminium hydroxide (d) Cimetidine

13. Which polymer is used in the manufacture of paints and lacquers ? **[JEE M 2015]**

(a) Polypropene (b) Polyvinyl chloride

(c) Bakelite (d) Glyptal

14. The concentration of fluoride, lead, nitrate and iron in a water sample from an underground lake was found to be 1000 ppb, 40 ppb, 100 ppm and 0.2 ppm, respectively. This water is unsuitable for drinking due to high concentration of : **[JEE M 2016]**

(a) Nitrate (b) Iron

(c) Fluoride (d) Lead

15. Which of the following is an anionic detergent?

[JEE M 2016]

(a) Cetyltrimethyl ammonium bromide.

(b) Glyceryl oleate.

(c) Sodium stearate.

(d) Sodium lauryl sulphate.

16. Which of the following statements about low density polythene is **FALSE**? **[JEE M 2016]**

(a) Its synthesis requires dioxygen or a peroxide initiator as a catalyst.

(b) It is used in the manufacture of buckets, dust-bins etc.

(c) Its synthesis requires high pressure.

(d) It is a poor conductor of electricity.

17. The formation of which of the following polymers involves hydrolysis reaction? **[JEE M 2017]**

(a) Nylon 6 (b) Bakelite

(c) Nylon 6, 6 (d) Terylene

18. Which of the following compounds will behave as a reducing sugar in an aqueous KOH solution? **[JEE M 2017]**

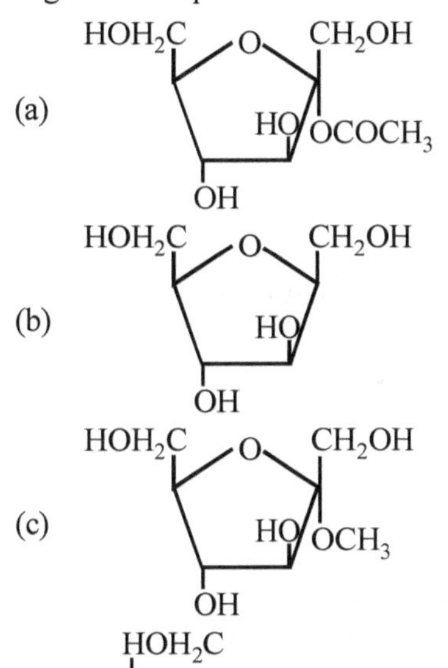

SOLUTIONS

PAST YEAR QUESTIONS JEE ADVANCED/IIT-JEE (2013 - 2017)

MCQs with ONE Correct Answer

1. (a)

$$CH_2 = \underset{\underset{CH_3}{|}}{C} - CH = CH_2 \xrightarrow{\text{Polymerisation}} \underset{\text{Natural rubber}}{-(CH_2 - \underset{\underset{CH_3}{|}}{C} = CH - CH_2)-}$$

Isoprene

$$\downarrow \begin{array}{c} H_2(\text{excess}) \\ \text{catalyst} \end{array}$$

$$\underset{\text{Ethylene}}{CH_2 = CH_2} + \underset{\text{Propylene}}{CH_2 = \underset{\underset{CH_3}{|}}{CH}} \xrightarrow{\text{Copolymerisation}} \underset{\substack{\text{Completely hydrogenated} \\ \text{Natural rubber}}}{-(CH_2 - \underset{\underset{CH_3}{|}}{CH} - CH_2 - CH_2)-}$$

2. (c) Step 1 :

Step 2 :

Diazocoupling

3. (c)

(IV)

The conjugate acid is stabilized by resonance with two different $-NH_2$ group. Hence electron density increases on N of $=NH$

(I)

The conjugate acid is stabilized by resonance with one $-NH_2$ group. Hence as compared to IV lesser increase of electron density on N of $=NH$

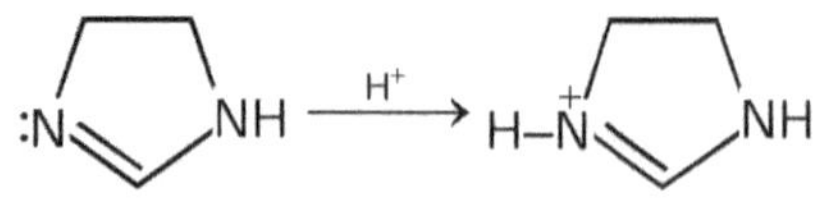

(II)

Lone pair is not involvd in aromaticity. Hence more available

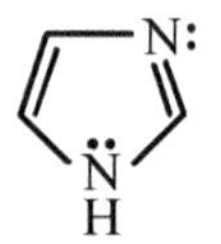

(III)

Lone pair is involved in aromatic sextet. Hence not available.

Hence the correct order of basic strength is

$IV > I > II > III$

MCQs with ONE or More Than One Correct

1. **(a, b, d)** In ice, water molecules are excessively H-bonded giving a cage-like structure which is lighter than water. Primary amines are more basic than tertiary amine, because the protonated $1°$ amines are extensively H-bonded and hence more stable than the corresponding protonated $3°$ amines.

$$R-\ddot{N}H_2 \xrightarrow{H^+} R-\overset{+}{N}H_3 \ ; \ R_3\ddot{N} \xrightarrow{H^+} R_3\overset{+}{N}H$$

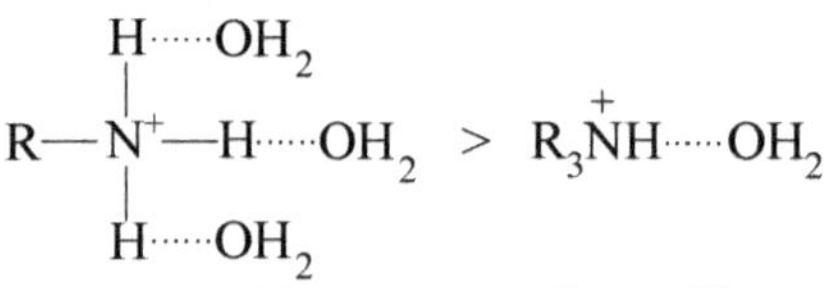

More stable   Less stable

Acetic acid undergoes dimerisation in benzene.

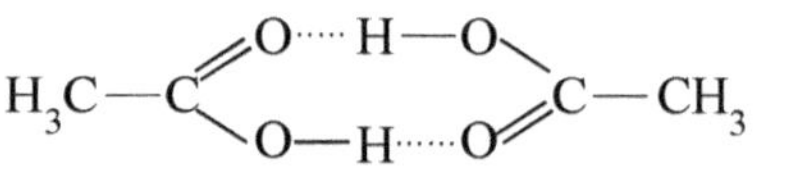

2. **(a)** $-\ddot{N}H_2$ group is acetylated by acetic anhydride in methylene chloride (solvent). Note that $-CONH_2$ group does not undergo acetylation because here lone pair of electrons is delocalised.

$$-CH_2-\ddot{N}H_2 + (CH_3CO)_2O \xrightarrow{CH_2Cl_2} -CH_2-NH + CH_3COOH$$

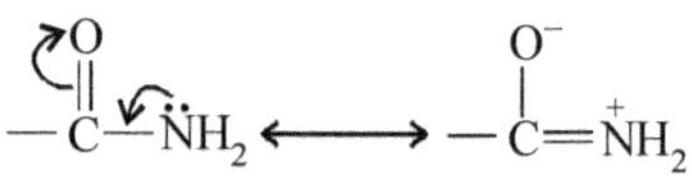

3. **(c)**

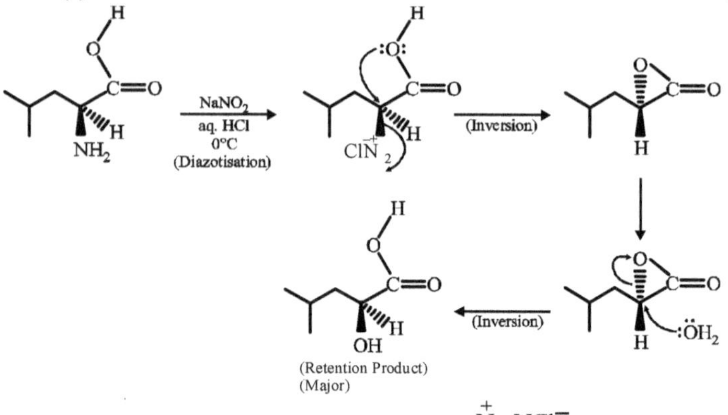

(Retention Product)
(Major)

4. **(a)**

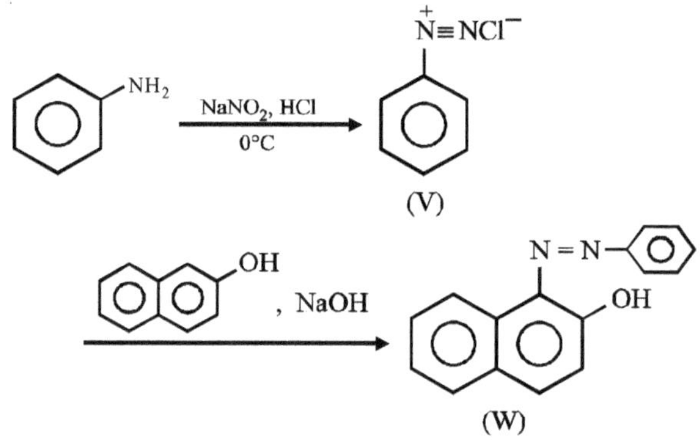

(V)

, NaOH

(W)

5. **(a)**

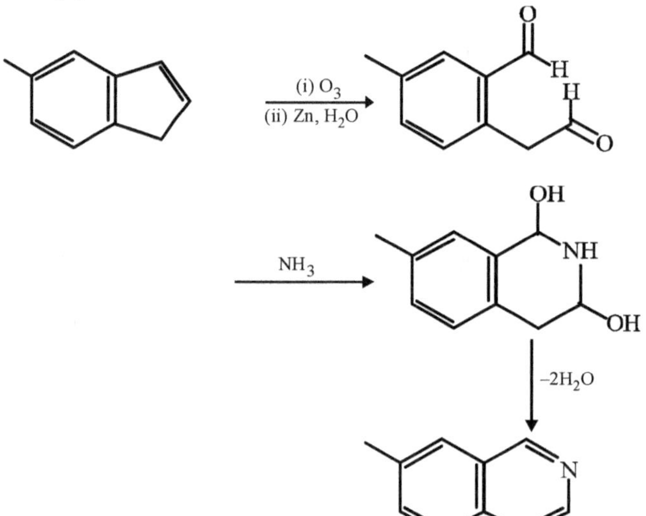

(i) O_3
(ii) Zn, H_2O

NH_3

$-2H_2O$

6. **(b)**

$\xrightarrow[\text{Pyridine}]{Ac_2O}$

Acetanilide

$\xrightarrow{KBrO_3/HBr}$

(Major)

$\xrightarrow{H_3O^+}$

$\xrightarrow[\substack{273-278 \ K \\ \text{(diazotisation)}}]{NaNO_2/HCl}$

$\xrightarrow[HBr]{Cu}$

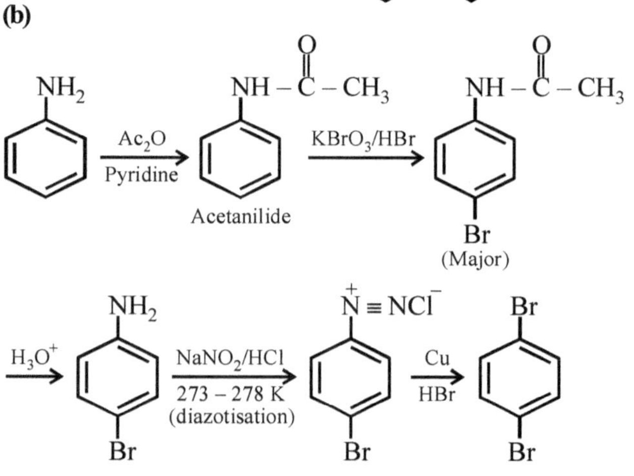

7. (a)

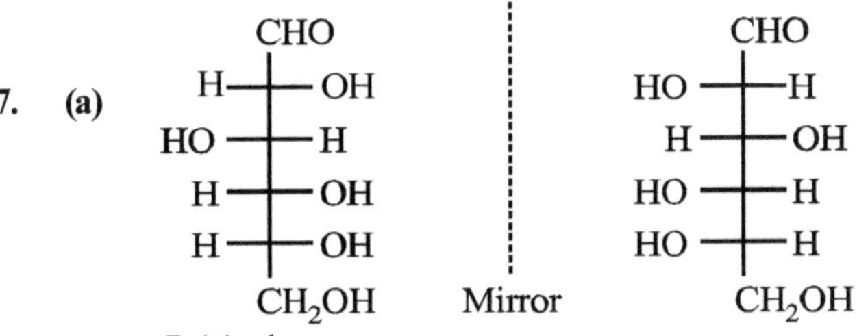

D-(+)- glucose   Mirror   L-(−)- glucose

8. (b, c) Invert sugar is an equimolar mixture of D-(+) glucose and D(−) glucose.

$$C_{12}H_{22}O_{11} + H_2O \xrightarrow{H^+} C_6H_{12}O_6 + H_2O \xrightarrow{+} C_6H_{12}O_6$$

+ sucrose   D(+)−glucose (+52°)   D(+)−glucose (−92°)

Invert sugar

- Specific rotation of invert sugar $= \dfrac{-92° + 52°}{2} = -20°$

- D-glucose on oxidation with Br_2-water produces gluconic acid and not saccharic acid.

Match the Following

1. (c) Scheme (III): $H \equiv H$ (Acetylene, **P**) $\xrightarrow[\text{Fe, 873 K}]{\text{red hot}}$ (benzene) $\xrightarrow{\text{Nitration}}$ (m-dinitrobenzene, NO_2, NO_2) $\xrightarrow{NH_4HS}$

(m-nitroaniline, NO_2, NH_2) $\xrightarrow[H^+]{NaNO_2}$ (m-nitro diazonium, NO_2, $\overset{+}{N_2}$) $\xrightarrow[\text{boil}]{H_2O}$ (m-nitrophenol, NO_2, OH) $+ N_2 + H^+$ ($C_6H_5NO_3$)

Scheme (IV): (resorcinol, OH, OH) **Q** $\xrightarrow[60°C]{\text{Conc. } H_2SO_4}$ (OH, OH, SO_3H) $\xrightarrow[\text{Conc. } H_2SO_4]{\text{Conc. } HNO_3}$ (O_2N, OH, OH, SO_3H) $\xrightarrow[\text{heat}]{\text{dil. } H_2SO_4}$ (O_2N, OH, OH) ($C_6H_5NO_4$)

Scheme (II): (nitrobenzene, NO_2) **R** $\xrightarrow{Sn/HCl}$ (aniline, NH_2) $\xrightarrow{CH_3COCl}$ (acetanilide, $NHCOCH_3$) $\xrightarrow[H_2SO_4]{\text{Conc.}}$ ($NHCOCH_3$, SO_3H)

$\xrightarrow{\text{Conc. } HNO_3}$ ($NHCOCH_3$, NO_2, SO_3H) $\xrightarrow[H_2SO_4, \text{ heat}]{\text{dil.}}$ ($NHCOCH_3$, NO_2) $\xrightarrow{OH^-}$ (NH_2, NO_2) ($C_6H_6N_2O_2$)

Scheme (I): (p-nitrotoluene, NO_2, CH_3) **S** $\xrightarrow[\text{(ii) } H^+, H_2O]{\text{(i) } KMnO_4, OH^-, \text{heat}}$ (NO_2, $COOH$) $\xrightarrow{SOCl_2}$ (NO_2, $COCl$) $\xrightarrow{NH_3}$ (NO_2, $CONH_2$) ($C_7H_6N_2O_3$)

Comprehension Based Questions

1. (a) 2. (b)

The reaction scheme shows o-dipropylbenzene (O) $\xrightarrow{KMnO_4/H^\oplus}$ phthalic acid (P) $\xrightarrow{NH_3/\Delta}$ phthalamide (Q) $\xrightarrow{Br_2/NaOH}$ o-phenylenediamine (R); phthalimide (S) reacting with $CH_3-\overset{Br}{\underset{}{CH}}-\overset{O}{\underset{}{C}}-OC_2H_5$ over KOH to give the N-substituted phthalimide, which on $H_3O^\oplus$ gives $CH_3-\underset{\underset{(T)}{NH_2}}{CH}-COOH$ Alanine.

Integer Value Correct Type

1. **(4)** According to question C – Terminal must be alanine and N – Terminal do have chiral carbon means it should not be glycine. So possible sequence is : Val Phe Gly Ala ; Val Gly Phe Ala ; Phe Val Gly Ala ; Phe Gly Val Ala

2. **(1)** On hydrolysis, the given peptide gives only one naturally occurring amino acid (glycine).

PAST YEAR QUESTIONS JEE MAIN/AIEEE (2013 - 2017)

1. **(b)**

$$R-\underset{\underset{Mol.Mass-16}{}}{NH_2} + CH_3-\overset{O}{\underset{}{C}}-Cl \xrightarrow{-HCl} R-\underset{\underset{Mol.mass-58}{}}{NH-\overset{O}{\underset{}{C}}-CH_3}$$

Now since the molecular mass increases by 42 unit as a result of the reaction of one mole of CH_3COCl with one-NH_2 group and the given increase in mass is 210. hence the number of –NH_2 group is = 210/42 = 5

2. **(d)** $A \xrightarrow{NH_3} B \xrightarrow{\Delta} C \xrightarrow[KOH]{Br_2} CH_3CH_2NH_2$

(I)   (II)   (III)

Reaction (III) is a Hofmann bromamide reaction formation of $CH_3CH_2NH_2$ is possible only from a compound $CH_3CH_2CONH_2$ which can be obtained from the compound $CH_3CH_2COO^- NH_4^+$ (B) in (II) reaction further propanic acid (CH_3CH_2COOH) on reaction with NH_3 produce $CH_3CH_2COO^-NH_4^-$ (reaction I) hence the reaction will be

$$\underset{(A)}{CH_3CH_2-\overset{O}{\underset{}{C}}-OH} \longrightarrow \underset{(B)}{CH_3CH_2COO^-NH_4^+}$$

$$\xrightarrow{\Delta} \underset{(C)}{CH_3CH_2CONH_2} \xrightarrow[Br_2]{KOH} CH_3CH_2NH_2$$

3. **(c)** Water-soluble vitamins dissolve in water and are not stored by the body. The water soluble vitamins include the vitamin B-complex group and vitamin C.

4. **(a)** Phenelzine is an antidepressant, while others are antacids.

5. **(d)** Glyptal is used in the manufacture of paints and lacquers.

6. **(a)** The maximum limit of nitrate in drinking water is 50 ppm. Excess nitrate in drinking water can cause disease such as methemoglobinemia ('blue baby' syndrome).

7. **(d)** Sodium lauryl sulphate ($C_{11}H_{23}CH_2OSO_3^- Na^+$) is an anionic detergent. Glyceryl oleate is a glyceryl ester of oleic acid. Sodium stearate ($C_{17}H_{35}COO^-Na^+$) is a soap. Cetyltrimethyl ammonium bromide

$$\left[CH_3(CH_2)_{15}\overset{+}{N}(CH_3)_3\right]Br^-$$ is a cationic detergent.

8. **(b)** High density polythene is used in the manufacture of housewares like buckets, dustbins, bottles, pipes etc. Low density polythene is used for insulating electric wires and in the manufacture of flexible pipes, toys, coats, bottles etc.

9. **(a)** Formation of Nylon-6 involves hydrolysis of caprolactum, (its monomer) in initial state.

Caprolactam $\xrightarrow[\Delta]{H_2O}$ $H_2N(CH_2)_5COOH$ (ε-Amino Caproic acid)

$\xrightarrow[Polymerise]{\Delta}$ $-(NH(CH_2)_5-\overset{O}{\underset{}{C}}-NH-(CH_2)_5-\overset{O}{\underset{}{C})_n}$ Nylon-6

10. **(b)**

The fructose furanose form reacting with acetic anhydride-type ester $\xrightarrow[-CH_3COOK]{Aq.KOH}$ Hemiketal $\updownarrow$ Ring opening $\rightarrow$ α-hydroxy ketone (a Reducing sugar) $\xleftarrow[Reagent]{Tollen's}$ ⊕ve silver mirror test